PRACTICAL PARALLEL COMPUTING

PRACTICAL PARALLEL COMPUTING

H. Stephen Morse

AP PROFESSIONAL
Boston San Diego New York
London Sydney Tokyo Toronto

This book is printed on acid-free paper. ∞

AP PROFESSIONAL
955 Massachusetts Avenue, Cambridge, MA 02139

An Imprint of ACADEMIC PRESS, INC.
A Division of HARCOURT BRACE & COMPANY

United Kingdom Edition published by
ACADEMIC PRESS LIMITED
24–28 Oval Road, London NW1 7DX

Library of Congress Cataloging-in-Publication Data
Morse, H. Stephen.
Practical parallel computing / H. Stephen Morse.
p. cm.
Includes index.
ISBN 0-12-508160-X
1. Parallel processing (Electronic computers) I. Title.
QA76.58.M67 1994
004'.35--dc20 94-32053
CIP

Printed in the United States of America
94 95 96 97 98 IP 9 8 7 6 5 4 3 2 1

dedicated to my children,
Kate and Paul,
whose on-board parallel processors
are a constant source of wonder

Contents

Preface xiii
Acknowledgments xvii

PART 1 Preliminaries 1

1 The Status and Future of Massively Parallel Processing 3

1.1 Technology Trends Favoring Parallel Architectures 4
- 1.1.1 Barriers to Clock Rate 5
- 1.1.2 Reliability 7
- 1.1.3 Memory Bandwidth 9
- Summary of Section 1.1 12

1.2 Obstacles Inhibiting Commercial Success 12
- 1.2.1 Availability of Application Software 14
- 1.2.2 Standards 16
- 1.2.3 Vendor Instability 18
- Summary of Section 1.2 19

1.3 Trends and Considerations 19
- 1.3.1 High-End Systems: The First TeraFLOP Computer 19
- 1.3.2 Low-End Systems: Desktop Supercomputers 21
- 1.3.3 Government and Policy Considerations 22
- Summary of Chapter 1 23

2 Can Parallel Machines Be Used Efficiently? 25

2.1 A Parallel Parable: Building a Wall 26
- 2.1.1 Replication 26
- 2.1.2 Locality of Communications 28
- 2.1.3 I/O Strategies 30
- 2.1.4 Miscellaneous 31

2.2 Amdahl's Law 32
2.2.1 Definitions 32
2.2.2 The Wall Revisited 37
2.2.3 Efficiency Depends on Problem Size 41
2.3 Examples 43
2.3.1 Database Queries 43
2.3.2 Latency versus Throughput 45
2.3.3 Load Balancing 47
Summary of Chapter 2 49

3 An Introduction to Hardware Architectures 51

3.1 Impacts of Hardware Architecture 52
3.2 A Primer on Interconnection Networks 55
3.3 SIMD Machines 60
3.3.1 A Top-Level Block Diagram 61
3.3.2 Strengths and Weaknesses 64
3.4 Distributed Memory MIMD Machines 67
3.4.1 A Top-Level Block Diagram 67
3.4.2 Strengths and Weaknesses 71
3.5 Shared Memory MIMD Machines 73
3.5.1 A Top-Level Block Diagram 76
3.5.2 Latency Hiding 78
3.5.3 Strengths and Weaknesses 82
Summary of Chapter 3 83

PART 2 Software Issues 85

4 Shared Memory Parallel Language Constructs 87

4.1 Basic Concepts for Shared Memory Parallel Programming 88
4.1.1 Lightweight Processes 89
4.1.2 Shared and Global Variables 92
4.1.3 Locks and Critical Regions 95
4.2 The Sample Problem on an SGI Challenge SMP 98
4.2.1 Overview of the Parallelization Strategy 98
4.2.2 Annotations 99
4.3 Observations and Considerations 106
Summary of Chapter 4 109

5 Message Passing 111

5.1 An Overview of the Message-Passing Library 111
5.2 The Sample Problem on an nCube 2 116
 5.2.1 The Parallelization Strategy 116
 5.2.2 Annotations 120
 5.2.3 Alternatives and Considerations 126
5.3 Express 127
 5.3.1 Overview of Express 128
 5.3.2 Annotations 132
 5.3.3 Alternatives and Considerations 137
5.4 Intel Paragon 138
 5.4.1 Overview of the Solution 138
 5.4.2 Annotations 140
 5.4.3 Alternatives and Considerations 143
5.5 Observations and Considerations 145
 Summary of Chapter 5 149

6 SIMD and Array-Based Languages 151

6.1 An Overview 151
 6.1.1 The SIMD Programming Model 152
 6.1.2 Array Languages and FORTRAN 156
6.2 MPL on the MasPar MP-1 157
 6.2.1 An Introduction to MPL 158
 6.2.2 Annotations 160
 6.2.3 Alternatives and Considerations 165
6.3 C* on the Connection Machine 167
 6.3.1 An Overview of C* 167
 6.3.2 Annotations 172
 6.3.3 Alternatives and Considerations 176
 Summary of Chapter 6 177

7 Linda 179

7.1 A Linda Primer 180
7.2 The Sample Problem in Linda 184
 7.2.1 An Overview of the Strategy 184
 7.2.2 Annotations 185
7.3 Observations and Considerations 191
 Summary of Chapter 7 193

8 The Development Environment for Parallel Software 195

8.1 Compilers 196
8.2 Debugging Parallel Code 200
8.2.1 SIMD Debuggers 202
8.2.2 Message-Passing Debuggers 203
8.2.3 Shared Memory Debuggers 204
8.3 Profilers and Load Balancing 205
8.4 Other Tools 208
8.4.1 Automatic Parallelization 209
8.4.2 Interactive Parallelization 211
8.4.3 Object-Oriented Approaches 212
Summary of Chapter 8 212

9 Operating System Issues 215

9.1 Multiple Users 216
9.2 Virtual Address Spaces 220
9.3 Scheduling 223
9.4 Virtual Processors 225
9.5 I/O 227
9.6 Open Systems 231
Summary of Chapter 9 233

PART 3 Management Issues 235

10 Benchmarking Parallel Applications 237

10.1 Dependence on Problem Size and Machine Size 238
10.1.1 Amdahl's Law Revisited 238
10.1.2 Measures of Effectiveness 240
10.1.3 Specifying Machine Configurations 244
10.1.4 Specifying Problem Sizes 249
10.1.5 Data-Dependent Benchmarks 252
10.2 Publicly Available Parallel Benchmarks 254
10.2.1 LINPACK Massively Parallel Computing 255
10.2.2 SLALOM 257
10.2.3 Others 258

10.3 Scaling Sequential Performance to Parallel Performance 259
10.4 Estimating Performance 262
10.5 Questions to Ask Vendors 266
Summary of Chapter 10 267

11 Porting and Developing Parallel Applications 269

11.1 Porting Strategies 270
11.1.1 Automatic Parallelization 271
11.1.2 Parallel Libraries 273
11.1.3 The Choice of Architecture 275
11.2 Developing Parallel Applications 278
11.3 Examples 283
11.3.1 Case 1: Porting an Image Processing Code to an SIMD Array 283
11.3.2 Case 2: Porting a Simulation to a Distributed Memory Hypercube 286
11.3.3 A Large Development Effort 290
Summary of Chapter 11 294

12 Matching Applications to Architectures 295

12.1 A Methodology 296
12.1.1 Performance Measures 298
12.1.2 Other Measures 301
12.1.3 Combining Measures for a Unified Result 303
12.2 Integrating a Parallel Machine into Existing Operations 306
12.2.1 Case 1: Turbo-Charging a Mainframe Application 306
12.2.2 Case 2: The MPP as Server in an Open System 308
12.2.3 Case 3: The LAN *Is* the MPP 312
Summary of Chapter 12 315

Appendix A The Sample Problem 317

Listing for Sample Problem 318

Appendix B SGI Challenge 323

Appendix C nCube 331

Appendix D Express 341

Appendix E Intel Paragon 349

Appendix F MasPar MP-1 355

Appendix G C* on the Connection Machine 363

Appendix H Linda 369

Appendix I Two Recent Machines 379

I.1 The SP-Series from IBM 379
- Node Architecture 379
- Interprocessor Communications 380
- I/O Software 382

I.2 Exemplar Series from Convex Corp. 383
- System Architecture 384
- System Software 385

I.3 Summary and Comparison 385

References 387

Index 393

Preface

This is the the book I wish I had had nine years ago when I first ventured into the realm of high-performance parallel processing. The contract to which I was then assigned involved selection of a parallel computer with nominal performance goals that were, at the time, truly staggering. This selection process, in turn, required an understanding of the full range of issues facing a parallel implementation.

> What are the hardware architecture options? How well do they match the customer's algorithmic and performance goals? Does the problem lend itself to parallelism; is there anything about it that might hinder a parallel approach? What about integrating such a machine into the existing computing environment? What about software—algorithms, operating system, software development support tools and environment, testing, benchmarking, etc.? What about risk, especially business risk for small high-tech start-ups? How can suitably balanced parallel I/O be accomplished?

The list goes on and, when the selection process began, the information required to answer these questions was scattered and clouded by misleading (or, at least, flawed) assertions from both sides of the border separating sequential from parallel vendors.

The remedy for this, and the key to making this book have value, has been the experience of working and consulting, over the intervening years, on the development of full-up, end to end parallel applications on a variety of equipment. The term "*practical*" in the title was chosen to capture this aspect of the book's intent. What it is that the vendors don't tell you, but that (it turns out) is critical, in a *practical* sense, to the success of the application. A proper appreciation for these "gotcha's" of parallel computing is, I think, of great value in moving parallel computing out of government-sponsored laboratories and into a commercial, pay-your-way setting.

The intended audience, then, are those who, like myself nine years ago, find themselves confronting the practical realities of parallel computing for the first time. An example of such a person (one I had in my mind's eye as the writing progressed) is a mid-level technical manager faced with a processing load that is increasing rapidly and with which the traditional vendor can no longer cost effectively keep pace. The possibility of shifting some of the computationally demanding applications off the main frame and onto an inexpensive but dazzlingly fast parallel processor is a dream that, I feel sure, has crossed the minds of many an MIS/ADP professional. At that point, however, the manager will be in the same situation I was in nine years ago—that is, faced with an array of practical questions about the technology that must be answered before solid choices and plans can be made and justified to upper management.

This book is addressed to a person in just that situation.

The top-level organization of the book separates the material into three parts:

Part 1: Preliminaries (Chapters 1–3)

Part 2: Software Issues (Chapters 4–9)

Part 3: Management Issues (Chapters 10–12)

Chapter 12 is the culmination of the book. It provides a structured, flexible methodology for selecting a parallel machine and for integrating it into existing operations. The material and level of detail in other chapters was chosen, in large part, to provide the necessary background for the discussion in Chapter 12. For example, Chapters 4 through 7 provide worked-out examples, based on a toy problem, of programs using several parallel languages. Since application software is, perhaps, the key missing ingredient in parallel computation, it seemed that an extended discussion was called for. As another example, Chapter 10 deals with benchmarking and performance estimation on parallel machines. Such a discussion is appropriate because, often, the hope of achieving greatly increased performance is the driving motivation for moving to parallel equipment. In Chapter 3, the reader will find a tutorial introduction to parallel hardware architectures. While we might be able to avoid such nitty-gritty matters when discussing sequential machines, the current state of the art in parallel processing does not allow hardware issues to be finessed.

My intent has been to provide a *balanced* assessment of the technology. This is *not* a sales brochure for parallel processing. Indeed, the view presented comes perilously close to: If you aren't *really sure* you need massively parallel computing, you had probably better think twice before getting involved with it. On the other hand, there has also been an attempt to debunk some of the more egregious and technically unsupportable charges sometimes made against parallel machines (see, for example, the discussion of *Amdahl's Law* in Chapter 2). The book is liberally sprinkled with examples and case studies. The tone is, at times, a trifle irreverent—the result of dealing in a field that is filled with the most extravagant claims and counterclaims, charges and countercharges. Still, despite these disclaimers, I hope the reader will also sense my genuine admiration for the technical pioneers who have made parallel computing a reality and who continue to work at the difficult remaining tasks of making it more broadly available and usable.

HSM
May 1994

Acknowledgments

The person who got this project going in the fall of 1992 was Tom Wheeler, at that time a senior technical manager with American Express. MRJ, Inc. had done some work for Tom on a consulting basis, and he approached the company with the idea of writing a volume on parallel computing as one in a series on open systems for which he was the editor. Tom was tragically afflicted with a brain tumor shortly after work began and died in the spring of 1993. Without Tom's initial impetus and vision, the book would never have been written.

Another shock came in the spring of 1993 when the intended publisher underwent a major reorganization. At that point, Alan Rose of Intertext took the book under his care and eventually found it a home at AP PROFESSIONAL. Being novices in the publishing world, MRJ is very grateful for Alan's help and patience. Without his initiative, the project might have foundered for lack of publishing interest.

As author, I am indebted to the management at MRJ for their support during the writing. Particular thanks go to my Division Manager, Scott Miller, who gave me flexibility in my schedule to free time for writing; and to Dr. Ed McMahon, President of MRJ, who made funding available to support the project. Ed also read through the entire draft manuscript and made a number of perceptive and valuable suggestions.

The example programs shown in Chapters 4 through 7 are intended to be compilable and runnable on the target machines. In many cases, the codes were actually prepared by technical staff from the vendors involved, and in all cases the sample code, comments, and annotations were reviewed by the vendors for accuracy. The companies involved were:

Silicon Graphics, Inc. (Power C on the SGI Challenge)
nCube Corporation (nCube 2)
ParaSoft, Inc. (Express)
Intel Corporation (Paragon)

MasPar, Inc. (MPL on the MP-1)
Thinking Machines Corporation (C* on the CM2 and CM5)
Scientific Computing Associates (Linda)

Many thanks to these companies and to their technical staff for helping to create and review these programming examples.

In many ways, the real heroes behind this book are the members of the parallel computing technical staff at MRJ. We are small, but we are very good; the material in this book owes its immediacy and relevance to lessons learned from *real* application development on *real* parallel equipment. Nothing focuses the attention like having to meet a deliverable—on time and in budget! Special thanks go to Steve Geyer, Alan Broder, and George Wilson who read portions of the text and tempered my more extravagant claims (e.g., on debugging) with a healthy dose of common sense and experience.

Finally, thanks to my wife, Mary, and my family for patiently enduring the emotional vicissitudes of authorship over the past 18 months.

PART I

Preliminaries

The three chapters of Part 1 constitute an introduction to the subject of parallel processing. The current status is examined in Chapter 1, including discussions of the performance potential of these machines and the reasons why they have, thus far, been so unsuccessful in the marketplace. Chapter 2 considers the merits of a commonly cited charge against parallel processors—that there are theoretical bounds on how many processors can be used efficiently on a single problem. The analysis concludes that the *size* of the problem being solved must enter into such a calculation in a critical way often overlooked by advocates of sequential and vector machines. Finally, Chapter 3 provides a tutorial introduction to the three major classes of parallel architecture and points out strengths and weaknesses in each case.

1

The Status and Future of Massively Parallel Processing

Asked to complete the sentence, "Parallel processing is ...," an honest technical assessment necessarily includes the characterizations "... painful" and "... inevitable."

If we view the vendors of high-performance computing as residing in two camps—traditional vector and sequential processing faced off against upstart parallel processing—both camps have strong vested interests in exaggerating or minimizing estimates of the kinds and levels of pain. The strong dependence of this pain both on the application and on the operational environment will defeat any "one size fits all" resolution of these opposing claims: There is justice on both sides. However, on the issue of *inevitability* there is broad agreement. Major vendors of traditional architectures have active R&D programs focused on the development of hardware and software for massively parallel processors (MPP). This amounts to a tacit admission, marketing hype aside, that they, too, have seen the technical handwriting on the wall.

For the most part, we will concentrate on the *pain* of parallel processing. What are the sources (expected and unexpected)? How can they be avoided or at least minimized? What characteristics of an application or an operational environment might facilitate a transition to parallel processing? At the outset, however, it is appropriate to consider carefully the *inevitability* of this technology. If MPP is inevitably in an organization's future, an understanding of the technology can enable wise decisions on timing, competitive advantage, transition planning, and integration. Were we to change "inevitable" to "avoidable" or even to "one option among many," then many organizations would (correctly) opt for the *status quo* or for conventional, less risky solutions. There is a lot at stake in the question of the inevitability of MPP.

The purpose of this chapter is to gather and present the relevant information on this question. While the author is familiar with the "gotcha's" of parallel processing, he is likewise convinced that the path to success for many organizations will inevitably include a substantial investment in parallel processing. The motivation for facing up to the pain is its inevitability.

The first of three sections will examine technology trends that converge to favor massively parallel hardware over traditional mainframes and vector machines. The reasons for the continuing market dominance of traditional machines will then be discussed in the second section. Finally, the third section looks ahead, at both high- and low-end systems, and considers the likely impact of government policy on these trends.

1.1 TECHNOLOGY TRENDS FAVORING PARALLEL ARCHITECTURES

If by *parallel* we mean *concurrent* or *simultaneous execution of distinct components*, then every machine, from a $950 PC to a $30 million Cray C-90, has aspects of parallelism. A more fruitful definition, for our purposes, is to observe that the total processing power of a machine can be found (subject to certain obvious provisos) by multiplying the *power of one processor* (measured, say, in MFLOPs or SPECmarks) by the *number of processors.* Using this simple observation, it is possible, for example, to achieve a processing rate of 1 billion floating point operations per second (that is, a *GFLOP,* or *Giga-FLOP,* in the technical argot of the industry) in several ways (see Figure 1-1).

In general, massively parallel approaches achieve high processing rates by assembling *large numbers* of relatively *slow* processors. Traditional approaches focus on improving the speed of the individual processors (often using forms of parallelism and latency-hiding invisible to the user) and assemble only a *few* of these *very powerful* processors for a complete machine.

From the point of view of an electrical engineer concerned primarily with hardware (power, bit error rates, footprint, cooling, costs of material/design/manufacture, reliability, etc.), both approaches have characteristic advantages and disadvantages. This section will briefly review some of these and will conclude that the massively parallel approach appears to be a clear winner.

	Number of Processors	x	Speed per Processor (MFLOPs)	=	Total Performace
Traditional	1		1,000		
↑	10		100		
	100	x	10	=	1 GFLOP
↓	1,000		1		
MPP	10,000		.1		

Figure 1-1. Approaches to building a GFLOP computer

1.1.1 Barriers to Clock Rate

Even casual users of PC-class equipment are aware that a computer has an internal "clock" and that the faster this clock "ticks" (measured in *MHz*, or millions of oscillations per second), the more responsive the machine (that is, the more rapidly it completes such tasks as screen redraw, spreadsheet computation, text reformatting, etc.). The last eight years have seen internal clock rates for commodity microprocessors increase from 6 MHz (1985) to 50 MHz or even higher for top-end machines (1993). Estimates of the *current* rate of increase for this class of machine are an approximate doubling every 18 months. If we pin 1993 at 50 MHz, this suggests that we might see clock rates for commodity microprocessors approaching 1 *nanosecond* (that is, a frequency of *1 GHz*, or 1 billion oscillations per second) by the turn of the century.

The significance of the clock rate in a computer is that, holding other things (such as the instruction set architecture) constant, useful measures of performance (such as MIPs, MFLOPs, SPECmarks, etc.) cannot increase faster than the clock rate. Provided that there is sufficient memory and bus bandwidth to service the increased demands that accompany high clock rates, we normally expect performance to increase proportionately to clock rate: Doubling the clock, for example, should double the performance. Reference [1] provides a clear introduction to the relationship between internal clock rate and achieved performance.

Naively, the rapid increase in clock rates for microprocessors seems to imply that one need only wait for succeeding generations of hardware, thus "riding the CMOS bow-wave" through the nineties and beyond to achieve ever more exalted levels of performance. Further, referring back to Figure 1-1, it seems there may be reason to hope that *individual processor* performance (the leftmost column) can increase indefinitely, thereby obviating the necessity of increasing the *number* of processors. High clock rates may (it is hoped) enable one to stay at the comfortable "traditional" end of the spectrum and avoid the fearful black hole of "MPP" lurking at the other end!

The close relationship between clock rate and performance is one key to understanding the *inevitability* of MPP. There are good reasons to believe there is a natural, physical barrier to practically achievable clock rates and that technology has already pushed close to that limit.

A complete discussion would take us into the nether regions of electrical engineering, materials science, and even quantum mechanics. An illustration close to the surface, however, is packaging and cooling. Power dissipation (and hence, heat) increases with clock rate and is considerably higher for components (such as SRAM or ECL) specifically designed for high clock rates than it is for components (such as custom CMOS microprocessors or DRAM) designed for more modest clock rates. This, in turn, requires increased attention to cooling—a facilities impact familiar to users of traditional mainframes and vector supercomputers.

This packaging problem is compounded by the fact that electrons can only travel a certain distance during a clock pulse (bounded by the speed of light). This distance shortens as the clock pulse decreases, approaching about a meter as the clock rate approaches 1 nanosecond per pulse (that is, a clock rate of *1 billion* ticks per second). This, in turn, requires very dense packaging of components (to keep them close together) and imposes rigid budgets on the lengths of wires interconnecting these components. This density makes it difficult to provide adequate coolant flow across parts to dissipate the heat. The miracle of a Cray computer is not that it runs so fast but that it doesn't melt down!

The lack of progress in the traditional supercomputer industry over the past few years exemplifies these problems. The Cray Y-MP was introduced in 1986 and had an internal clock rate of 6 nanoseconds (167 MHz). Five years later, the next generation Cray C-90 was introduced with an internal clock rate of 4 nanoseconds (250 MHz)—a mere 50 percent increase in clock rate. (Note: The C-90 achieves an *aggregate* sixfold peak performance improvement over the Y-MP8 by quadrupling the number of vector pipelines from 8 to 32.) One may reasonably suppose that had faster clock rates been achievable by Cray Research (say, 2 nanoseconds, or 1 nanosecond per pulse), they would have been incorporated.

The experience of Cray Computer Corporation (a spin-off of Cray Research headed by the guru of vector supercomputers, Seymour Cray) with Gallium Arsenide (GaAs) has been no better. The original design of the Cray 3 called for a 1-nanosecond clock; it was subsequently scaled back to 2 nanoseconds, and (as of this writing) it has not yet achieved sufficient hardware stability to attract a customer. Again, the complexity of the EE tasks associated with such high clock rates appears to have surpassed the means of even the most gifted of supercomputer architects.

If clock rate limitations impose a fundamental barrier (of, say, 1 nanosecond) for processing power on a single processor, the only alternative to achieving ultra high aggregate performance lies in the right-hand column of Figure 1-1: Increase the number of processors. This is the heart of the argument regarding the *inevitability* of MPP. It shows that the only feasible path to achieving, for example, a TFLOPs (1 *trillion* floating point operations per second) machine lies at the MPP end of the spectrum. We will take up this issue again, in a slightly different guise, in Section 1.3.1.

1.1.2 Reliability

MPP also has inherent advantages in system reliability when compared with traditional architectures. The key lies in the alternative VLSI technologies, which are summarized in Figure 1-2, used by each approach.

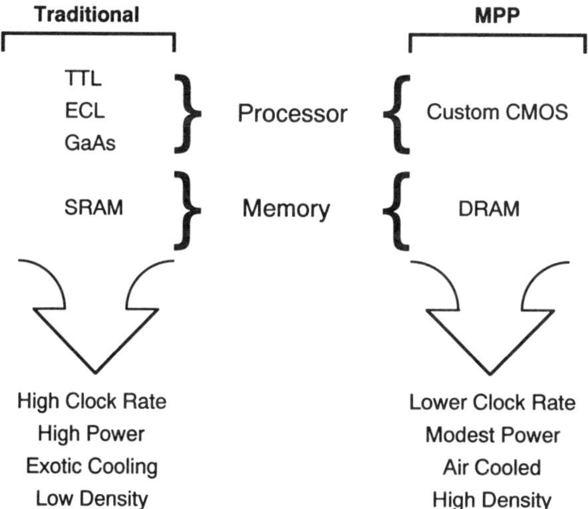

Figure 1-2. MPP and traditional VLSI approaches contrasted

A single processor for traditional mainframes and vector supercomputers is built from a fairly large number (50 or more) of specialized chip types. The high clock rates employed require VLSI technologies such as ECL, TTL, and GaAs. The relatively low device density for these technologies (perhaps a few tens of thousands of devices per chip) requires these multiple chips to be spread across a large board area. We may thus view the processor as comprising a large number of chips, of different chip types, spread across (perhaps) several boards and hence having a relatively large number of interchip connections. Further, memory bandwidth requirements (see Section 1.1.3) dictate use of SRAM, with similar high-power/low-density characteristics.

The *speed* of the processor is being paid for in several ways: increased chip count, decreased device density, increased board space, increased power dissipation, and increased number of interchip connections.

Alternatively, the custom CMOS microprocessor (the well-known "CPU on a chip") and commodity DRAM memory are the lifeblood of an MPP. The relatively slow processing rate of the microprocessor (when compared with a traditional vector processor) is well matched to the slower retrieval rate of DRAM. Thus, the MPP approach wins the *density* and *power* contest hands-down. For a given amount of board area, an MPP approach chooses to trade off reduced speed per processor for higher density and lower power—custom CMOS microprocessors and commodity DRAM. While a single MPP processor is slower than a single traditional CPU, many more of them (and significantly more bits of memory) can be fit into the same board real estate. And, since custom CMOS at standard clock rates (20 to 50 MHz is typical) dissipates less power than its ECL/TTL/GaAs counterparts, the packaging and cooling requirements are reduced.

Another advantage of the custom CMOS/DRAM approach is that these technologies are at the heart of the burgeoning commercial market in microprocessors—PCs, workstations, embedded microprocessors, DSPs, etc. This market incentive has resulted in what can only be described as a stunning acceleration both in microprocessor capability and in DRAM densities. Current commodity custom CMOS microprocessors are fabricated at .7 micron line widths, resulting in 2 to 3 million transistors per chip. As line widths decrease (perhaps to .3 microns by the turn of the century), additional functionality (especially large amounts of on-chip memory) and higher clock rates follow. Similarly, commodity DRAM memory densities are quadrupling about every three years. Pegging 16 MB DRAM to 1992, we can expect 256 MB DRAM parts (that is, 4 million 64-bit words) on a single chip before the turn of the century.

All this comes "for free" to the MPP designer, since these developments are driven by strong market forces quite independent of MPP considerations. Also observe that the very best point on the $/MFLOP curve is provided by the custom CMOS/DRAM combination.

These matters are well illustrated by the processor design of the nCube 2 parallel supercomputer. A single processing node (one cabinet of the nCube 2 can have up to 1,024 of these nodes) comprises 11 chips: one custom CMOS microprocessor and 10 commodity DRAM chips. These reside on small daughterboards, measuring 1.25" × 3.25", which are mounted (like bathroom tiles) on a large motherboard, which contains the interprocessor network wiring. A single motherboard, containing 64 processor nodes, each with 16 MB of SECDED DRAM, has a peak processing rate of over 200 MFLOPs (over 400 MIPs), provides 1 GB of addressable memory, dissipates less than 200 watts, and is air cooled.

As the title of this section indicates, perhaps the most significant benefit of the custom CMOS/DRAM combination is in system reliability. The two worst enemies of reliability are chip count and clock rate. The dependence on chip count is obvious: The more parts, the greater the likelihood that one will fail. The dependence on clock rate is tied primarily to increased heat but also reflects materials stress associated with more frequent transistor state changes. In any case, a system that can provide a given level of performance with fewer chips and at a lower clock rate will, other things being equal, have a substantial advantage in increased MTBF. Both transistor density (and, hence, reduced chip count) and clock rate favor the CMOS/DRAM approach, and this, in turn, makes MPP attractive—perhaps inevitable—based on reliability considerations.

1.1.3 Memory Bandwidth

The third consideration that suggests the inevitability of MPP is memory bandwidth. Any particular memory technology—SRAM, DRAM, FRAM, etc.—has a characteristic interval of time—call it T_R—required to either store or retrieve a data word. A typical value of T_R for commodity DRAM is 80 nanoseconds, or 12.5 MW per second. A typical value of T_R for SRAM is 10 nanoseconds, or 100 MW per second. The number of bytes in the word, multiplied by the number of words per second, yields the *memory bandwidth* of a memory device constructed with the given technology.

Example: An 80486-based microprocessor has a 32-bit bus and hence can fetch one 4-byte word from memory per memory reference. Using 80-nanosecond DRAM, a supporting memory device can provide

$$12.5 \text{ MW/sec} \times 4\text{B/W} = 50 \text{ MB/sec}$$

of memory bandwidth. Note that the bandwidth depends on the memory device and the word size, *not* on the clock rate of the microprocessor. ■

One way to increase memory bandwidth is to increase the number of bytes in a word. For example, when Cray Research moved from the Y-MP to the C-90, it doubled the memory word length from 8 bytes to 16 bytes. (In effect, each memory reference provides *two* 64-bit words.) Another approach is to decrease T_R. Again, in the change from the Y-MP to the C-90, the SRAM used to implement the memory went from $T_R = 15$ nanoseconds (Y-MP) to $T_R = 6$ nanoseconds (C-90).

One of the critical, but often overlooked, facts about DRAM is that the value of T_R for DRAM has remained fairly constant despite extraordinary improvements in bit storage density. Thus, as custom CMOS microprocessor clock rates have dramatically increased, DRAM retrieval times have remained in the 50- to 80-nanosecond range. This widening mismatch has had a marked impact on the design of microprocessor-based machines (such as MPPs).

The most effective way to increase memory bandwidth is to parallelize—that is, to have multiple independent memory devices, called *memory banks*, all active concurrently. Eight such devices, for example, can provide up to eight times the bandwidth of a single memory bank.

A common rule of thumb is that there should be about two words of memory bandwidth for each floating point operation. The desired processing rate, together with the value of T_R and the word size of the machine, can be used to calculate the number of memory banks required to meet this goal.

Example: Supposed a machine is intended to provide 20 GFLOPs of double precision (8 bytes/word) floating point power. The corresponding memory bandwith requirement is then approximately 40 GW/sec = 320 GB/sec. If high-speed SRAM with $T_R = 10$ nanoseconds is used, then

$$(40 \text{ GW/sec})/(100 \text{ MW/sec}) = 400$$

memory banks are required. If the memory is to be implemented in slower DRAM with TR = 80 nanoseconds, then

$$(40 \text{ GW/sec})/(12.5 \text{ MW/sec}) = 3{,}200$$

memory banks are required. ■

We have already noted the advantages accruing to slower CMOS/DRAM in packaging, reliability, and cost. The large number of DRAM memory banks needed to provide adequate bandwidth, however, raises another concern: How is it possible to connect one, or even a few, processor(s) to hundreds or thousands of distinct memory banks?

The answer provided by traditional mainframes and supercomputers is to tackle the problem head-on. Using SRAM reduces the required number of memory banks (since T_R is shortened). Further, an extremely high performance *cross-bar switch* is used to provide *uniform* access (that is, *equal in time* access) from every processor (currently, on the order of 10 to 20) to every memory bank (currently, on the order of several hundred). The circuitry of this cross-bar switch and the wire lengths required to implement it are a major obstacle to increasing the clock rate. The advantage is that every processor has immediate, rapid, and uniform access to all of memory. This is the the hallmark of a *shared memory* computer (see Section 3.5).

The answer to the question, How do we connect it up? given by MPPs is simple and elegant: Put a processor at each memory bank! The processor has full contention-free use of the bandwidth provided by its private memory bank. In fact, the processor/memory bank pair looks very much like a stand-alone microprocessor assemblage. Instead of providing a small number of processors uniform access to a large number of memory banks, the MPP approach provides private, nonshared memory bandwidth to each of a very large number of processors. The term *distributed memory* is used to describe such a configuration.

The downside, however, is that the processor can only directly access *its own* memory; it cannot directly access data held in the memory private to any other processor. Astute readers, perhaps already familiar with MPP technology, will immediately raise the objection, What if, in the course of an application, a processor *needs* the data held, not in its own private memory bank but in the memory private to another processor? This is, indeed, the price that MPP pays for its elegant solution to the problem of memory bandwidth. Notice, however, that the difficulty concerns primarily the type of application being executed, not hardware limitations per se. As we will see, all MPPs provide the capability—some better than others—to move data from one private memory to another. The frequency with which a given application requires such data movement, and the robustness of the hardware facilities that support the movement (usually a low-latency point-to-point network of some sort), will strongly affect, on a case-by-case basis, how well a given MPP machine executes the application. The efficiency of MPPs will be taken up at length in Chapter 2. For the moment, it is enough to observe how MPPs provide a natural, cost-effective, and elegant solution to the problem of very high aggregate memory bandwidth.

A similar approach has been taken by manufacturers of RAID (*R*edundant *A*rrays of *I*nexpensive *D*isks) mass storage devices. Using inexpensive commodity Winchester drives, a word of data is spread across multiple disks, including several "extra" disks that provide error-correcting codes should one of the units fail. The bandwidth of any single drive is poor by DASD standards, but we are allowed to multiply by the number of disks to calculate total bandwidth. Using parallelism to provide high bandwidth from inexpensive commodity parts is the common theme behind both RAIDs and MPPs and is what places them at such favorable cost/performance points.

Summary of Section 1.1

The theme of this section has been the *inevitability* of the eventual success and widespread use of MPP technology. The arguments are based primarily on hardware considerations: fundamental limits on clock rates, packaging, reliability, memory bandwidth, and cost/performance. While conceptually separable, these factors are tightly coupled in the design of any actual machine and must be weighed against other factors, particularly actual cost (including software) and actual delivered performance on real applications. In the following section, we will consider why, given all the advantages of MPP listed above, the technology has remained outside the mainstream of high-performance computing; that is, we begin to focus on the *pain* of parallel processing.

1.2 OBSTACLES INHIBITING COMMERCIAL SUCCESS

That there is market resistance to accepting MPP technology is beyond dispute. Supercomputing has been estimated to have a worldwide market of perhaps $1.5 billion; of this rather small pie, MPP has perhaps 20 percent. These are not figures to gladden the hearts of potential investors.

Note: These figures would change considerably were we to include *symmetric multiprocessors* (SMPs) in our calculations. These shared memory computers have been in the computing mainstream for some time. The reasons for distinguishing SMPs from "parallel processing" have, in part, to do with their place on the spectrum shown in Figure 1-1. They are well towards the top, with numbers of processors on the order of 4 to 10. We will have more to say on this subject in Section 3.5.

Thus, MPPs are properly thought of as on the fringe of the computing universe (proponents might substitute "frontier" for "fringe"). Nevertheless, these machines have found niches here and there, often as dedicated production machines for compute-intensive applications on which they offer dramatic cost/peformance advantages. Examples include seismic processing in the oil industry, molecular modeling in the pharmaceutical industry, and SQL/OLTP database processing in the retail industry. Why have these remained "niches" instead of rapidly growing markets?

Before answering this question, we should dispel one widely held misconception. It is frequently suggested that MPPs are *special-purpose* (as opposed to *general-purpose*) machines. The idea conveyed by this criticism is that there are only a small set of applications that can be executed efficiently on highly parallel hardware. The speaker of this phrase (often a vendor of traditional hardware) clearly intends to exclude from this short list any that might be of interest to his or her audience.

If, however, we mean by *general purpose* the characteristics programmable and efficient on a wide range of applications, then massively parallel processing has clearly and convincingly shown itself to be general purpose. As we will see in Chapter 2, the inefficiencies in parallel processing usually have much more to do with *problem size* than with domain-specific idiosyncrasies of the application. Over the past 10 years, MPPs have been programmed—*efficiently* programmed—for applications in virtually every area of interest to both the research and commercial worlds. It would be far more difficult, in 1994, to list applications *not* suitable for parallel processing (provided only that the problem size is sufficiently large) than the reverse. A partial list of successes includes:

- artificial intelligence, including neural nets, case-based reasoning, production systems, robotics, and pattern recognition
- scientific visualization
- finite element analysis, including a wide variety of ordinary and partial differential equations in statics, electromagnetics, and computational fluid dynamics
- standard computer science algorithms, including sorting, searching, and tree and graph processing
- optimization, including linear, dynamic, and integer programming
- database operations, including SQL and OLTP
- simulation, including event-driven simulations and Monte Carlo techniques

- signal processing, including ultra-large FFTs, image processing, SAR, CAT scans, computer graphics, seismic processing, character recognition, and ultra high speed communications

As we will see, resistance to MPP technology has more to do with practical implementation considerations than with inherent limitations on efficiency or applicability. MPPs *are* general purpose.

Returning now to the key question, three areas of difficulty stand out for special consideration: (1) lack of quality application software; (2) lack of industry standards; and (3) vendor instability. We will look at each in turn.

1.2.1 Availability of Application Software

Just as the availability of production-quality third-party software (over 1,500 applications is typical) has fueled the current market explosion in high-performance workstations, its absence is the single greatest factor holding back market penetration of MPPs. With few exceptions, an organization considering incorporation of MPP faces a substantial software porting and/or development effort. In Chapters 11 and 12, we will consider strategies in these areas. For the moment, we will focus on why the "build versus buy" option for MPP applications so often, of necessity, reduces to "build."

Consider the situation of a company that develops and markets application software. Given a decision of whether to spend scarce development dollars on MPP codes rather than other alternatives (additional features for existing products, for example), there are at least five factors strongly mitigating *against* an investment in MPP:

- small installed base
- high cost of porting
- lack of standards
- validation
- vendor instability

We will briefly consider each in turn.

1. **Small Installed Base:** As we noted, market share for MPPs is miniscule by any reasonable standard. Most large machines are in government labs with large support staffs for application development. A number of smaller machines are on university campuses, used primarily for research and training. While the *existence* of an application might help to *create* a market, it is harder to sell hardware + software than it is to sell

software alone. Users with budgets to purchase software for execution on centralized facilities are excluded. The basic issue: Who am I going to sell to?

2. **High Cost of Porting:** Chapter 11 will discuss the many factors that potentially complicate a software port from a traditional architecture to an MPP. To briefly summarize a complicated subject, MPPs require a programmer to be conscious of the underlying hardware in ways long obsolete on sequential machines. This often (but not always) entails substantial alterations in data layout, control flow, data movement, and even fundamental algorithms. Failure to take these matters into account will result in potentially crippling inefficiencies, obviating the reason for moving to the MPP in the first place. A software port to an MPP can be lengthy, costly, and risky.
3. **Lack of Standards:** The good news is that every MPP supports both UNIX and standard network protocols (EtherNet, TCP/IP, HIPPI, FDDI, NFS, etc.) and hence is a natural candidate to act as a *server* in an *open system.* The bad news is that application development languages, and underlying hardware architectures, vary wildly from vendor to vendor and from machine to machine. Even if a language standard were to be adopted, the need to optimize algorithms to the target hardware may necessitate substantial recoding.

Example: The right choice for a large sort on an SIMD 2-D mesh may well be a backwards/forwards *mesh sort,* while the right choice on an MIMD hypercube may well be a *bitonic sort.* Having a common language for the two machines does not help, since the fundamental algorithm has to change to accommodate the peculiarities of the underlying hardware. The notion that "parallel is parallel" is fallacious; there is a different flavor of "parallel" for each machine. ■

4. **Validation:** Testing a software port to an MPP can be an eye-opening experience. Just because the results of serial and parallel versions disagree, it is not clear that the serial version is always right (even though it may be the legacy code). This is especially true for numerical codes, where convergence and accuracy may depend on rules of thumb that change as problem size increases.

   As we have noted, MPPs usually need large problems to be used efficiently. If growth in the problem size (say, for example, the dimensions of a matrix) causes the numerical properties (e.g., convergence rate, accumulated round-off error) to change, algorithms that worked well on smaller problems may no longer work in the new regime. Further, it is often true that mathematical/algebraic restructuring will cause operations to be performed in different orders on the sequential and parallel machines. Abstract mathematics may say that the sum of a set of numbers doesn't depend on the order in which they are added (that is, addition is *associative*), but floating point hardware can only approximate this ideal. These and other similar considerations make the validation of parallel codes a potential can of worms that software vendors would just as soon avoid, especially if results could cast doubt on their existing sequential offerings.

5. **Vendor Instability:** In Section 1.2.3, we will consider some of the reasons for high mortality among MPP companies. The prospect of porting software to a machine that will soon be defunct is cause for concern. Even if the company remains afloat, however, many MPP vendors pay no attention to instruction set compatibility between machine generations. The tendency has been to "wipe the slate clean" when design of the next machine is begun and to make design decisions based on "beauty and light" rather than market considerations. The result is that application codes developed for one generation of machine must often be scrapped, or substantially modified, when the next generation is introduced.

   (Note: The transition from the nCube 1 to the nCube 2, where upward binary compatibility was maintained, is in striking contrast to this general industry trend. Another positive example is the transition from the MasPar MP-1 to the MP-2. Similarly, MPP designers using commodity microprocessors inherit the the instruction set standards from generation to generation. Things in 1994 are considerably better than they were four years ago.)

The academic/research/technical–challenge atmosphere typical of MPP development teams (let's face it: These people are in it for *love*, not for *money*, and it drives the marketing staff *crazy!*) undoubtedly contributes to what must be considered a lack of market discipline in MPP design decisions.

1.2.2 Standards

The UNIX operating system, often running on a high-performance workstation that serves as user interface and front end, is ubiquitous among MPP vendors. In addition, all major vendors are committed to support networking standards—NFS, EtherNet, TCP/IP, HIPPI, FDDI, and, in the near future, ATM/SONET. This makes MPPs ideally suited for insertion as *servers* in an *open systems network.*

Standardization is weak, or nonexistent, in the areas of languages and underlying hardware architectures. We'll look briefly at each in turn.

Regarding programming languages and paradigms for MPPs, the current status is chaotic. Every vendor provides its own proprietary version of C and/or FORTRAN with parallel extensions, libraries, compiler directives, and modifications tailored to its own hardware. None of these proprietary versions are supported by other vendors (to do so, I suppose, would be an admission of weakness). A software port from one MPP to another can be more difficult than a port from a traditional machine to an MPP.

There are some software houses that provide libraries that run on more than one machine. Examples include Express from ParaSoft, Linda from SCA, STRAND, and PVM from Oak Ridge Labs. The idea is that an application written using one of these packages will run on any machine on which the package has been hosted—including, in some instances, a network of workstations.

The lack of standards in languages is more than equaled by the extreme diversity in hardware architectures. Table 1-1 summarizes some of this diversity for three major architectural features—the node processor, the network

Table 1-1. MPP Architecture Diversity

Machine	Node Processor	Network	Control
Thinking Machines CM-2	Bit Serial + Floating Point	16:1 Multiplexed Hypercube	SIMD
Intel Paragon	i860	2-D Mesh	Message Passing MIMD
Kendall Square KS-1	Custom	Hierarchy of Rings	Cache-Based Shared Memory
nCube 2	Custom	Hypercube	Message Passing MIMD
Thinking Machines CM-5	SPARC + Vector Units	Fat Tree	Synchronized MIMD
MasPar MP-1	4-Bit Custom + Floating Point	2-D Mesh + Router	SIMD
Cray T-3D	DEC Alpha	3-D Mesh	Message Passing MIMD

topology, and the control paradigm—for several MPPs. The significance of this diversity lies in the tight coupling that must occur between the hardware and the algorithm that is mapped onto it. This coupling is what makes porting and software development for MPPs difficult and is a major and recurring theme of this book. The algorithmic differences required as we move from one MPP architecture to another render the language issue, in some sense, moot.

In Chapters 4 through 7, we will look at the major programming paradigms for parallel machines. Even within a single paradigm, however, there are substantial proprietary differences among vendors that frustrate portability. While the need for standards—both in languages and in hardware—is given lip service by MPP vendors, the actual definition of and adherence to standards is, in a practical sense, nonexistent.

1.2.3 Vendor Instability

The MPP industry has experienced an extremely high mortality rate. Casualties among MPP vendors over the past six years include Ametek, BiiN, Multiflow, WaveTracer, Alliant, the BBN TC2000, FPS (though the hardware has been resurrected with a Cray Research label), and Myrias. Reasons for these failures are not hard to find. Whether a separate company or a group associated with a large parent corporation, the MPP vendors are small. Based solely on system sales, most are not profitable and must rely on the continued support of venture capital, the government (via DARPA, the DOE, NSF, or other agencies with an interest in high-performance computing), or the parent corporation. For most MPP casualties, the source of largesse eventually disappeared.

This financial dependence makes the design/development teams vulnerable to pressure. It is no accident, for example, that DARPA-sponsored Thinking Machines moved to shoehorn floating point accelerators and FORTRAN into an elegant bit-wise architecture. Similarly, we are not surprised to find Intel microprocessors (the i860 and 80x86) in the Intel-sponsored Paragon machine. DEC-sponsored MasPar, needless to say, uses a DEC workstation as its front end. When DOE announced support for software development on Cray Research's MPP, we were not surprised to learn that Cray intends to support Oak Ridge Lab's PVM message-passing paradigm. Similar relationships exist between Oracle and nCube and between DARPA and the Intel/CMU iWarp project.

An organization considering incorporation of MPP must be concerned about the continuing financial health of the MPP suppliers. This, in turn, has made it difficult for the MPP industry to generate an installed base broad enough to become self-supporting. Lack of a market-driven discipline among MPP vendors has not helped this problem. The entry of a large stable supplier, with broadly based contacts throughout the business community and with the business savvy to understand customer requirements, would do wonders for the commercial health of the MPP industry.

Summary of Section 1.2

The current lack of commercial success of MPPs can be attributed primarily to lack of high-quality application software. Other factors—lack of standards and vendor instability—contribute to the problem but are fixable, or at most annoying, if the software problem can be addressed. For the present, organizations considering the incorporation of MPPs must continue to ask the question, *Where is the software coming from?*

1.3 TRENDS AND CONSIDERATIONS

In this section, we will gaze into the crystal ball and attempt to discern the future pattern of MPP technology development. We will look at this both from the point of view of high-end systems (Section 1.3.1), where maximum performance is the major issue, and from the point of view of low-end systems (Section 1.3.2), where cost/performance is key. A final section considers the role of government policy and funding in how these will play out over the next few years.

1.3.1 High-End Systems: The First TeraFLOP Computer

Most MPP vendors, and their design teams, have drunk the heady brew of *speed* and are in hot pursuit of the Holy Grail of high-performance computing: the first TeraFLOP computer, capable of a sustained rate of 1 trillion (10^{12}) floating point operations per second. It is reminiscent of the period, during the 1920s and 1930s, when new flight endurance and speed records were almost daily events, sure to sell lots of papers to a public in need of heroes. It is a bit embarrassing to watch the various vendors vying with one another in their marketing hype for the title of "World's Fastest Supercomputer." A game of leapfrog has been going on for some time (the Japanese have lately been doing well in this game with their vector processors), and the latest release of Jack

Dongarra's LINPACK benchmark suite is devoured eagerly by design teams from Cambridge, to Minneapolis, to Beaverton, to Tokyo.

As we showed in Section 1.1.1, it now appears certain that the first TFLOP computer (estimates variously place its advent between 1996 and 2000) will be an MPP. Figure 1-3 illustrates this. Recall that total performance of a full machine can be found (subject to certain obvious provisos) by multiplying the number of processing nodes by the processing power at each node. On a log/log graph, level curves of constant total processing rate turn into straight lines. Figure 1-3 shows the lines corresponding to a 1-GFLOP and a 1-TFLOP computer, with four of the major contenders (Cray, Intel, Thinking Machines, and nCube) in more or less their current positions (first quarter, 1993) and with an informed guess (an arrow) about their future directions.

Now, consider where, along the 1-TFLOP line, the various arrows are heading. In particular, all the arrows have a very *substantial horizontal component!* Now, "horizontal" means "more processors," and "vertical" means "faster processors." A strong horizontal component means MPP: attaining high aggregate performance by increasing the number of processors. If we consider the region along the TFLOP line towards which the arrows are pointed and then look down to its projection on the *x*-axis, we see that the first TFLOP computer *will* have several thousands of processors—an MPP by anyone's definition.

The quizzical reader may well ask: What could anyone *do* with a TFLOP computer? Good question. Among the research community in the National

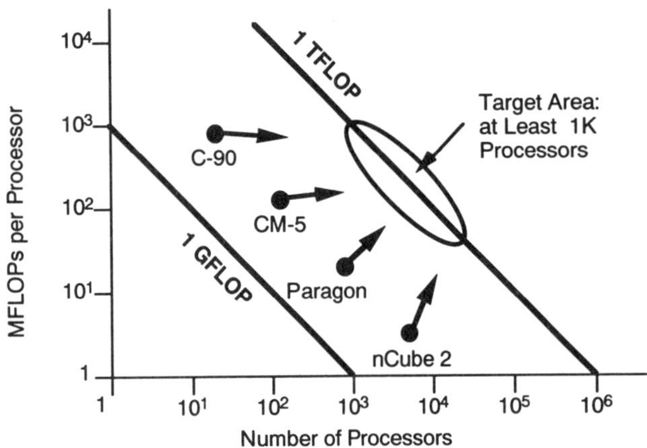

Figure 1-3. The first TFLOP computer *will be* an MPP

Labs, are those with problems already formulated that are fully suitable for such processing rates. It remains to be seen which companies, in the commercial arena, will find the insight to formulate tasks for such a machine that can result in a competitive advantage—advanced design methodologies, accelerated testing procedures, database mining, more precise financial models, improved use of exploration resources, etc. The availability of this level of computational power will, we can be sure, create a whole new set of winners and losers in a variety of, as yet unforeseen, industries. Good luck!

1.3.2 Low-End Systems: Desktop Supercomputers

Some in the MPP industry have not been so intoxicated by the pursuit of speed at all cost as to lose sight of what is probably the most likely path to financial success for MPPs. Even at the generous rate of $100/MFLOP (as of second quarter, 1993), rates are around $500/MFLOP for MPPs and much higher for traditional vector supercomputers), a TFLOP computer would cost $100 million. You're asking for a *lot* of competitive advantage to justify such an expenditure from a commercial enterprise; even the government might think twice about a pricetag like that.

However, at $100/MFLOP, a mere $2 million would procure 50 GFLOPs of performance—as much as the fastest supercomputer available in 1993. And a $100,000 investment would provide 2.5 GFLOPs—about the power of a full-up Cray Y-MP from 1990 and packaged in an air-cooled cabinet about the size of a laser printer.

What are the impacts on the way we do business of having a supercomputer in every department? On each engineer's desk? No one, to my knowledge, has adequately addressed this issue. Its revolutionary potential approximates that of microprocessors introduced in the early 1980s. The Joker in the deck is that these levels of performance are only achieveable using the distributed memory approach characteristic of MPP (see Sections 1.1.3 and 3.3), with its attendant software problems and lack of standards.

The "right" way for these issues to be wrung out is through market forces. The potential market for MPP is far greater at the low end than at the high end. It will be through businesses recognizing the potential for productivity gains and competitive advantage, and demanding the technology to support it, that both the software and the standards issues will be resolved. In the meantime, supported by continued government funding for R&D, the knights on the MPP design teams continue their quest for TFLOP computing. The wisdom of this approach will be considered in the next section.

1.3.3 Government and Policy Considerations

In 1991, after a lengthy period of wrangling among the various government agencies with a finger in the supercomputing pie, Congress passed the HPCCI (High Performance Computing and Communications Initiative). It consolidated funds from existing programs, added some additional funds, and resliced the pie. A major sponsor of this legistation was Vice-President (then Senator) Gore.

The funding provided by this initiative is distributed among a number of programs that are overseen by a variety of agencies. Much of the money goes to the National Labs (overseen by DOE) and to the four major Supercomputer Centers (overseen by NSF). In addition, the bill provides for construction and operation of a "Data Superhighway" to interconnect supercomputing resources on a very high performance network. In theory, this will provide researchers anywhere on the network access to computing resources elsewhere—"anytime anywhere supercomputing."

Some of the money from the HPCCI has gone to support R&D efforts by supercomputer and MPP vendors. Beneficiaries include Thinking Machines Corp., Intel, and Cray Research. In addition, all supercomputer vendors compete for hardware procurements that may be funded by the HPCCI.

The National Labs and DoD-related agencies are the largest accounts for all domestic supercomputer vendors. This, together with additional money the government provides for R&D effort, has made the entire industry extremely dependent on the government and highly attuned to perceived government requirements. It is not clear that this is a healthy situation.

Supporters of this arrangement suggest: (1) that the industry would collapse without government support, and (2) that maintaining U.S. worldwide supercomputer leadership is critical to the national security. Without venturing an opinion on (2), opponents suggest that the threatened collapse really reflects the unhealthy symbiotic relationship that currently exists between the government and the supercomputing industry and that the cure is to force supercomputer vendors to find and demonstrate commercial applications that can be justified in dollars and cents. The truth, no doubt, lies somewhere in the middle, but the continued dependence of high-performance computing on government largesse must be viewed as a temporary expedient, the sooner removed the better.

In this regard, the previous section suggested that the most likely place to find a profitable market in the commercial arena is not in the high-end systems but in the low-end systems. All major MPP vendors have offerings under $1 million, some even under $100,000. The marketing and software for these systems, however, lags, and there is no doubt that the major focus of the MPP vendors remains the glamorous goal of TFLOP computing. Weaning companies away from government (or parent corporation) support by forcing attention on profitability could be useful in building the low-end market, which is, for most potential commercial users of MPP, the place where MPP can have the most immediate impact. Recent changes, for example, at ARPA indicate that the government is increasingly aware of these issues and is prepared to accept a more Darwinian approach (based on competitive commercial success) to architecture evolution.

Summary of Chapter 1

We have argued, based primarily on hardware considerations, that MPP will inevitably (some would argue that the transition is already well underway) replace vector supercomputers as king of the high-performance mountain. However, due primarily to poor application software, but also abetted by lack of standards and vendor instability, MPP remains on the fringe of the computing world. As the knights of MPP pursue their quest for the Holy Grail of TFLOP computing, the most attractive potential commercial market for MPP, at the low end, goes largely untended.

2

Can Parallel Machines Be Used Efficiently?

There is an a priori argument that purports to show, from general principles, that it is *impossible* to use a large number of processors efficiently on a single problem. It is the purpose of this chapter to examine this argument in some detail (don't worry; nothing more complicated than addition and multiplication is required). The conclusion will be, not that the argument is wrong, but that there is a critical assumption about *problem size* that should be made explicit whenever the argument is used.

The argument goes by the name of *Amdahl's Law* and is part of the repertoire of marketeers from vendors of traditional architectures. The dreaded trinity of "fear, uncertainty, and doubt" now has a fourth companion to demoralize the unknowing. We hope to remove the mystery surrounding this argument so that the user can, with confidence, make his or her own assessment regarding the potential inefficiencies of a proposed implementation.

The chapter begins with an extended metaphor comparing the implementation of an application on a parallel processor to the task of building a wall. The masons correspond to the processors, the finished wall corresponds to the complete task, and the portion of the wall assigned to each worker corresponds to the part of the job (often based on a partitioning of a large data set) assigned to each processor. The idea for this metaphor comes from Dr. Geoffrey Fox's book, *Solving Problems on Concurrent Processors* [2]. A surprisingly large number of basic concepts in parallel processing can be simply illustrated using this analogy, and it will provide a good example for testing our analysis of Amdahl's Law.

A word of encouragement. The ideas are intuitive and natural, and the amount of math is minimal. Reflection on this material *now* will pay dividends as the book proceeds.

2.1 A PARALLEL PARABLE: BUILDING A WALL

We propose an extended metaphor for the situation where a problem is to be executed on a parallel processor. Consider, for the moment, the task of building a long wall. Both the ancient Chinese and Romans faced such a task, and for similar reasons—they wanted to provide a defense against incursions by barbarians. Further, both used a similar strategy (a highly parallel strategy) for accomplishing the task.

They partitioned the entire wall length into many shorter segments and assigned each of these segments separate, independent workers (or small teams of workers), all of whom were active *simultaneously*. If, on a given day during the building of Hadrian's Wall, an observer had surveyed the entire length, thousands of Roman legionnaires might have been seen spread along the entire wall length, each legionnaire working on the (relatively) short stretch to which he had been assigned. As days passed, the entire wall grew in height as each soldier gradually added brick and stone to his own segment. It is clear, I think, that up to thousands of legionnaires could be profitably employed in this endeavor, since the wall was very long (73 miles).

A modern-day *sequential* approach to this problem would be to first manufacture a large, fast, expensive *wall-building machine*. The machine would be lined up at one end, pointed in the right direction, the switch flipped, and the machine would go chugging along, laying bricks at an incredible rate, until it at last reached the other end.

In our metaphor, the legionnaires working on stretches of the wall correspond to processing nodes in a *parallel processor*, each assigned a part of the total application. In the next few sections, we will consider both advantages and disadvantages of this highly parallel approach from several points of view.

2.1.1 Replication

The wall-building metaphor illustrates one of the central motivations behind MPP: the *replication* of both *hardware* and *software*. Let's take up software first. Just as a legionnaire working on the wall corresponds to a processor (one among many) working on an application, so also the program executed by the processor corresponds to the instructions given to the legionnaire, describing how he is to complete his section of the wall. Note that: (1) the problem of building a short stretch of wall is "just like" the problem of building a long stretch of wall, and (2) all the short stretches of wall are interchangeable.

First, this means that if legacy code for wall building already exists, possibly large amounts of it may be reusable in the concurrent version. A change of parameters—say, for wall *length*—may be all that is required to prepare much of the instruction set for the individual processors. Second, it means that it is not necessary to prepare a different program (instruction sheet) for each processor (legionnaire); the instructions can be prepared using a duplicating machine, *replicating* the program once per legionnaire. This style of parallel programming is called *SPMD*—*s*ingle *p*rogram/ *m*ultiple *d*ata. Each processor works on a unique, independent local data set, while the program used to drive the processor is replicated—a single program run multiple times concurrently on different (multiple) data sets.

This is clearly advantageous for software development. Existing sequential code may be reused, and the software development effort does not grow with the number of processors. Usually, in fact, the number of processors to be employed is a *run-time variable* reselected on each new occasion to match the particular problem size. Thus, the same program can run successfully on both different problem sizes and on different machine sizes (where the "size" of the machine is the number of processors).

Replication of hardware is also illustrated by the example. From the point of view of the legionnaire commander, the legion consists of a large number of conceptually identical "units." No one legionnaire, or group of legionnaires, is distinguishable from any other; idiosyncrasies between them are abstracted away. Just the same point of view is taken with respect to parallel architectures. Like the individual flowers on an azalea, once nature has learned how to make one, it can make billions. The nonrecurring engineering costs in MPP are therefore spread over a large set. We noted in Section 1.1 that the custom CMOS/DRAM combination is at the heart of MPP architectures. These technologies are what make replication of hardware in MPPs technically feasible. In fact, it was the realization that microprocessors could be used in this way that was (and remains) the most significant impetus for the development of MPPs.

Replication is not without its potential "gotcha's." For example, consider the replication of read-only data structures (such as look-up tables). Suppose the algorithm, for example, calls for a legionnaire to look up a value from a handbook based on locally differing conditions (e.g., slope of the ground). Each legionnaire must have his own copy, and the replication may be onerous, both in overhead of distributing it and in memory used to store it. Of course, machines (shared memory machines, in particular) may be able to avoid this problem by providing a single central copy available to all the workers. As we shall see, however, the number of independent processors that can be efficiently supported on a shared memory machine is quite small (30 or so), and contention for access to the shared structure must be mediated. An important and recurring theme of this book is: *There is no free lunch in parallel processing!*

2.1.2 Locality of Communications

One problem faced by the parallel approach that does not arise in the sequential approach is the portion of the wall *shared* by two adjacent legionnaires. The boundary region is typical of MPP solutions. The underlying data set or work to be accomplished may be partitioned, but adjacent pieces will be shared by two (or more) workers/processors, and arrangements will be required for coordination, data exchange, and cooperation.

In an actual application, this will require both data and control (synchronization) to flow across the *boundary* shared by the processors. This adds overhead, both in time for data movement and in additional software to control the exchange. The amount of data, its frequency, and the ability of the underlying hardware to move the data efficiently will all be important factors in how well a given application performs on a given MPP, and we will return to these matters at greater length in, for example, the sections on benchmarking (Chapter 10). For the moment, observe that *general* communications (*any* soldier to *any* soldier) are *not* required. In fact, in this wall-building example, any given soldier only needs to communicate with two other soldiers—his right- and left-hand neighbors.

This is a significant advantage and is a characteristic of the wall-building problem that makes it especially attractive for parallel implementation. It means that the underlying hardware (for this problem) only needs to provide a limited and highly structured communications capability—right-hand and left-hand shifts—rather than a completely general capability. Further, the right/left conceptual model maps easily and naturally onto the underlying two-dimensional hardware world of computer chips and printed circuit boards.

In general, problems that exhibit *locality* and *structure* in their required data communications patterns are, to that extent, well suited to MPP implementation. Any particular machine will have an underlying interconnection network within which some pairs of processors are closer together than others. If the *logical* pairwise communications requirements of the problem can be mapped onto the *physical* processors in such a way that the distance between communicating processors is minimized, this can be a significant performance boost to a parallel implementation. Such a mapping, however, usually requires conscious knowledge by the programmer of the underlying hardware interconnection scheme—hypercube, 2-D mesh, fat tree, or whatever (see Section 3.2).

This is only one example, among many, of potential complications in the programming task for MPPs. The good news, however, is that many problems exhibit extremely simple and highly localized communications requirements. This regularity can arise in several ways. Image processing, for example, naturally exhibits a two-dimensional arrangement. If we break the image up into equal area squares, for example, any given subimage will have four neighbors (up, down, left, right), or eight if corner-crossings are required. A similar two-dimensional decomposition can arise in matrix operations. A time-oriented problem can often be decomposed into nonoverlapping time intervals, giving rise to a natural one-dimensional left/right (before/after) pattern similar to the wall. Even seemingly general problems, such as sorting, have a natural underlying logarithmic structure (based on successive doubling) that maps well onto, for example, a hypercube interconnection scheme.

A further theoretical observation, but one that is of great importance to the range of applicability of MPP, is that the *boundary* of a problem tends to grow significantly less fast than its *interior.* In our wall metaphor, for example, we see that the amount of work devoted to the edge (where the communication is required) does not change at all, no matter how long or short the stretch of wall assigned to a given soldier. In a two-dimensional problem, the boundary is the perimeter, and it grows *linearly* with edge length, while the interior grows as the *square* of edge length. Even in a general problem, such as sorting, the parallelizable "interior" grows linearly, and the nonparallelizable "boundary" grows logarithmically.

The significance of this observation is its impact on how inefficiencies change with problem size. Since (briefly) overhead inefficiencies tend to be associated with the boundary, they increase much more slowly than the parallelizable part of the problem associated with the interior. This is the key to why MPPs need large problems to be used efficiently. The problem has to be large enough so that the fraction of time spent in overhead (the boundary of each subproblem) is small relative to the problem as a whole. Since the two parts of the problem (inefficient boundary and efficient interior) change at different rates as the problem size grows, their ratio changes. The fraction of time spent on the inefficient boundary can be made quite small by choosing a sufficiently large problem.

The impact of the need to communicate across boundaries can be greater on software than on hardware. Even if only a small (say, less than 1 percent) of the execution time is spent in communications, the code to implement that communications can be a substantial portion of the total code and will ordinarily not be available from legacy codes. Indeed, much of the effort associated with a software port to an MPP is directed to this portion of the problem: supplying the additional code necessary to provide communication between processors across subproblem boundaries.

2.1.3 I/O Strategies

If we return briefly to the sequential solution to the wall-building problem, we see that the large, fast wall-building machine will have a large appetite for data. We can, in our mind's eye, imagine the dump trucks rolling up beside the machine and emptying large loads of bricks to keep the hoppers full. These dump trucks provide high bandwidth (measured in megabricks per second?), and their absence or poor performance will clearly affect the ability of the wall-building machine to maintain its performance rate.

What of the parallel approach? The poor man's dump truck is a wheelbarrow, and we imagine the legionnaires trudging to the depots (hopefully, several along the wall length) to fill up with bricks and return. Clearly, the wheelbarrow is very low bandwidth, at least when compared to a dump truck. However, observe that *every* soldier has *his own* wheelbarrow, and, therefore, we are allowed to multiply the bandwidth of one wheelbarrow by the total number of soldiers to compute the total bandwidth into the wall. With up to thousands of soldiers at work, it is not hard to see that the aggregate bandwidth in the parallel approach could equal, or exceed, the bandwidth provided by the high-performance sequential approach.

This strategy is exactly analogous to that adopted by MPP architects for their I/O subsystems. Typically, a modest (by Cray standards) communications path is provided to each processor in the array, together with the means for many (or all) of the processors to drive these channels simultaneously. The modest bandwidth of the individual link is then multiplied by the number of links (that is, the number of processors) to obtain very high aggregate I/O bandwidth.

Another closely related approach to I/O is to dedicate a subset of the processors (often physically located near the edge of the array) solely to I/O on behalf of the full array. The interconnection network—the same one we mentioned in the previous section—is used to link these specialized I/O processors to the rest of the array. Requests for I/O service generated by processing nodes are passed to the I/O nodes. The I/O bandwidth is, therefore, tied to the number of I/O processors (rather than the full array), but the I/O processors are dedicated to their specific task. Just as in RAID technology, software is often provided by the vendors automatically and invisibly to spread files across multiple I/O nodes. This allows many I/O nodes to be simultaneously involved in a single file access and, hence, can dramatically improve file access bandwidth.

2.1.4 Miscellaneous

We have nearly exhausted the utility of our extended wall-building metaphor, and the reader no doubt is concocting the counter-examples that indicate various ways in which the analogy breaks down. During a briefing on this subject, the author was once challenged, "How about building a skyscraper? You can't build the sixtieth floor at the same time you're building the tenth." Another participant (destined for greatness?) responded, "Sure you can. Just construct the building sideways, and then stand it upright at the end!" An ingenious solution and typical of the kind of thinking sometimes needed to discover the way in which a problem can be parallelized.

Other capabilities overlooked by the example but sometimes key to implementation success include:

- broadcast capabilities, in which a datum is made available from a central controller to all the processors
- reduction, in which data or results held by processors are combined (say, by summation or by applying the maximum operator) and made available to a central controller
- synchronization, in which all the processors must reach a common point in the control stream before any can proceed to the next step
- load balancing, in which care is taken that the work done by any processor is about equal to the work done by any other, so that processors are kept as busy as possible over the course of the task
- nonuniform tasking, where some (perhaps small) subset of processors is assigned a substantially different task—say, to build a gate or a tower somewhere along the wall

Real-world problems may be able to make use of these or other capabilities, and parallel architectures with specific hardware support for these requirements will have a corresponding performance advantage on such applications. It is, however, quite remarkable how many real applications are well modeled by our original no-frills example. Even where additional capabilities might appear to be useful in theory, a brute-force approach will often be adequate in practice. In short, the author believes that for the majority of applications that might be considered for parallelization, the "build a wall" conceptual scheme is adequate (providing some ingenuity and resourcefulness is applied) for discerning the opportunities for and evaluating the appropriateness of parallelism.

In the next section, we take up the most common argument against massive parallelism. As we shall see, it is *problem size* that is usually determinitive in whether an MPP can provide an efficient solution.

2.2 AMDAHL'S LAW

In this section, we will consider the most frequently used, and potentially damaging, argument against the idea that many—up to thousands or more—processors can be used efficiently to solve a problem. The first goal (Section 2.2.1) is to be more precise about what is meant by the term *efficiently* and to provide the formal statement of Amdahl's Law. In the following section, the wall problem from Section 2.1 is reexamined to discover what Amdahl's Law has to say in this simple case. Finally, in Section 2.2.3, some easily understood and illustrative examples taken from standard applications are considered to see how efficiently we might expect an MPP to perform on them. The major conclusion of Section 2.2 is not that Amdahl's Law is *wrong* but that its effects depend critically on *problem size.*

2.2.1 Definitions

We begin with definitions for two basic terms in assessing the performance of parallel processors: *speed-up* and *efficiency.* The idea behind these terms is simple. The reason to have multiple processors is to execute the problem faster. Hopefully, the more processors applied, the faster the problem can be executed. However, intuition will suggest that adding more and more processors, thereby executing the problem in less and less time, cannot continue indefinitely. Sooner or later, inefficiencies in the hardware (for example, coordination among the processors to decide which one gets what piece of the problem) will start to dominate the time spent in useful work. It is common, for example, to find problems in which adding more processors beyond a certain point actually makes the problem run *longer. More* is not necessarily *faster* when it comes to parallel processing.

Example: Intuition suggests that the same principle applies in the workplace. For a given size job—say, building a piece of application software or doing a financial analysis—there is an optimal number of people that can be profitably assigned to the task; beyond this number, productivity actually decreases. ■

Ideally, we would like these inefficiencies to be minimal, and it will help to have a notion of how far from the ideal a given implementation has departed. In the ideal case, where there are no inefficiencies, the time to execute the problem will decrease in proportion to the number of processors. To formalize this, we introduce the following terms:

N : the number of processors

T_N: the time to execute the problem using N processors

As N increases, T_N should decrease: *Increasing* the number of processors from 1 to N should result in *decreasing* the run time by $(1/N)$; that is:

$T_N = T_1/N$ in the ideal case

or, doing some algebra,

$T_1/T_N = N$, in the ideal case.

Formally, we define the ratio T_1/T_N to be the *speed-up. Ideally*, the speed-up on N processors will be *equal* to N. *In practice*, because of inefficiencies, it is *less* than N; that is, we usually have:

$T_1/T_N \leq N$, in practice.

The ratio of the *actual* speed-up on N processors to its *ideal* is our measure for *efficiency*. Formally,

efficiency = (actual speed-up)/(ideal speed-up)

= (speed-up on N processors)$/N$.

Because the speed-up is at most N, we see that

efficiency ≤ 1.

Often, efficiency is translated into a percent:

efficiency% = efficiency $\times$ 100%.

Clearly,

efficiency% $\leq$ 100%.

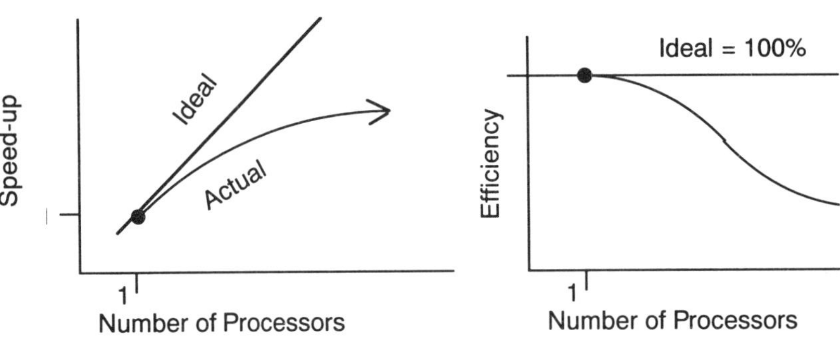

Figure 2-1. Notional graph showing drop-off in speed-up efficiency as number of processors increases

Figure 2-1 contains notional graphics illustrating how speed-up and efficiency decrease as the number of processors increases.

***Example*:** Table 2-1 shows an example of measured run times on a problem (this happened to be a bitonic sort on 32-bit integers on an nCube 2) for varying numbers of processors (that is, for different values of N). The ideal *run time*, *speed-up*, *efficiency*, and *efficiency* % (as defined above) are calculated in each case. ■

Intuitively, low values of *efficiency* represent wasted system processing power. If, for example, we use 20 processors, but only obtain a speed-up of 5 (that is,

Table 2-1. Measured Results for a Sort

# of Nodes	Measured Run Time	Ideal Run Time	Actual Speed-up	Efficiency %
1	86.70	86.70	1.0	100%
2	49.72	43.35	1.94	97%
4	27.69	21.68	3.13	78%
8	17.04	10.84	5.09	64%
16	10.59	5.42	8.19	51%
32	7.49	2.71	11.65	36%

the problem only runs five times faster when 20 processors are utilized), then the *efficiency* % is

$$\text{efficiency\%} = 5/20 \times 100\% = 25\%.$$

In effect, we are only getting about 25 percent of the machine, due to inefficiencies of whatever sort.

We are ready now to turn to Amdahl's Law. The intention of Amdahl's Law is to show that there is an upper limit to the speed-up that can be achieved on a problem, *independent of the number of processors*; that is, Amdahl's Law claims that, for any given problem, there is a bound—call it *B*—such that

$$T_N \geq B,$$

no matter what the value of N. Heuristically, no matter how many processors we apply to the problem in parallel, we can't execute it faster than the limiting time *B*. This, in turn, means that the speed-up is bounded above by

$$\text{speed-up on } N \text{ processors} = T_1/T_N \quad T_1/B.$$

Now, consider the definition of *efficiency* (as illustrated in the previous equations). We see that the numerator (the *speed-up*) is bounded above, while the denominator (*N*, the number of processors) can increase (at least conceptually) to arbitarily large values. The lower bound, *B*, suggested by Amdahl's Law means that, for large values of *N*, the efficiency decreases towards 0.

We can summarize this situation as follows. Amdahl's Law suggests that we cannot speed up execution on a problem indefinitely. As more and more processors are added, the machine will be used less and less efficiently. The observed speed-ups will fall farther and farther away from the ideal of linear or proportional speed-up, and, correspondingly, the efficiency will become very poor as machine size grows. In short, MPPs cannot be used efficiently.

Where does this lower bound, *B*, on run time come from? The argument goes as follows. The total run time for a problem on a single processor, T_1, can be broken up into two components. Part of the problem will be *parallelizable.* This is the part of the problem where adding additional processors really does speed things up—perhaps at even very close to ideal rates. Let us call the time spent to execute this part of the problem T_P.

There will also be another part of the problem—the *inherently sequential* or *nonparallelizable* part of the problem. This is the part of the problem that won't speed up by adding more processors, since it must (at least conceptually) be executed *at least once* by *every* processor included in the processing array (or by a single processor acting as a surrogate, while the rest of the array is idle). If we call the time spent in this part of the problem T_S, we have:

$$T_1 = T_S + T_P.$$

The term T_S is the lower bound, *B*, discussed above. We can reduce the T_P term by adding more processors (in fact, we can reduce it by a factor of [1/*N*] if we add *N* processors); but, we can't reduce the T_S term at all. We have:

$$T_N = T_S + (T_P/N) \quad T_S.$$

Some examples will help to illustrate the point.

Example: Suppose that, for a given application, the total run time on a single processor is 25 minutes, of which 20 are parallelizable. We have:

$$T_1 = T_S + T_P$$

$$25 = 5 + 20$$

If we were to parallelize with $N = 5$ processors, then

$$T_5 = T_S + (T_P/5)$$

$$9 = 5 + 4.$$

The ideal speed-up with 5 processors is 5, but in this example the actual speed-up attained is

$$\text{speed-up} = T_1/T_5 = 25/9 = 2.67$$

Thus, our efficiency is

$$\begin{aligned}\text{efficiency} &= (\text{speed-up})/N \\ &= 2.67/5 \\ &= .56\end{aligned}$$

and

$$\text{efficiency\%} = 56\%$$

The machine is only being used at 56 percent of capacity. If we repeat the same calculation with $N = 20$ processors, we obtain:

$$T_{20} = 5 + 1 = 6$$

$$\text{speed-up} = 25/6 = 4.2$$

$$\text{efficiency} = 4.2/25 = .17$$

$$\text{efficiency\%} = 17\%$$ ■

Increasing the number of processors from 5 to 20 speeded up the execution (from 9 seconds to 6 seconds) but at the cost of reducing the efficiency from 56 percent to 17 percent. On this example, a parallel machine with 20 processors could only obtain a speed-up of 4.2 (instead of an ideal 20) and could only be used at 17 percent of its capacity. A bit of reflection will convince the reader that it is the T_S term—the 5 seconds that do not decrease no matter how many processors are used—that is the underlying culprit.

It should also be observed that the *speed-up* and *efficiency* calculations are without units; that is, the same result would have been obtained if the run times had been measured in milliseconds or in hours. It is the *ratio* of T_S to T_P—or, even better, the ratio T_S to T_1 that is important. In this example, it was the fact that T_S was one-fifth (20 percent) of the single-processor run time that was critical. It said, in effect, that T_N can never become lower than $T_S = (.2) * T_1$, so that the speed-up is bounded above by

$$\text{speed-up} = T_1/T_S \leq T_1/(T_1/5) = 5.$$

Putting this into our efficiency equation, we have

$$\text{efficiency} = (\text{speed-up})/N \leq 5/N,$$

no matter how large the value of N may be. In fact, the maximum possible speed-up, 5, suggests that no more than about 5 processors ought to be put on the problem, due to ever decreasing efficiency. Certainly, an MPP with hundreds or thousands of processors would be a waste.

The key point is that the *fraction* of total run time spent in the nonparallelizable part of the problem, T_S/T_1, imposes a hard bound on speed-up, independent of the number of processors. The larger the fraction of total run time that is nonparallelizable, the less efficient an MPP is in executing the problem.

2.2.2 The Wall Revisited

The last section observed that it is the *fraction of total run time that is nonparallelizable* that is the determining factor in when inefficiency begins to dominate. When, for example, T_S was as high as 20 percent, then a limit of $1/.2 = 5$ is placed on speed-up. If T_S were 40 percent of run time, then a limit of $1/.4 = 2.5$ is placed on speed-up. If T_S is 5 percent, then an upper limit of $1/.05 = 20$ is placed on speed-up. (Ah, you say, things are looking a little better!) If T_S is 1 percent of total run time, then speed-up is only bounded by 100. If T_S is .1 percent of run time, then speed-up is only bounded by 1,000—not much of a bound at all and suggesting that up to 1,000 processors (clearly in MPP range) could be used efficiently. Thus, the critical question regarding Amdahl's Law is: *What fraction of the total run time is, in fact, nonparallelizable?*

If this fraction is large on a particular problem, then MPPs can't be used efficiently. If, however, it is fairly small (say, less than 1 percent), then the theoretical limit imposed on MPP efficiency by Amdahl's Law has been removed.

Clearly, we cannot answer the question of efficiency once and for all; it depends on the problem. And, when Amdahl wrote the paper containing this argument, he said as much. However, he went further. He analyzed a number of typical FORTRAN codes current at the time (1966) and asserted that the portion of time spent in T_S is "typically" between 5 and 30 percent. If true, speed-ups of at most a factor of 20 (corresponding to 5 percent) are achievable, strongly suggesting that MPPs can never be used efficiently. It is in this version that Amdahl's Law makes great marketing copy for vendors of traditional sequential machines.

What needs to be understood, however, is that the ratio of T_S to T_P is not constant, even for a given *type* of problem such as, say, matrix inversion. As we saw in Section 2.1.1, the parallelizable and nonparallelizable parts of a problem vary with problem size. Typically, the parallelizable part grows much more rapidly than the sequential part, because it is associated with the *interior* of the problem, not its boundary. As the problem size changes, the ratio of T_S to T_P (that is, T_S as a fraction of T_1) changes too, and, typically, T_P grows much faster than T_S. For many problems, we can make T_S an arbitrarily small fraction of T_1 just by making the problem size large enough.

When Amdahl wrote his paper, typical problem sizes substantiated his estimate. For those problem sizes, appropriate to that generation of machine, the fraction of T_S suggested by Amdahl was correct, and, in fact, MPPs *cannot* be used efficiently on problem sizes typical of the early 1970s. However, for large problems, in which T_S has become a very small fraction (typically much less than .1 percent), very large speed-ups are possible, and MPPs can be used quite efficiently. An example will help to make these ideas more concrete.

> ***Example:*** Let us return to the wall-building problem and analyze it in terms of Amdahl's Law. The reader's intuition should be that on a wall 73 miles long, lots (up to thousands) of soldiers can be used efficiently. As we will see, this is correct, and the reason *why* it is correct is the same reason why MPPs can be used efficiently.
>
> Let us consider the parallelizable and nonparallelizable parts of the wall problem. The parallelizable part corresponds to building the *middle* part of the wall—the nonends. Adding more soldiers will proportionately de-

crease the length of wall any given soldier has to build. The nonparallelizable part corresponds to building the ends of the wall—a soldier's shared boundary with right- and left-hand neighbors. Even if a given soldier has a very short stretch of wall to build, he still must attend to the two ends. Notice that this corresponds to the "interior/boundary" observation we made in Section 2.1.2.

In order to focus more clearly, let us suppose that a typical soldier can build one yard of wall per day and that it takes him three days for each end—a total of six days for the two ends. Let L be the total length of the wall in yards (for a 73-mile wall, L is 73 ¥ 1,760 = 126,480 yards). We can now calculate T_1, the total time required to build the wall using one soldier:

$$\begin{aligned} T_1 &= T_S + T_P \\ &= 6 + 126{,}480 = 126{,}486 \text{ days.} \end{aligned}$$

We also see that the ratio of T_S/T_1 is quite small—less than .005 percent, with a corresponding speed-up limit of about 21,000—suggesting that an MPP approach might be appropriate.

Let us suppose we choose to use $N = 1{,}000$ soldiers. Then each soldier has a length of wall 126,480/1,000, about 127 yards per soldier. We can calculate $T_{1,000}$, the time it takes to build the wall with 1,000 soldiers:

$$\begin{aligned} T_{1,000} &= T_S + (T_P/1{,}000) \\ &= 6 + 127 = 133 \text{ days.} \end{aligned}$$

The corresponding speed-ups and efficiencies are:

$$\begin{aligned} \text{speed-up} &= T_1/T_{1,000} \\ &= 126{,}486/133 = 951 \end{aligned}$$

$$\begin{aligned} \text{efficiency} &= (\text{speed-up})/1{,}000 \\ &= 951/1{,}000 = .951 \text{ (or 95\%)} \end{aligned}$$

In this problem, we could use 1,000 soldiers with about 95 percent efficiency.

Suppose we try to use $N = 10{,}000$ soldiers. Then

$$\begin{aligned} T_{10,000} &= 6 + 13 = 19 \text{ days} \\ \text{speed-up} &= 6{,}657 \\ \text{efficiency\%} &= 67\% \end{aligned}$$

Notice that by the time we get to 10,000 soldiers, each individual soldier is spending almost one-third of his time on the T_S portion of the problem.

Things are quite different if the wall is only 10 miles long. In this case, using $N = 1{,}000$ soldiers, we find

$$T_{1,000} = 6 + 18 = 24 \text{ days}$$

speed-up = 733

efficiency = 73%

By the time we try to use $N = 10{,}000$ men on the 10-mile wall, we have

$$T_{10,000} = 6 + 2 = 8 \text{ days}$$

speed-up = 2,200

efficiency% = 22%

The reader may verify that for a 1-mile wall, the efficiency with $N = 1{,}000$ soldiers is only 22 percent, and the efficiency with $N = 10{,}000$ soldiers drops to 3 percent. In this last case, each soldier has less than a full yard of wall to build but must still spend the full six days building the two ends. ■

The main conclusion of this discussion is that MPPs *need large problems in order to be used efficiently*. In particular, the problem must be large enough so that the nonparallelizable fraction of the problem, T_S, becomes extremely small. Because the nonparallelizable part of the problem grows at a different and slower rate than does the parallelizable part (often because the boundary of the problem grows more slowly than its interior), we can make the nonparallelizable fraction arbitrarily small simply by increasing problem size. This, then, is the theoretical reason why Amdahl's Law does *not* "prove" that MPPs cannot be used efficiently. It is also the most significant single practical observation that can be made by an organization considering a conversion to MPP technology. The key question to ask is: Do I have a large enough problem to be appropriate for an MPP?

This is also illustrated in Figure 2-2, where the notional speed-up and efficiency graphs from Figure 2-1 have been revised to reflect problem size. There is not a single curve but a family of curves—one for each size of problem in the application domain. Notice that large problems remain close to the ideal for large numbers of processors. Alternatively, if we hold the number of processors constant, increasing the problem size improves both speed-up and efficiency.

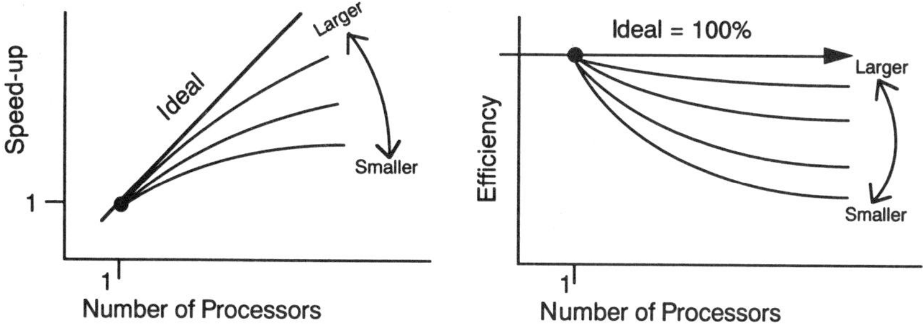

Figure 2-2. Different problem sizes have different speed-up and efficiency curves

2.2.3 Efficiency Depends on Problem Size

The observations made in the preceding section have a number of consequences concerning how one should assess the applicability of MPP technology. First, it should be clear at this point that a complete evaluation ought to extend over at least two parameters: (1) the *size of the problem*, and (2) the *number of processors*. In the wall problem, these were, respectively, *L*, the length of the wall, and *N*, the number of soldiers. Table 2-2 illustrates this. With columns labeled by wall length, *L*, and rows labeled by number of soldiers, *N*,

Table 2-2. Speed-up and Efficiency Depend Both on Number of Soldiers and on Wall Length

Number of Soldiers		Wall Length in Miles: 1	10	25	50	75	100
1	*t:*	1,766	17,606	44,006	88,006	132,006	176,006
	s:	1	1	1	1	1	1
	e%:	100%	100%	100%	100%	100%	100%
100	*t:*	24	182	446	886	1,326	1,766
	s:	73.6	96.7	98.7	99.3	99.6	99.7
	e%:	74%	97%	99%	99%	100%	100%
1,000	*t:*	8	24	50	94	138	182
	s:	221	734	880	936	956	967
	e%:	22%	73%	88%	94%	96%	97%
5,000	*t:*	7	10	15	24	33	42
	s:	251	1,760	2,934	3,667	4,000	4,191
	e%:	5%	35%	59%	73%	80%	84%
10,000	*t:*	6	8	10	15	20	24
	s:	294	2,200	4,400	5,867	6,600	7,334
	e%:	3%	22%	44%	59%	66%	73%

t: days; s: speed-up; e%: efficiency%

each cell contains the time to complete (t) as well as the computed values of speed-up (s) and efficiency% (e%).

When we hold the value of L (the problem size) constant, the speed-up increases while the efficiency decreases as we add processors. Similarly, if we hold the machine size, N, constant, *both* the speed-up *and* the efficiency increase as we increase the problem size, L. MPPs typically are available with a large range in the number of processors. (As an extreme example, nCube 2 products extend over three orders of magnitude: from 8 to 8,000 processors.) It is, therefore, possible to select the *size* of the machine to match the problem, or the range of problems, on which it is to be applied—an important consideration during benchmark activities (see Chapter 10).

Second, an interesting problem arises in computing T_1 when the problem size increases to the point where an MPP might be appropriate. The technical details of this issue are well discussed in [3]. For our purposes, it should be clear that *actually measuring* T_1 in our wall example (namely, the time it would take a single soldier to build the entire wall) would be inconvenient. Often, in a benchmarking effort, we can only measure values of T_N for large values of N when the the problem is large. Since T_1 is not directly measureable, a model and some arithmetic are needed to estimate T_1 and, hence, to calculate the speed-up and the efficiency.

Example: As a quick example, suppose that T_{500} and T_{800} are measured for our wall example (that is, benchmarks executed using 500 and 800 processors, respectively). Using our model (and remembering that now T_S and T_P are variables to be computed rather than known a priori), we have:

$$T_{500} = T_S + (T_P/500)$$

and

$$T_{800} = T_S + (T_P/800)$$

If, for example, $T_{500} = 87$ and $T_{800} = 57$, it is possible to solve these equations and find that

$$T_S = 7$$

$$T_P = 40{,}000$$

and, hence

$$T_1 = T_S + T_P$$

$$= 7 + 40{,}000 = 40{,}007$$

Once T_1 is known, we find that for $N = 500$,

$$\text{speed-up} = T_1/T_{500} = 460$$

$$\text{efficiency\%} = 460/500 \times 100\% = 92\% \blacksquare$$

Third, there are a number of ways in which a problem can be "big," in the sense of being appropriate for MPP execution. Ordinarily, the best way is to have very large data requirements (which translates into large physical memory and/or storage). As we discussed in Section 1.1.3, an MPP places its processors close to lots of distinct (distributed, in the jargon) memory banks. A large number of memory banks means a very large physical memory and the ability to hold potentially extremely large data sets "in core." A smaller processor (or a small number of processors) might need constantly to reference secondary storage for its data and, hence, pay very high I/O overheads. Further, there is a natural parallelization strategy by spreading the large data set evenly across all of the processors in the array. This type of parallelism, called *data-level parallelism*, is the most common (and appropriate) way of making a problem "big." The next section will take up this issue by looking at some simple, real-world examples.

2.3 EXAMPLES

In this section, we will illustrate some of the ideas introduced by our wall-building metaphor using examples based on real-world applications. Our purpose is to convince the reader that these applications really do embody the characteristics described above and that they should be suitable for efficient execution on massively parallel hardware. Later in the text, we will consider implementation issues. At this point, the examples are offered as illustrations of the basic ideas underlying parallelization.

2.3.1 Database Queries

Perhaps the simplest database operation is to search through a set of records for those that match a pattern or condition. The SQL paradigm formalizes and standardizes this activity. Heuristically, we are thinking of queries such as:

- find all the flights into Denver that arrive before 5:00 P.M. on February 17

- find all the taxpayers in the Boston metropolitan area with incomes less than $55,000 and who reported no deductions for mortgage interest payments
- find all articles that reference papers from the *Journal of Pharmaceutical Geriatrics* dated between 1980 and 1985

In fact, these queries are simple by today's standards. SQL queries involving literally hundreds of conditions are commonplace, and the task of deciding whether even a single record lies in the set can be formidable and time-consuming. The task of searching *all* the records in a database with millions of entries can stress the computational power of even the largest and most expensive mainframe.

The natural approach to parallelizing this problem is to partition the large database into equal-sized (counted, say, by number of records) subsets, one subset for each processor in the MPP array. Since each processor has a small set of records to search, and since each one searches its assigned records concurrently and independently, we should expect a significant performance improvement, even when using a very large number of processors.

In this problem, there is no "boundary" between processors; each processor works completely independently of the others and communicates only with a central controller to receive the pattern for search (a broadcast operation) and to report back the results of the search (a reduction operation).

> ***Example***: This situation has been likened to a game of Bingo. The "broadcast" corresponds to the call of the next value, which must fan out rapidly to all the players. The "reduction" corresponds to the declaration of "Bingo" by the winner, which must return rapidly back to the central caller. ■

Provided the machine supports broadcast and reduction operations efficiently, the sequential part of the problem (T_S) will be minimal, even when the number of records to be searched by a single processor is fairly small.

It is likely that on a real problem the I/O to obtain the data from secondary storage will dominate total run time on an MPP. Thus, in an efficient implementation, considerable attention is paid by designers to ensuring high, parallel bandwidth into the processor array. One way to accomplish this is to spread the file across a number of storage devices, each serving a small subset of the complete MPP array. Each I/O device operates independently of and concurrently with the others, thereby providing high aggregate bandwidth into the processor array. If the database is too large to be held in physical memory, we can envision a series of repeated "load/process, load/process" steps until the complete file has been examined.

Database operations are naturally highly parallelizable and of great interest to the commercial world. For this reason, software and hardware to support parallelized database operations have found a market—one of the few success stories in parallel applications. NCR Corp. (now a subsidiary of AT&T) markets the TeraData database machine, an MPP dedicated solely to database functions. NCR also markets a modestly parallel machine (the 3600) to support a high-performance user interface to the database engine. Another example is the port of the Oracle RDBMS to the nCube 2 parallel processor (although this is primarily targeted at OLTP). Finally, there are a number of in-house, highly specialized MPP database applications in situations where extensions to existing hardware cannot provide a growth path to the desired levels of performance. References [4] and [5] provide a good introduction to the subject of parallel databases.

2.3.2 Latency versus Throughput

A standard way of measuring performance can be conceptualized as:

(work accomplished)/(time).

A common example is MFLOPs—millions of floating point operations per second. The *work accomplished* is a million floating point operations; the *time* taken to do the work is a second. However, because we have divided to get our measure, the same answer would have resulted had we done 500 floating point operations in half a millisecond, or 3.6 billion floating point operations in an hour. In all cases, the *rate* is the same: More work, in more time, can be equivalent (in this measure) to less work in less time.

> ***Example***: A man driving an old, deteriorating car was stopped by a policeman for speeding. When the officer announced that the car had been traveling 50 miles per hour in a 35 mile per hour zone, the driver protested that this could not be true since, as he said, "This car won't run an hour." ■

> ***Example***: An old chestnut in parallel processing observes that if one woman can come to term in nine months, then (clearly) nine women can deliver a child in only one month. ■

The truth hidden in these jokes is that very often we are not concerned about *rate* so much as about *elapsed time to do a single job*. The elapsed time to accomplish a single instance of a job is commonly termed its *latency*. It may or may not be that a parallel processor can decrease the latency—that is, can execute the job faster—than a sequential processor. The joke about delivering the child hinges on observing that *this* task is *not* parallelizable. However, it is *always* true that a parallel processor can increase the rate, just by running several instances of the job concurrently. It is true that *nine* women can deliver *nine* children in *nine* months, for a processing *rate* of one child per month. The numerator (amount of work) increases, while the denominator (time to execute the total amount of work) remains constant.

An approach that attempts to decrease the *latency* of a job is often referred to as *parallelizing the inner loop*. In this approach, we work hard at making a single job run faster, rather than on running several instances of the job on multiple processors, in the same elapsed time as a single job on one processor. The alternate strategy is (appropriately) called *parallelizing the outer loop*. When parallelizing the outer loop is an acceptable strategy, it is almost always easier and less expensive than the alternative.

Other names for parallelizing the outer loop are *increasing the throughput* and *embarrassingly parallel*. The point of the second definition is that the opportunity for parallelism is so obvious, one should be embarrassed for having to mention it at all. Even so, parallel professionals (including the author) all have stories in which an embarrassingly parallel solution remained undetected for an embarrassingly long time. The point of the first definition is that *throughput* is related to *rate* and, hence, does not directly reflect *latency*.

Vendors of parallel hardware love problems where throughput, rather than latency, is the primary requirement. A typical example might be, Our machine can compute 6,000 mandelbrot sets in an hour. Fine, but suppose I want a *single* mandelbrot set in 10 milliseconds. The throughput (processing rate measured in jobs per time) is the same in both cases, but the operational impact is quite different.

There are many applications where throughput, not latency, is the driving requirement. One example is on-line transaction processing (OLTP). Here, it is not so important that a *single* transaction be completed very rapidly but that an *aggregrate* (entering the system with some known stochastic characteristics) be processable at a specified rate. For example, if it is desired to handle, say, 500 transactions per second, it is *not* necessary that each one be processed in 2 milliseconds. In fact, a typical response time (latency) for a given transaction might be on the order of 1 to 5 seconds. This is a situation ideally suited for parallel processing.

Another example arises in optimization problems. Here, a large space must be searched for the point where some function takes its maximum (respectively, minimum) value. Often, it is easy to compute the value at any point, so that a simple strategy is to repeatedly evaluate the function at many points, testing each time against the best value thus far obtained. Again, it is not so important that any single point be evaluated rapidly but that many points be evaluated in some given, longer period of time. A parallel approach is indicated.

A final example is Monte Carlo simulations. Because they are typically driven by random number generators, it is important to run the simulation a large number of times, with different random number seeds, so that the probability distributions of the variables of interest can be found. As with our other examples, it is not so important that a single instance be run rapidly (low latency) as it is that a large number of independent cases be run in a given time (high throughput).

If we rephrase this discussion in terms of Amdahl's Law, the point is that the sequential part of an embarrassingly parallel problem is negligible in practical terms. The reason is that the separate instances of the problem are completely independent (no shared boundary). Thus, arbitrarily large numbers of different instances can be executed concurrently with no loss of efficiency. The only caveat is that there are at least as many job instances as processors—a veiled way of saying that the size of the problem (number of instances) should match the size of the machine (number of processors).

2.3.3 Load Balancing

An implicit assumption made in the analysis of Amdahl's Law (Section 2.2) was that the amount of work done by each processor (soldier) is about equal once the problem (wall) has been partitioned. While it is not so costly if a few processors have *less* work to do than most, it can be disastrous if one, or a few, have substantially *more* work to do. The reason is that the problem (or stage of the problem) is not complete until *all* processors have completed; none can move onto the next task until all have finished. Thus, if one processor takes a great deal longer to complete than the rest, the excess time will be spent by the idle processors in *waiting* rather than *working*. This can be a source of inefficiency.

Example: Returning again (and for the last time!) to the wall-building example, it might be that terrain affects the rate at which a soldier can complete his section of the wall: Steeper terrain results in slower progress. Were we to divide the wall evenly by length, soldiers assigned to hilly places would take longer than their comrades to complete the work.

One strategy to deal with this is to assign wall lengths based not on *length* but on *estimated time to complete.* This assumes that we have a priori information enabling us to make that calculation (in the wall example, knowledge of the terrain and knowledge of the difference in building rates based on slope). Another strategy is to make the initial division using the simple "equal lengths" algorithm and then monitor progress, adjusting wall-length assignments dynamically as appropriate based on observed completion rates. This has the advantage of accounting for other kinds of irregularities (trees in the way, a more difficult path to the brick depots, etc.) besides terrain, but it adds overhead, since some of our soldiers must be used as monitors. ■

It is well known that the observed run time for many algorithms can be highly data dependent—based not just on the *size* of the data but on the *values* of the data and on their *relative position* in the underlying data structure. Examples of algorithms that strongly exhibit such dependence are:

- sorting
- numerical iterative techniques, where convergence is the stopping condition, and different input data can result in different numbers of iterations required to achieve the desired error bound
- optimization techniques (such as linear programming), in which the number of steps to reach the optimum is highly data dependent

Faced with such a situation, the parallel algorithm designer may go to great lengths to assure an even division of labor.

Example: Suppose we are sorting a large array and that the keys to be sorted lie between, say, 1 and 10,000. It would be a mistake to assume that half the elements in the array lie below 5,000 and the other half above 5,000 (that would only be true if the key values are evenly distributed throughout the key space, and, typically, they are not). Thus, for example, if we wished to distribute the array evenly over 100 processors, it would be an error to assign to processor #1 the elements whose keys lie between 1 and 100, to processor #2 those between 101 and 200, etc. Such a distribution would almost certainly leave many processors with far more than 100 elements and other processors with far fewer than 100 elements.

What is wanted is an estimate (in the simplest case) of the *median* value: the number (probably different than 5,000) for which half the keys lie below, and half lie above. This requires a calculation to determine the median, which adds overhead and reduces efficiency. However, these calculations can more than repay this inefficiency by balancing the load. Such calculations are typical of parallel algorithms that, for reasons of load balancing, must equally partition data over a large processor array. ■

Example: A typical large problem is to optimize a function over a space that can be represented as a tree. Each node of the tree is a possible solution, and the algorithm is to "walk" the tree, evaluating and comparing values at various nodes with the current best (this technique is called *branch and bound*). To parallelize this algorithm, we should assign various parts of the tree to different processors and have each processor search its subtree concurrently with and independently from the other processors. The problem is that unless we know the complete structure of the tree in advance, it is likely that some processors will be assigned subtrees that are deep (and, hence, require more time to complete), while others are assigned subtrees that are shallow (and, hence, can be completed quickly). Elaborate schemes to dynamically repartition the work based on completion rates experienced at run time have been developed for this type of problem (see, for example [6]). While these schemes require some overhead, they substantially improve the observed run time by keeping as many processors as possible busy over the length of the run. The ability of the algorithm designer to devise such techniques is often determinative as to whether an MPP is used efficiently on a given application. ■

Summary of Chapter 2

A commonly raised objection to parallel processing, Amdahl's Law, suggests that the inherently sequential, nonparallelizable part of a problem imposes a bound on possible speed-up and, hence, on the number of processors that can be used efficiently. We have argued that the fraction of the problem that is nonparallelizable changes with problem size and, typically, can be made arbitrarily small as the problem size becomes large. The conclusion, that *MPPs need large problems to be used efficiently*, was then tested against our intuitions (using an extended metaphor based on building a long wall) and against some real-world examples. Some other potential sources of inefficiency (difficulty of reducing latency and load balancing) were then examined. The conclusion of this chapter is that the efficiency of an MPP depends on problem characteristics (such as size) and cannot be either denied or affirmed without considering the specific characteristics of the problem and the algorithmic approach taken to parallelize it.

3

An Introduction to Hardware Architectures

Nobody (that is, nobody *I* know) likes to worry about hardware, in the nitty-gritty sense of busses and instruction sets and memory bandwidth, etc. One contributing factor to the widespread use and success of traditional, sequential architectures is that *most* of the time the user need not be concerned with hardware details. *Virtual memory* (that is, allowing the programmer to pretend there is a much larger physical memory than is actually present and providing hardware support to minimize the performance impacts of that illusion) is a dramatic success story of this kind. Even more important, and a point stressed by Leslie Valient [7], is that the same basic *hardware abstraction* can be efficiently applied to literally hundreds of different vendor products. An application designer can hold in the mind's eye an abstract view of a machine applicable to different physical machines—DEC VAXs, IBM RS6000s, PCs, or NeXT workstations. When compared to the current situation for parallel hardware, the differences in the programming models for these machines are minimal. This is not to say that differences may not be found by looking closely enough at the hardware implementations, operating systems, and software libraries. What is common, however, is the underlying set of assumptions and operations out of which more elaborate constructs are fashioned. At this level, all the sequential machines mentioned are essentially interchangeable from a programmer's perspective.

Unfortunately, such a commonly accepted and broadly applicable hardware abstraction does not yet exist for parallel machines. In Chapters 4 through 7, we will examine in more detail the major programming paradigms for parallel machines. They all grow out of, and are optimized for, fundamentally different hardware platforms. The unfortunate consequence is that at this point in the development of parallel processing *some* knowledge of the major hardware categories and of their strengths and weaknesses is required.

The three modest goals for this chapter are: (1) to introduce basic terminology necessary for further reading; (2) to properly arm the reader to listen to vendor presentations; and (3) to explain how the hardware architecture necessarily impacts the software. Annotated references are sprinkled throughout the text to point interested readers to more detailed discussions.

An introductory section amplifies the theme of the impact of hardware. Interconnection networks (a basic component of all MPPs) are then discussed. The final three sections take up the three major hardware categories: SIMD, distributed memory MIMD, and shared memory MIMD.

3.1 IMPACTS OF HARDWARE ARCHITECTURE

The distinguishing feature of a supercomputer is its speed, and we suggest the following analogy: The relationship between a supercomputer and a commodity processor is similar to that between a race car and a family sedan. A race car owes its speed to a collection of specialized (that is, nonstandard) features—in the engine, the drive train, the suspension, the transmission, the fueling, etc. A race car without these features, or a racing team that attempts to avoid their use, defeats the *raison d'être* of the race car. Similarly, what makes a supercomputer fast is a collection of specialized (that is, nonstandard) features—in the memory subsystem, the interconnection netwok, the instruction set, the packaging, the register organization, etc. A programmer who does not use these special features will get not a race car but a very expensive Buick. The only way to get the speed from a supercomputer is to utilize those specialized, nonstandard features of the machine *that make it fast.*

In practice, an algorithm designer must structure the program to take advantage of whatever special features the target machine may offer. On a Cray Y-MP, for example, this means using *vectorizable loops* whenever and wherever possible. Often, this requires restructuring a "natural" approach to remove factors (index dependencies, logical branches, subroutine calls) whose presence could prevent use of vector instructions. Similarly, the designer must avoid using features of the machine that are inefficient. In the older Cray X-MP models, for example, this meant recognizing the potential for memory bank conflicts and sizing (or resizing) arrays to avoid them.

This type of fundamental algorithm restructuring is a general characteristic of programming supercomputers, but it is especially and uniquely true for MPPs. Any given MPP will have some types of operations it performs well, and others it performs poorly. The task of an application developer is to select an algorithm and an implementation of it that maximizes use of the efficient, and minimizes use of the inefficient, parts of the machine.

> ***Example***: As we will see shortly, an SIMD machine is naturally suited for broadcast and reduction operations. These same operations, however, may have considerable overhead when performed on a distributed memory MIMD machine. An algorithm developer targeting an SIMD machine (such as a CM-2) will *look* for opportunities to use broadcast and reduction operators; he or she will, in fact, *choose* algorithmic approaches that *require* such operators. The same developer targeting a message-passing machine (such as an Intel Paragon) will think quite differently, choosing algorithmic approaches that *avoid* broadcast and reduction operators in favor of what the Paragon does best—namely, multiple independent control streams. ■

This example illustrates why language standards for parallel machines only address part of the problem. The fundamental algorithms used in the two cases will be quite different, even if the same language is used to write them both (see Section 1.2.2). These algorithm differences defeat the desired goal of portability and a shared abstraction.

The implications of this observation—that fundamental algorithmic restructuring may be required when an application moves from a sequential platform to a parallel one, or from one parallel platform to another—are pervasive and are at the heart of why application software (and, hence, market acceptance) has been so long coming to MPPs.

In preparation for coming material, we introduce some terminology. The first top-level discriminator for MPPs is between *SIMD* and *MIMD:*

- **SIMD**: **S**ingle **I**nstruction **M**ultiple **D**ata
- **MIMD**: **M**ultiple **I**nstruction **M**ultiple Data

The second-level discriminator, within MIMD machines, is between

- **Distributed Memory**
- **Shared Memory**

This taxonomy is illustrated in Figure 3-1.

The meaning of these distinctions and their implications for application programming and execution will be discussed more fully in succeeding sec-

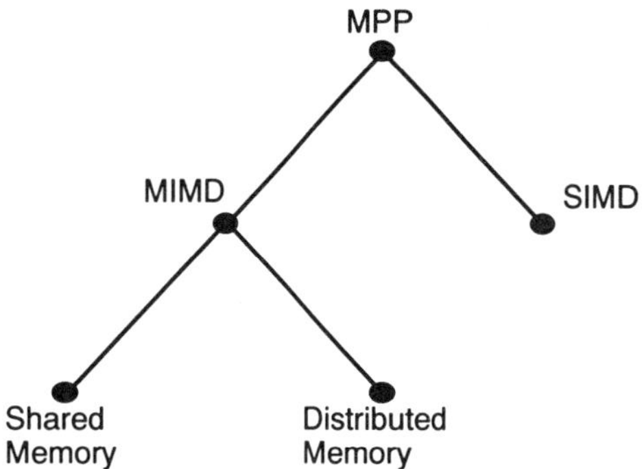

Figure 3-1. A top-level taxonomy of parallel architectures

tions. To facilitate that discussion, however, we remind the reader of the three basic components of a standard, vanilla-flavor sequential processor. These are illustrated in Figure 3-2.

The component labeled S is the *storage* or *memory* of the processor. It holds the instructions for the program to be executed, the data on which the program will operate, and the data produced as output by the program. In programs requiring substantial I/O, S also serves as a staging area for data moving to and from secondary storage. The component labeled C is the *controller* or *CPU*. Its task is to fetch instructions from storage and decode them. The result of this decoding is low-level signals sent to the third component, labeled P, the *processor*. It receives the signals from the controller (in slave-mode), fetches data from and stores data to the storage component, S, and operates on the data as instructed by the controller (e.g., performs floating point arithmetic, tests conditions, calculates addresses, etc.). The three major MPP architecture classes can be characterized by various arrangements of these three components.

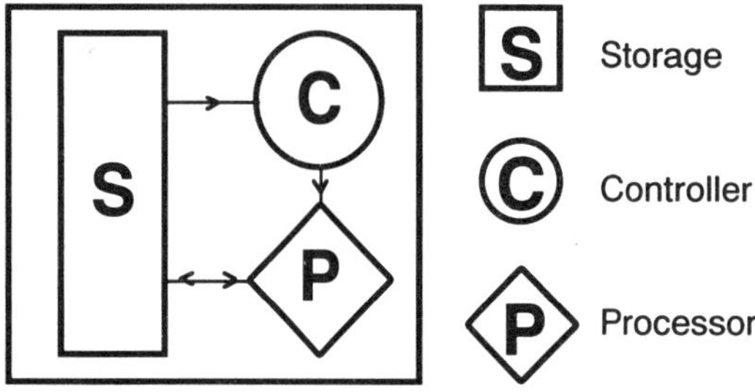

Figure 3-2. The three major components in a standard sequential computer

3.2 A PRIMER ON INTERCONNECTION NETWORKS

No matter what the architecture class, every parallel processor requires an interconnection network to enable processors to share data (like the soldiers in the wall-building example, who must cooperate across shared boundaries). In many machines, this network is also used to support I/O operations.

The term "network" is used today in many senses. So that there is no confusion, the networks under consideration here are not standard, off-the-shelf networks like EtherNet, FDDI, SNA, or HIPPI. Rather, our focus is on very high speed, low-latency networks that are intimately tied to the hardware internals of the machine. As a point of reference, a typical performance goal for an MPP is to move a packet of data as small as a single word between processors in about the same time it takes to operate on that data. Compared with the software protocol layers involved in commercial LAN technology, we are talking about two to three orders of magnitude improvement in latency. This can only be achieved by implementing virtually the entire transfer directly in hardware.

As we saw in Chapter 2, the fraction of run time spent in the sequential (nonparallelizable) part of the problem is the key to MPP efficiency. Typically, the sequential part is where interprocessor communication is required. The ability to perform this communication rapidly is, therefore, frequently *the dominant factor* affecting overall performance on an application. As MPPs have moved through successive generations, improvements in interconnection technology have tracked well with corresponding improvements in memory bandwidth, memory density, and microprocessor performance. This is essential in order to maintain an overall balance between system components.

> ***Example***: In a telling comment on supercomputer architectures, Ken Batcher once defined a supercomputer as a machine that turns a compute-bound problem into an I/O-bound problem. The hidden message is the need to maintain *balance*. It does not help to scale one part of the machine without providing corresponding improvements in other system components; to do so is simply to trade one set of problems for another. In MPPs, we do not wish to turn compute-bound problems into communication-bound problems. ■

The model for MPP int erprocessor communication networks is the *point-to-point network*. This is well modeled by a graph, in which the *nodes* of the graph represent *switches*, and the *edges* of the graph represent wires connecting switches to each other. Often, but not always, there will be a processor closely

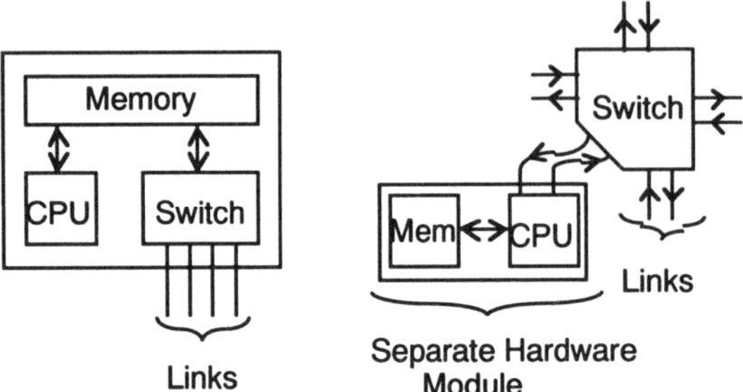

Figure 3-3. Alternate approaches for connecting the node processor to the network

bound to each individual switch. The processor uses the switch as its entry point into the network. It can dump data into the switch (data that are destined for some other processor), and it can receive data from the switch (data orginated by some remote processor). For this reason, the distinction between the switch and its closely associated processor becomes blurred in some discussions.

From a packaging viewpoint, there are two major approaches, illustrated in Figure 3-3. In the first, the switching logic is very closely tied to the processor. Often, the switch is implemented on the same chip as its associated processor. Examples include the CM-1, CM-2, and AMT DAP in the SIMD world; and nCube, the Transputer, iWarp, and the KS-1 from Kendall Square in the MIMD world. In these implementations, it is usually possible for a processor to send and/or receive multiple concurrent messages, a potential source for additional parallelism. It is in these implementations that the switch/processor distinction is most fuzzy.

The second packaging approach physically separates the processing node hardware from the switching hardware. A processor has a single path to its associated switch element. The decoupling of the switch hardware from the processor supports *heterogeneity* in the choice of processor. For example, in the Intel Paragon, some processor nodes are used strictly for I/O and can be implemented using 80486 chips. Other nodes are for computation and can be implemented using i860 chips. The switches in the underlying network are, however, identical in both cases. The penalty associated with this second packaging strategy is in decreased levels of integration (more boards, more chip types). The benefit is in greater flexibility of node architecture. No SIMD machine uses this packaging approach for its network. MIMD machines include the Intel Paragon, the CM-5 from Thinking Machines, and the new T-3D MPP from Cray Research.

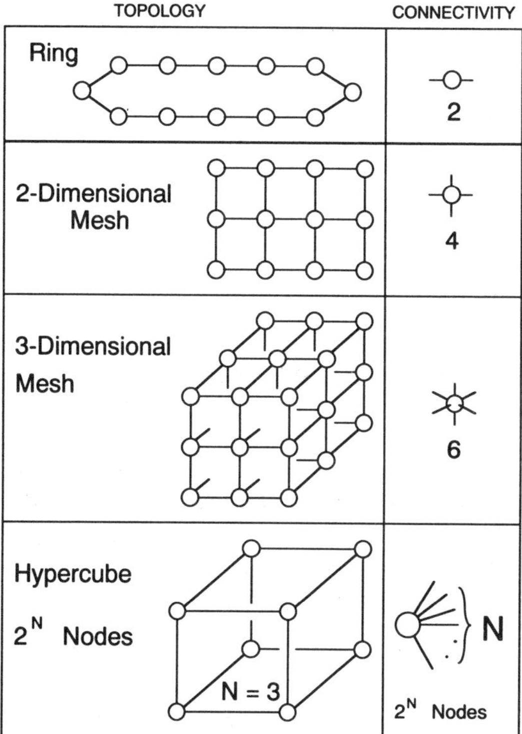

Figure 3-4. Some commonly used network topologies

Because not all pairs of nodes can have links (too many wires would be required), there is always a pattern used to decide which pairs of nodes will be linked and which will not. This pattern is called the *topology* of the network, and Figure 3-4 shows four easily understood and widely used topologies: a *ring, two-* and *three-dimensional meshes,* and a *hypercube.* This figure also illustrates *connectivity*—that is, how many "nearest neighbors" a node has in the underlying topology.

Major performance characteristics of an MPP interconnection network (besides topology) include:

- *link bandwidth*—the number of bytes of data per second that can flow between switch nodes across a direct link. This will be a function of the number of pulses per second (clock rate) and the number of bits sent per pulse.
- *switching latency*—if two processors need to exchange data, but there is no direct link joining them (or their associated switch nodes), then they

must rely on intermediate nodes to relay the message, one step at a time, from the sender to the destination. As the message moves from node to node, there will be additional time spent in each switch as the message header is received on an input port, the switch is made to the appropriate output port, and the transmission of the message continues. Greater latency can result in reduced performance penalty if the message must pass through a large number of intermediate nodes. Switching latency in current interconnection networks is very low—on the order of 100 to 200 nanoseconds—because of the adoption of *wormhole routing* (see [8]) techniques. This has replaced outdated *store-and-forward* techniques (characteristic of early MPP products), which required time-consuming memory references as part of the flow control protocol.

- *processor independence*—that is, whether a processor must be interrupted to help service communications activity. Current hardware implementations usually permit the processor to continue processing concurrently with message transmission, receipt, and routing. This permits some amount of communications overhead to be hidden behind useful computation.
- *contention*—it may happen that two messages, simultaneously received as inputs by a switch, both require use of the same output port. One must wait, and a protocol is required to make that decision and to halt transmission of the losing message until the needed port becomes available. (Alternatively, hardware may be provided to time-share the physical port between the two competitors.) The delay caused at the destination node, as it waits for the delayed message, can result in reduced performance.

Ultimately, competing network implementations must be evaluated based on cost and delivered performance. Abstractly, however, the scarce resource in an interconnection network is *wires.* The thing to hold constant, when comparing two otherwise equivalent networks, is the total number of wires. The theoretical expression for this is the *network bisection constant*: How many wires need to be "cut" to divide the network in half (see, for example [9]).

Now, there are at least two useful things to do with the available wires. One is to increase link bandwidth. This is done by sending *multiple bits between links on a given clock pulse.* The cost is in additional wires to carry those bits. Instead of a single wire (which can carry 1 bit per clock), we might, for example, provide eight wires so that a total of 8 bits can be transmitted per clock. Additional link bandwidth can be had at the cost of additional wires on each link.

The other use that can be made of the wires is to increase the *connectivity* —that is, the number of pairs of nodes that have direct links between them.

Having more direct neighbors (links) in the underlying topology can mean shorter distances for the message to travel and reduced contention.

> ***Example***: In a 2**10 = 1,024-node hypercube, each node has 10 nearest neighbors (that is, any switch has a direct link to 10 other switches). Assuming each link is implemented with a single wire, this is a total of 1,024 × 5 = 5,120 wires. In a corresponding 32 × 32 = 1,024 node two-dimensional mesh, each node has only four neighbors—up, down, left, and right. This is only 2,048 links. In order to keep the total wire count the same in comparing these alternatives, we should give the two-dimensional mesh two or three (10/4 = 2.5) additional wires on each link. *Fewer links* are balanced by *increased link bandwidth.* ■

Both approaches have advantages and disadvantages in reducing total message latency, increasing total usable bandwidth, and reducing the likelihood of contention. The argument about the proper balance between *more links* and *wider links*—that is, how best to use the wires—has reached religious proportions among MPP vendors and typically forms a major part of a marketing pitch. The *practical* answer, of course, is that any given problem will use one alternative more efficiently than another; if several applications are to be run, this aspect may well be a wash. Benchmarking and cost, rather than theory, ought to be used to resolve the question in any given instance.

What *can* make a difference, however, are *programming strategies* that minimize the distance messages must travel along the network. Any particular application will impose problem-specific communications requirements between logical nodes. The programming goal, then, is to map communicating pairs of *logical* nodes onto *physical* nodes that have direct links between them. This can dramatically reduce both latency and contention during interprocessor communications. Unfortunately, in all but the simplest cases, the compiler is not able to make the optimal logical-to-physical assignment. This is an important example of how specific knowledge of the hardware (in this case, the network topology) is required for efficient programming.

A long-time goal for MPP vendors is to provide a network with such high performance that parallel programmers need no longer include network topology considerations in efficient program design. The machine should behave as if it were completely interconnected—direct, rapid, contention-free communications between all pairs of nodes. The current reality is that there is still a great deal of additional performance to be had (up to an order of magnitude, depending on the problem) by taking the logical-to-physical node mapping into account.

Different vendors have adopted differing strategies on this issue, which amounts to trading off ease of programming against performance. Some vendors, opting for ease of programming, do not allow the programmer to "see" the underlying topology through the programming language; they insist that the compiler make the logical-to-physical node assignment. At the other extreme, other vendors provide no programmer support at all for this function; the programmer must make the logical-to-physical assignment in even the simplest cases.

A vendor's stance on this issue is important, and the "right" answer depends on whether ease of programming (with attendant performance penalties) is the goal or whether a more demanding programming paradigm is acceptably balanced by increased performance. In the author's opinion, an organization that is willing to face up to the problems of programing an MPP *at all* is accepting very little additional cost by having the added capability to perform the logical-to-physical assignment. A vendor that raises the "assembly language" spector at this point in a discussion should be dismissed as either technically naive or deliberately obfuscating.

Example: John Gustafson asks: What is the difference between a used car salesman and an MPP salesman? The answer: The used car salesman knows when he is lying. ■

When performance is not an overriding goal, an emerging use of an LAN of workstations is to treat the workstations as processing nodes of a parallel machine and to use the LAN as the interconnection network. The term *cluster* is used for such a configuration. This strategy works best in cases where only a very small portion of the application requires interprocessor communications. The lack of adequate interprocessor bandwidth will quickly bring many applications to a grinding halt, and true supercomputer performance levels cannot be obtained over a broad range of problems. For problems that *do not* require interprocessor communications, however, this approach can be very cost effective, for it avoids the part of an MPP purchase price associated with implementation of the network. Further, since many LANs are idle during off-hours, this approach can put wasted machine cycles to effective use.

3.3 SIMD MACHINES

In this section, we consider one of the three major classes of parallel architectures, those based on an SIMD control structure. Successive sections consider a top-level block diagram (3.3.1) and strengths and weaknesses (3.3.2).

3.3.1 A Top-Level Block Diagram

Recall that in Figure 3-2 the job of the controller, C, is to fetch and decode the sequence of instructions to be executed. The processor, P, in turn, is driven by these decoded signals (in slave-mode) fetching data, operating on it, and storing it back to memory, S. The key idea behind an SIMD machine is that instead of driving only a *single* processor, the controller drives an entire *array* of processor/memory units.

This is illustrated in Figure 3-5. The controller, C, has private storage, S, to hold the program and global scalar variables. The decoded instructions are then broadcast, one by one, to the entire array of processors, $P_1, P_2, \ldots, P_N$, Each processor, P_K, has associated with it a private memory bank, S_K, for storing data. Whatever instruction is broadcast by the controller, *all* processors execute in perfect lock-step synchrony. If, for example, the controller issues the instruction sequence: "Fetch the values from memory locations *A* and *B*, add them, and store the result in memory location *C*;" then *all* the processors perform this sequence of operations in parallel, each using values for *A*, *B*, and *C* obtained from its local, private memory unit (processor P_K referencing memory unit S_K). In effect, there is not a single value of, for example, the variable *A* but as many different values as there are processor/memory

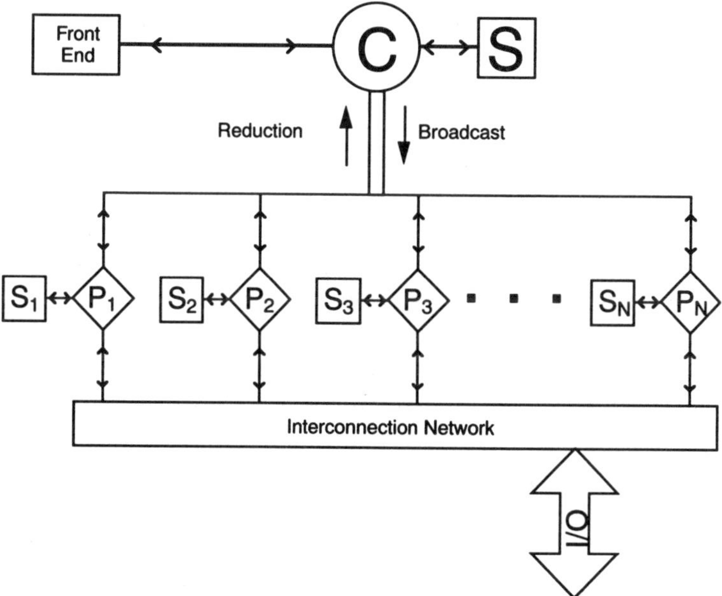

Figure 3-5. A generic SIMD configuration

banks in the machine. If there are 2,000 processors in the array, then the decoded instructions are executed 2,000 times, concurrently, on 2,000 different instances of data.

An SIMD machine requires a fan-out tree (wiring) to support the broadcast of the instructions from the controller to the array. This can also be used to broadcast global data values to the array and, in reverse, can be used to collect data from the array at the central controller (for example, a global OR, in which the final value arriving at the controller is FALSE only if each processor participating in the operation input a FALSE). The existence of this fan-out tree is the reason why, in the previous section, we asserted that SIMD machines support broadcast and reduction operations efficiently.

Most (but not all) SIMD machines can selectively put individual processors to sleep. While asleep, the processor does not listen to or execute the instructions broadcast by the controller. This is required when dealing with sections of code such as the following:

```
if ( A is even ) then

        B = A / 2

else

        B = 3 * A + 1

end if
```

Each processor performs the test to see if its local value of `A` is even. Those for which the test is **`TRUE`** stay awake; the rest go to sleep. The controller then issues the instructions corresponding to the **`if`** part of the branch: `B = A / 2`. Next, the sleepers and wakers change roles, and the controller issues the instructions corresponding to the **`then`** part of the branch: `B = 3 * A + 1`. This is necessary, since there is only a single controller, and it cannot issue more than a single instruction stream at a time. Each branch must, therefore, wait its turn (processors sleeping in the meantime), and the controller must service each of the branches one after the other. The reader will see the potential for inefficiencies if a very long **`switch`** structure is encountered!

We recall from Figure 1-1 that the total power of an MPP is approximated by multiplying the number of processors by the capability of each processor. Where do SIMD machines fit in this spectrum? Early SIMD machines (the MPP from Goodyear and the CM-1 from Thinking Machines, for example) used *bit serial processors*; each processor could perform a single bit-wide operation per clock. Even basic operations (like floating point addition) can take hundreds of clock cycles on a bit-wise processor. The advantage of this design choice is that (because they are so simple) many processors can be placed onto a single chip (16 per chip in the CM-1), so that very large arrays of processors can be constructed (up to 2**16 = 65,000 nodes in the CM-1).

When Thinking Machines changed generations from the CM-1 to the CM-2, they added floating point coprocessors to boost floating point performance—one floating point chip for every 32 bit serial processor. It then became more convenient to think of (and compile for) the machine as 2**11 = 2,048 floating point nodes (instead of 65,000 bit-wise nodes). Other SIMD machines, such as the AMT DAP or the MasPar MP-1, have *more* but *less powerful* nodes than their typical MIMD counterparts. The MP-1, for example, has up to 2**14 = 16,000 nodes, each of which uses a 4-bit internal bus and is capable of about 75 KFLOPs. Returning to Figure 1-1, we see that SIMD machines tend to lie near the extreme lower end of the spectrum—lots and lots of very basic processors.

A variety of I/O strategies are utilized by SIMD vendors. The CM-1 and CM-2, for example, utilize the interconnection network (together with I/O processors at the "edge") to move data into and out of the array. The AMT DAP, however, gives the I/O subsystem direct access to registers at the local nodes. An entire "plane" of data can be up- or downloaded to the array in a single clock. In order to achieve very high I/O bandwidths, it is often necessary to use secondary storage units that have been specially designed to support these bandwidths. In particular, a large SIMD machine requires more bandwidth than can ordinarily be provided over standard networks. When very high performance is required (and why else would one use an MPP?), the proprietary storage system provided by the vendor must be used. When the data reside on other devices or are required by other components of the network, an I/O bottleneck can result. This can be a major obstacle in integrating these machines as *servers* in an *open system.*

As we observed in Section 1.1.3, and in common with other MPPs, SIMD machines provide high aggregate memory bandwidth by giving to each processor its own private memory bank. This enables the total memory bandwidth to increase as the number of processors increases and permits an SIMD MPP to scale to very large configurations.

Finally, it is typical for an SIMD machine to use a *front end.* This is ordinarily a workstation running UNIX, and it provides the interface to the broader network. The compiler for the SIMD machine resides on the workstation (as does software to schedule the hardware among competing users), does accounting, and provides (through remote log in) access to the machine by users on the network. The front end may or may not take direct part in executing applications. The controller of the SIMD MPP can, if it is sufficiently powerful, itself take on the role of the front end.

3.3.2 Strengths and Weaknesses

The two most powerful aspects of an SIMD architecture, when compared to its MIMD competitors, are (1) built-in synchronization among processors, and (2) highly efficient broadcast and reduction operators.

First, as we will see in greater detail shortly, an MIMD machine has many control streams in operation concurrently. Each control stream will take its own path through the code, branching and iterating based on local data values. After only a short time, these control streams will diverge, some running farther ahead and some falling behind. At specified points (and, for an MIMD machine, the fewer the better), the processors need to "sync up"; that is, a protocol is executed to assure that all processors have reached the same point in the code and can participate in a global, cooperative action. None of this is an issue in an SIMD machine. The nature of the control hardware ensures that all processors are in lock-step and, hence, are always synchronized.

Second, this totally synchronized action permits a much freer use by the programmer of operators that require cooperation by all processors—operations such as broadcast, global summation, parallel prefix, and loops that require testing some global condition. An MIMD machine must pay synchronization overhead each time such operators are used; on an SIMD machine, they are "for free." Further, the fan-out tree used to distribute instructions to the array also supports rapid data movement between the array and the controller.

Another advantage sometimes mentioned for SIMD machines is that the memory required to hold the program instructions is only needed once, at the controller. This means that the local processor memories can be devoted entirely to data. The situation is different in an MIMD machine; one copy of the program is required at each processing node. A related issue is the hardware (i.e., chip and board space) needed to replicate the controller functionality at each processing node of an MIMD machine. Given the high density and low cost of custom CMOS/DRAM, this factor is not nearly as important as it once was.

Some SIMD vendors provide software to simulate more processors than are physically present. For example, even though the machine may have only, say, 2**14 = 16,000 processors, the compiler and operating system will execute programs that were written for a much larger number of processors. In effect, the compiler inserts an inner loop, invisible to the user, and lets one processor do the work of several. This capability for *virtual processors,* when it is supported, can be a powerful and useful enhancement.

A potential advantage mentioned by Seitz [9] is based on granularity. He suggests the metaphor that filling a container with pebbles is analogous to mapping an application onto a parallel machine. Small pebbles can efficiently fill a greater variety of container shapes; because the pebbles are small, they can more easily fit into odd-shaped crevices than can larger pebbles. Thus, the smaller the granularity of the subproblem size, according to the metaphor, the more efficiently the machine can adapt to the idiosyncrasies of a variety of problems. Because SIMD machines typically use many basic processors, the problem granularity for SIMD machines is very fine. For example, on an image processing application, it is typical to assign pixels to processors on a one-to-one basis.

One of the cost advantages of an SIMD machine is the hardware implementation of the interconnection network (see Section 3.2). This is simplified by built-in synchronization and, hence, can be much less expensive than an MIMD implementation. Often, interprocessor wiring on an SIMD machine is direct register-to-register; data transfers are one-clock synchronous "shifts," and the complexity of routing protocols and elaborate switching hardware is avoided. The corresponding downside is the difficulty of maintaining global synchronization as machine size increases to multi-GFLOP performance levels. The fan-out trees, which distribute the synchronous clock and the instructions can become a limiting factor in large SIMD machines.

The most serious disadvantage to an SIMD machine has already been mentioned—namely, the necessity of having to step through all data-dependent code branches separately, one after the other.

> ***Example:*** An electromagnetics code developed for an SIMD machine illustrates this problem. The code operates on a three-dimensional cube in space and partitions the cube into thousands of subcubes, like children's building blocks tightly packed to fill a box. Boundary conditions are imposed on the exterior, and the code proceeds, using very small time increments, to propagate the wave into the interior. There are four types of subcubes: corners, edges, face cubes, and interior cubes. Unfortunately, each type requires a different processing flow. The code is very efficient for the interior cubes—there are very many of them. But, by the time the code branches are taken to handle the edges and then the eight corners, most

of the machine is "asleep," while only a few processors remain "awake" to execute the command stream. This creates inefficiencies that can, depending on specifics of the problem, offset the very high efficiency on that part of the code dealing with the interior. ■

Another disadvantage for SIMD machines is in sharing the resource among the user population. Since there is only a single controller, the machine can only be assigned to one user at a time; time-sharing and space-sharing are not possible. Some vendors provide the capability to partition the machine into as many as four independent submachines, each with its own separate controller. In this configuration, the machine appears to users as four separate, individually schedulable resources, each about one-fourth as powerful as the full-up machine.

Three years ago, the issue of SIMD versus MIMD appeared to be quite open. As of 1993, at least for top-end systems, it now appears that MIMD has won. The last major adherent to the SIMD model among supercomputer-class vendors, Thinking Machines Corp., introduced the CM-5 in the middle of 1992, and it was a distributed memory MIMD machine. One of the advantages of SIMD, rapid synchronization across a large array, has been supported in the CM-5 by a separate low-latency network very similar to the fan-in/fan-out tree used in an SIMD machine for broadcast/reduction. Further, the CM-5 associates a separate processor, acting in some ways like an SIMD controller, to each user and associated subarray. Thus, the CM-5 attempts to retain some of the strengths of its SIMD heritage within a basic MIMD structure.

This does not mean that SIMD will vanish from the MPP scene. There are some application areas, particularly in signal and image processing in embedded applications (e.g., tracking), where there is an excellent match with the SIMD paradigm and in which the SIMD architecture offers packaging advantages (multiple simple processors with small amounts of memory, often implemented on the same chip). For the low end of the market, where, for example, a lab might need to turbo-charge one aspect of an often-repeated calculation, the cost advantages of an SIMD machine, and the naturalness of its programming paradigm for many scientific applications, can make it an attractive alternative.

As we will see in Chapter 4, the SIMD programming paradigm is especially powerful for many application areas, and there is increasing interest in implementing this paradigm on top of underlying MIMD hardware. Array operations in FORTRAN 90 are an important example of this trend (see Chapters 4 and 5).

3.4 DISTRIBUTED MEMORY MIMD MACHINES

The following sections describe and assess the second major category of MPPs—machines with an MIMD control structure which provide separate, private memory banks to each processor.

3.4.1 A Top-Level Block Diagram

Recall the three components described in Figure 3-2: the controller, C; the processor, P; and the storage or memory, S. In an SIMD machine, a single controller drives a multitude of slave processors, each with its own private storage. In distributed memory MIMD machines (*DM-MIMD*), not only the processors and storage are replicated, but also the controllers. This is illustrated in Figure 3-6. What is apparent immediately is that each of the replicated processing nodes (or, more loosely, processors) looks like a replica of the original vanilla-flavor sequential computer pictured in Figure 3-2. Each is capable of storing and executing its own program, on its own data, completely independent of, and asynchronous with, all other processing nodes. The term *multicomputer* is sometimes used for this type of architecture, and the name fits.

Figure 3-6 grossly simplifies the interconnection network. As discussed in Section 3.2, this is often the most expensive, difficult, and critical component of the entire system. Its system-specific characteristics (topology, routing, la-

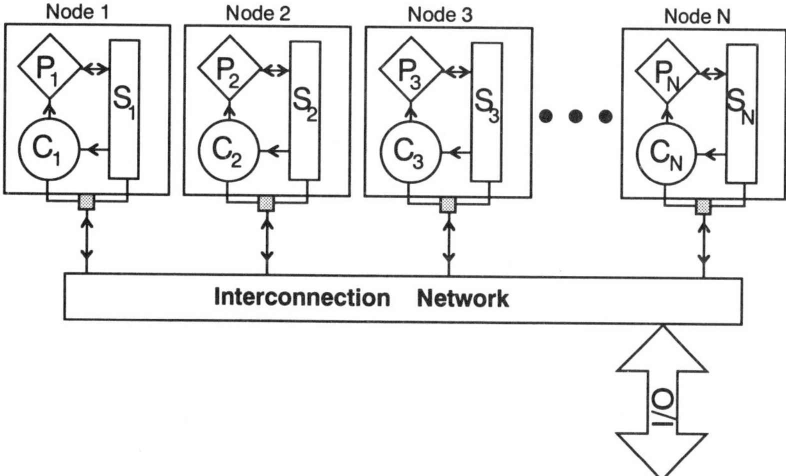

Figure 3-6. A generic DM-MIMD configuration

tency, bandwidth, contention, etc.) differentiate DM-MIMD machines from each other and contribute to the industry lack of standards.

MPP vendors would *like* users to think of their machines as Figure 3-6 suggests—with all processors more or less the same "distance" from each other on the high-performance interconnect, which is abstracted to a "communications server." This would ease the programming task, since the assignment of logical-to-physical nodes on the network becomes irrelevant to performance and, hence, compilable. The reality (as we pointed out in Section 3.2) is that there is still a lot of performance to be gained by paying explicit attention to the internals of the network.

The problem we noted on SIMD machines concerning execution of code branches is not an issue on DM-MIMD machines:

```
if ( A is even ) then
      B = A / 2
else
      B = 3 * A + 1
end if
```

Typically, a separate instance of this code is held by each of the processing nodes. As each controller comes to this point in its copy of the program, it will fetch its own local, private value of the variable `A` (which varies from node to node) and perform the test. If the test succeeds, it will execute the **`if`** portion of the branch taken; if the test fails, the **`else`** portion is executed. Note that, on any given processor, *one or the other* branch is taken, *not both.* On the SIMD machine, however, both branches had to be issued by the single controller, first on behalf of the processors on which the test has succeeded and second for those on which the test failed.

Since the processors in an MIMD array are acting independently and asynchronously, each taking locally determined paths through the code based on local data values, at any given instant of time the various nodes may be found at (perhaps) widely separated points in the code. The times at which they complete sections of code can, therefore, differ considerably. It is common practice to include points in the code where the processors synchronize; that is, points beyond which no processor proceeds unless and until it has been reached by all processors. This style of programming, called *loosely synchronous,* is in common use for DM-MIMD machines and is supported by several languages, libraries, and language extensions.

Synchronization points are illustrated in Figure 3-7. Processors in the array reach the synchronization point at different times, the faster ones waiting for the slower. Once synchronized, all processors can participate in a global activity (e.g., a global summation or finding a maximum). The overhead for synchronization is not a problem faced by an SIMD machine: All processors in an SIMD machine respond in lock-step to a *single* controller; synchronization is built into the architecture. This is in sharp contrast to the multiple, independent, asynchronous behavior typical of an MIMD array.

A complete processing node for a DM-MIMD machine comprises: (1) a microprocessor, (2) DRAM (typically anywhere from 8 to 64 MB), and (3) an interface to the interconnection network. As noted in Section 3.2, in some implementations the network interface is tightly coupled to the microprocessor architecture itself, which permits very high levels of integration. In other cases, the microprocessor is an off-the-shelf commodity part, and additional circuitry is required to support the network interface.

As with network topologies, the choice of microprocessor for the processing nodes is a matter of bitter dispute among vendors of this machine type. The advantage of a home-grown, proprietary microprocessor is that communications can be tightly coupled to the processor—in the best case, placed directly on-chip. On the other hand, large chip manufacturers are always at the leading edge of performance and density, so that by sacrificing high levels of integration in favor of COTS, the architect can be assured of the most

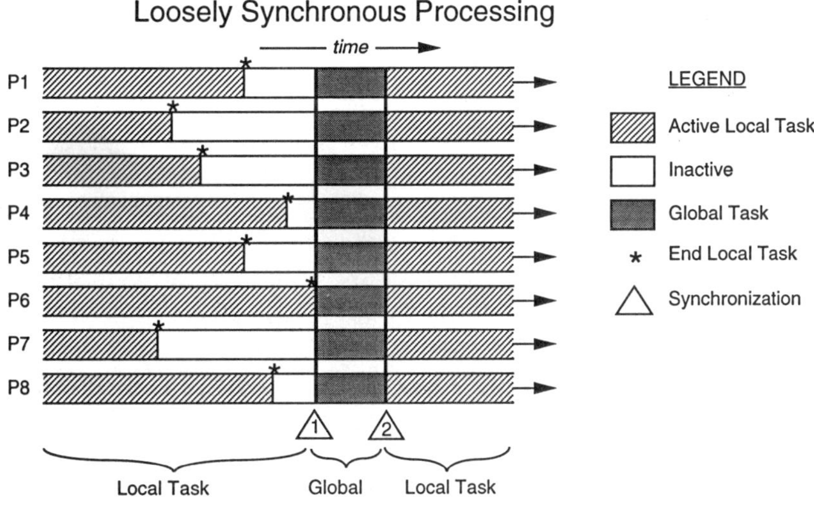

Figure 3-7. Some processors must wait until others reach synchronization point

recent and powerful of processors. Further, off-the-shelf microprocessors often have large amounts of high-quality software available because of the PC/workstation market. While this software is not strictly parallel, it can be a useful base from which parallel applications and system software can evolve.

This type of architecture supports configurations that vary considerably in size—from as few as eight or so nodes up to a few thousand. For some vendors, the number of nodes is constrained to be a power of 2 (16, 32, 64, 128, 256, etc.); others are more flexible. Some vendors utilize a front end, usually a UNIX-based workstation, in a role similar to that on an SIMD machine; others use the node processors directly to support the user interface, accounting, and compiling. UNIX is ubiquitous as the operating system both on the front end and on the individual processing nodes.

The typical mode for sharing a DM-MIMD resource among users is *space-sharing.* When a user attaches the resource, he or she requests a subarray of a certain size (number of nodes). The central resource controller keeps track of which nodes of the machine are in use and attempts to assign a group of free nodes of the requested size. When the user job or session completes, the nodes are released back to the controller. The typical programming style for DM-MIMD machines leaves the number of nodes a run-time variable, so that the user can request a subarray of size appropriate to the job. For example, it is typical to do code development and debug on a small array—as small as a single node—and then move to larger arrays for final testing.

I/O strategies for these machines are of two types. One approach is to provide each processor node an independent path to the I/O subsystem. The other is to utilize the interconnection network, perhaps designating certain nodes as I/O processors on behalf of the entire array. In the least expensive but most constraining approach, the front end itself can perform I/O on behalf of the array; this can be a serious sequential bottleneck for arrays comprising more than just a few processors.

When compared to SIMD machines, DM-MIMD arrays fall toward the middle of the spectrum indicated in Figure 1-1. The processing nodes, which utilize custom CMOS microprocessors, are continuing to improve both in performance and in the size of the individual node memory. COTS microprocessors include the i860 (Intel Paragon), SPARC (CM-5 for Thinking Machines), and DEC's Alpha (the T-3D from Cray Research). The nCube developers continue their tradition of utilizing a highly integrated proprietary custom microprocessor/router.

These microprocessors are currently sustaining on the order of 2 to 20 MFLOPs, and this will continue to improve as we move through the nineties. A plausible TFLOP machine in the 1997–1999 time frame might consist of

2**13 = 8,000 microprocessors, each with a sustained rate of 2**7 = 128 MFLOPs (perhaps twice that, peak), and each with 16 MW (= 128 MB) of DRAM memory partitioned into four or eight memory banks per node (multiple memory banks support the high bandwidth requirement of the processor, a result of the mismatch between accelerating microprocessor performance rates and relatively flat DRAM retrieval rates). All of the technology to support such an architecture is already "in the pipe," completely independent of MPPs, based on commercial market pressures for workstations, PCs, and other microprocessor applications. The principal value added by an MPP architect is design and fabrication of the interconnection network.

3.4.2 Strengths and Weaknesses

We begin by listing some of the reasons why the industry has settled on the DM-MIMD architecture as the most promising approach to TFLOP performance levels. Many of these reasons have already been mentioned, in passing, at scattered points in the text. Here, we want to list them together to get a sense of their force and direction.

1. **Memory Bandwidth:** DM-MIMD exhibits the classic MPP solution strategy: hundreds or thousands of independent memory banks are needed to sustain TFLOP processing rates; place each bank (or a small group of them) at each processing node in a large array.

2. **Size of Memory:** The only electrically feasible approach to achieving the TByte memory sizes necessary for TFLOP computing is to take advantage of the extraordinary increases in DRAM bit-per-chip densities. This, in turn, means accepting DRAM's significant limitations in longer retrieval times. DM-MIMD uses this approach.

3. **Microprocessors:** In parallel with improvements in DRAM, the custom CMOS microprocessor industry is on an exponential growth curve in chip complexity and processing speed. While the mismatch to DRAM retrieval rates widens, the basic processing rates can be expected to exceed 200 MFLOPs (peak) by the turn of the century. DM-MIMD utilizes this technology.

4. **Packaging and Reliability:** The custom CMOS/DRAM combination enables packaging strategies that are conservative and inexpensive when compared with mainframe approaches. Low chip counts (based on higher transistor densities) lead to greatly increased MTBF, and replication leads to small, inexpensive *least unit of repair.*

These first four observations are central to why DM-MIMD architectures can scale to TFLOP levels of performance.

5. **Compiler Technology:** Because each node of a DM-MIMD machine is "really" just a microprocessor, one feasible (and widely used) programming approach is to supplement an ordinary sequential language, such as C or FORTRAN, with a subroutine library to support message passing among the nodes. This approach allows the MPP developer to utilize standard compilers but puts the full burden of parallelization (via use of the library) on the user. There are significant savings in not having to develop a parallelizing compiler or invent new syntax.
6. **Ability to Emulate Other Paradigms:** A number of programming approaches (see Chapters 4 through 7) have been proposed for use on MPPs. While these are historically rooted in hardware differences, they embody a variety of powerful parallelizing abstractions that can considerably ease the software development task. Any of these paradigms can be used, with varying degrees of efficiency, on DM-MIMD hardware. The hope is to decouple the fight over programming standardization from hardware considerations. As is clear from discussions elsewhere, the author remains dubious about how successful such a decoupling can be in practice.
7. **Sharing:** The ability to divide a DM-MIMD array into subarrays and allocate them independently to separate users is a major advantage to an organization intending to use the MPP as a shared resource. This is typical, for example, of open system operational environments. Other MPP approaches, and SIMD in particular, are not so flexible.

The major disadvantages of the DM-MIMD architecture are in synchronization overhead and memory usage inefficiencies. We have already mentioned, in Section 3.4.1, how the loosely synchronous programming approach inserts points in the control flow that ensure the entire array is together (see Figure 3-7). If, for example, one of the processors takes considerably longer than the others to arrive at the synchronization point, the time spent waiting is a source of inefficiency. The job of designing the program so that this situation does not arise is called *load balancing* and can be a significant part of algorithm and software development. Profiling tools are available to produce diagrams, such as that in Figure 3-7, to assist in detecting and correcting these problems.

There are several ways in which DM-MIMD machines use memory less efficiently than their SIMD and shared memory counterparts. First, the message-passing capabilities provided by the interconnection network require a certain amount of buffer space to hold incoming messages until the running process is ready to receive them. Depending on the number, size, and frequency of these messages, a considerable amount of node memory may be required for this purpose. Second, each node must hold its own copy of the program to be executed. In SIMD machines, a single copy for the controller suffices. In shared memory machines, the processors can share a single copy of the program. Third, global data structures (such as, for example, the *twiddle array* used in FFTs) can pose a problem. It is faster for each processing node to have its own private copy; access time is minimized since there is no need to send for an array value over the network. The price for this efficiency is increased memory usage.

We mentioned, in Section 3.2, how an LAN of workstations can be treated as an MPP by using the LAN as the interconnection network. The architecture type of such a configuration is clearly DM-MIMD, and the programming paradigms (in particular, message passing) developed for DM-MIMD are the most suitable for such an arrangement. The term *cluster* is now commony used to describe such a configuration.

3.5 SHARED MEMORY MIMD MACHINES

The difficulty in explaining the architecture issues for shared memory machines lies in a basic confusion, perpetrated by all parties, concerning shared memory as a *hardware architecture* versus shared memory as a *programming paradigm*. Briefly, shared memory as a programming paradigm has one clear advantage over its competitors: It moves data using the simplest of all programming mechanisms, by *naming* it. We saw, for example, how in a DM-MIMD world, the meaning (that is, the value) associated with a variable varies depending on which processor (and its local memory bank) is considered. This is what is meant by the "*MD*" in the *MIMD* designation—and we might call it *m*ighty *d*isturbing.

While this approach is not *formally* ambiguous (in the computer science sense that deterministic results can be obtained), it is *psychologically* ambiguous to the beginning parallel programmer. A variable *ought* to mean the same thing no matter who (that is, what processor) refers to it; its value should not depend on hardware context—at least that is the position taken by proponents of shared memory as a programming approach. Shared memory also has the advantage of being closer to the standard sequential progamming abstraction: a single large address space as opposed to multiple distinct address spaces. This close association can considerably ease both the compiler task and the job of porting applications to the parallel environment.

Whatever the merits of this point of view, it rests on an assumption about the underlying hardware that is either difficult or impossible to implement—namely, that all of this large address space is *uniformly distant* from the processor(s). In practical terms, it should not matter *which* variable the processor references: The *time to retrieve* a variable from memory (*memory latency*, in the technical argot) ought to be the same for all the variables.

Now, the *facts* are that uniformity of memory reference, even in conventional sequential machines, is an illusion—an abstraction, the creation of which is the goal of a good deal of both hardware and operating system software in all modern architectures. At the moment a program references a variable, that variable can physically be in a number of different possible locations, some of which are very close to the processor (fast access), and some of which are distant from the processor (slow access). This is illustrated in Figure 3-8, which shows how latency (that is, memory access time) increases depending on whether the variable being referenced is found in a local register, cache, main memory, or secondary storage (with thanks to John Gustafson for introducing me to this diagram).

There are dozens of approaches in current use that attempt to ensure, based on statistical behavior of program execution or on compiler analysis of the memory reference patterns, that when a variable is actually referenced by the processor it will be as "close" to the processor as possible. This means *moving* the data, *before* it is referenced, so that it will be in the fastest part of memory (register or cache) *when* it is referenced.

These techniques have been very successful on traditional sequential programs and rely heavily on the statistical property of *locality of reference:* When one variable is referenced, the odds are that nearby variables will soon be wanted. So, instead of moving just a single variable to fast memory, we move several of its neighbors (the *memory page* in which the variable resides) as well. These nearby data will then be waiting in fast memory ready for use when required.

Lots of things start to go wrong with this approach when we move to many (more than, say, 10 or 20) processors and when the data sets on which the program operates become very large. To mention just one potential problem among many, it is common in very large problems to step through memory with a "stride" (that is, the distance between successive memory addresses) that exceeds the size of a page. Faced with such a situation, a page-based caching scheme will bring superfluous data into fast memory on each successive reference, and machine execution will creep along at the bandwidth of slower main memory rather than faster cache. In a virtual memory machine relying heavily on disk back-up, this can actually result in a disk reference for each variable and a consequent horrendous performance penalty.

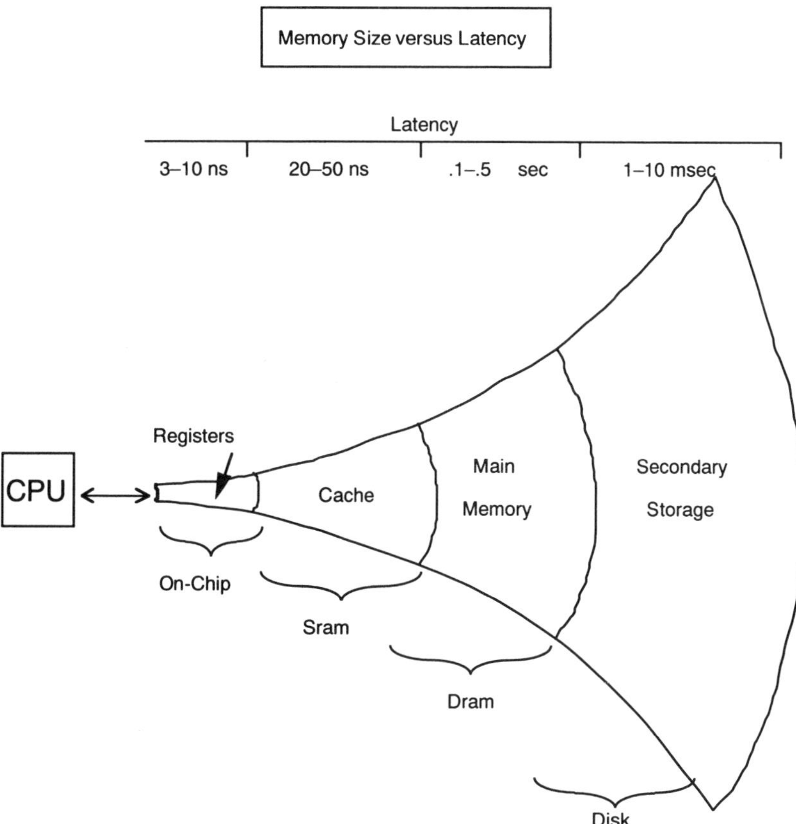

Figure 3-8. Fast access memory is smaller and closer to the CPU

All this is to put the reader on notice. A *shared memory* machine is not, in practice, a *uniform reference* machine, even though the programming paradigm encourages the programmer to pretend that it is. For the shared memory programming paradigm to work (that is, to provide acceptable performance) in practice, the underlying hardware (and supporting compiler/operating system software) must be able to mask effectively the nonuniform latency problem. A major argument of this section will be that such latency hiding has only proven itself effective on fairly small numbers of processors and even then requires a tremendous amount of additional hardware.

From the MPP point of view, the additional hardware (and board real estate) needed to support the uniform access abstraction could be put to better use: more processors and more memory. The trade-off ultimately becomes one of ease of programming versus higher performance. MPP vendors hope that as more experience is gained and software standards evolve, the "ease of programming" penalty will also ease and will eventually become competitive with the shared memory paradigm. A point of view heard on occasion is that software developers have become spoiled by all the virtual memory hardware support; "real men map the physical memory" is the motto of some MPP programmers, in search of the elusive (and illusory) last 1 percent of performance.

> ***Example***: We suggest an analogy with the *CISC* versus *RISC* instruction set controversy. The putative benefit of CISC was that it eased the task of the compiler writer. It was eventually realized, however, how much in performance was being given up for this ease; and, at the same time, compiler technology was itself improving. The triumph of RISC (performance over ease) in high-end microprocessors may be taken as an omen of a similar victory of DM-MIMD over simpler, but less powerful, SM-MIMD. ■

The reader will have the opportunity to form an independent judgment of these matters when we describe alternative programming approaches in Chapters 4 through 7. Our goal here is to present the shared memory hardware approach, including the two major latency-hiding mechanisms: vectorization and caching. The difficulties that lie in the path of extending this architecture to truly MPP levels of performance will then be discussed.

3.5.1 A Top-Level Block Diagram

Recall the three components from Figure 3-2: the controller, C; the processor, P; and the storage, S. In a shared memory parallel machine, the approach is to replicate several copies of C/P and to provide a single uniformly accessible instance of S. This is commonly termed a *symmetric multiprocessor* (*SMP*) and is by far the most commercially successful and prevalent of parallel architectures. The C/P pair is usually just called a *processor*. These ideas are illustrated in Figure 3-9.

The reason for the commercial success of this architecture derives from the way it is usually used. The operating system, using standard virtual memory addressing hardware logic, "tricks" each individual processor into thinking it has a private, nonshared memory. To the processor and the application running on it, the machine looks like an ordinary sequential processor. The existence of the other processors and the fact that the memory is actually being shared is hidden. Thus, an SMP can execute multiple user jobs concurrently, providing each user the illusion of having a complete sequential machine for

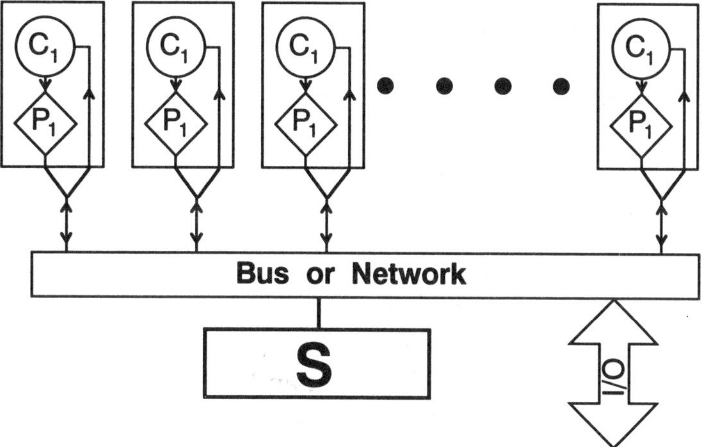

Figure 3-9. A generic SMP configuration

his or her own use. The "time-sharing" approach is now supplemented by "space-sharing" the separate processors allocated to the job stream.

One supremely important consequence of this approach is that *no modification to existing sequential software is required.* The sequential programming paradigm is preserved, in toto. Parallelism is used, not to speed up a given job, but to execute multiple, independent jobs concurrently.

The reader may be a bit uneasy about all this. Things are quite different here than in the previously discussed approaches. What about using *all* the processors on a *single* job? Isn't that what we really mean by *parallel*? To which the author replies: Yes, but what is being described is how, in daily practice, these machines are being used. Further, if we consider Figure 1-1, we will find that the shared memory approach lies at the far top end of the spectrum: SMPs typically have on the order of 4 to 20 processors. They do *not* use the basic MPP approach of replicating processors at each of a large number of independent memory banks. Instead, they attempt to provide each of the processors more or less uniform access to all memory banks (the collection of memory banks being, in the aggregate, the memory component, S).

The reason for the small number of processors is that the memory is a shared resource and, hence, a bottleneck. The total available memory bandwidth remains constant, independent of the number of processors. When the number of processors has increased to the point that memory bandwidth has been exhausted, it does no good to add more processors: They cannot run faster than the memory bandwidth available to support them. As a practical matter, memory bandwidth runs out somewhere between 4 and 20 processors.

Example: The difference between shared memory and distributed memory can be illustrated, somehat irreverently, by hogs gathered around a trough. Even if the trough is large, the space around it is quickly occupied, after which any remaining hogs must wait. The single shared trough imposes an upper bound on the number of hogs that can be supported. The solution, taken by the distributed memory architects, is to give each hog its own trough! ■

Although not widely employed, it is possible to "parallelize" a single application across the multiple processors of an SMP. The MIMD control approach has each of the C/P units executing an independent control stream, each operating (under program direction) on separate subsets of data held in the shared memory, S. The processors are the soldiers, each operating on a designated subset of the full data set (the wall) held in the large shared memory.

The shared memory is also used as the mechanism for processors to communicate. When processor C_K wishes to send data to C_M, the data are placed (by C_K) at a data location (that is, in a variable) known to both processors. At a later time, C_M can then reference the location, and a data transfer has taken place. Note that the programmer must arrange to ensure that "later" is enforced and that C_M does not access the shared location before C_K has placed the data there. This issue of synchronization between the processors (also called a *race condition*) is a typical feature of programming shared memory machines. It is also important to distinguish *global variables* (varia-bles referring to regions of memory accessible to multiple processes) from *local variables* (variables private to a particular process). It is also typical to have more logical *processes* active than there are physical *processors* to execute them. The logical-to-physical mapping, based on time-slicing and a prioritization scheme, is handled by the operating system.

The next section will describe the two major approaches to hiding memory latency on shared memory machines.

3.5.2 Latency Hiding

As we discussed briefly in the introduction to Section 3.5, the practical efficiency of the shared memory programing approach will depend, critically, on the ability of the underlying hardware to sustain the illusion of *fast, uniform reference* to the address space. As soon as this illusion breaks down (that is, as soon as run-time inefficiencies make it apparent that some variables are really a lot farther from the processor than others), ease of use of the paradigm is subject to serious challenge, based on inefficiency.

Two basic approaches have been used by vendors to address this issue. The first is *vectorization*, illustrated by machines from Cray Research. High-memory bandwidth is provided by using multiple memory banks, and a very high performance cross-bar switch provides all processors (up to 16 in the latest C-90) uniform access to all the memory banks. This is the crucial point: It takes no longer to reference a variable in one bank than in any other. The programming abstraction of "uniform access" is a physical reality for such a machine. The *cost* of this uniform access, however, is the trip back and forth across the switch that connects the processors to the memory banks. Many clock pulses elapse (say, 15 to 20) while the reference traverses the switch to the memory bank, completes the data retrieval, and retraces the path back across the switch to the issuing processor.

A vectorizing machine hides this latency by exploiting the fact that, often, it is possible to precompute a large number of memory references in advance. This is especially true of mathematical codes utilizing matrices; the exact memory locations of data to be referenced follow a simple pattern based on a starting location and a constant "stride" between successive addresses. When such a "vectorizing" operation is encountered, the hardware can queue up a long string of memory references and can issue them at full clock speed, *not waiting for one to complete before the next is issued.* The cost of the trip back and forth across the switch is paid only once for the entire set. Once the first reference is complete, the successors follow right behind, at full clock rate, just as if the processor was right next to the memory, with no switch in the way.

This approach requires data structures, and operations on them, that support the ability to recognize and precompute regular memory references. On any given application, speed will be contingent on the ability to hide successfully the long latency imposed by the cross-bar switch, in effect by pipelining many memory accesses concurrently. What it means to "vectorize an application" is to restructure the application in a way that maximizes the opportunities for using this capability.

The second major approach to latency hiding is by using *cache memory*. Figure 3-10 is an augmentation of Figure 3-2, showing the interposition of the cache between the controller/processor pair and main storage. Briefly, the cache is a small amount of very fast memory (typically SRAM and increasingly on-chip). When the controller or processor makes a memory reference, the hope is that the requested data are found in the cache; this permits the memory reference to be completed rapidly, thereby hiding the higher latency of a reference to main memory (typically implemented in slower, but less expensive, DRAM). As noted earlier, for standard sequential programs the statistical properties of *locality of data* can be exploited to obtain very high cache

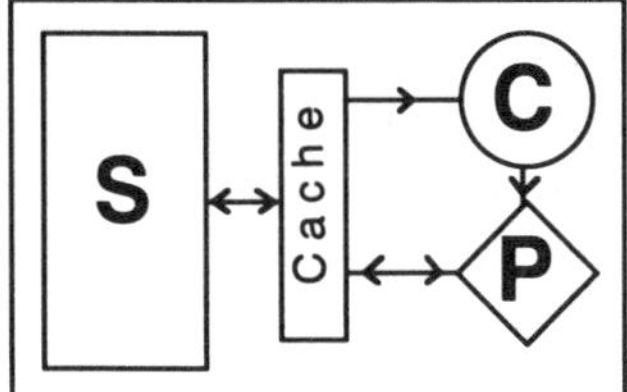

Figure 3-10. Fast access cache is placed between main memory and the CPU

hit rates: A typical figure is that 98 percent or more of memory references are found in the cache. The larger the cache, the greater the cache hit rate. This improves performance by allowing the processor to operate at the much higher memory bandwidth provided by the cache. It is one way in which the mismatch between slower DRAM memory retrieval rates and faster microprocessor operation rates can be bridged.

Figure 3-11 shows that caching can be used to improve performance on an SMP architecture. Each processor has its local cache and only references the global shared memory, S, when necessary. However, a difficulty now arises that was not present in the uniprocessor case. It is now possible for a single *logical* variable to be *physically replicated* in the caches of several processors. This is not a problem so long as the variable is "read only." However, what happens if the value of the variable is altered by one of the processors? How is this event to be conveyed to the others, warning them that their local values are no longer valid?

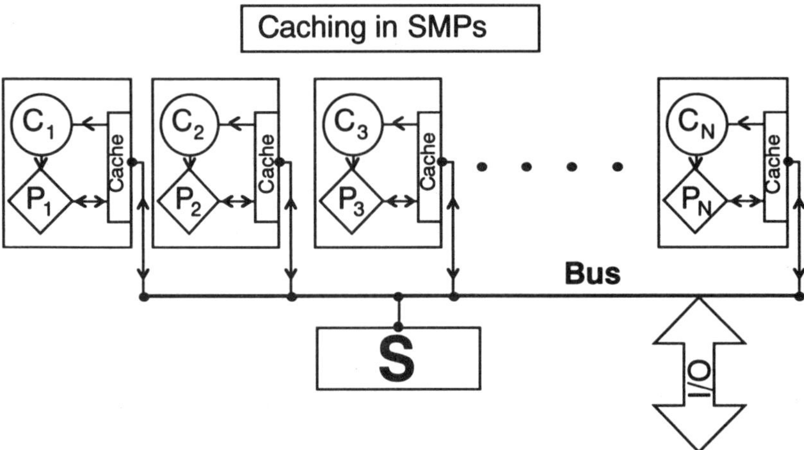

Figure 3-11. Adding caches to each node of an SMP can improve performance

This is known as the *cache coherency* problem. A complete text could be written on various approaches. What we want to observe, for the moment, is that the $C_K/P_K/$cache triple in Figure 3-11 looks very much like the $C_K/P_K/S_K$ triple from our description of DM-MIMD machines in Section 3.4 (see Figure 3-6). The contoller/processor, with its cache, is a baby step away from being a stand-alone processing node in a DM-MIMD architecture!

Vendors and academics have noticed this resemblance. Their hope is to make a DM-MIMD machine that appears to the user as a shared memory machine and to do this by treating the local memory at the processing node as if it were a cache. Some sort of hardware/software to support this abstraction is, of course, required. In effect, data flow between the processing nodes in the DM-MIMD machine not by explicit message passing but by a virtual memory/cache coherency protocol supported by the hardware and operating system and invisible to the user. The idea is to get the best of both worlds: all the memory bandwidth scalability of DM-MIMD with the ease of programming of shared memory—truly a marriage made in heaven, *if* it works.

The reader is right to detect some skepticism from the author at this point. Simply put, as we have noted several times, the practical success of the shared memory paradigm depends on maintaining the illusion of *uniform memory access.* Picture in the mind's eye a machine physically consisting of several hundred separate MIMD processors, each with its local memory, spread across the interconnection network at various relative positions and distances. Now, picture a programmer developing an application on which the relative positions of data in this array are not taken into account but in which a local memory reference is treated by the program no differently than a reference to a variable held in another processor's memory. *That* is the problem. The *machine hardware* will treat those two references very differently—completing one rapidly and the other much more slowly. The *program* treats them as if they were the same.

Only if the distance (relative latency) between data and processor is explicitly recognized can the application be structured so as to minimize it. Perhaps, in simple cases, a compiler might help lay out data across the array in an efficient manner. But, at least at this point in parallel processing, only simple cases can be handled. If the programmer *does* take into account the relative locations of processors and includes this explicitly in the program, the advantages (in increased simplicity) of the shared memory paradigm have been lost. Again, there is no free lunch in parallel processing!

Reference [10] provides an excellent survey of attempts to support the shared memory programming abstraction on networks of workstations. The Linda programming paradigm is the best known of these approaches (see Chapter 7). Both the Butterfly and the TC2000 from BBN were machines that attempted to support the shared memory paradigm for MPPs on a physically distributed platform. Currently, the KS-1 from Kendall Square Research has adopted this approach, with extensive hardware support for virtual memory and cache coherency not seen on previous hardware. The stated goal for the KS-1 is to provide the commercial appeal of an SMP with the scalability (to hundreds of processors) of a DM-MIMD MPP. The perceived commercial payoff for successfully marrying DM scalability with SM programmability will undoubtedly keep this part of the architecture space active for years to come. References [10–15] provide an excellent introduction to this important part of the parallel architecture space.

3.5.3 Strengths and Weaknesses

The most significant SMP characteristics have already been mentioned in the foregoing discussion. These include:

- close resemblance to sequential programming and operating system paradigms
- the ability to share the machine among users by executing their existing sequential applications with little or no modification
- simple approach to data movement, using the shared memory as the data transmission mechanism
- *uniform* memory access is incompatible with large numbers of processors (MPP), compromises proposed to address this, and their weaknesses

Two other items are worth noting. First, because the memory is shared, the data structures in it can be shared. Important examples include the code segment and look-up tables required by the algorithm. This avoids the replication (and additional memory usage) required in distributed memory architectures. Similarly, I/O facilities can be shared, including virtual memory (that is, once a page of memory has been touched by one processor in the array and brought into core, it is available for the others, as well).

Second, let us return to the subject of latency versus throughput from Section 2.3.2. There we noted the difference between two situations. Suppose, for example, that the task is to accomplish 10 jobs in a total of 10 hours. Two possible solutions are:

1. use a machine that can run one job per hour, and then run the 10 jobs, one after the other, on the single machine (reduced latency per job)
2. find a machine that can run one job in 10 hours, and then replicate the machine 10 times, running all 10 jobs concurrently (increased throughput)

One advantage the first approach has over the second is that the same resources are *reused* by the successive jobs; that is, if, for example, the memory requirement for one instance of the job is 60 MB, then the first machine only needs a total of 60 MB of memory, which is then reused by each of the successive jobs. The second solution requires a total of 600 MB—60 MB in each of the 10 processors. The compensating advantage of the second approach is that its lack of speed (on each individual machine) may enable it to utilize less-expensive components. The 10 slower machines may, in aggregate, cost less than the single fast one.

The first approach (reduced latency) is characteristic of shared memory architectures, the top end of the spectrum from Figure 1-1. The second is characteristic of MPPs.

Summary of Chapter 3

Our goal has been to show how the basic hardware architecture for a parallel machine inevitably impacts algorithm design and implementation. The topology (that is, wiring pattern) of the interconnection network is an important example: The programmer must try to position processors needing to communicate so that they are close together on the network; the "right" solution can vary dramatically based on topology differences. Similarly, the algorithm must take advantage of what the machine does well (broadcast and reduction on SIMD machines, multiple independent control streams on DM-MIMD, etc.) and avoid what the machine does poorly (multiple data-dependent branching on an SIMD machine, synchronization and global operations on a DM-MIMD machine, etc.). The difficulties of marrying a shared memory programming paradigm (with its underlying assumption of uniform memory access) to the scalability of a distributed memory architecture (in which the latency of memory references is highly nonuniform) were discussed at some length.

A major observation is that, at the high end, MPP vendors have converged on DM-MIMD for the hardware architecture. There is far less agreement on the proper programming approach, with message passing, array/SIMD, and shared memory all having adherents. This will be taken up at greater length in Part 2.

PART 2

Software Issues

As noted in the preface, the major purpose of this book is to present enough information about parallel processing to enable a manager to make intelligent decisions about whether this technology is "right" for his or her organization. A key consideration, in many instances, is the programmability of the machine. Questions arise about the languages used to program these machines, the operating systems they employ, and the development environment (including tools to assist in porting existing codes to a parallel machine).

The approach we have adopted for *parallel languages* is to present complete, coded solutions to a "toy" sample problem in each of a number of different currently available languages. Some explanation of this process may be appropriate at the outset. First, the problem itself was coded in ordinary sequential C. A description of the problem and a listing of the solution can be found in Appendix A. It would be well to become familiar with the problem now, before attempting to tackle the parallel versions.

The sample problem was constructed in order to illustrate a number of features of parallel machines: I/O (both file and terminal), broadcast and reduction operations, loop dependencies that make parallelization more difficult, decomposition of large data sets, etc. The problem itself is fairly simple (calculate some statistics on a set of test scores), so that hopefully little effort need be spent on the purpose and meaning of the code.

Seven sample solutions are then presented, each one using a different dialect of C (or, alternatively, a different library of C subroutines): one representing a shared memory paradigm (Chapter 4); three representing a message-passing paradigm (Chapter 5); two representing an array/SIMD paradigm (Chapter 6); and one using Linda (Chapter 7).

Each chapter begins with an introduction to the key ideas underlying the programming approach. Then, the specific solutions are presented. Listings of actual code are provided in the appendices, and detailed annotations are provided in the text. The intent is to make as clear as possible for the reader exactly how each language identifies and expresses the parallelism in the problem. In this way, the reader can get a sense of the difficulty (or ease) of writing a parallel application.

The language C was chosen as the baseline out of consideration for the intended audience: FORTRAN is not widely used in the commercial world. Had the audience been, for example, the research community or the National Labs, a different choice might have been made. Also, there are aspects of the sample problem that are somewhat artificial. A real application suitable for a supercomputer-class MPP would be much larger than that presented here, and considerably more attention would have to be paid to I/O than is paid here. Nevertheless, the reader should come away with a good feel for the types of parallelism a programmer looks for in an algorithm or application and the type of tools a language provides to assist in expressing and exploiting that parallelism.

In addition to the four chapters on parallel languages, two additional chapters are provided dealing with other aspects of parallel software. Chapter 8 is concerned with the software development environment: automatic parallelization, debuggers, profilers, etc. Chapter 9 takes up operating system issues. These two chapters are perhaps the most technically demanding of the entire book. The material they contain may, however, be critical to making an informed decision about the suitability of parallel processing for a particular application and operational environment.

4

Shared Memory Parallel Language Constructs

The author broaches this topic only with trepidation, for it is a subject about which many companies have strong, and often conflicting, opinions. It is also an area that is currently in flux. Standards have yet to emerge, industry leaders have yet to commit to one or another of the alternative approaches, and the business implications of all these matters are substantial.

Shared memory systems are more burdened by their history than are other parallel machines, primarily because they have been much more successful. There already exists a large and growing market for symmetric multiprocessors (SMPs), and, hence, customer expectations and commitments exist that constrain proposed solutions. When other factors, such as competitive advantage and standards battles, are thrown in, the current mix is volatile.

At the heart of this topic is the issue of the next generation of UNIX. It is generally recognized that this will have to provide additional capabilities to handle "lightweight processes" or *threads*, which will be discussed in more detail later in this chapter. An example of such a system, called *Mach*, has been around for some time and has actually been used as the kernel by several vendors. At the moment, however, the situation is chaotic. Different vendors have their own proprietary multiprocessing operating systems for their SMPs (while still supporting standard UNIX for sequential processes) and their own programming language interfaces to these facilities.

While there are common themes and capabilities as one moves from one vendor to another, there are still no standards. Hence, third-party software vendors have been very selective about developing fully parallelized applications in this environment. Typically, parallelism on SMPs (when it is used at all) is accomplished directly through UNIX—creating separate, independent UNIX processes by the *fork* call and allowing them to communicate via *pipes* or *shared memory regions* (implemented via the page tables). Such approaches require a fair degree of UNIX programming skill and (as we will see) often impose unacceptable levels of performance overhead, particularly when the child processes need to appear and disappear rapidly, frequently, and dynamically. More often, opportunities for parallelism are simply ignored.

Irrespective of the operating system, however, is the separate issue of the "right" set of programming constructs that will allow a programmer to express (hopefully, quickly and easily) the parallelism in a problem. Ideally, these constructs might even permit a smart compiler automatically to detect opportunities for parallelism in existing codes (automatic parallelization). Even better, it might be possible for the *same* source code to be compiled for *either* a sequential machine *or* an SMP. Only one version of the source need be maintained, with enhanced execution on an SMP should one be available. These, at least, are some of the motivations underlying the development of SMP parallel language constructs.

We will begin our discussion with an introduction to the major concepts that must, in one way or another, be addressed by any shared memory programming paradigm (Section 4.1). Section 4.2 then presents a solution to the sample program on a particular SMP—the Challenge Power Series from Silicon Graphics. Section 4.3 presents several observations and considerations.

4.1 BASIC CONCEPTS FOR SHARED MEMORY PARALLEL PROGRAMMING

In this section, we will discuss three key ideas that the shared memory programmer must keep in mind and whose expression and manipulation must be provided by the shared memory language constructs. The key ideas are:

- creation and control of separate control streams
- synchronization of activity between the control streams
- use of local and shared memory to enable data passing and coordination between the control streams

Separate subsections are provided for each of these topics.

4.1.1 Lightweight Processes

The basic scheduling problem for a symmetric multiprocessing operating system is illustrated in Figure 4-1.

Logical processes (that is, jobs and user programs) are entered into a work queue, and the operating system is responsible for getting the work done. In a *single processor* system, the major resource is time on the single CPU. Each process in the queue, based primarily on priority, is assigned time-slices during which the CPU performs its processing. In a *multiprocessor* system, however, there are several CPUs available. The basic idea of resource sharing stays the same, but an additional dimension—sharing time on multiple CPUs, instead of just one—has been added.

UNIX (and all other general-purpose operating systems) already has facilities to create new processes on the work queue—primarily the *fork* command. However, this is inadequate for parallel processing because of the size of the data structures—the *state*—needed to describe a standard UNIX process. This state includes a considerable amount of information, which implements the virtual memory, flags and signals, priority, access privileges, file conditions, and other data structures needed by the operating system to provide the complete environment for the process. All these must be created whenever the process is spawned and deleted/updated when it suspends or terminates. Further, during the swapping operation (exchanging one executing process on a CPU for another), the complete execution state for the process must be

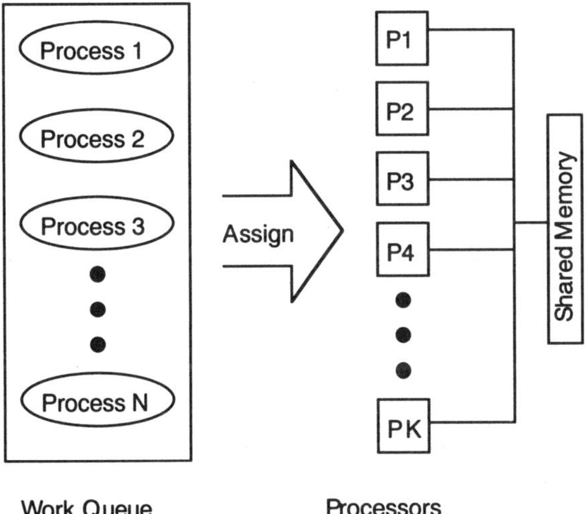

Figure 4-1. Logical processes must be assigned to physical processors

saved, including registers, virtual memory translation structures, file pointers, and other similar data, which reflect the current operational condition of the process. Again, the amount of state associated with the process is large and adds to the overhead of swapping during time-sharing.

For many problems, parallelism does not need all of this baggage, and having to create it and manage it wastes time and degrades performance. This observation led to the idea of *threads* or *lightweight processes.* The idea is that these can be scheduled (that is, assigned to processors and executed) in much the same way as ordinary UNIX processes but that they *share* much of the heavyweight state of their parent process—which is now called a *task* (to reduce confusion). (We have borrowed the terms *thread* and *task* from Mach terminology.) These ideas are illustrated in Figure 4-2.

A task consists of multiple threads, which are the executable (that is, schedulable) entities. The task is where the heavyweight state data structures are stored. Threads, on the other hand, are much more ephemeral. They can come and go quickly, without a great deal of system overhead. Threads are the right construct, from an operating system point of view, to efficiently support fine-grained parallelism on SMPs.

Even though the figure shows only one active task, it is possible to have more than one task (and its threads) active. An ordinary UNIX process becomes a task that has only a *single* thread, and ordinary UNIX time-sharing is done by letting the tasks compete (based on priority) for CPU time, just as always. However, when real parallelism (as opposed to multiple job execution) is the

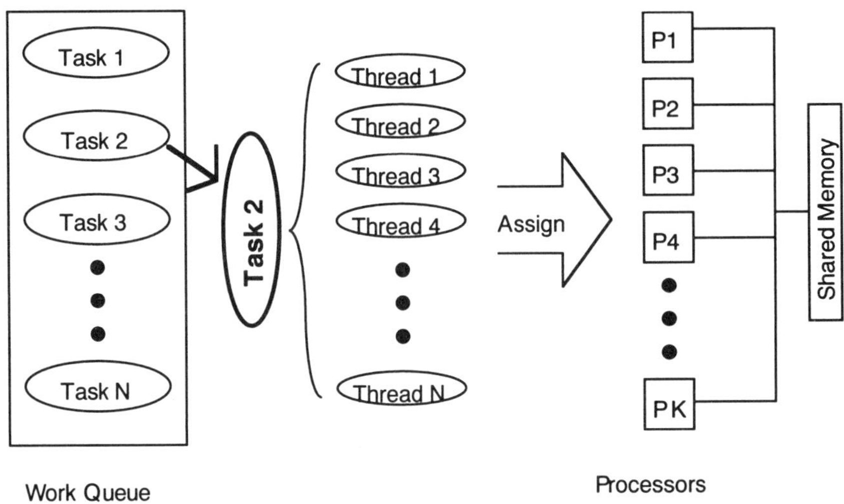

Figure 4-2. A task consists of several independent threads

objective, there are advantages to having only a single task and its threads executing at one time. Typically, in a parallel application, the threads will cooperate with each other, and a stage of processing in one thread may depend on the prior completion of a result in another. If only some of the threads are active, they may be delayed by the fact that the thread on which they depend has not yet been scheduled. For the same reason, it is usually a good idea to have exactly as many threads as there are processors (or at least not more threads than processors). To summarize, having all the threads for a task execute concurrently (which corresponds to the programmer's conceptual model) can improve efficiency, and ordinarily the operating system will attempt to ensure that this is done.

The programmer's view of all of this is that the *task* takes the form of the main executable program, and the *threads* take the form of *parallel regions* inside the program. These regions cue the compiler that the work can be subdivided into separate, lightweight executables that cooperate on completion of a section of code. This is illustrated in Figure 4-3.

The shift back and forth between sequential and parallel regions is a striking feature of this programming style. As we will see, even within a parallel region there are sometimes portions of code that should be executed by only a single process (terminal I/O is a common example)—a kind of sequential island in the parallel ocean.

It is common for the programmer not to take explicit account of the number of physical processors or logical threads. This permits use of library routines that create variable numbers of threads, dynamically at run time, based on system loading. Code that uses these facilities can execute without modification on SMPs with differing numbers of physical CPUs. The programmer merely indicates the opportunity for parallelism in a block of code and allows the compiler, together with the run-time system, to make the low-level deci-

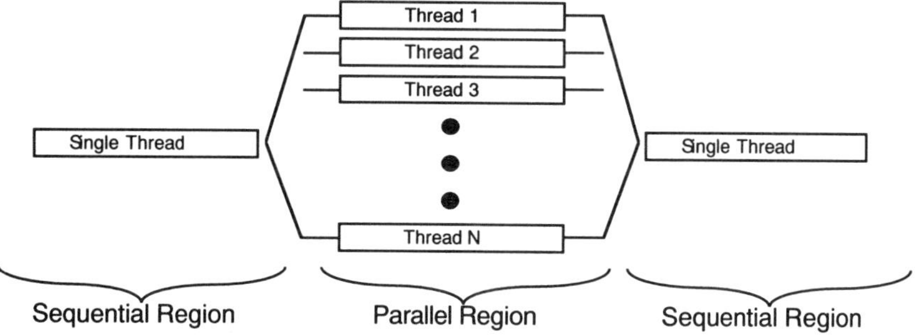

Figure 4-3. Sequential and parallel regions

sions about how many threads to create. One consequence of this is that the order of operations can vary from run to run. Bugs that only show up when, say, at least five threads are active may go undetected simply because the run-time environment happened to use four or fewer. The advantages of a nondeterministic run-time environment (portability, ease of programming) are a mixed blessing.

Another factor, which is often overlooked but that can have a substantial effect on performance, is thread-to-processor *reassignment.* The issue arises because of an interaction between UNIX time-sharing and processor caches. As we have seen (Figure 3-11), SMPs typically improve their performance by the use of high-speed associative caches local to each processor. During execution of a task and its threads, each processor's cache will become saturated with the data and instructions needed by the thread that is executing on it. When the task is swapped out (together with its threads), the physical cache state remains. When the task is later swapped back in, it would be nice if the *same* threads were reassigned to the *same* physical processors on which they were executing prior to the swap. This will permit reuse of the cache state and, hence, will improve performance.

4.1.2 Shared and Global Variables

The notion of variables that are "seen" by more than one part of a program—say, by multiple, independent subroutines—is commonplace for sequential languages. The COMMON block implements this notion in FORTRAN; and in C, the *scope* of a variable can extend across multiple blocks. It is a simple way for the results of one function to become available to another without having to pass the values explicitly in the calling sequence of the function. It is also a way to make shared data structures, such as look-up tables, globally available to any routine that needs them. When a subroutine names a variable, its programmer must be aware of whether or not the variable can be "seen" by other subroutines. If so, some additional care must be taken so that these other routines do not corrupt the values and that the updated value of the variable is consistent with the requirements of those routines. Dealing with these issues is one of the motivations behind the ideas of private data types and object-oriented programming.

A somewhat analogous situation arises in the shared memory paradigm. This is illustrated in Figure 4-4.

Typically, multiple independent threads will execute concurrently (in parallel). Consider the following line of code executed by one of the threads:

```
x_var = y_var + z_var;
```

A critical element in understanding this line of code is whether other threads also "see" the values of the variables being referenced. Some variables are completely *local* to the thread—modifications to these variables are not seen beyond the scope of the thread itself. Other variables are *shared* across multiple threads. The very same variable is "seen" by all the threads; when one thread modifies this variable, the modification is made to the shared instance and, hence, will be experienced by all the other threads as well.

In the line of code above (reference is made to Figure 4-4), `x_var` and `y_var` are both *local* variables to whichever instance of a thread is executing. Each thread has its own private copy of `x_var` and `y_var` (a separate, private copy for each thread), so that modifications made by any thread to its own, local copy are not seen by, and do not affect, any other thread. On the other hand, the variable `z_var` is a *shared* variable. The value of `z_var` is the same across all the threads, because only a single memory location, seen by all the threads, is provided. Thus, the line of code

```
z_var  =  x_var  +  y_var;
```

acts very differently from the preceding line of code. Any thread executing this line of code will *change* the value of `z_var`, and this change will then immediately become visible to and affect the processing of any other thread that references `z_var`.

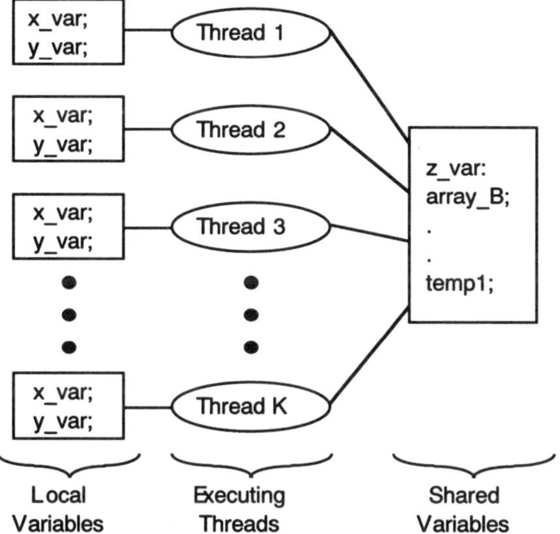

Figure 4-4. Local and shared variables in the shared memory model

The notion of local and shared variables is fundamental to the shared memory paradigm. The fact that the memory is uniformly accessible to all the processors is the basis for interprocessor communication, and the ability to designate certain variables as shared is the way in which this capability is implemented. On the other hand, we do not want all variables to be accessible to everyone. Local, private variables ease the programmer's task, since they greatly restrict the number of possible culprits when something goes wrong and a variable "goes south."

All shared language paradigms provide mechanisms for the programmer to distinguish between local and shared variables. In effect, this becomes part of the *declaration* of the variable, although many variations have been tried where the "shared versus local" distinction is piggybacked on top of other existing constructs (e.g., COMMON blocks, subroutine parameters, call-by-reference, etc.). One of the first things to do when confronted with an unfamiliar shared memory language is to become clear on how the language distinguishes between shared and local variables.

There are two especially common types of errors that arise as a result of the difference between local and shared variables. One type has to do with controlling access to the global variables, and this will be discussed at greater length in the next section. The other type of problem arises because a *local variable can hold an address of a global variable.* This is especially detrimental in C, which has a long history of rather free use of address logic (pointers). Even though the variable that holds the address may be local, the memory location referenced by the address may be global.

This capability is certainly required. For example, we might want each thread to process a separate row (or group of rows) of a matrix. Rather than copy the entire row over into the local address space of the thread, it is much more efficient to simply pass the address of the first element of the row and allow the thread to access the data directly as it sits in the global memory area. The associated penalty for this power is that now the thread has an address, which, in effect, gives it the ability to reference the entire array (and, in C, other unrelated data structures that may happen to be nearby in memory). For "reference," in the previous sentence, one could substitute "wreak havoc." The programmer is lulled into a false sense of security, believing that because the variable is "local," it cannot do damage outside the scope of the thread in which it is referenced. Not so! Experienced programmers will have been burned often enough to avoid the more common pitfalls, but this is a debugging danger, continually lurking for the unwary, that is unknown in the sequential world. Many (most?) SMP vendors provide specialized debugging facilities to help the programmer detect and correct this type of problem.

The interaction of concurrent threads with the memory allocation routines (`malloc` and `free`) is another source of potential confusion, especially in dynamic data structures (linked lists, B-trees, red-black trees, etc.). Coordinating the manipulation of these structures among multiple, concurrent processing flows can be a nontrivial exercise in logic. These matters are not exactly easy even in the sequential world. The coordination of multiple accesses to shared variables and the interaction between shared and local variables are additional sources of complication in a shared memory environment.

4.1.3 Locks and Critical Regions

The problems involved with updating shared data structures have been around for a long time. A well-known example is in on-line transaction processing—say, for airline reservations. A record in the national database corresponds, say, to a particular flight. Agents access this record from remote terminals to see what seats are available and to enter reservations. It is important in this environment to ensure that two different agents (say, one in Albany and another in Cleveland) do not access this single, national record *at the same time.* Otherwise, they might both think that seat 16C on the flight is still available, and, thus, both reserve it. This would result in the same seat being reserved for two different customers.

Fortunately, the databases used by the airline industry are smart enough to *lock out* one of the agents until the transaction by the other one has completed. By enforcing *sequential access* to the record, the DBMS ensures that the second agent will find, when at last access to the record has been granted, that seat 16C has already been booked (perhaps only seconds ago).

Exactly the same kind of situation can arise in a shared memory SMP, as the following example shows.

Example: Suppose that each of four separate concurrently executing threads on an SMP has a local variable—say, `x_var`. Different values have been assigned to `x_var` by each thread, and it is desired to find the maximum of these values and to store this in a shared variable called `max_val`. This situtation is shown in Figure 4-5, where the values of `x_var` in each of the threads are 4.2, 7.5, 6.6, and 4.8, respectively. Clearly, the correct answer for `max_val` should be 7.5 at the end of the computation.

Suppose that each of the four threads were to execute the following line of code:

```
if( x_var > max_val ) max_val = x_var;
```

What will be the effect?

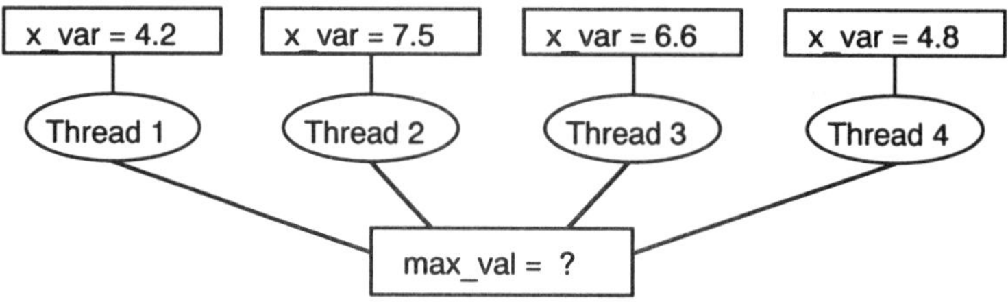

Figure 4-5. Calculating a global maximum

As each thread reaches this point in the code (and, typically, the threads are executing asynchronously, so that they reach this point at different times), it will: (1) copy the current value of max_val from shared memory to its own local registers; (2) compare this value against its locally held value of x_var; and (3) if x_var is larger, store back into max_val the larger value.

Will this give the right answer? Like the agents accessing the airline record, all will be well so long as two threads do not attempt to access max_val at the same time. However, as Figure 4-6 shows, this need not be the case.

The separate blocks represent time intervals, and the values display the state of max_val as time progresses. Two errors have occurred. First, Thread 2 begins execution at the fourth time slot, before Thread 1 has completed. Thus, Thread 2 uses the "old" value of max_val (0.0) for comparison instead of the "right" one (4.2). If only it had begun execution two ticks later, all would have been well. Note, however, that all is still OK. By luck of the draw, the result of the comparison is the same in either case. Since 7.5 is larger than 0.0 (as it would have been larger than 4.2), the result at the eighth time slot is correct (but only by good luck).

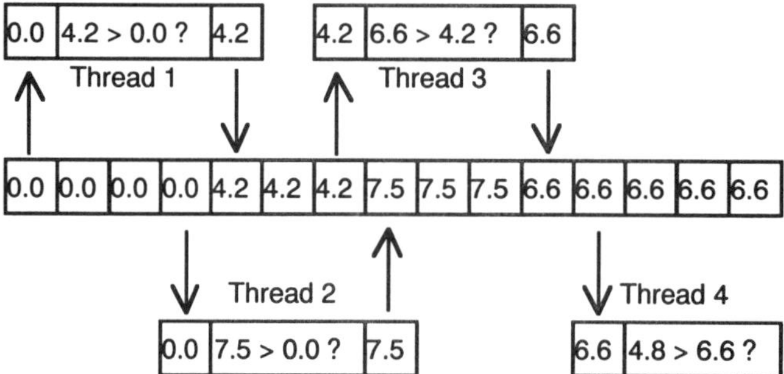

Figure 4-6. Example of a race condition

The same type of error occurs at the seventh time slot: Thread 3 starts execution before Thread 2 has completed. This time the result is serious, since the comparison goes differently in the two cases. When Thread 3 writes back the result, it overwrites the correct value, and the final answer is in error. ■

This type of error, which depends on the order of execution of the concurrent processes, is called a *race condition.* Clearly, the correct fix is to ensure that the "next" thread does not begin execution until the previous one has finished. It does not matter in what order access to the global variable is granted; it only matters that the access is "one by one." Figure 4-7 shows a serialized execution sequence that gives the correct answer.

The most common way to ensure sequential access to a shared variable is by means of a *lock.* In the abstract, the lock has two states—on and off. Before a thread can begin execution, it first *tests the lock* to ensure that it is off. If not, the thread *waits* some amount of time and then tests again. This process (called a *spin-wait* or *spinning on a lock*) is repeated until at last the lock returns off. The thread then immediately sets the lock to on (that is, it *takes control* of the lock). It then executes the code sequence, updating the shared variable if necessary. Finally, just before continuing to the next code block, the thread *resets* the lock to off (that is, it *returns control* of the lock) so that the next thread can have access.

All parallel languages for shared memory machines provide a *lock* mechanism. One of the side effects of a lock is that many threads can be simultaneously waiting for access to the same shared variable, and, hence, all could be spinning on the same lock. In hardware terms, this means that they are all repeatedly reading and testing the same global memory location. This, in turn, can result in significant increases in bus traffic and, hence, reduced performance. A common remedy is to require the thread to wait a fixed amount of

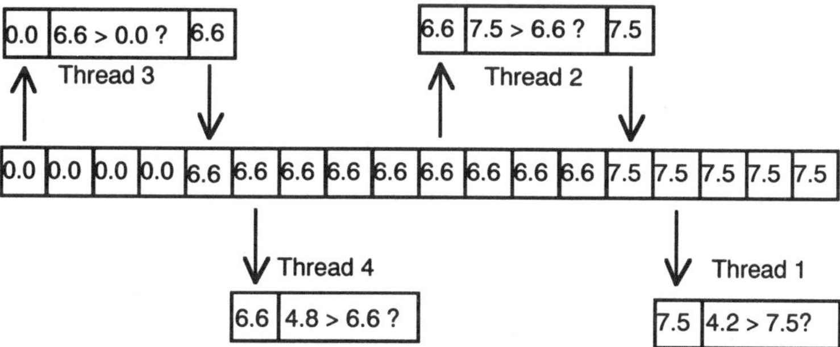

Figure 4-7. Sequential access solves the race

time before retrying the lock. Another approach is to provide a small number of hardware registers that are globally accessible to all the processors on a single clock tick. Both approaches are aimed at reducing bandwidth demands on the global shared memory that can result from locks.

Another approach, from a language standpoint, for implementing locks is the notion of a *critical region*. Conceptually, this is a sequence of code that must be executed "one at a time" by the threads. The *implementation* of a critical region is by means of locks, but the programmer need not be concerned about this. The programmer merely designates the code region as critical, and the compiler and run-time system take care of inserting the proper mechanisms (including wait delays and/or switch registers) as appropriate.

The most frustrating thing about bugs resulting from the incorrect use of locks is that they can go for many runs without appearing—either because the threads *happened* (by chance) to arrive at the shared variable sequentially or because the data values were such that the right answer appeared even though the underlying logic was in error. Further, it is often difficult or impossible to duplicate the error, since the order of arrival of the threads at shared variables changes from run to run (based on system loading and other factors that cannot be replicated). *Race conditions are one of the most notoriously difficult bugs to find.*

4.2 THE SAMPLE PROBLEM ON AN SGI CHALLENGE SMP

In this section, we will present a parallelized solution to the sample problem using the parallelizing language constructs provide by Silicon Graphics on their Challenge SMP products. The author wishes to thank the technical staff at SGI for their help in preparing this solution.

In Section 4.2.1, we give a brief overview of the parallelization strategy and working assumptions about the operational environment. In Section 4.2.2, we present the detailed annotations to the solution code, which can be found in Appendix B.

4.2.1 Overview of the Parallelization Strategy

We assume that the code will execute on a Silicon Graphics Challenge Series computer. This is a cache-coherent SMP in the classic architecture pictured in Figure 3-11. This machine can have up to 36 distinct processors, but the code as written will execute correctly on as few as one. The file system can be either private to the SGI box or can be provided by a shared file system on the LAN. Similarly, the user's workstation from which the code is executed can be either remote or directly attached to the SGI. The operating system is IRIX, SGI's multiprocessor version of UNIX.

The basic parallelizing strategy is to partition the large scores array into smaller pieces, handing one subset off to each of a number of independent threads. The actual number of threads created in any given run will be determined by the compiler in conjunction with the run-time system. Each thread processes its portion of the large array, using the main `for` loop as the partitioning mechanism. Next, the threads must cooperate to obtain global values corresponding to the local values they have calculated (e.g., a global maximum based on the locally computed maximums). A critical region of code is defined to ensure sequential access to the global shared variables. A second loop is parallelized to compute the scaled scores array. At this point, the parallel region ends, and the final portion of the code executes sequentially.

Things to notice as we proceed through the detailed code include:

- the code, as written, will compile and run correctly on either a single processor machine or a multiprocessor SMP
- the actual number of processors and threads is not known or used by the program/programmer
- large amounts of the sample problem code have been reused "as is," without modification
- use of several parallelizing constructs including shared versus local variables, parallel regions, critical regions, synchronization, and single processor regions,,
- influence of FORTRAN on parallel loops

4.2.2 Annotations

line 3: The executable module has the same form as the original sample problem and maintains the basic appearance of a sequential flow of control.

lines 4–13: The same set of variables used by the sample problem.

lines 14–18: All of these variables will be replicated, once for each of the parallel threads created. Thus, storage is allocated for these variables not *once*, but *once per thread*. The " `l_` " notation has been introduced to alert the reader to this fact.

lines 19–33: All this code is identical to the code from the sample problem, and it executes in exactly the same way—namely, sequentially. In particular, notice that I/O still occurs sequentially. During this portion of the code, a single thread is active on one processor of the SMP. It is executing exactly as if the entire code were vanilla-flavor sequential C.

line 34: This signals the compiler to begin a parallel region. The use of the **#pragma** directive permits these lines to be ignored entirely by nonparallelizing compilers—this characteristic of **#pragma** is actually part of the ANSI C language specification.

line 35: There are a number of possible modifiers that can follow the **parallel** pragma. As we explained in Section 4.1.2 above, the threads need to know which of the variables are local and which are to be shared. The **shared** pragma allows the programmer to specify a list of the shared variables. Notice that these variables have already been declared in the function header (lines 4–13). The default on the SGI is that variables will be treated as shared unless otherwise noted. There is also a subtlety with the num_scores variable. On the one hand, it needs to be shared by all the threads, since it tells the total number of scores to be processed. On the other hand, it is a read-only variable and will not be modified during the parallel region. In this case, it is possible to use a different construct:

```
#pragma byvalue ( num_scores )
```

The effect of this would be to create a read-only copy of num_scores in each thread's address space, initialized to the current value of num_scores. This can have performance advantages, since cache coherence on num_scores need not be maintained (this has the effect of reducing bus traffic). Notice that the scope of a **#pragma** only extends to the the first EOL—hence, the use of "\" to lexically spread the arguments to the **#pragma** across multiple lines.

line 36: Here is the list of local variables. Separate copies of these variables will be created for each thread. Thus, for example, when we read

```
047>   curr_score = scores[ i ];
```

in line 47, there are separate values for i and for curr_score—one for each active thread. However, since scores is a shared variable (see line 35 above), only the single scores array is referenced. These new local variables needed by the parallel version were declared in lines 14–18. However, memory space is actually only allocated at this point, when the threads are created.

line 37: This "`{`" and its paired "`}`" at line 72 define the extent of the parallel region. This is the portion of code that the separate threads will execute. Ordinarily, there will be one thread for each processor, and the scheduler will arrange to schedule all threads at once for a given time slot in the UNIX time-sharing scheme. These threads are exactly the "lightweight" processes described in Section 4.1.1. One way of visualizing what is taking place is to imagine a number of *independent and identical* subroutines, each executing the code from lines 37 through 72. The local variables are (as intuition suggests) local variables in each subroutine. The shared variables are common (global) across the subroutines, such as COMMON blocks in FORTRAN.

lines 38–42: The local variables for each thread must be initialized in the same way that the global, shared variables were initialized in lines 29–33.

line 43: The **`pfor`** pragma is the mechanism for parallelizing certain types of C `for` loops. Part of the education of a user in this parallel strategy is to learn the rules for when and how the **`pfor`** pragma applies. The basic rules are:

1. the `for` loop should really be a FORTRAN DO loop in disguise—that is, it should be governed by an index variable running between two *known* limits with a *known* step size
2. the iterations of the loop should be completely independent—that is, the loop index should be able to run through its values *in any order whatsoever* and still obtain the correct answer

The C `for` loop, of course, is considerably more flexible than this and often is written with data-dependent exit conditions. These types of `for` loops cannot be used with the **`pfor`** construction. Sometimes they can be rewritten (e.g., the number of iterations can be computed) and sometimes not. Similarly, `while` loops that are really DO loops in disguise must be rewritten to conform to this syntax.

The **`iterate`** key word signals the identification of the index (which must be a local variable), its limits, and the step size. This is a C-izing of the FORTRAN DO loop from which this construct grew. This construct is the one of most interest to many FORTRAN programmers, and we are simply seeing its translation into C.

line 44: This "`{`" and its paired "`}`" at line 54 define the scope of the **`pfor`** pragma. In fact, it simply brackets the main `for` loop of the program.

lines 45–53: The effect of the **`pfor`** pragma, acting on this `for` loop, is to hand off different subsets of iterations to different threads. Each thread is given a different subset of the scores to process. In this sense, the loop as written is initally confusing, for it seems to suggest that *all* the threads execute *all* the iterations of the loop (as they did in line 42, where each thread executed the entire `for` loop over its local instance of `l_hist` array). In fact, without the **`pfor`** pragma, this is exactly what they *would* do.

Note that the programmer does not know how many threads have been created nor how many or which iterations have been given to each thread. This is usually a convenience; let the compiler decide the low-level details. Ordinarily, the range of the index would be divided into contiguous intervals (e.g., with 50 iterations and 10 threads, Thread 1 would do 1–5; Thread 2 would do 6–10; etc.). However, directives are available to alter this (for example, have Thread 1 do iterations 1, 11, 21, 31, 41; Thread 2 do iterations 2, 12, 22, 32, 42; etc.). It is also possible to do load balancing when the different iterations of the loop might take different lengths of time. Under this scheme, a thread would receive an index (much like a take-a-number machine at a bakery) and process it to completion. It would then report back for more work. Threads with easy iterations complete quickly and get more work; threads with more difficult iterations take longer to complete. The overall effect is to spread the total amount of work more evenly across the threads.

There are a number of other considerations that must be mastered in order to become proficient in using the **`pfor`** construct. Nested **`pfor`** constructs are not allowed—for example, when they occur inside subroutines called inside a **`pfor`** loop. In general, the interaction of the **`pfor`** pragma with the other pragmas (**`critical, one processor`**, etc.) is a bit tricky and not immediately intuitive.

The values (for example, `l_sumsc` or `l_hist`) that hold in a given thread at the end of the loop need not be the same from run to run. The reason is that the subset of the scores array given to each thread differs from run to run, since the number of threads created can vary. These intermediate values may not be of much use during debugging, since it is difficult to relate them back to the subset of the scores array from which they were derived.

Failure to use **`local`** variables for the threads (see lines 15–18 and line 36) would be a key error. It is in this loop that the local variables come into play. In subsequent lines, they will be combined into global variables.

line 54: Closing the scope of the **`pfor`** pragma opened at line 44.

lines 55–63: It is in this section of code that the partial values computed by each thread are combined into the global values. The need to enforce sequential access to the shared variables has been explained in Section 4.1.3. Each thread, one by one in turn, gains control of this section of code and executes it. After each thread has had its turn, the global variables (such as `min_scores`) will hold the correct value.

line 55: The mechanism used here to enforce sequential access is the **`critical`** pragma. Other mechanisms are available, including locks explicitly declared and controlled by the programmer.

From a logical viewpoint, it would have been possible to put this critical region inside the **`pfor`** loop (lines 45–53). Conceptually, instead of creating local values for its portion of the scores array, each thread would go directly to the global, shared values, using the **`critical`** pragma to enforce sequential access. While this is correct from a logical standpoint, its use would not improve performance at all. Each global variable would have to be accessed *once for each element of the* scores *array*—something the sequential sample problem was already doing. The way the code is written here, sequential access to the global variables occurs once per thread, not once per score.

line 56: This "**{**" and its paired "**}**" at line 63 define the scope of the **`critical`** pragma.

lines 57–62: These are new lines of code. Here is where the reduction from the local values (per thread) to the global values occurs. Note that the entire histogram array must be updated *by each thread.*

line 63: Closing the scope of the **`critical`** pragma.

lines 64–71: Beginning here, the flow of control from the sample problem changes. The only computation that remains to parallelize is the scaling of the scores array—that is, an updated version of the scores array is computed, with the average of all the scores being subtracted from each one individually (lines 50 and 51 from the sample problem). We will perform only the part of the calculation needed to parallelize the scaling and nothing else. This means:

- computing in each thread the value of the average for use by the thread on its portion of the scores array
- scaling the scores array
- updating the shared, global value of average for later output to the file

line 64: The **`synchronize`** pragma illustrates a subtlety of the shared memory paradigm. Recall that with the parallel region bounded by the brackets at lines 37 and 72, separate threads are independently executing separate copies of the code. The underlying idea is that each thread is a true sequential control stream in which processing proceeds to the *next* statement as soon as the *previous* one has completed.

If we consider the **critical** pragma, for example, each thread will wait its turn for access to the **critical** region. As each completes, however, the paradigm assumes that (without any additional direction) each thread will immediately proceed to the next portion of code. Since the threads are released one by one from the **critical** region, the first threads to complete will run on ahead of the others, getting a headstart on the next block of parallelized code to be executed.

For the next few lines of code, this would result in an error, since the correct, global value of `sum_scores` (needed in line 65 to compute the average) is not known until the last thread has completed its pass through the **critical** region. What we want is for the first threads to *wait* until the last thread is finished. This is the function of the **synchronize** pragma. It imposes a barrier beyond which no thread can proceed until it has been reached by all the rest.

These ideas are illustrated in Figure 4-8. This figure represents processing time, increasing from left to right. Six threads each, one after the other, enter the critical region: Thread 5 first, then Thread 1, then Thread 3, and so on. This sequential behavior is enforced by the critical pragma. However, because of the presence of the synchronization barrier, each thread *waits* until all the others have completed before entering the next block of code. In this example, Thread 4 is the last to complete; when it is done, all the rest are released to continue the processing flow.

lines 65–66: Each thread computes its own local value of average, using the (now correct) value of `sum_scores`.

lines 67–69: Another example of the **pfor** pragma—this time used to break up the scores array for scaling. Each thread is given a subset of the array to process, and the programmer does not need to be concerned about the details of the partitioning.

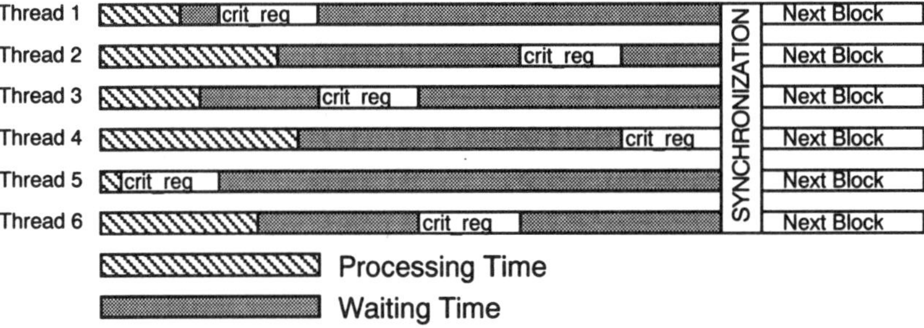

Figure 4-8. Critical region and synchronization

lines 70–71: The **one processor** pragma is how the programmer can switch back to a single sequential processing flow, if desired, without having to terminate the parallel region. Because there is operating system overhead associated with the creation of threaded regions, this directive permits single processor execution without penalizing the program a second time for thread creation. One side effect of the **one processor** pragma is synchronization. No thread will proceed beyond the **one processor** block of code until the processor executing it has finished. These ideas are illustrated in Figure 4-9.

Thread 4 is the first to reach the one processor block, and it begins execution. As the other threads complete Block 1 (first Thread 6, then Thread 1, and so on), they wait until Thread 4 has completed the one processor block. In this example, Thread 3 does not finish Block 1 until after Thread 4 has already finished the one processor block. It, therefore, can proceed directly to Block 2 without waiting at all. The overall effect is that the **one processor block** was only executed by a single thread, as in ordinary sequential processing flow.

In the sample code, the **one processor** block is used to prevent more than one thread from storing its local value of `l_average` to the global shared value. All the threads have the correct value, but only one need save it. Another common use of **one processor** blocks is file and terminal I/O. There is usually no advantage on an SMP in attempting to parallelize I/O operations. In the sample solution, this is the reason why the input and output remain serial, and only the major loops have been parallelized. Had we needed to perform I/O in the midst of the calculation, the **one processor** pragma could have been used to serialize this section of code.

line 72: Ending the parallel region begun at line 37. From this point on, conventional sequential single processor execution is utilized.

line 73: This line has been shifted out of its original position. The scaling of the scores array is placed inside the parallel region, and this calculation has been moved outside. This resulted in a rearrangement of the order of the code.

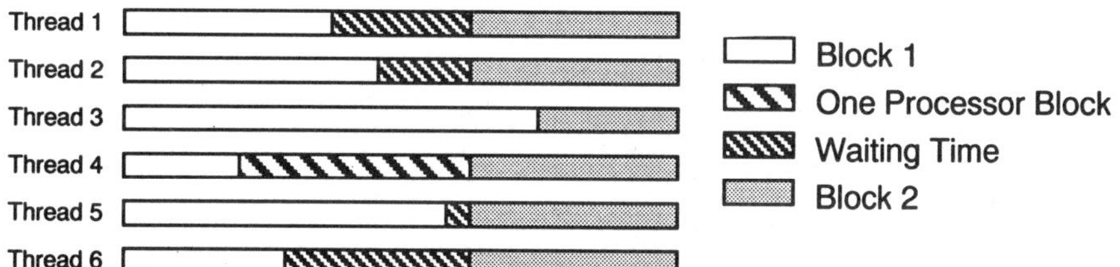

Figure 4-9. Processing flow for one processor block

lines 74–82: No attempt has been made in this solution to parallelize this loop. Since it is on the shorter histogram array, this makes sense. On other occasions, the array on which the prefix operation is performed may be larger, and explicit parallelization would then be appropriate. All this code is reused, as is, from the original sample problem.

lines 83–93: Identical to the original sample problem.

4.3 OBSERVATIONS AND CONSIDERATIONS

Undoubtedly, the greatest advantage to the programmer from the shared memory paradigm is being relieved of the responsibility of decomposing the large data arrays and placing them in disjoint address spaces. Provided that the processing flow matches one of the basic patterns provided by the parallelizing directives (in particular, the FORTRAN DO loop model with independent iterations), the compiler/run-time system can automatically decompose the arrays and initiate concurrent threads.

There are also several capabilities provided by SMP parallelizing extensions that we have not looked at. If we drop down a level to the operating system, there are routines directly available to by the programmer to generate threads and deal with them by thread identifiers, rather than relying on the compiler to make these decisions. At this level, the decomposition of the control flow becomes explicit. This gives greater control and flexibility but comes at the expense of increased software complexity. The set of compiler assists provided by a vendor at the source language level is largely market-driven: What capabilities are in most demand? We have already seen the influence of FORTRAN in this regard, since the scientific community has traditionally been a major purchaser of high-end equipment.

There are also a number of tools that are available to assist in the analysis of existing sequential code. Two, in particular, are worth mentioning. The KAP product from Kuck & Associates is targeted at precisely the SMP programming model. It is now available—either as a source code front end or as a stage in the compiler—for virtually every SMP on the market. Versions are available that support both FORTRAN and C. In the ideal situation, the tool can accept nonparallelized source and produce a modified source with parallel extensions inserted with little or no programmer assistance required. However, there are many characteristics of real codes that can inhibit this process. The section on automatic parallelization (Section 8.4.1) discusses this in greater detail.

Another useful tool in the SMP environment is the collection of FORGE tools from Applied Parallel Research. These are based on technology developed at Rice University by Ken Kennedy, and their major strength is in interprocedure analysis. The value can be seen when it is recalled that to be effectively parallelized using threads, separate iterations of the loop being parallelized must be independent. If the loop contains a subroutine call (which, in turn, may contain other subroutine calls, etc.), it may be a long and difficult process to decide whether or not, buried deep in the calling hierarchy, there is a dependency. The use of COMMON blocks and shared variables further complicates this analysis. A partial solution is not to attempt to parallelize the outer loop; just parallelize tight inner loops for which independence can be assured. As we showed in the discussion of Amdahl's Law, however, there are often performance advantages for keeping the granularity of the parallelism as coarse as possible. Having a tool that can assist this analysis can be valuable in understanding the structure of the program and moving the parallelizing loop out as far as possible in the calling hierarchy.

It is sometimes asserted, in defense of the shared memory programming model, that this is the model taught in most CS graduate schools. The model referred to is the *PRAM* (**p**arallel **r**andom **a**ccess **m**emory) model. However, the PRAM model suffers from a fatal flaw that renders it virtually valueless from a practical point of view. It allows the programmer to consider very large numbers of processors, all with uniformly fast access to a very large memory. As we have seen, the number of processors that can actually be attached to a shared memory is fairly small—say, 20 to 40 at the top end—before memory bandwidth is exhausted (recall the discussion in Section 3.5). The PRAM model, on the other hand, encourages use of very large numbers of processors. Since no physical shared memory machine can actually support so many processors and still maintain uniform memory access, the algorithms developed using the PRAM model have almost no practical utility.

The greatest value of PRAM is that it has helped many CS graduate students do research leading to degrees.

During the annotations, we asserted that it was, in fact, possible to parallelize the computation of the percentile array, even though it has a loop dependency. The following example shows how this can be accomplished.

Example: Suppose that we wish to compute the summation prefix of an array $A = \{a_1, a_2, a_3, \ldots, a_N\}$; that is, we want to compute an array $S = \{s_1, s_2, s_3, \ldots, s_N\}$ such that

$$s_K = a_1 + a_2 + a_3 + \ldots + a_K$$

$$= s_{K-1} + a_K, \quad K = 1, 2, 3, \ldots, N$$

The loop dependence shows up in the second line, where the *K*th value of *S* depends on its (*K*–1)th value.

The idea is to break up the long array into subarrays and to compute the summation prefix on each subarray independently—that is, in parallel. The true value of the summation prefix for the index that begins each subarray is then computed, and this value is used to adjust the prefix values for the subarray.

This process will be illustrated using four threads on an array of 20 elements (see Figure 4-10). In Step 1, an ordinary summation prefix is performed on each subarray. If we have four threads, for example, each thread would be given five array elements. Note that it is important that the *first* thread be given the *first* five elements; the *second* thread must have the *second* five elements; and so on. This step is parallelizable by an ordinary **pfor** pragma.

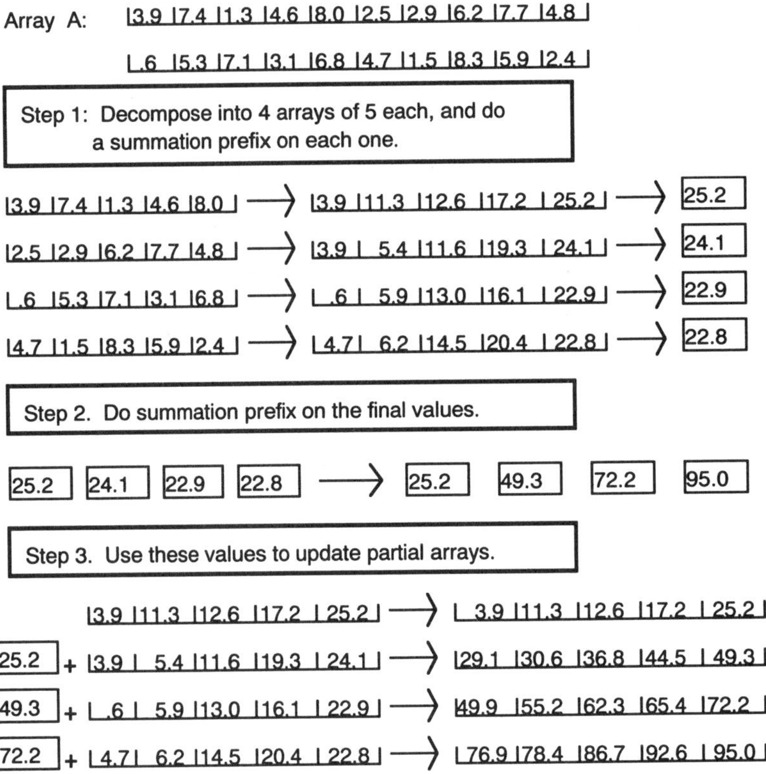

Figure 4-10. Parallelizing the summation prefix operation

In Step 2, an ordinary parallel prefix is done again but this time on the final values in the subarrays calculated in Step 1. This is sequential and would be accomplished using a **one processor** pragma, preceded by a synchronization to ensure that all threads had completed Step 1 before Step 2 begins. Since there are only as many values to sum as there are threads, this step will not be lengthy.

In Step 3, the partial sums from Step 2 are summed into the partial sums computed in Step 1, and the computation is complete. Again, this step is parallelizable. No work need be done on the first subarray; and for each of the others, we are simply summing a constant into each element. Again, a **pfor** will suffice. ■

Summary of Chapter 4

The major functionality required for shared memory multiprocessors—lightweight processing threads, shared and local storage, and synchronized access to shared variables—has been discussed and illustrated in the solution of the sample problem. There was a considerable amount of code reuse, and the programmer did not need to consider the actual number of threads required or write additional code to partition the data arrays. We have also described some of the subtleties associated with the paradigm—for example, the need for care in synchronizing threads and the potential for a local pointer to hold the address of a shared variable. The interactions of the pragmas with each other (e.g., scope, nesting, and subroutine calls) must be understood and mastered before the full power of the machine becomes available. Even so, our example shows that for many codes, a substantial amount of parallelism can be uncovered and expressed on a shared memory machine using a few simple language constructs.

5

Message Passing

In Chapter 3, we noted some of the advantages of a distributed memory hardware architecture. These included the ability to scale, realistically, to very large numbers of processing nodes. The penalty associated with this architecture, however, is in the software. Effort is needed to detect and express the parallelism in a problem in a way that takes maximum advantage of the machine's potential.

Simply based on the current performance leaders in MPPs—Thinking Machines, nCube, Cray, Intel, and Meiko—it would appear that distributed memory MIMD machines (DM-MIMD) have "won" the architecture battle at the high end. Message passing is the natural programming approach for such machines. As we will see, however, in some instances the programmer can be shielded from some of the complexities of message passing by well-constructed library routines that can perform low-level data partitioning and coordination.

Section 5.1 gives a top-level overview of the basic capabilities required from a set of message-passing extensions. We then consider three separate solutions of the sample problem: the nCube 2, from nCube, Inc.; the Express library from ParaSoft Corp.; and the Paragon, from Intel Corp. Considerations and additional observations are then presented in Section 5.5.

5.1 AN OVERVIEW OF THE MESSAGE-PASSING LIBRARY

Conceptually, the idea behind message passing is clear and unambiguous. We imagine a number—possibly a very large number—of independent processors, each with its own private program and data. Data are exchanged among these processors by means of *messages* sent between pairs of processors. The message is originated by one node (the *sender*), transmitted across the interconnection network, and eventually accepted and acted upon by the destination node (the *receiver*). A node may act as sender at any time, originating messages of various sorts for various receivers. Similarly, any node will have a *pending message queue*, which holds messages that have been sent to it and that are awaiting processing. The result of sending a message to a destination node is that the message will be posted in the pending message queue at the destination processor. The receiver can then, at its own discretion, retrieve messages and act upon them.

This situation is illustrated in Figure 5-1. Three processors are shown—A, C, and M—together with the current status of their pending message queues. We see that Processor A has sent messages to both C and M and has received messages from processors C, E, and K. While this diagram correctly illustrates the conceptual situation, implementation details differ from machine to machine.

To the message-passing system, the network appears as a service—something that ensures delivery from the sending node to the destination and that maintains the message queues. In practice, the properties of the network may be important in program design. For example, Processor A may be considerably closer, in the underlying network topology, to Processor C than it is to Processor M. Messages between A and C will be delivered faster and will cause less network contention than messages between A and M. Taking advantage of these performance characteristics requires the programmer to consciously map the *logical* sender/receiver pairs of the algorithm onto the *physical* network. This mapping is unknown in sequential code (or, for that matter, in the shared memory paradigm, which, nevertheless, has its own complexities in

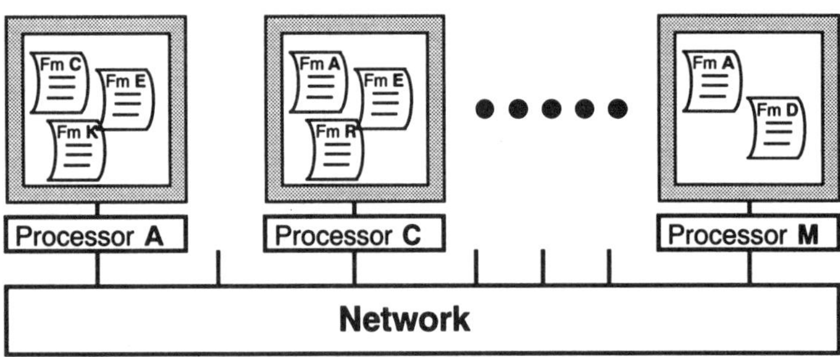

Figure 5-1. Message queues in a message-passing system

the memory hierarchy) and is one source of additional complexity in the message-passing programming model. A considerable amount of work has been done by DM-MIMD vendors to shield the programmer from this side effect of the architecture—either by trying to improve the network performance so that its topology does not affect overall performance (or, more realistically, does not affect it very much) or by supplying optimized library routines that hide these details behind a convenient, easily understood programming interface.

If we think about what is necessary to implement a message-passing scheme, the following capabilities stand out:

- Each node must be able to address the other nodes. In particular, a node should know its own address and be able (relative to this address) to calculate the addresses of the other nodes on the network.
- Each node must be able to create and send messages, using the addressing scheme, with confidence that the message will be delivered to the receiving node and placed in its message queue.
- Each node must be able to peruse its own message queue, remove messages from the queue, and move the data into its own process address space.

To implement these capabilities, the standard sequential library for the processing nodes will be supplemented by (at least) three library routines: *send*, *receive*, and *context*. These are the programmer's interface to the messaging system, and we will discuss each in turn.

The purpose of *context* is to tell the calling node its own node number and the size of the array in which it resides. It is typical to write programs that will run correctly on arrays of varying sizes and where the array size itself is a run-time variable. Similarly, a process running on a node in the array will often want to calculate addresses relative to its own—for example, predecessor/successor in a linear array or left/right/up/down in a two-dimensional array. Other information may also be provided, but these two—node id and array size—are critical.

The *send* routine is used to transmit a message to a destination node. Typically, a message is a contiguous set of bytes in memory and is specified by the *starting address* and the *number of bytes*. Next, the *id of the destination node* must be provided. Finally, it is typical to provide a *message_type* field (usually an integer variable). This field can be used by the receiving node to select messages of interest from the message queue by matching against the *message_type* and/or the *id* of the sender.

The *receive* routine is used to remove messages from the message queue. The system must be told where to put the data, typically by designating a starting address and a maximum number of bytes that will be accepted. In addition, the receiving node may specify which messages are of interest by using two matching fields: the *id* of the sending node (that is, "I'm only interested in messages from node 16.") and the *message_type* (that is, "I'm only interested in messages whose message_type is 7."). Wild cards are provided, and the messaging system will report the selected values if wild cards are used. When more than one match exists, the earliest message (where "earliest" is appropriately defined) is selected.

Example: Consider the following code fragments executing on two different processors, **A** and **B**.

Code fragment from processor **A**:

```
•
•
msg_typ = 5;
dest = 'B';
send( buf, 30 * sizeof( int ), dest, msg_typ);
•
```

Code fragment from processor **B**:

```
•
•
msg_typ = -1;   /*  wild card */
sender = 'A';
length = receive( buf1, 200, &sender, &msg_typ );
•
```

The result of the **send** expression (executed by **A**) will be to post in processor **B**'s message queue a data structure that is 120 bytes long (120 = 30 * 4). Associated with that message will be identifying information: The message came from processor **A** with message_type = 5. The result of the **receive** expression (executed by **B**) will be to copy the 120 bytes of data into processor **B**'s address space, beginning at the address buf1. No more than 200 bytes are acceptable, and the value of `length` will be set to 120, the actual number of bytes copied. Processor **B** has specified that the message must come from processor **A** but indicated that it did not care about the type of the message (-1 being the wild card). The actual message type— in this case, 5—will be placed in the variable msg_typ. ■

What happens if no message in the message queue matches the submitted fields? In this case, the process *halts* (suspends) until a matching message is delivered; that is, the **receive** expression is *blocking*. This is the primary mechanism for synchronizing activity among the various nodes. The programmer can use messages to signal a node that it is now permitted to continue to the next stage of processing. Until the message is delivered, the receiving process will halt. In this way, a node can be prevented from running on too far ahead of the others; or, further processing can be delayed until global results are complete and have been delivered to the entire processor array.

Most message-passing systems provide one additional service called *test*. This allows the calling process to see whether or not any messages currently exist in the message queue and what their properties are (how long they are, who they are from, etc.). The test routine is nonblocking, and the local code can branch depending on the results of the test. (For example, it might find out the size of the incoming data and use `malloc` to dynamically allocate local memory to hold it.)

Using these four primitives—**context**, **send**, **receive**, and **test**—quite elaborate and powerful additional capabilities can be constructed. These include *broadcast* operations (one node wishes to transmit a value to all other nodes), *reduction* operations (say, finding the global sum of the local values held in each processor), and *synchronization* (a barrier past which no processor proceeds until it has been reached by all the rest).

One frequently used programming style for message-passing systems is *S*ingle *P*rogram *M*ultiple *D*ata (SPMD). This means that the *same* program is executing in each of the processing nodes. Since each node knows its context (that is, its own node number and the size of the array of which it is a part), the node can use this information both for branching and for partitioning of large data arrays or loop iterations.

Another frequently used style is to designate a single node—which could be the front end or a high-performance graphical workstation—for a special role. This node would typically act as the *master*, doling out work as appropriate to the other *slave* nodes that report in for work. This style requires at least two major code modules: the module that will run on the master node and the module that will run (typically replicated once per processor) on the other nodes in the processor array. Such an approach might be useful, for example, where the front end is to drive a complex user interface, including (perhaps) graphics displays. There is no need for this interface code to be replicated across the processor array, and in many instances this display software may already exist as a COTS package. In such a situation, the processor array accelerates the computational part of the problem (CAD/CAM is a typical example), reporting results back to the master processor for display to the user.

It is not ordinarily necessary to write separate code for each processor; a single program will do. All of the sample solutions adopt this approach. While it is possible, in a theoretical sense, to have different programs executing on each node, such an approach is significantly more complicated and is usually avoided. One important exception to this rule, however, is *parallel event-driven simulation* [16] , in which the various nodes in the array take on the roles of different object types—military objects in a battlefield simulation, for example. See also [17] for an example in which heterogeneous programming has been successfully used.

5.2 THE SAMPLE PROBLEM ON AN nCube 2

Our first solution will be on an nCube 2 parallel processor. This is a distributed memory machine with a point-to-point hypercube interconnection network. The hypercube topology will be significant in how the problem is parallelized. It permits very rapid logarithmic reductions in which the pairs of nodes that communicate are nearest neighbors in the interconnection topology. This keeps routing delays to a minimum and ensures that there is no contention for shared link bandwidth.

Section 5.2.1 provides a hypercube primer and explains the parallelization strategy. Section 5.2.2 provides detailed annotations. Section 5.2.3 discusses alternative approaches and practical considerations. The author wishes to thank the technical staff at nCube for their help in preparing this solution.

5.2.1 The Parallelization Strategy

A hypercube is a geometrical object with N = 2**D nodes and D * N/2 edges. The "D" in the preceding expressions is called the dimension of the hypercube, and "N" is the total *number of nodes*. For example, if D = 6, then the hypercube has N = 2**6 = 64 nodes, and D * N/2 = 6 * 32 = 192 edges.

The nodes are numbered from 0 to N-1 (in a dimension 6 hypercube with 64 nodes, they would be numbered from 0 to 63). It turns out to be easy to decide which pairs of nodes have edges (that is, direct network links) between them. If the node number is written as a binary integer (that is, a sequence of 0's and 1's representing the powers of 2 that make up the number), then two nodes have an edge between them if their binary representations *differ by exactly one bit.* (For readers with the right background, the nodes have a *Hamming Distance* of 1.)

Example: Consider node number #23 in a dimension 6 hypercube (so, there are 2**6 = 64 nodes, numbered 0 to 63). The binary representation for this node is:

```
#23  ~  010111.
```

If we toggle each of the bits in turn, we can name each of node #23's nearest neighbors (that is, the nodes to which #23 has a direct network connection):

```
010110  ~  #22
010101  ~  #21
010011  ~  #19
011111  ~  #31
000111  ~  #7
110111  ~  #55  ■
```

Figure 5-2 shows the numbering scheme and edges for a dimension 3 hypercube (that is, with 2**3 = 8 nodes numbered 0 to 7).

A common and powerful operation on hypercubes is for the nodes to successively pair up, first with neighbors in the first bit, next with neighbors in the second bit, and so on. Suppose, for example, that it is desired to find the *minimum* of all the values held in each of the nodes. On our dimension 3 hypercube, this can be accomplished in three steps (see Figure 5-3).

The operation is to find the smallest value (represented by letters) in the array. In Step 1, each of the nodes names one of its nearest neighbors by

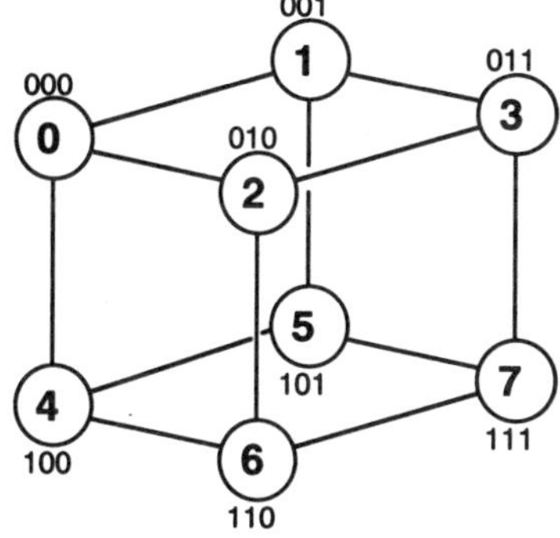

Figure 5-2. A dimension 3 hypercube

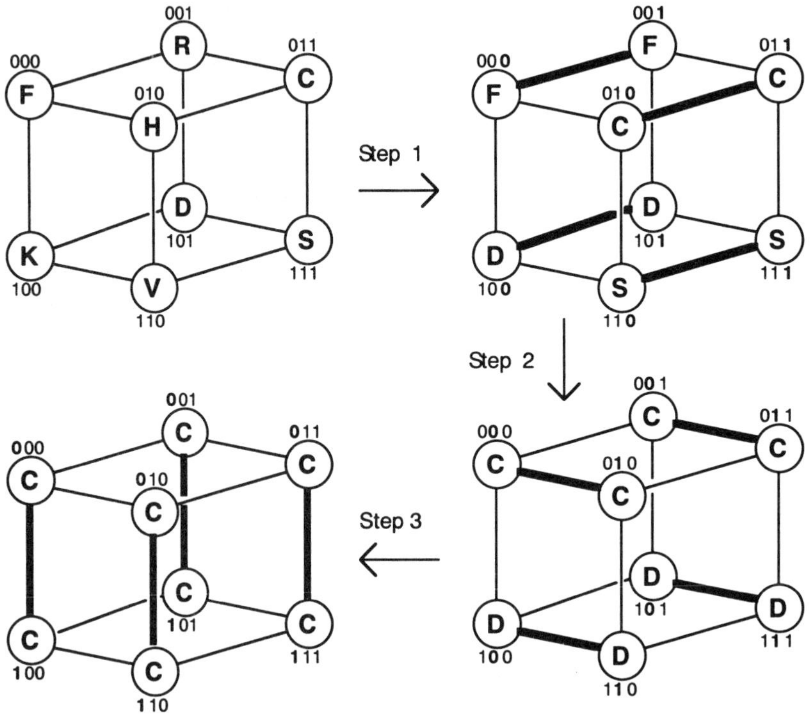

Figure 5-3. Example of logarithmic reduction in a hypercube

toggling their *first* bit. For example, node #5 ~ 101 names node **100** ~ #4; at the same time, node #4 is naming node #5. Nodes #4 and #5 have *paired* along their common edge by toggling the first bit in their respective addresses. The nodes exchange values (using **send** and **receive**), compare, and retain the smaller value. The situation after Step 1 is shown: Nodes #0 and #1 each hold **F** (the minimum of **F** and **R**); nodes #2 and #3 each hold **C** (the minimum of **C** and **H**); and so on.

In Step 2, the process is repeated, but this time pairing occurs by toggling the *second* bit in the address. In our example, nodes #5 ~ **101** and #7 ~ **111** are paired. Again, paired nodes exchange values, compare, and retain the smaller.

In Step 3, the *third* bit is toggled. This time node #5 ~ **101** is paired with node #1 ~ **001**. Paired nodes exchange values, compare, and keep the smaller. We see that at the end of this step, *all the nodes hold the correct, global minimum*!

This same process can be used for many global operations: finding a global sum or product; broadcasting a value to all nodes; finding a global maximum; etc. It is extremely efficient for the following reasons:

- during each step, all nodes are active
- pairs of nodes that communicate are nearest neighbors in the hypercube topology
- during any step, no edge is required by more than a single pair—that is, there is never any *contention* among nodes for a shared communications path
- the number of steps is the *logarithm* of the number of nodes—for example, 2**10 = 1,024 nodes can accomplish the global operation in just **10** steps

The nCube library contains routines that perform exactly these types of operations very efficiently, without requiring explicit intervention by the programmer. In the sample solution, we show both approaches: (1) using the nCube library routines, and (2) writing a code sequence that implements this operation—looping one-by-one over the bits, toggling them to name a nearest neighbor, exchanging data values, and performing the update. It is an easily learned and very powerful procedure that underlies a good deal of hypercube programming.

The four basic message-passing operations—context, send, receive, and test—have system-unique names on the nCube: They are, respectively, `whoami()`, `nwrite()`, `nread()`, and `ntest()`. The basic approach is to partition the large input scores array across the processors. After each node gets its context (using whoami), a library routine is called that does the partitioning automatically—relieving the programmer of the partitioning arithmetic. Each processor `seeks` to the part of the input file that holds the subset of scores for which it is responsible and reads them in. Then, local statistics (max, min, sum, sum of squares, and histogram) are computed by each node separately and concurrently on the subset of scores held by the node. Global values for these quantities are then obtained by using the optimized nCube library functions (a roll-your-own version is also provided for illustration). No attempt is made to parallelize the percentile calculation, primarily because it is so small (only 1,601 entries). However, summation prefix can be parallelized, and this would be appropriate for larger arrays (see also the Express solution in Section 5.3.2). Next, each node scales its own portion of the scores array using the global average. Output then occurs, with each node again seeking the proper position in the file and writing the portion of the updated scores array for which it is responsible.

Things to notice as we proceed through the detailed code include:

- all the nodes are executing the same program (that is, SPMD), branching as appropriate based on node id and local data values
- logarithmic time reduction using the hypercube topology
- a good deal of code can be reused from the sample problem
- most of the additional coding is in the I/O operations; no explicit message passing is required
- the code will execute correctly on any dimension hypercube (including dimension 0, a single node)

5.2.2 Annotations

line 3: The header file for the nCube library.

line 4: This program will be executed by every processor in the array—a classic example of the SPMD programming model.

lines 5–15: These declarations are identical to the sample problem. Note that they are replicated, once per processor.

lines 16–20: New declarations required for the parallel program. Several—`pid, hid, target, msgtyp,` and `mask`—are dummy variables for subroutines that will be called later on and do not contribute to the processing flow or logic. Two others—`array_size` and `my_offset`—have been introduced for typographical convenience. The only variables that contribute essentially to the computation are: `me, dim, num_start,` and `num_here`.

line 21: The **`whoami`** routine is the nCube equivalent of `context` (see Section 5.1). The variable `me` returns with the address (that is, the hypercube node number) of the node on which the call was made. The variable `dim` holds the dimension of the hypercube. It is not necessary for the program to execute on the entire physical machine. Typically, during the preexecution phase, the user will specify the dimension of the cube on which the program is to run. The operating system will then "carve out" a subcube of that dimension and ensure that the "0 to N-1" numbering scheme used by the program is correctly mapped to the physical numbering in the hypercube. The `pid` variable is the standard UNIX process id (yes, you *can* do process time-sharing on each node). The `hid` variable is the address for the front end. As we discussed in Section 5.1, some applications use a master/slave programming approach in which a separate program is written for the front end. This variable permits messages to flow between the front end and the processor array.

line 22: C shorthand for computing 2**`dim`.

line 23: The nCube I/O facilities include at least two major types of capabilities. First, the I/O can be done through the front end—typically a workstation connected to the LAN and using the network file system. This limits I/O bandwidth to LAN rates and can become a serial bottleneck for large configurations. Second, nCube provides a separate, high-speed, and parallelized I/O subsystem. A typical configuration might include a RAID disk array, frame buffer, and HIPPI network interface. The I/O operations defined here will operate correctly on either arrangement. The file name supplied by the user, and in particular its path, will implicitly specify on which of these file systems the file resides.

The **`nglobal`**() and **`nlocal`**() calls shift the system back and forth between two I/O modes. In the first, **`nglobal`**(), only a single I/O operation occurs, even though the call is made by all the nodes. On input, for example, a *single* record will be read and broadcast to *all* the nodes. On output, all the nodes write the same record, but only a single instance is sent to the file. The second I/O mode, **`nlocal`**(), performs separate I/O operations for each of the nodes. For example, if each of the nodes issues an `fread` call, then separate records will be read—a different record for each node. Figure 5-4 illustrates the difference between **`nglobal`**() and **`nlocal`**() for a dimension 3 (that is, 8-node) hypercube.

Terminal I/O is often in **`nglobal`**() mode, as is the case here.

lines 24–25: Every node in the array receives the input file name. Only a single line is printed to the screen.

line 26: Switch to **`nlocal`**() I/O mode. Now (until the next shift, at line 70), each node will perform its own file I/O independently of all the others.

lines 27–31: Each node opens the file. If one of the nodes were to fail in the file open operation, it would print the fact and its node id, `me`, to the user's screen (line 29).

line 32: Every node reads the same first record, the total number of scores in the file. Note that each node is now maintaining its own private file pointer.

line 33: A utility provided by nCube assists in partitioning the large scores array evenly over the processor array. The same routine is used at all nodes, so consistency is maintained across the entire array. The routine returns the starting address to be used by the processing node in the scores array, `<num_start>`, and the total number of scores to process, `<num_here>`. This utility partitions the data array as evenly as possible over the processor array.

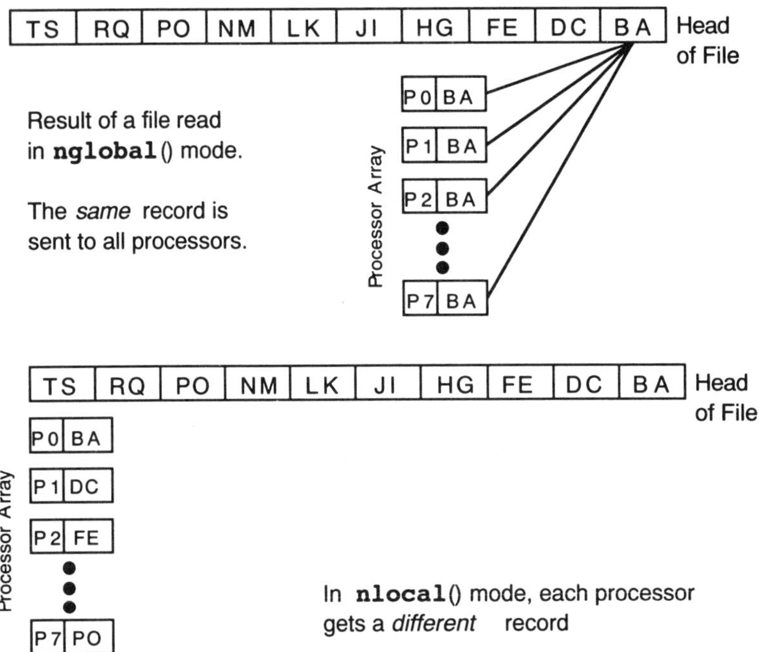

Figure 5-4. The difference between `nlocal` and `nglobal` I/O modes

line 34: Each node allocates only the amount of memory it needs to hold the portion of the scores array it has been assigned.

line 35: Each node positions its private instance of the file pointer to the place in the scores array where its subarray begins. The extra record is for `num_scores` at the beginning of the file.

line 36: Identical to the sample code, except that only part of the array—<`num_here`> records—are held by any given array processor.

lines 37–50: Identical to the sample problem code, except that the array runs from index <`0`> to index <`num_here`> rather than from <`0`> to <`num_scores`>. The variables `sum_scores`, `sumsq_scores`, `min_scores`, `max_scores`, and `histogram[]` at this point hold only values corresponding to the portion of the scores array held in each processor in the array.

lines 51–55: The local values held in each processor are now combined into global values. The nCube library provides optimized subroutines for this purpose, based on the logarithmic doubling idea explained in Section 5.2.1. The `target`, `msgtyp`, and `mask` variables provide additional capabilities not required for this problem. Note that *every* node in the array ends up with the correct global value. It is as if the reduction operation has been combined with a broadcast operation. The explanation in Section 5.2.1 shows how this is accomplished in logarithmic time without additional overhead.

line 51: A global minimum using the `min_scores` variable.

line 52: A global maximum using the `max_scores` variable.

lines 53–54: Global sums using first the `sum_scores` variable and next the `sumsq_scores` variable. Arithmetic will be carried out in double precision.

line 55: A global sum, but this time element by element on the `histogram` array.

line 56: An alternative approach to lines 51–55. The advantage is that it decreases the total number of message stages. For each of the library routines in lines 51–55, the hypercube will go through a complete logarithmic message-passing protocol, such as the one described in Section 5.2.1. For example, on a 2**9 = 512-node system, each of the subroutine calls results in nine message stages, for a total of 5 * 9 = 45 message stages. Given the very short length of all but the final message, the bulk of the time will be spent in message start-up overhead. By packaging all the variables into a single structure, this alternative subroutine only requires nine message stages and, hence, reduces the message-passing overhead. The details of this subroutine are presented in lines 86–116. (Given that the sample problem is already I/O bound, however, this is likely to provide almost no noticeable improvement in overall run time.)

lines 57–67: Identical to the sample problem code. Note that this calculation is performed redundantly by each of the processor nodes. This does not add extra time, however, since it has to be done by at least one node anyway. To bracket the code with something like

```
if( me == 0 )
{
CODE BLOCK
}
```

would force only one processor to execute the CODE BLOCK, but would not improve overall run time.

line 62–67: This solution does not attempt to parallelize the percentile computation. The primary reason is that the histogram array, on which the summation prefix is performed, is so short. In other circumstances, however, a parallelized version of the prefix operation could be constructed and used, and it runs in logarithmic time on the hypercube.

lines 68–69: Each node scales only the part of the scores array it holds. Since the global value of sum_scores is known to the entire array, each can compute the correct global value of average (line 57) and use it in the scaling loop in line 69.

line 70: The next few values to be written to the file are common to all the nodes. Changing the I/O mode back to **nglobal**() has exactly this effect. Even though all the nodes perform the fwrite operations, only one instance is actually appended to the file. The situation is exactly the reverse of the fread operation illustrated in Figure 5-4.

lines 71–77: Identical to the sample problem code. The **nglobal()** in line 70 ensures that only one copy of these values is actually written to the file, even though all the nodes execute the fwrite statements.

line 78: An idiosyncrasy of the nCube I/O system. UNIX does buffered I/O and typically waits until the buffer is full, or for input, to actually write the data to the disk. Since we are about to switch to **nlocal()** I/O mode (line 79) and each node will perform a seek operation (line 81), it is important that the data be in the file and not in the buffer. This line accomplishes that objective.

line 79: Shift to **nlocal()** I/O mode preparatory to writing the pieces of the scaled scores array back to the file. Since each node holds its own portion of the array, we want each of the I/O operations to have effect—not just one.

line 80: Each node will seek to the correct place in the file, moving past the preexisting data (num_scores and the scores array), past the data just written in lines 72–77 (min_scores, max_scores, average, standard_dev, the histogram array, and the percentile array), and finally past the initial portion of the array supplied by other nodes (that is, as far as <num_start>). This line of code computes the total number of bytes in this offset.

line 81: seek to the correct file position, prior to writing.

line 82: Write a total of <num_here> scaled scores, begining at the offset found in line 80.

lines 83–85: Close the file and exit. One consequence of this will be to release the subcube allocated for running this program back to the operating system.

lines 86–116: An alternative approach for combining the local values held in each node into global values. The basic approach is the same as that described in Section 5.2.1. The nodes pair up by toggling bits—the first bit in step 1, the second bit in step 2, and so forth, up to the number of bits in the address. At each step, the pairs exchange the "current best" values and update them.

After <dim> stages, where <dim> is the dimension of the hypercube, the computation is complete.

line 86: The declaration of the subroutine. The five quantities for which global values are desired are min_scores, max_scores, sum_scores, sumsq_scores, and the histogram[ ] array.

line 87: The message will want to have the data packed into a contiguous array of bytes in memory. A structure is as good a way as any to do it.

line 88: We'll need two copies: one to hold our own current best version of the data and the other to receive the message data sent, in each stage, by our neighbors.

lines 89–91: Declare local variables.

line 92: The context of the node is available at any point in the subroutine calling hierarchy. We could have passed the node id and array size in the subroutine calling sequence, but this is just as easy.

lines 93–97: Pack the values passed in the subroutine call parameters into my local structure.

line 98: We won't use the message_type matching capability of **nread**, but we'll need to supply a value for the field. Here it is.

lines 99–109: Here is the main loop. At each stage, the node <me> names its neighbor, <my_neighbor>,by toggling the appropriate bit in <me>. At the same time, of course, the neighboring node will be naming <me>, thus forming a pair connected by a direct, nonshared hypercube edge (see the explanation in Section 5.2.1). Data are exchanged across this edge between the pairs, values are updated, and the next stage can begin.

lines 99–100: The number of bits to be toggled is the same as the dimension of the hypercube.

line 101: This performs the bit-toggling. This is one of the first lines of code learned by a hypercube programmer. Learn it once and use it often!

line 102: The node sends its current values in the temp_message structure off to the neighboring node. Note that it would be an error to do the next **nread()** operation *before* the **nwrite()**. The reason is that the neighboring node is also executing the same code and, hence, will also be waiting to receive data. Since the receive operation is *blocking*, both nodes will hang, waiting for a message that never comes. This is a common error for beginning message-passing programmers.

line 103: Retrieve the data sent by your neighbor. A key point is that the "sender" field is not filled in by a wild card but rather by the actual node id `<my_neighbor>` to be paired on this step. Failure to do this could result in an error. Not all nodes in the array need be at the same place in their control flow. Other nodes of the hypercube may have completed stages beyond the stage currently being processed by `<me>`. If so, other neighbors (not yet reached in `<me>`'s loop) may have already posted messages, which are waiting in the message queue. It is therefore important to select the *right* message from the message queue; matching on the "sender" id is the right way to do this. Another reasonable technique is to reset the `message_type` variable to the current value of `<i>` and to match on this field.

lines 104–108: Update the local `temp_message` structure using the data received from the neighboring node in the `input_message` structure. At the end of these lines, the `temp_message` structure holds current best values for the max and min and has summed the neighboring values into the global sum variables.

line 109: Ready to process the next neighbor.

lines 110–114: The `temp_message` structure now holds the correct global values. Unpack them back to the input variables passed in as parameters in the subroutine call.

lines 115–116: Return to the calling routine.

5.2.3 Alternatives and Considerations

As we have noted, the sample problem is unrealistic in several respects, most notably in the extent to which it is dominated by I/O. It is likely that improvements in the I/O portion of the system would swamp any other optimizations. For nCube, this means finding reasonable ways to parallelize the file input and output operations. Run-time improvements will require use of the high-performance I/O subsystem; I/O through the front end will not be satisfactory.

One reason to use the nCube-supplied library routines (**imin**, **imax, dsum**, etc.) is that communications efficiencies are available that cannot be had using **nread** and **nwrite**. These routines can use the knowledge that data will be *both* sent *and* received along a single, nonshared link to bypass some the ordinary checking and copying that must be done if the message traffic is completely asynchronous. There may or may not be enough savings here to compensate for the reduced number of messaging stages associated with the **find_global_values** subroutine. In any case, these library routines will ordinarily contain low-level optimizations not otherwise available except through assembly programming.

An interesting trade-off is in the operating system that is to run at each node in the processor array. Since this code must be duplicated in each node's memory, there are memory efficiencies in keeping this operating system down to a minimum. On the other hand, many programmers are used to all the services of full-up UNIX, and this could become very expensive in duplicated memory utilization. One capability that does not make sense in this context is virtual memory. If the array nodes must be constantly referencing the disk system for pages, the performance of the system will be dramatically reduced. Typically, applications should be able to execute in the *real* memory available at each node. Since nCube can provide up to 64 Mbytes per processing node, this should not be a problem for most applications.

Space is also taken up by the operating system to implement the pending message queue. If the messages are very long and if a given node finds itself acting as a central controller or repository, the size of memory allocated for the message queue can sometimes be of concern. System parameters are available to control this, and the debugging facilities can show the status of the message queue (including space available) at any point in the processing flow

Processing on MIMD hypercubes has a long history, going back to the Cosmic Cube developed at Cal Tech by Charles Seitz and his students in 1983. Several commercial and research clones were almost immediately forthcoming, including nCube, the Intel iPSC, Ametek, and the Mark II and Mark III hypercubes at JPL. There is abundant literature available for algorithms on DM-MIMD machines. Only one of these machines (the nCube 2) is still commercially available with a physical hypercube interconnection scheme. The trend has been to shield the user from the topology of the network, and a variety of interconnections (2-D and 3-D meshes, fat trees, etc.) are now being employed by DM-MIMD manufacturers. Reference [2] is an excellent introduction to programming on MIMD hypercubes, and it includes a number of completely worked examples and sample codes.

5.3 EXPRESS

The Express parallelizing library is a product of ParaSoft Corp. Its genealogy extends back to the Crystalline operating system first developed at Cal Tech for the Cosmic Cube and later used on the Mark II and Mark III hypercubes at JPL. However, its current implementation extends well beyond that initial beginning. It contains a number of capabilities designed to assist the user in partitioning data arrays across a distributed memory MIMD parallel processor and to permit the user to operate on those arrays, conceptually, as single structures instead of piece by piece. While Express provides a basic set of message-passing primitives, it is often possible to program using only higher-level abstractions (such as global sum, broadcast, synchronization, etc.) without the explicit need to pass messages at all (that is, all the message passing can be hidden behind the higher-level operators).

One of the powerful features of Express is that it can often shield the user from logical to physical node address translation. We will illustrate this in more detail in Section 5.3.1. This translation process is at the heart of optimizing data placement on the processor array so as to minimize communication overhead. Since Express runs on a variety of MIMD machines—including hypercubes, meshes, LANs of workstations, and even shared memory machines—programs written using the Express libraries will beenefit from portability and a high degree of optimization across a variety of parallel hardware platforms.

5.3.1 Overview of Express

Express utilizes a classic message-passing paradigm that executes on a number of different parallel hardware platforms—primarily DM-MIMD but also shared memory. What makes it attractive is a powerful library of operators that shields the programmer from the hardware internals of the machine on which the program is executing. This has two advantages. First, the programmer does not have to think about the details of the underlying network topology (what nodes are nearest neighbors, for example). By using the Express library routines, which automatically partition and map the data sets and independent loops, the programmer can be assured of optimal data placement in the processor array. Second, code written using Express will be portable—and *efficiently* portable—across various platforms. By simply linking into the Express library for the new machine, the optimal data distribution will be performed without programmer intervention.

Of course, the programmer always has the option of doing explicit message passing, and there are some problems where that is appropriate. In many (perhaps most) cases, however, the interprocessor communications will fall into one of the standard prototypes already provided by Express. In the solution for the sample problem, for example, the entire computation (including parallelizing the summation prefix) can be accomplished without a single explicit send or receive operation.

At the heart of the Express view of the world is the distinction between the *physical* number (that is, address) of a node in the processing array and its *logical* number in the program. The message-passing scheme must use physical node addresses; the programmer, on the other hand, conceptualizes the array in a pattern that matches the algorithm—most typically, a one-, two-, or three-dimensional grid. In the conceptual model, edges connect nodes (logical nodes) that need to exchange data. What is required for efficiency is a *logical to physical mapping that maintains adjacency*. Nodes that are logically adjacent in the algorithm should be mapped to physical nodes that are physically adjacent (or, if that is not possible, at least as close together as possible) in the underlying network topology.

Figure 5-5 illustrates this problem using a three-dimensional hypercube as the underlying physical interconnection network.

Suppose that we wish to treat the nodes as a linear array, numbered 0 through 7, with (logical) links between successors: 0 connected to 1, 1 connected to 0 and 2, 2 connected to 1 and 3, etc. By the phrase "connected to," we mean that in our algorithm these nodes will need to exchange data, so we envision messages traveling between them. It would be nice, then, to have physical network links in the underlying network topology connecting the pairs of nodes that are logically connected in the algorithm.

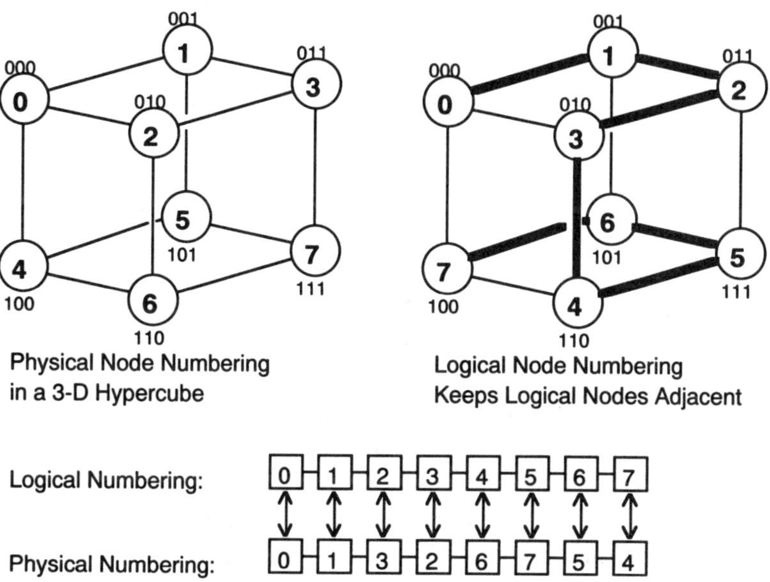

Figure 5-5. Logical and physical numbering schemes in a 3-D hypercube

Unfortunately, if we choose the most naive approach—just assign logical node K to physical node K—this will not occur. We see, for example, that physical nodes 1 and 2 are adjacent in the logical mapping, but there is no direct hypercube wire between them in the underlying physical network. A similar situation exists between physical nodes 3 and 4—they are actually at opposite corners in the hypercube, and two intervening message "hops" are required in messages sent between them.

The second diagram in Figure 5-5 shows a more promising arrangement (for the cognoscenti, we have a simple *Gray Code* on the hypercube nodes) in which the logical linear array has been placed onto the physical hypercube in such a way that logically adjacent nodes *do* have physical network connections between them. Figure 5-6 illustrates the same issue, but this time on a three-by-four mesh interconnection.

In a real application, code will be required to make the logical to physical assignment (and the reverse mapping, as well). Further, suppose that instead of a simple linear (1-D) logical array, we wished to treat the processor array as a 2-D or 3-D grid (perhaps even with end-to-end wraparound, a torus!). How is the optimal logical to physical mapping to occur? What are the algorithms to compute it? What happens when I want to port the code from, say, a hypercube to a 2-D mesh: Must the mapping be recomputed from scratch?

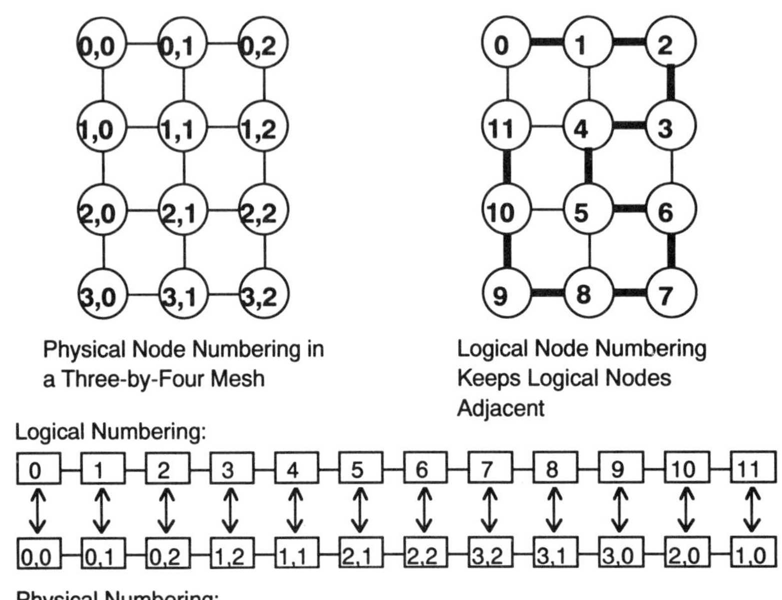

Figure 5-6. Logical and physical numbering in a three-by-four mesh

An important service provided by the Express library is that it performs the optimal logical to physical mapping and does so in a way that is transparent and portable. The user merely specifies the logical arrangement desired: linear array (or ring); 2-D mesh (or torus), including the size along each dimension; etc. An Express routine (**`exgridcoord`**) then computes, for any *physical* node, what its *logical* address is. The programmer can then use this logical address freely in developing the algorithm, confident that the underlying physical address (about which he or she does not care) has been selected in an optimal fashion.

Because of this simple interface, applications using the Express library are efficiently portable across a number of different hardware platforms. The internals of, for example, **`exgridcoord`** for a hypercube will be different than for a fat tree, but the programmer interface is identical. In either case, the optimal logical to physical assignment will be selected by Express; the programmer need not know or care about the physical interconnection scheme.

There is a good deal more to it than just this. For example, there are routines that allow the programmer to communicate directly between logical nodes—say, for example, to pass data `left` in a logical ring—and the Express system will automatically convert `left` to the correct physical address and perform the message passing without further intervention by the programmer. Even more important in many cases, the logical mapping cooperates with the I/O subsystem to help spread and reassemble large data arrays as they move between the I/O subsystem and the processor array. We will see this in the sample problem, in the interaction between the **`forder`** call and the **`fmulti`** I/O mode.

A fair amount of literature exists on the issue of optimal logical to physical mapping in DM-MIMD machines. The goal is to minimize message-passing overhead while retaining an intuitive and expressive programming interface. While simple cases (logical grids and meshes) can be handled easily and can cover many real applications, it turns out that the fully general problem (in which virtually arbitrary pairs of nodes must communicate) is very difficult—NP-complete in the fully general case. For such an application, profiling capabilities that watch and display network loading patterns can help to improve performance. The idea is to detect pairs of logical nodes that communicate heavily, and then (under programmer control) force them to be adjacent in the underlying physical network. Express provides a profiling tool for exactly this purpose.

In the FORTRAN world, much of HPF (High Performance FORTRAN) is aimed at the issue of optimal data placement across the processor array. How much can be done automatically? Is there a portable language syntax that retains optimal, or close to optimal, performance as we move between different machines? What set of primitive operations on arrays can be efficiently implemented on a large variety of architectures and interconnection topologies? Express can be thought of as a good first cut at this set of problems. In a practical sense, it is doubtful that HPF can improve much on the tool set Express provides. In the author's opinion, the debate shifted long ago from technical merit to "turf," the "not invented here" syndrome, and perceived competitive advantage.

Things to notice as we proceed through the detailed code include:

- use of the classic SPMD strategy: The same program executes on each node, with branching based on node id and local data values
- the entire problem can be parallelized without use of explicit message passing
- explicit parallelization of the percentile calculation using a global summation prefix operation
- the way in which **`exgridinit`** and **`exgridcoord`** cooperate with library routines, including I/O, to shield the user from low-level partitioning arithmetic
- use of library functions to perform optimized global reduction operations
- use of **`forder`** to control partitioning of the scores array for input and output
- extensive reuse of the original code
- portability: The same Express program can execute on a variety of hardware platforms, including processor arrays of varying sizes

5.3.2 Annotations

line 3: The header file for the Express library.

line 4: This global structure is used to return context to the calling process. Among others, fields are provided for the local node address in the processor array (`.procnum`) and the size of the array (`.nprocs`).

line 5: Like the other message-passing examples, the programming model is SPMD: The same program will execute on each node of the processor array.

lines 6–17: Local declarations. There is one change from the sample program: The variable `temp1` is no longer needed (see lines 60–72). Also, even though the percentile array is statically allocated at length 1601, in this solution the percentile array will actually be decomposed across the processor array, so that only a fraction of this space will actually be needed. Since the amount of memory used is so small in this case, it hardly matters. But, for a larger array, it might be preferable to dynamically allocate space once the run-time storage requirements are known.

lines 18–20: The additional variables needed by the parallel version.

line 21: This is how Express returns context to the calling node. The globally declared structure `cparm` has been used for this purpose (line 4).

lines 22–23: The same issue arises here regarding I/O mode as arose for the nCube (see Figure 5-4). Whereas nCube uses the terminology **`ngobal()`** and, respectively, **`nlocal()`**, Express uses the terminology **`fsingl()`** and, respectively, **`fmulti()`**. The effect is the same. The default mode in Express is **`fsingl()`**. Thus, even though all the nodes execute the `printf` statement, only a single line of output is written to the user's screen. Similarly, the user only enters a single character string for the file name—not a separate one for every node. This string is then broadcast to the entire array.

lines 24–28: The nodes open the file. In **`fsingl()`** mode, a single file pointer is maintained and shared by all the processors. In **`fmulti()`** mode, a separate pointer is maintained for each node.

Most DM-MIMD machines provide a variety of file systems, including a fully parallelized I/O subsystem as well as, for example, NFS. The type of the file system is ordinarily determined as part of the file path; a particular node in the path will have been *mounted* with the pointer to the appropriate set of drivers. Express cooperates seamlessly with this capability. If the file name points to a parallelized file, Express can and will utilize this additional performance. The type of the file system (native, parallelized, NSF, etc.) is completely independent of the **`fmulti()`** and **`fsingl()`** I/O mode designators.

line 29: Position the pointer to the start of the file.

line 30: In **`fsingl()`** mode, all the processing nodes receive the single input value for `num_scores`.

lines 31–32: These two lines perform the logical to physical mapping. The initial parameter—1—to **`exgridinit`** tells Express to treat the processors as a one-dimensional array. In more complex situations, two- or three-dimensional meshes (or toruses) can be specified. The call to **`exgridcoord`** then returns the *logical* address of this node, given its *physical* address as input. This assignment has been optimized under the assumption that most communications between nodes will be along the edges defined by the mesh;

the logical to physical assignment has been made to minimize communications along these paths. Thus, each node now has *two* addresses: its *physical* address in the machine (held in `cparm.procnum`) and its *logical* address in the conceptual array, (described in the call to **`exgridinit`** and held in the local variable `myslot`). See Section 5.3.1 for additional discussion on this topic.

line 33: Express has the ability to partition input data arrays based on estimates of load (processing time) and will attempt to balance the load as much as possible. This call executes that function.

line 34: Here is where each node in the array finds out what portion of the large `scores` array it will process. This is returned as a starting position (`score_first`) and a total number of elements (`score_vals`).

line 35: Each processor allocates only the amount of memory it needs to hold its subset of the scores array.

line 36: The next I/O operation will be one at a time to each node. We therefore shift to **`fmulti`** mode.

line 37: This call tells the I/O subsystem where to place each successive block of data. It matches the *physical* order of the data elements coming off the file to (in this case) the *logical* numbering of the nodes. This ensures that logical processor 1 receives data block 1, logical processor 2 receives data block 2, and so on. It, therefore, works in conjunction with the `fread` and `fwrite` statements in lines 38, 83, and 85 to properly order the data subsets as they move between the sequential file and the processing nodes.

line 38: The third field (`score_vals`) still specifies *how many* bytes to read but because of the action of **`forder`** in the preceding line, the data blocks are routed to the appropriate processing nodes according to their logical ordering. We see how the Express library routines interact with each other to shield the user from the details of partitioning and spreading the data across the processor array.

lines 39–52: Exactly as in the sample problem, except that each node only processes the subset of the scores array it has been given (hence, the length of the loop is `score_vals` instead of `num_scores`). At the end of line 52, each node has a local copy of the statistics variables.

lines 53–57: These library routines perform the global reduction operations—finding the global max and min, for example, and the global sums for `sum_scores`, `sumsq_scores`, and the `histogram` array. These routines implicitly cause message-passing to occur among the processing nodes, but the programmer is shielded from the details. In addition, the internals of these routines will vary from machine to machine to reflect the optimal messaging strategy for that machine and its network topology. For a hypercube, a logarithmic reduction scheme (as we described in Section 5.2.1) will be used. For a 2-D mesh, row-column broadcast rings may be selected. For an LAN of workstations, a master/slave protocol may be used. The programmer does not care and need not be concerned. And, should the code be ported to a different MIMD architecture, the version of the Express routines for that machine will be optimized to it without requiring any recoding (just recompilation and linking in the new version of the Express library).

As we saw in Section 5.2.2, the use of separate reduction operations leads to additional messages. Packing all the data into a single structure, which is passed once across the array, can save message overhead. The problem is that such a roll-your-own scheme must be tailored to the specifics of the machine (especially the network topology) and, hence, is not portable.

lines 58–59: All nodes compute the average and standard deviation. They can do this, since *every* node ends up with the *global* value of `sum_scores` and `sumsq_scores`.

lines 60–72: Unlike other MIMD solutions, this one illustrates how to parallelize the summation prefix operation at the heart of the percentiles calculation. As with other solutions, based on the length of the calculation and programming complexity, the programmer may elect the simpler sequential approach. The basic parallelizing strategy is simple. Each node individually does a summation prefix using a subset of the histogram array. Using the final values in each subarray, a global summation prefix is performed using message passing between nodes. In Express, a library routine is available for this purpose. The individual results are then adjusted. Figure 4-10 outlines the basic steps of the operation: (1) local prefix operation (lines 60–67); (2) global prefix operation (lines 68–69); and (3) correction of local values (lines 70–72).

lines 60–61: The call to **`exgridsize`** performs the same function as it did at line 34, but this time partitioning the histogram and percentile arrays. After the call, each node knows the subset of the histogram array it will be responsible for: the starting element (`percent_first`) and the total number of elements (`percent_vals`).

line 62: Because the truncation of the percentile array has been moved outside the main loop (to line 72), there is no need for the `temp1` variable.

lines 63–65: Logical processor 0 is initialized as before, but the other processors will process subsets of the histogram array that are interior and, hence, must begin with the last preceding value. Note that in all nodes we initialize `percentile[0]`; that is, we will use the *initial* portion of the percentile array to hold results in each node. This will be useful at line 83, since output will start at index 0, where it should. However, we see that we have allocated more memory for the percentile array (at line 15) than is needed. Another approach is to locally allocate memory using `percent_vals`, rather than allocating the memory statically during the declarations. Had we declared:

```
16>  float * percentile;
```

we could have inserted

```
63>  percentile =
     (float *)malloc( percent_vals * sizeof(float) );
```

at this point and saved a bit of space.

lines 66–67: The truncation at line 48 in the sample problem was what caused the inclusion of the temporary variable `temp1`. Since we have moved that operation to a separate loop (lines 71–72), we can use `percentile[i-1]` directly. Note that the percentile array is used from the beginning (beginning with index `<0>` up to index `<percent_vals-1>`), while the interior of the histogram array is used (beginning with index `<percent_first>` up to index `<percent_first + percent_vals–1>`).

lines 68–69: Each node initializes the variable `pref_sum` to the final (largest) of the values computed in the preceding loop. Then, the Express library routine **`exprefop`** is called to perform a global summation prefix on the values of `pref_sum` held in the various nodes. The order of summation is dictated by the logical numbering of the nodes (`myslot`, as computed by **`exgridcoord`** at line 32). Internally, **`exprefop`** has been optimized for the network topology of the machine on which it is executing. On a hypercube, for example, this operation can be accomplished in logarithmic time. The programmer is not required to do explicit message passing; all that is hidden inside the call. And, as before with the combining operations (lines 53–57), this call is portable from machine to machine.

lines 70–72: The locally computed values of the percentile array can now be adjusted, using the global prefix summation held in the variable `pref_sum`. This is also where the truncation of the percentile to an integer takes place. This line completes the parallelization of the percentile calculation.

lines 73–74: Each node scales the subset of the scores array assigned to it in the call to **`exgridsize`** (line 34).

line 75: The first few items to be written to **`file 1`** are only written once, although copies are held in each node. The current I/O mode is **`fmulti`** from line 36. We shift back to **`fsingl`**.

lines 76–81: These file operations only occur once, even though the call occurs in every node. This is the effect of the **`fsingl`** call in the preceding line.

lines 82–85: Both the percentile array and the scaled scores array have been distributed piece by piece across the processor array. Each node must contribute its part, and the subsets must be correctly interleaved back into the sequential file. The **`forder`** call (line 37) cooperates with the **`fmulti`** I/O mode to ensure that this happens under programmer control. The order of writing back to the file will be the *logical* node numbering (because `myslot`, the *logical* node number, was passed as the parameter to **`forder`**). This is an example of how **`exgridcoord, forder`**, and **`fmulti`** cooperate to shield the programmer from the details of partitioning and reassembling the data set.

line 82: Shift to **`fmulti`** I/O mode.

line 83: The percentile array, currently in pieces in the processor nodes, is reassembled and written to the file.

line 84: Flush the buffer before the next output operation.

line 85: Now the scaled scores array is reassembled and written to the sequential file.

lines 86–88: Close the file and exit.

5.3.3 Alternatives and Considerations

The Express solution to the sample problem is one of the few that explicitly parallelizes the summation prefix operation in the computation of the percentile array. The array is so short that not much performance is gained on this particular example. In any case, the solution shows the reader an excellent, coded example of the parallelization strategy.

The cooperation between the I/O subsystem and the Express coordinate function means that the semantics of the standard I/O library calls (e.g., `fwrite` and `fread`) have changed in a subtle way. This, in turn, means that Express must be able to interface to the system I/O facilities at a level invisible to the user to accomplish the desired added functionality. As we saw with the nCube, and as we will see again with Paragon, there are different I/O options and file system approaches available—some via the front end (which are relatively slow and pose a sequential bottleneck) and others that deal directly with the high-performance I/O subsystem. Express accomplishes this directly through the file name—some file path names lead to the parallel I/O subsystem, others to NFS, etc.

As we mentioned briefly, Express can be used to develop parallel applications on networks of workstations. The LAN serves as the interprocessor communications mechanism, and the Express library enables the processes on the various platforms to coordinate and exchange data. In this environment Express can be an efficient means for parallelizing coarse-grained applications that do not require significant amounts of interprocessor communications. In open systems settings where high-performance workstations are underutilized or idle during off-hours, Express can be an effective means for putting these cycles to constructive use.

5.4 INTEL PARAGON

The Paragon is a massively parallel distributed memory MIMD (DM-MIMD) supercomputer produced by the Supercomputer Systems Division of Intel Corporation. In its larger configurations, it interconnects up to several hundred processing nodes (using the Intel i860 processor) on a high-performance network. The technology for the network is derived from work done at Cal Tech by Bill Dally and Charles Seitz. Routing chips connected in a two-dimensional grid provide input ports to the network at each processing node and to nodes implementing the I/O subsystem.

The next few sections briefly introduce the parallelizing language structures, show the sample problem solution, and discuss alternatives and considerations.

5.4.1 Overview of the Solution

The Paragon solution is very similar to the others we have seen. The large scores array is decomposed into smaller subarrays, which are handed off to the processors. Each processing node calculates local statistics using its locally held values. Global values are then computed using the Paragon library. Like other solutions, this one does not parallelize the summation prefix operation in the percentile calculation, since the array is so small. Under other circumstances, parallelizing the prefix operation would be both possible and appropriate. The statistics are then output, and the processor array cooperates in writing the scaled scores array.

The most remarkable feature of this solution is the ease with which the I/O operations are accomplished. The standard C I/O library has been replaced by a proprietary I/O library. Its syntax is familiar, and its effect is to greatly simplify the part of the problem that requires spreading data across the processor array or, on output, assembling the disjoint pieces of the array for sequential output. In the proposed solution, I/O operations that are only to occur once (that is, the analogue of the **`fsingl()`** mode in Express) are enforced by bracketing the statements in an "`if`" test based on processor id. For example, we see code sequences such as the following:

```
if( mynum == 0 )
{
CODE BLOCK ONE
}
```

The effect of this is to ensure that only node 0(that is, the node whose `id = mynum = 0`) will execute CODE BLOCK ONE. If CODE BLOCK ONE contains I/O operations, they will only be performed once—by the node whose id satisfies the "`if`" test.

A similar construct is:

```
if( mynum == 0 )
{
CODE BLOCK TWO
}
else
{
CODE BLOCK THREE
}
```

Here, node 0 executes CODE BLOCK TWO, while all the other nodes execute CODE BLOCK THREE. One use for this is to have node 0 read in data from the file and then *broadcast* it to the other nodes in the array. In the meantime, the other nodes are executing a *receive* statement to obtain the data. The fully symmetric `fread` operations previously encountered have been replaced by an asymmetric local read plus broadcast. The symmetric **`fsingl()`** and **`fmulti()`** I/O modes have been replaced by an asymmetric "if . . . then . . . else" branch based on node id.

This problem solution also illustrates how I/O libraries other than the standard C library may be needed to get access to the full capabilities of the system. Other MPPs share this characteristic. Fortunately, the syntax is similar enough to the C library that the transition should appear intuitive.

Things to notice as we proceed through the detailed code include:

- the solution is fully SPMD: all nodes execute the same program
- the solution executes correctly on processor and data arrays of varying sizes
- the I/O library automatically provides for partitioning and reassembling of linear data structures
- "if . . . then . . . else" tests based on node id are used to switch between sequential and parallel I/O
- the Paragon library provides reduction and broadcast operations that shield the user from explicit message passing
- a significant amount of the original sample problem code was reused

5.4.2 Annotations

lines 3–4: The header files for the Paragon message-passing and I/O libraries.

line 5: Every node in the processor array will execute a copy of this program—the classic SPMD programming model.

line 7: The standard C I/O library is not used for file I/O; the Paragon I/O library is used instead—hence, the difference in type for the file descriptor.

lines 8–16: Identical to the sample program.

lines 17–24: The additional variables needed in the parallelized version.

lines 25–26: The library routines **`mynode()`** and **`numnodes()`** are used to return the context for the calling node. This code will run correctly on any number of nodes— down to and including a *single* node. The size of the array is a run-time variable returned by **`numnodes()`**.

lines 27–36: Here is where the file name is read and distributed to all the nodes in the array. A single node—in this case, node 0—does the terminal I/O and then broadcasts the results to all the other nodes. They, in turn, read the data. Instead of each node issuing its own I/O read request, they share the results using a broadcast.

line 27: Only node 0 will execute lines 29–31.

lines 29–30: Prompt the user for the file name and read it in. The standard C library is being used.

line 31: Broadcast the file name (read in at line 30) to the rest of the array. The fact that `PID = 0` (set at line 19) is what triggers the broadcast. Depending on the physical configuration of the subarray on which the program executes, this broadcast may be optimized by having intermediate nodes participate in the operation.

lines 34–36: All the nodes *except* node 0 execute these lines.

line 35: Here is where the other nodes in the array receive the data sent to them by node 0. Notice that they match on the first field, which is the *message type* `(= =1)`.

lines 37–41: Each processor in the array opens the file. Note that the Paragon I/O call **`open`** is used instead of the C library **`fopen`**. The functionality and syntax, however, are synonymous.

line 42: Two I/O modes are used in this problem solution. Both are similar to the **`fmulti()`** mode from ParaSoft, since I/O operations are not shared: Every read or write from a node results in a separate I/O operation. The difference between the two modes is that `M_LOG` does not specify the order in which the separate I/O operations will occur: It is first come, first served. In the `M_SYNC` I/O mode, however, the order of the I/O operations is forced to correspond to the number of the processor nodes in the array: Node 1 will read (or write) first, node 2 second, and so on.

Both of these I/O modes will be used. This line of code sets the initial mode to `M_LOG`.

lines 43–51: Identical in function to lines 27–36, except that I/O is to the file rather than the user's terminal. Only node 0 executes the first branch.

line 45: First, read in the size of the file using the Paragon file I/O library. Note that if this had not been guarded by the "if. . . then. . . else" clause, all the processors would have executed the I/O operation, and the (shared) file pointer would have moved deep into the scores array.

line 46: Now, broadcast the result to the processor array. Again, it is the fact that `PID == 0` that alerts the system that a broadcast operation is underway.

lines 48–51: The nodes other than node 0 execute this branch.

line 50: Receive the data broadcast from node 0 at line 46. Note that nodes match on the message type field again (this time, `MSG_TYPE2 == 2`). This enables them to distinguish between the two broadcasts at lines 31 and 46. A late-starting node might have *both* messages waiting in its queue— the match on message type enables it to select the correct one.

lines 52–54: Each node calculates the *length* of the subset of the scores array it will process (`my_scores`). We will switch to the `M_SYNC` I/O mode to ensure that the order of reading in the scores corresponds to the order of the processors in the array.

line 55: Only allocate the amount of memory needed to hold the assigned subset of the scores array.

line 56: Switch to the `M_SYNC` I/O mode. This will force the order of the **cread** operations from the various nodes to correspond to their node id order.

line 57: The `M_SYNC` I/O mode ensures that the **`cread`** operations will be done in the order of the node numbering: Node 1 will receive the first set of records; node 2 will receive the next set; and so on.

lines 58–70: Identical to the sample program, except that the array length is shorter— `my_scores`, instead of `num_scores`. At the end of this segment, each processor in the array holds the partial statistics on the subset of the scores array it has been allocated.

lines 71–75: These are the global reduction operators— max, min, and summation. The call to **`gisum()`**, in line 75, does the summation reduction on the entire histogram array element by element. Note that the program is responsible for providing the necessary work space needed by the intermediate message-passing steps— `itmp`, `dtmp`, and `work`. This at least puts the programmer on notice that these operations are not without some memory effect. At the end of these lines, every node in the array has the correct global value for all the statistic variables.

lines 76–86: Identical to the sample code. Even though only one copy of, say, the percentile array is needed, all the nodes compute it (with no run-time penalty, since they are all working concurrently). No attempt is made to parallelize the summation prefix operation in the calculation of the percentile array. This makes sense on this problem, because the percentile array is so small. In other circumstances, parallelizing a summation prefix is possible and would be appropriate.

lines 87–88: Each node scales its local subset of the scores array. This was possible, since each node got the *global* value of `sum_scores` at line 73 and, hence, could compute the correct value of `average` at line 76.

lines 89–98: Only one processor needs to do this part of the file output—we've chosen node 0, but any other would do as well. The Paragon I/O library has been used.

line 99: The `M_SYNC` I/O mode set at line 56 will ensure that the order to the **`cwrite`** operations corresponds to the order in which the **`cread`** operations were executed at line 57.

line 101: The Paragon library routine is used to close the file opened at line 37.

5.4.3 Alternatives and Considerations

When compared with the nCube and Express solutions, the Paragon solution illustrates some of the potential variety and power of the I/O capabilities of MPPs. In general, the syntax of the standard C library is not sufficiently expressive to capture the variety of I/O configurations and I/O modes that may be appropriate for a given application. Like Paragon, MPP vendors provide a richer set of I/O functions to support this increased capability. For I/O-bound applications, these I/O facilities can be the critical element in achieving good overall system performance.

Even though an SPMD programming style was adopted, the Paragon solution did much more branching based on node id than was done in the other solutions we have considered. In each case, it will be seen that the branching was for the purpose of guarding I/O operations. It is just to avoid such node-dependent branching that the **`fsingl()`** and **`nglobal()`** I/O modes are provided in Express and nCube. The Paragon can also support such a style, but this capability is not illustrated by this solution.

When a user submits a program for execution on the Paragon array, he or she also requests a certain number of nodes on which the program is to execute. The operating system then looks for a contiguous set of array nodes to assign to the job. The advantage of a contiguous set of nodes is that the global operations—broadcast, global sum, etc.—can be optimized if the nodes preserve the structure of the underlying 2-D physical grid. However, the system is not restricted to contiguous blocks of processors. If, say, 12 nodes have been requested, the system has the ability to assign any subset of 12 nodes to the problem: In effect, the 12 nodes become a *logical* grid, even though they may not be *physically* contiguous in the processor array.

The fact that the assigned collection of nodes may not be contiguous in the underlying physical grid means that some variation in performance (due to changes in communications overhead) may be experienced from run to run. The goal of Paragon is to provide interprocessor communications with such high performance that such variability will be without practical consequence. Extensive algorithm optimizations based on assumptions about the grid topology will be ineffective if the actual physical configuration on which the program executes does not match these assumptions. Again, Paragon hopes that the high performance of the interconnection network will hide such hardware details and run-time consequences from the user.

Example: While the underlying network topology for the Paragon is a 2-D mesh, the processor id returned by **`mynode()`** is a number between 0 and `(nprocs-1)`. How this number maps onto the network topology is unclear—*intentionally* unclear. The idea is that the performance of the network is such that, in effect, we can treat all processor nodes as if they were nearest neighbors (adjacent) in the underlying physical network. If no pairs of nodes are "closer together" than others (measured in reduced latency), there is no need for the programmer to worry about "where" the nodes are with respect to each other in the physical processor array. ■

This abstraction is undoubtedly easier for the programmer. And, in simple problems such as this one, it is also realistic. The potential problem is that even though the message latency is close to equal across the array, the number of intermediate links being used by the message increases when the nodes are far apart in the underlying topology. Figure 5-7 illustrates this point.

When nodes A and B communicate, only two intermediate links are used. When nodes C and D communicate, six intermediate links are used. Even if the time spent by the network transmitting the message is identical in the two cases, the fact that *more links are used* in the second case means that other messages needing the links will have to wait. Or, alternatively, since all the links are required to complete the message transaction, the chances are greater in the second case that some other message will already be using one of the required links, so that the C to D message will be delayed as a result of competition for the shared resource—link bandwidth.

Generally speaking, communication between nodes that are at a distance over the network will increase the contention and, hence, reduce overall performance. If the messages are short or if not much communications band-

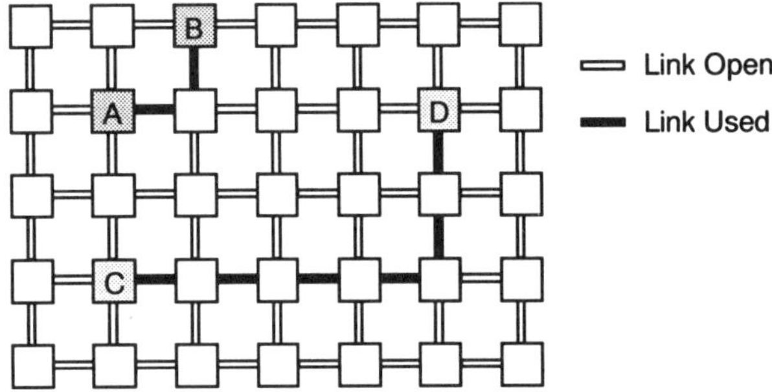

Figure 5-7. Advantages of adjacency in a 2-D mesh

width is required, this effect will not be noticeable. For communication-bound problems, however, it can be the dominant factor in overall performance.

In its larger configurations, the Paragon is capable of delivering tens of GFLOPs of performance on scientific vectorizing codes. This puts it at the forefront of supercomputer performance levels and makes it suitable for "Grand Challenge" problems— weather prediction, the human genome, very large scale computational fluid dynamics, etc. The sample problem, even with several million elements in the scores array, is very small by these standards and does not at all exercise the performance potential of such a machine.

5.5 OBSERVATIONS AND CONSIDERATIONS

Having seen, at this point, four complete solutions of the sample problem (one shared memory and three message passing), the reader is no doubt convinced that there is not much more juice to be squeezed from this orange. Just to show off a little, and perhaps to indicate that things can sometimes get a bit harder than they have appeared so far, let us consider one more level of parallelization—that is, parallelizing the histogram itself.

We saw, for example, that the calculation of the percentile array can be parallelized using a summation prefix operation. Each processor (or thread, in the case of the shared memory solution) is responsible for part of the percentile array, and the computation begins by each processor, in parallel, performing a local summation prefix on the corresponding part of the histogram array. A little thought will show that a given processor does not need to know all of the histogram values—it need only know the subset of histogram values corresponding to the portion of the percentile array for which it is responsible. It is also clear that the most expensive part of the global reduction operations was, in fact, the part relating to the histogram. An entire copy of the histogram array is passed between processor pairs during this stage—overwhelming the amount of data exchanged relative to the max, min, sum, and sumsq variables.

It might, therefore, occur to the perceptive reader that instead of each processor having a *complete* copy of the histogram array, it might be more efficient to assign each processor only *part* of the array—say, the part of the histogram array that corresponds to the portion of the percentile array it will need in the parallelized summation prefix operation.

As soon as this is suggested, however, the difficulties of parallelizing the histogram computation become apparent. Each processor has a subset of the scores array, but these scores will mostly belong to portions of the histogram array held by other processors. Let's consider a few possible algorithmic approaches.

As one alternative, suppose that each processor examines its set of scores, one by one in turn, and sends messages to the processor(s) holding the portion of the histogram array corresponding to each score. For example, consider processor, say, #23. It will loop through its set of scores. When it comes to a score element with value 842, it will calculate which processor in the array is responsible for the histogram slot #842. It will then send a message to that processor indicating that one more score has been found with that value, so that the #842 histogram slot should be incremented by one. Of course, each processor will not only send messages but will also have to read and process the set of messages that have been sent to it—reading them and incrementing its portion of the histogram array appropriately. To make this point a little differently—each processor will do double duty as a *sender* of messages (to other processors based on score values) and as a *receiver* of messages (based on the portion of the histogram array assigned to it).

The biggest difficulty with this approach, and the reason why it would probably not be implemented in practice, is the amount of message traffic that would be generated. The messages are truly general—any node may need to communicate with any other—so that the economies of clever logical to physical mapping are of no use. Further, the message buffers of the receiving nodes (that is, all nodes) would be stressed. Finally, there are load-balancing considerations: A node holding a portion of the histogram with lots of values would receive far more message traffic than nodes whose histogram values occur infrequently.

How can we address these difficulties? Another possible approach would be to pass the entire scores array through every processor. We might imagine the processors forming a ring. At each stage, each processor examines the subset of the scores array it currently has and increments its portion of the histogram array only if it sees a corresponding score; the other scores it simply ignores. The stage ends by having each processor relay to the next processor (its successor) in the ring the set of scores just examined; of course, it will also receive the next set of scores to examine from its predecessor in the ring. After every node has looked at every score, the distributed histogram calculation will be complete.

The major problem with this approach is that it will not speed up the calculation. In the sequential approach, the single processor examined the entire scores array. The same thing is done in this approach. If the histogram array is large enough, some speed-up could arise from the fact that a single processor solution might experience virtual memory paging effects; however, this algorithm is really a surrender, not a victory, for parallelization.

It turns out that the best approach is probably to *sort* the scores array first, and then use the message-passing approach first discussed above. The effect of sorting the array will be to drastically reduce the *number of messages* any given processor will have to send and (*mutatis mutandis*) the number of messages it will have to receive. After sorting, the set of scores corresponding to any given histogram slot will be held in one or (if the string of identical scores spans a processor boundary) at most a few other processors. In fact, rather than arbitrarily splitting the histogram array into equal slots per processor, the algorithm could use the sorting to accomplish the splitting. In any case, it is clear that parallelizing the histogram computation on a sorted scores array is a far simpler and more rapidly accomplished task than parallelizing it on a randomly distributed array.

What are the downsides of this approach? First, of course, there is the overhead of the sort itself. It turns out, however, that sorting is one of the things parallel machines do very well. For large data arrays, the sequential part of the sort (recalling Amdahl's Law) falls off rapidly, and nearly linear speedups (as a function of the number of processors) can be expected. On hypercubes, for example, sorts are available that are nearest-neighbor and contention-free (see, for example [2, Chapter 18]). Perhaps the biggest expense in this approach will be the extra memory required. While parallel sorts are typically in-place, the algorithm as presented in the sample problem requires that we write the scaled scores array out in the same order in which it was read in. Sorting the scores array would destroy that order, so a separate copy will be required, thereby doubling the memory requirements. One solution might be to do the scaling and writing of the scores array *before* the calculation of the histogram. Then, the same space used to hold the initial scores array could be used to do the sort.

Perhaps the reader now has a sense of why automatic parallelization poses such a difficult problem. It is not hard to find solutions that work in the sense of "get the right answer, eventually." It may be much more difficult to find solutions that optimally balance the various constraints for any given implementation: constraints on memory, the network topology, the application requirements, etc. Changes in any of these open up or preclude possibilities, and the selection of one approach may have a domino-like effect on other portions of the algorithm. Even in a very simple code like the sample problem, subtleties can arise as soon as we try to do more than the very minimum amount of parallelization. Fortunately, in many instances the application has enough inherent, coarse-grained parallelism that good speed-up can be had with only a minimal additional effort.

Another message-passing library is receiving attention from scientific processing centers. Called PVM (*P*arallel *V*irtual *M*achine), it is intended to operate in a *heterogeneous* computing environment (see [12, 13] for a description and some benchmark results). A computing center may have a variety of hardware platforms—traditional vector supercomputers, MPPs, SMPs, and high-performance workstations, for example. Various parts of a complete application might execute more efficiently on one or another of these platforms. PVM intends to provide a flexible way for the programmer to orchestrate this process, executing functions on the most appropriate machine and efficiently moving data between the machines (including the headaches of data format conversion). The abstraction (ideally) is that the entire processing center, with all its different hardware platforms, can be programmed as a *single computing resource.* The PVM library was developed and is supported by Oak Ridge National Laboratory, and it is publicly available. There are versions of PVM that execute on LANs of workstations. PVM is thus an inexpensive way to turn the LAN into a parallel processor.

The strongest arguments against message passing have to do with the consequences of splitting up single, large arrays into separate pieces. The I/O can become more complicated, and conceptually simple operations on the array can turn into lengthy and obscure messaging protocols. The library routines (broadcast, reduction, etc.) can shield the programmer from much of the low-level detail, but the fact that a single logical structure has been decomposed to reflect hardware considerations seems, to many, a high price to pay.

The strongest argument in favor of message passing is that it puts the programmer in direct touch with the part of the problem that will most affect performance—namely, how far the data are from the processor that will operate on it. Messages are nothing more than a programmer-controlled way to move data to (that is, into the private memory of) the processor that needs it. This is done automatically in shared memory caching systems but with the disadvantage that cache coherency imposes upper bounds (due to hardware considerations) on the number of processors that can be effectively used. Message passing forces the programmer to become conscious of data movement—this is both its strength (improved performance) and its weakness (increased programming complexity).

Because DM-MIMD appears to have won the parallel architecture battle at the high end, and because message passing is the natural model for this hardware, explicit message passing is perhaps best viewed as a kind of *assembly language* for DM-MIMD machines. Much of the time, library routines will be available to do what is needed, perhaps with some small but acceptable performance penalty. For those instances where the library does not provide the needed capability, or in which the performance penalty is too high, roll-your-own explicit message-passing routines optimized to the network topology and application idiosyncrasies can be constructed. Each organization must judge into which category its intended applications fall and, hence, how much (or little) programming complexity can be expected. These matters are taken up at greater length in Chapters 11 and 12.

Summary of Chapter 5

The sample problem was solved using three different message-passing libraries. Some of the complexities of parallelizing both the percentile calculation (using summation prefix) and the histogram calculation (using a sort) were discussed. The difficulties in distributing and collating data during I/O were illustrated, together with the capabilities provided by various vendors to simplify this for the programmer. Similarly, both explicit and implicit message-passing operations (e.g., reduction, broadcast, synchronization) were illustrated by the examples. The natural fit between message passing and DM- MIMD architectures virtually guarantees that message passing—in some form—will continue to play an important role in high-performance computing.

6

SIMD and Array-Based Languages

In this chapter, we will consider parallel languages that use an SIMD programming model. At the outset, it is important to separate the *language constructs* from the *physical* hardware on which the language will execute. The constructs that we will present were initially motivated by SIMD hardware considerations—both large processor arrays and vectorizing machines. It soon became apparent, however, that the expressive power of these constructs was ideally suited to the large vector operations characteristic of scientific processing. User demand—particularly in scientific organizations—for these constructs increased. As things stand today, most supercomputers—irrespective of their internal hardware details—offer languages that incorporate, to a greater or lesser extent, the large array manipulation capabilities of these languages.

Our approach will be to begin with the SIMD hardware-based conceptual model (Section 6.1.1) and then show how the ideas led to more generalized array-based languages, particularly the more recent versions of FORTRAN (Section 6.1.2). We then present solutions of the sample problem in two proprietary SIMD versions of C: MPL on the MasPar MP-1 (Section 6.2) and C* on the Connection Machine (Section 6.3).

6.1 AN OVERVIEW

The following two sections trace the ideas in the SIMD programming model from their origins in the SIMD hardware architecture (6.1.1) to current instantiations in array language constructs (6.1.2).

6.1.1 The SIMD Programming Model

The SIMD programming model is based, conceptually, on the top-level hardware architecture shown in Figure 3-5. A single controller broadcasts instructions, one by one, to a large array of processors operating in slave-mode. Whatever instruction is issued, *all* the processors execute in lock-step. The only exception to this is that certain processors may be "put to sleep" for a while—during such periods, they are *inactive* and do not respond to the controller's directives.

In addition to the instructions broadcast to the processor array, however, it is usually convenient to also have an ordinary scalar instruction stream executing on a conventional, sequential front-end processor. The idea is that some types of inherently sequential processing—for example, terminal I/O or loop tests—are best executed using an ordinary sequential processor operating on ordinary sequential data structures.

If we examine a program using SIMD array syntax, we will see a mixture of instructions: some intended for the processor array and some intended for a standard sequential processor associated with the front end. These ideas are illustrated in Figure 6-1.

The instruction stream contains two types of instructions: (1) those destined for the scalar, sequential part of the machine, and (2) those destined for the processor array. These two types of instruction are interleaved, and one task of the controller is to route them to the appropriate part of the machine. Note that the scalar processor has its own memory (shaded in black), just as each processor in the array has its own local memory (also in black).

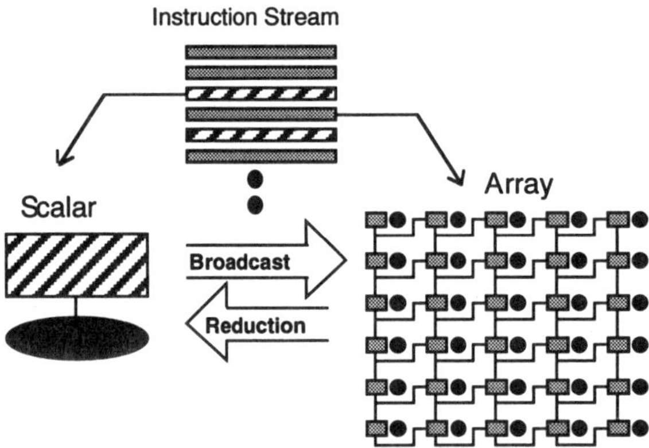

Figure 6-1. The SIMD programming model

In addition to the two types of instructions—scalar and array— it is necessary to move data back and forth between the array processors and the scalar unit. The generic term *broadcast* refers to data movement *from* the scalar processor *to* the array. In the simplest case, a single variable held in the scalar unit is sent to the entire processor array. However, if some of the processors in the array are inactive ("asleep") when the broadcast occurs, the effect is to send the data to just the active processors. In the extreme case, when only a *single* processor is active, data can move between the scalar unit and a single processor in the array.

Similarly, when data move *from* the processor array *to* the scalar unit, we use the generic term *reduction.* There are a number of different forms of reduction. Global sums is a typical example: Each processor in the array holds a local copy of a variable, and the intent is to find the sum of all these values and to place the result in the memory of the scalar unit. Other examples include: global max and min, global logicals ("and," "or"), global products, and selective extraction of data from a single processor's memory (by making all the other processors inactive).

Another required capability is to move data between processors in the array. These are special types of array instructions and can be thought of as *send* and *receive* primitives similar to those we encountered in message passing. Figure 6-1 shows a portion of the processor array as a six-by-five 2-D mesh. In typical SIMD machines, there may be upwards of several thousand processors in the array, and the interconnect topology can be more complex. Whatever the details of the network, however, the language must enable the programmer to arrange for and control interprocessor communications. SIMD-style languages often provide high-level operators that shield the programmer from the hardware details of the interconnect topology and that can be optimized for the hardware of the target machine.

Another required capability is to arrange for processors to become inactive ("go to sleep") during stretches of the computation. In the typical case, each processor will test a locally held value; those that pass the test (for example, "Is x greater than 5?") will remain active, and the rest will become inactive until further notice. Since these tests can, themselves, be *nested,* a variety of language constructs are available to successively undo the "sleep" directives issued to the array—much like successively removing masks that have been overlaid on the processor array.

I/O operations must be provided for both the scalar unit and the processor array. Typically, terminal I/O is done through the scalar unit using the standard I/O library. An additional set of library functions is provided for the processor array.

The most natural way to distinguish between scalar and parallel *operations* is to first distinguish between scalar and parallel *data variables.* When data variables are declared, it is determined (by special, additional syntax devoted to this purpose) whether the variable will reside on the scalar unit or on the processor array. In the first case, language contructs are identical in meaning and syntax to sequential language usage: a standard, sequential C program will compile and run on an SIMD machine but will execute solely on the scalar unit without involvement by the processor array!

In the second case, the operations will be performed on the distributed data structures on the processor array. Thus, in reading an SIMD program, it is critical to keep in mind which variables are *scalar* (operated on by the scalar unit) and which are *parallel* (operated on by the processor array).

A simple way to indicate broadcast and reduction operations is to *mix* scalar and parallel variables in a single expression. If the left-hand side of an assignment is a scalar and the right-hand side involves parallel variables, a *reduction* is indicated (data are moving from the array to the scalar unit). Similarly, if the left-hand side of the assignment is a parallel variable and the right-hand side involves scalars, we are dealing with a *broadcast* operation (data are moving from the scalar unit to the processor array). By keeping Figure 6-1 in mind and remembering that some variables are on the processor array while some are in the scalar unit, the reader will quickly be able to sort out the meaning of many SIMD expressions in an intuitive, commonsensible manner.

Example: The following toy example illustrates some of these ideas using a simple syntax. In its declaration, any variable preceded by the key word **parallel** will reside on the processor array; other variables (declared in the ordinary fashion) will reside on the scalar array.

```
float s_x, s_y, s_z[20];
int s_i, s_curr;

parallel float p_x, p_y, p_z[20];
parallel int p_i, p_curr;
```

Each processor in the processor array now holds five variables: two ordinary floats, one array of 20 floats (note that every processor in the array has 20 elements), and two ordinary ints. The scalar processor has the same collection. Consider the following expressions:

```
001>     s_x = 2. * s_y + s_z[ s_i ];
```

Since all the terms in this expression are scalar terms (that is, held in and manipulated by the scalar unit), this is an ordinary C expression: Add twice the value of s_y to the <s_i>-th element of the array s_z, and store it in s_x.

Next, consider the expresion:

```
002>            p_x = 2.* p_y + p_z[ p_i ];
```

All the variables in this expression are parallel variables (even the "2."— a separate copy of which is in each processor) and will be executed in parallel by all (active) processors in the processor array. *Every* processor will take its *local* value for p_y (which can vary from processor to processor), multiply it by 2., and add it to the <p_i>-th element of the local array p_z.

Finally, consider

```
003>    p_x = 2. * s_y + p_z[ s_i ];
```

The mixture of scalar and parallel variables indicates a broadcast operation is also involved (*broadcast,* since the left-hand side of the assignment is a parallel variable). In this case, the scalar variables s_y and s_i are held in the memory of the scalar unit. Copies of these values must be distributed to the processor array (by broadcast). Each processor can then use its local copy to complete the indicated operations on the parallel variables. ■

The power of languages based on this SIMD model is that the programmer is able to operate on entire arrays of data with simple, intuitive expressions. In the example above, if the processor array has, say, 2**13 = 8,192 elements, then statement 002> is simultaneously executed 8,192 times—once per processor—on 8,192 distinct local values. It is *as if* the variable p_x were actually an *array* of 8,192 different values. The single statement in 002> has the same effect as if a "for" loop were automatically inserted to perform the operation on each of the array elements.

Example: Consider the declarations:

```
    float p_x[8192], p_y[8192], p_z[20][8192];

    int p_i[8192];
    int j;

005> for( j=0; j<8192; j++)
006>        p_x[j] = 2. * p_y[j] +  p_z[ p_i[j] ][j];
```

This bit of code has the same effect as the code in line 002> above, treating the parallel variables explicitly as arrays. The major difference is that this code *says more than it needs to.* It specifies exactly the order in which the variable `j` will run through its range, when in fact *we don't care!* We just want *all* the values of `p_y`, `p_i`, and `p_z` to be operated on as if at once—that is, *as if in parallel!* Statement 002> above says what we want done much more clearly than statements 005> and 006>. This is the power of SIMD array-based languages. The loop in statements 005> and 006> *sequentializes* what is, conceptually, a simple and natural *parallel* operation. The language construct in statement 002> is simple, powerful, and says no more than is necessary. ■

The toy syntax introduced above illustrates the basic idea but finesses a number of issues that are important in practice. For example, how shall we handle mismatches between the physical array size (8,192 in our example) and the logical array size required by the application? Also, our syntax has not dealt with ways to specify interprocessor communications, nor have we given examples of reduction operations. In Sections 6.2 and 6.3, we will see worked-out examples of fully elaborated SIMD syntax suitable for complete problem solutions.

6.1.2 Array Languages and FORTRAN

The preceding section illustrates a very attractive feature of SIMD-type languages. By operating on entire arrays as single entities, they relieve the programmer of having to sequentialize (through DO loops or "for" loops) what are naturally parallel (that is, concurrent or nonordered) operations. If we think back, for example, to Chapter 4 on the shared memory paradigm, the critical element determining whether or not a "for" loop could be parallelized was whether the *order of execution of the iterations* of the loop mattered, logically, to the final answer. The array syntax captures this idea perfectly: Just add this set of elements one by one to that set, and I don't care how or in what order you do it.

Various machines are free to respond to such a request in the manner most suited to their hardware. The SIMD machine says: Fine, I'll do them all at once, in parallel. Other machine architectures will use other approaches. A shared memory machine, for example, will set up independent threads, each assigned a subset of the elements to deal with. A distributed memory machine will similarly break the larger set into subsets and give each to a separate processor. A vector machine will cheerfully use its vector instruction set, perhaps after having first done a preliminary partitioning of the control stream based on shared memory ideas. In any case, each of these parallel machine architectures knows what to do with a statement like

a = b + c

where a, b, and c are themselves similarly dimensioned arrays.

Thus, the SIMD array syntax generalizes to other parallel machines and appears to capture an important (some scientific users might say *the most* important) type of parallelism.

This observation—that the SIMD array syntax appears to be efficiently parallelizable across a variety of machine architectures—was one of the major motivations behind two new versions of FORTRAN: FORTRAN 90 and High Performance FORTRAN (HPF). In each case, basic FORTRAN is extended to provide array syntax and associated operations. An important additional feature of HPF is that it permits the user to specify details about how very large arrays are to the decomposed and spread out across distributed memory machines. The advantage of this capability will be understood by recalling the need for efficient interprocessor communications. Data placement on the array is at the heart of minimizing network latency and contention.

Naively, it might be imagined that such a capability is exactly the parallel language standard for which the parallel community has been searching. Unfortunately, it is not that easy. Irrespective of language syntax, each parallel machine will have some types of operations it does very well and others which it does somewhat poorly. Thus, the algorithm choices (selectively exploiting the individual machine's strengths and avoiding its weaknesses) will be machine specific even if the language used in each case is the same. Standardizing the language cannot address the problem of hardware-specific algorithm differences.

No similar standardized array syntax has emerged for C, although work is underway to specify such a standard. Our examples (in Sections 6.2 and 6.3) are taken from vendor-specific extensions to C.

6.2 MPL ON THE MASPAR MP-1

In this section, we will consider a solution to the sample problem on the MP-1, an SIMD array processor from MasPar, Inc. The following sections will introduce the machine and its C-like language, MPL. The annotated solution is then presented, followed by a brief discussion of alternatives and considerations. The author wishes to thank members of the technical staff at MasPar, Inc., for help in preparing the solution to the sample problem.

6.2.1 An Introduction to MPL

The MasPar MP-1 is an SIMD array processor. The individual nodes in the array have a full instruction set, including built-in floating point assist. Two types of interprocessor communications are available: the XNET, which treats the processor array as a two-dimensional grid and provides very rapid data transfers to any of a processor's eight nearest neighbors (see Figure 6-2), and a general router (based on a three-level switch), which permits *any* pair of processors to communicate.

MPL provides natural C-like extensions supporting each of the four major types of SIMD characteristics: scalar versus array variables, broadcast and reduction operations, interprocessor communications, and inactivating portions of the array. We'll look at each in turn.

First, variables that are to reside on the processor array are indicated by the key word **plural**. The effect is to create a separate instance of the variable in every processor—exactly like the key word **parallel** we used in the toy syntax in Section 6.1.1. Predefined variables assist the programmer in navigating around the processor array. For example, **nproc** holds the total number of processors in the array (the MP-1 comes in various sizes and this permits code portability); and **iproc** is a **plural** variable that tells each processor its index between 0 and (**nproc- 1**). Similar variables are available if it is desired to treat the array as a two-dimensional grid.

Second, broadcast operations are accomplished by *typecasting*. When a scalar variable is recast as a **plural** variable (using standard C typecasting syn-

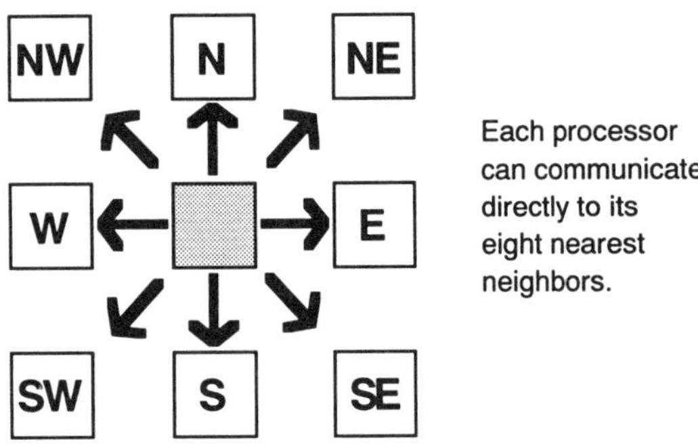

Figure 6-2. XNET communications on the MasPar MP-1

tax, including the **plural** key word), the effect is to create a variable of the indicated type and value in each processor's local address space. Thus, for example, if s_x is a scalar variable and if p_y and p_z are **plural** variables, the line of code

```
p_z  =  p_y + (plural int) s_x ;
```

has the effect of transferring the single scalar value of s_x to each processor in the array, adding it to the local values of p_y, and storing it in the local instance of p_z. As with standard C, there are type promotion rules to resolve mixed-type expressions where the programmer has not indicated casting explicitly. The line of code

```
p_z  =  p_y  +  s_x ;
```

will have exactly the same effect as the previous line, following the type promotion rules.

In reading this line of code, no clue is given that the variables are of mixed type (**plural** and scalar). The only way to resolve the issue is to go back to the original declarations of the variables. Overloading of the operators in this way (that is, where the meaning of the operator in any situation is derived from the type of the operands) makes for code that is compact but that can be difficult to read.

Reduction operations are done through the MPL library. There are functions to compute global sums, maximum, minimum, summation prefix, etc. For example, if s_x is a scalar integer variable and p_y is a **plural** integer variable, the line of code

```
s_x  =  reduceAdd32( s_y ) ;
```

will store in the variable s_x the *sum* of the local values of s_y held in the processor array (the "**32**" in the function name is one of several modifiers tailored to different data types—in this case, 32-bit integers).

Third, two capabilities are provided for interprocessor communications. The XNET is used when nearest-neighbor communications in the two-dimensional grid are adequate. The XNET has lower latency and higher bandwidth than the router, but the router has the capability to exchange data between arbitrary pairs of nodes. Either of these may be appropriate, depending on the particulars of the problem. In the case of the router, the address (that is, processor id) of the destination node must be provided along with the data to be transferred. With the XNET, addressing is always relative—for example: All nodes send a datum to your northwest neighbor. The sample solution gives an example of use of the router. In fact, however, many of the reduction and

I/O operations use the XNET implicitly to accomplish data movement across the array.

Fourth, making processors inactive is accomplished using the standard C "if" statement when the test is performed on **`plural`** variables. Each processor performs the test on its local values. The processors that fail the test then become inactive throughout the scope of the "if" statement. An accompanying "else" can be used to switch the processors between active and inactive: Those that failed the initial test become active for the "else" block, while those that passed the test initially now become inactive. We will see several instances of this usage in the sample problem solution.

Things to notice as we proceed through the detailed code are:

- there is a single flow of control in which some instructions refer to the scalar unit and some to the processor array
- ordinary C arrays typically become **`plural`** variables spread out across the processor array
- use of library routines to perform global reduction and scan operations
- parallel I/O library routines to support direct I/O to and from the processor array
- use of standard "if" statements to inactivate portions of the processor array
- elegant use of the router command to perform the data-dependent histogram computation

6.2.2 Annotations

line 3: The header for the MPL parallel libraries.

line 4: Unlike MIMD, the SIMD style has only a single flow of control. Parallelism will arise not by multiple independent processors executing a replicated program but by the processor array operating in lock-step synchrony to the instructions issued by the single master controller.

lines 5–11: These are scalar variables residing in the scalar unit. All the arrays—scores, histogram, percentile, etc.—have been shifted out to the processor array, as well as some of the other variables (`curr_score, temp2`).

lines 12–14: Three additional scalar variables.

line 15: A *pointer* is allocated in each processor. This will be used to reference the data array in each processor allocated at line 29 and read in at line 31.

lines 16–17: The histogram and percentile arrays now become single integers, one per processor in the processor array. In fact, there are many more than 1,601 processors, so not all the processors will be used. We will test on processor id to exclude (make inactive) the ones we don't need. Were that not the case, we would have to do some arithmetic to spread the data array over the processor array.

lines 18–19: Some local variables needed in each processor.

lines 20–27: Identical to the sample problem. This code is being executed on the scalar unit exactly as if it were an ordinary sequential processor (which, in fact, it is).

line 28: A calculation to see how many scores will be assigned to each processor. This is necessary in case the number of scores is not an even multiple of the number of processors. The variable **nproc** is predefined and holds the actual number of processors in the array. This program will be able to execute successfully on MasPar machines of various array sizes.

line 29: Space is allocated in each processor's memory to hold its portion of the scores array.

line 30: Not all the memory allocated in line 29 will necessarily be used. We will use a "-1" as a flag to indicate whether an array element does not receive input from the scores array.

line 31: The scores data are read into the processor array. The input is blockwise: The first set of records goes to processor 0, the next set to processor 1, etc., until the scores array is exhausted. If the size of the scores array is not an even multiple of the number of processors (**nproc**), there may be some processors (near the end) that receive no records at all; and there may also be one processor that does not receive a full set of records. We will have to deal with this explicitly during output (see lines 69–80). To do this, we will use the **plural** variable my_num. The function **p_read** returns, to each processor, the actual number of elements it received. For a processor near the beginning, receiving a full set of scores, its local value of my_num will be the maximum: local_scores. For a processor near the end, receiving none of the scores array, its local value of my_num will be 0.

lines 32–35: Initialize the statistical variables, as in the sample problem.

line 36: This sets the local value of histogram to 0 in all the processors. Recall that histogram is a **plural** variable. An alternative expression is:

```
036>  histogram = (plural int) 0;
```

This makes it explicit that in this context 0 is a local constant in each processor of the array—not a scalar constant in the scalar unit. Compare this line to line 33, for example, which has its usual meaning since `max_scores` is a scalar variable.

line 37: There is only one control stream and, hence, only one loop (unlike the MIMD examples, where there was a separate instance of the loop in each processor). The variable `i` is a scalar variable in the scalar unit.

lines 38–52: The body of the "for" loop. Unlike the MIMD loops, the reduction operations will take place inside this loop rather than outside.

line 39: A broadcast has implicitly occurred in the expression `scores[ i ]`. The scalar variable `i` will be recast to type

```
(plural int) i ;
```

The compiler may choose to set up a local variable in each processor, with each processor incrementing its local copy of `i` directly. The logical effect would be the same, and it would save having to perform a broadcast at each loop step (that is, a broadcast of the current value of `i` to the processor array). The programmer could force this to occur by declaring `i` to be a **`plural`** variable. The same situation arises in the loops at lines 30 and 59.

A related subtlety is that if all the instances of the local scores array begin at the same memory location, then the scalar unit might broadcast not `i` but the actual address of `scores[ i ]`. That is, the address calculation

```
scores + i
```

might be done in the scalar unit, broadcast to the array, and the dereferencing

```
*( scores + i ) = scores[ i ]
```

would be done in the local processors. Again, the programmer has the capability to force one or another interpretation by explicit typecasting.

line 40: Not all the processors may have received a full set of scores values during the **`p_read`** at line 31. Because of the initialization at line 30, the values for these array elements will be `-1`. This test makes inactive all those processors in the array whose value is `-1`. Only processors for which `curr_score` is *not* `-1` will execute lines 42–50. The fact that the variable `curr_score` is a **`plural`** variable signals that an active/inactive determination is being made.

lines 42–49: Unlike the MIMD solutions, the SIMD solution has put the global reductions inside the main loop over the local scores values. The global reductions are repeated each time through the loop, instead of once outside the loop. The hardware architecture of SIMD machines makes reduction operations much more efficient than on MIMD machines; hence, there is no need to restructure the code to reduce or eliminate their use. This is an example of a fundamentally different approach to algorithms between SIMD and MIMD machines, based on taking advantage of what the machine does best. We see reductions for max, min, and global sums.

line 50: An elegant, compact, and powerful construct. If I am a processor whose local value of `curr_score` is, say, 855, I want to notify processor #855 to add 1 to its value of histogram. Think of processor #855 as a destination: I need to send a message to processor #855 saying, "Increment your value of histogram." In the meantime, all the other processors in the array are similarly naming their associated destinations, based on their locally held values of `curr_score`.

The "**`router`**`[ curr_score ]`" construct names (and sends a message to) the destination processor whose id matches the local value of `curr_score`. The remainder of the line tells each processor to increment its local value of histogram by 1 for every message it receives. If processor #855 receives, say, 17 messages, it will increment its value of histogram 17 times, once for each of the 17 processors whose local value of `curr_score` was 855.

In effect, each processor is doing double duty: first, as a searcher through its local portion of the scores array and, second, as keeper of the histogram cell corresponding to its processor number. As a searcher, it sends a message to histogram keepers to update their local histogram cells. As a histogram keeper, it receives these messages and increments its local histogram cell accordingly. The syntax of this line of code elegantly combines these functions into a single, powerful expression.

A subtlety (that turns out not to be a problem) is that *destination* nodes are not affected by the "inactive" test made at line 40. Even if a processor is currently inactive, it will nonetheless wake up long enough to process incoming data from the **`route`**r call. However, no inactive processor will *send* data (which is good, because `-1` is not a valid **`router`** address!).

lines 53–54: At this point in the code (after the loop is complete), the correct global values of the statistics are held in the scalar variables. Lines 53 and 54 compute the average and standard deviation in the scalar unit on scalar variables.

line 55: The heart of the percentile calculation is the summation prefix operation. This is available via the **`scanAdd`** library call in MPL. The parallel variable `scanval` is used to hold the result. As a result of this call, we have, for each value of `i` from 1 to 1600:

```
scanval[ i ]  =  histogram[ 0 ] +
    histogram[ 1 ] +
                          .
                          .
                      histogram[ i-1 ]  ,
```

the value of `scanval[i]` being held in processor #i as a **`plural`** variable.

lines 56–57: Completing the percentile calculation using the plural variable `scanval` computed at line 55. Notice that the entire adjustment is made with a single statement. Each processor, in parallel, updates its own local values for `scanval` and `percentile`. This is a classic example of array syntax.

lines 58–59: Each processor scales its local values of the scores array. We don't bother to mask off the processors whose `scores` values are `-1`, because this flag is no longer needed. Again, the statment inside the loop is itself an implicit loop over the processor array, using classic array syntax.

lines 60–64: Identical to the sample problem and with the same effect. These lines are executed on the scalar unit.

line 65: The variable **`iproc`** is a predefined **`plural`** variable and holds (in each processor) its id, between 0 and (**`nproc–1`**). Since the histogram and percentile arrays each have 1601 elements, only processors with ids between 0 and 1600 need output their local values. Without this test, *all* the processors would output their values, even though only 1601 values are actually wanted.

lines 67–68: These lines are only executed by processors with ids between 0 and 1600 (see line 65); all the others have been rendered inactive. First, the histogram is written out to the file (line 67), and then the percentile array (line 68).

lines 69–80: Outputting the scaled scores array is a bit more tricky. Some of the processors (at the beginning of the processor array) have a full set of `scores` values, one processor may have a partial set, and the rest don't have any `scores` values. Fortunately, we have saved the actual number of scores in each process to the plural variable `my_num`, computed as part of the **`pread`** at line 31.

lines 69–72: Only those processors with a full set of `scores` values remain active for the execution of line 71; all the rest become inactive. The fact that the test is performed on a **`plural`** variable signals active/inactive determination.

line 73: How many scores are in the one processor that holds a partial number of scores? Note that this can be 0 even if **`nprocs`** does not evenly divide `num_scores`. For example, suppose we have 100 processors, and `num_scores = 810` is the number of elements in the scores array. We see that `local_scores = 9`. The entire array will fit into exactly 90 processors @ 9 scores per processor with 10 processors left over holding no scores.

If the number of scores had been 815, the 91st processor would have had to hold the extra 5; that is,

```
last_few = 5 = 815 % 9.
```

line 74: This line is executed in the scalar unit on scalar variables. If there are no leftover scores, then we're done; so don't execute lines 75–80.

lines 76–79: Line 76 is executed on **`plural`** variables and will be used as an active/inactive mask. Exactly one processor will have the value of `my_num` equal to the number of leftover scores calculated at line 73. All other processors become inactive while this processor outputs the rest of the scores.

lines 81–82: Executed on the scalar unit, exactly as in the sample problem.

6.2.3 Alternatives and Considerations

Quite a bit of code in the sample solution was devoted to the potential mismatch between the size of the scores array and the number of processors in the processor array. In particular, if the scores array is not an even multiple of **`nproc`**, the remainder is a nuisance, adding additional code for very little additional functionality.

One approach to this kind of problem, which is typical of SIMD machines, is to agree to always round the file size up to the next largest convenient size, packing the remaining spaces with dummy data if necessary. At the cost of a small amount of additional disk usage, the code can become much more compact and efficient. Alternatively, UNIX truncation commands could be used to trim the excess if required.

It is also possible in MPL to have direct control over the placement of the data on the processor array during I/O. For example, each processor in the array can maintain its own file pointer independent of the others and can read the block of data beginning at its pointer instead of accepting the default. This can be useful is keeping continuous blocks near each other in the XNET—say, for block-type matrix manipulations.

An important capability offered by the MP-1 is the use of indirect addressing within each processor's local address space. For example, consider the following sequence of code:

```
plural int var_1, var_2, list[10];
     .
     .
var_1 = list[ var_2 ];
```

The semantics of this expression say that each processor in the array is to find the value in the local 10-long `list` array pointed to by `var_2` and assign this value to `var_1`. Since the values of `var_2` will vary from processor to processor, each processor will be looking into potentially different address locations. The MP-1 supports this capability directly. Other SIMD machines would have to execute a loop:

```
for( i=0; i<10; i++ )
if( var_2 == i ) var_1 = list[ var_2 ];
```

The "if" statement acts as a mask; in each loop iteration only those processors are activated whose value of `var_2` agrees with the current value of `i`. The MP-1 has addressing arithmetic at each processor node and so can execute the statement without resorting to such a loop.

A capability offered by some SIMD languages, but not supported by MPL, is the notion of *virtual processors*. The idea is that some data arrays are larger than the physical number of processors in the machine (scores was such an array in our example). Despite this physical limitation, we would like to allow the programmer to pretend that the machine is large enough to assign one processor to each array element. The compiler and run-time system are responsible for inserting the necessary loops, hidden from the user, to create this illusion. Consider, for example, how easy output was on the histogram and percentile arrays, where we knew that each element had its own processor. The arithmetic using **`nproc`** and **`iproc`** was not necessary for those arrays, though it was for the much larger scores array. Similarly, the main loop at lines 37–52 could have been dispensed with. Conceptually, each processor would have only one value of the scores array so that the reduction operations could be performed directly instead of iteration by iteration. The effect is as if **`nproc`** is as large a value as we need to hold the entire data array, one per processor.

The single thread of control in MPL (and other SIMD languages) is an advantage sometimes overlooked by MIMD advocates. Since each line of code is executed one by one in order, just as in ordinary sequential code, the debugging task can be considerably simplified. Single-stepping the execution has a natural meaning, and the debugger can probe for data values in the array with knowledge that no processor has "run on ahead" of the others (a common event in MIMD-style programming with its multiple, independent, unsynchronized threads of control).

6.3 C* ON THE CONNECTION MACHINE

In this section, we will consider a solution to the sample problem using the C* parallel language from Thinking Machines Corporation. This language executes on Connection Machine systems, both SIMD (the CM-2) and DM-MIMD (the recently introduced CM-5). A brief overview of the language is followed by the detailed annotations for the solution to the sample problem. A final section takes up alternatives and considerations. The author wishes to thank members of the technical staff at Thinking Machines Corporation for their help in preparing the solution to the sample problem.

6.3.1 An Overview of C*

As with our discussion of MPL, we will consider how C* provides the four basic types of functionality needed for an SIMD array language: (1) distinguishing between scalar and parallel variables; (2) broadcast and reduction operations; (3)making portions of the processor array inactive; and (4) interprocessor communications. While other languages we have looked at provide functionality using calls to library routines, C* incorporates much of this functionality into its syntax. As we will see, this makes for compact, powerful, and elegant expressions.

First, parallel variables in C* are indicated using the **shape** key word. Every parallel variable has a **shape**, and there are operators for creating and manipulating **shape**s. A parallel variable (that is, one that has a **shape**) resides on the processor array. Conceptually, a **shape** is a Cartesian grid with dimensions specified by the programmer; hence, the array notation (using brackets) can be borrowed from standard C to reference elements in the parallel array. However, the brackets indicating the parallel array dimensions and their sizes are placed *before* the parallel variable rather than *after* it. Consider the following:

```
001>  shape [1000][1000]matrix_shape;
002>  float:matrix_shape  A1, A2;
003>  int:matrix_shape  J;
```

Line 001> declares a **shape**—matrix_shape—with two array dimensions, each with 1000 elements. Line 002> then declares two parallel variables whose

shape is matrix_shape and which hold floating point values. Conceptually, we imagine the arrays A1 and A2 spread across the processor array. In fact, the language encourages us to think of a one to one correspondence between processors and parallel array elements. Neither the physical number of processors, nor the explicit logical to physical assignment, enters into the syntax. This feature, called *virtual processors* in Thinking Machines parlance, is a powerful abstraction that relieves the programmer of much low-level detail. Similarly, line 003> declares a parallel variable whose **shape** is matrix_shape and which holds integer values. The three parallel variables—A1, A2, and J—all reside on the processor array.

It is possible to refer to specific elements of a parallel variable using the array coordinates in its **shape**. For example, if x is an ordinary scalar variable, the statement

```
004>    x = [236][815]A1;
```

assigns to x the value from the indicated element in the parallel array A1. Only the processor that holds this particular array element will participate in this statement. The prefix-array notation on parallel variables is key to interprocessor communications (discussed below). Also note that ordinary C is a proper subset of C*—scalar variables and arrays declared without the **shape** syntax are ordinary C constructs held in and operated on by the scalar unit.

More than one **shape** may be declared in a program, and many different parallel variables may be assigned to each **shape**. However, during any given stretch of code, a particular **shape** is distinguished as the **current shape**. The significance is that subroutines and system library functions are written (at compile time) to operate successfully on *any* **shape** but must be told *which* **shape** to use for any particular call (that is, the **shape** to use is determined dynamically at run time). The **current shape** is designated by the key word **with**, as in:

```
005>  with( matrix_shape )
006>  {
          BLOCK OF CODE
007>  }
```

The block of code between the brackets will use matrix_shape as the default **current shape**.

Second, broadcast and reduction operations are handled using typecasting and simple syntax extensions. Consider the following:

```
008>  shape [5000]shape_A;
009>  float:shape_A list_one, list_two;
010>  float x, maximum;

011>  with( shape_A )
012>  {
013>    maximum = >? list_one;
014>    list_two = (float:shape_A)x;
015>  }
```

Line 013> is an example of a *reduction* operation—in this instance, finding the *maximum* element in the `list_one` parallel array. Similar operators are available for minimum, sum, product, and logical operators. Notice that `maximum` is a scalar variable residing in the scalar unit, while `list_one` (since it has a **`shape`**) is a parallel variable residing on the processor array.

Line 014> is an example of a *broadcast* operation. The value of the scalar variable `x` is assigned to every element in the `list_two` parallel variable. As in C, there are type promotion rules in C* so that

```
016>  list_two = x;
```

would work just as well as line 014>. Finally, a statement like

```
017>  list_one = 2. * list_two – x;
```

doubles each element in the parallel variable `list_two`, subtracts the scalar value `x`, and assigns the result, element by element, to the parallel variable `list_one`. This is the classic SIMD array language syntax: The statement operates on *all* elements in the parallel variables concurrently. Not having to sequentialize this operation by explicitly writing the implied loop over the elements in the array is what makes array languages like C* so attractive.

Third, the C* language uses the key word **`where`** as the mechanism to render processors inactive. Consider, for example:

```
018>  shape [2000][2000]matrix_shape;
019>  float:matrix_shape  array_A;

020>  with( matrix_shape )
021>  {
022>     where( array_A < 0. )
023>     {
                BLOCK OF CODE

024>     }
025>  }
```

The block of code between the brackets at lines 023> and 024> will only be executed by processors whose local value of `array_A` is nonnegative—those for which the value of `array_A` is negative will be inactive. Like the ordinary C **`if`** statement, **`where`** can be accompanied by an **`else`**, causing the active and inactive sets to interchange. The key word **`everywhere`** is also available to temporarily make the entire array active. In the solution to the sample problem, this capability is not required.

In Thinking Machines parlance, the set of processors (or, more precisely, the locations in the **`shape`** grid) that are active at any given moment is called the *context.* Thus, the **`where`** construct is used to *set the context* for the array. Since **`where`** clauses can be nested and since called subroutines inherit context from the caller, keeping track of context is a potentially subtle affair. There are also interactions between context and the interprocessor communications facilities. Context is near the top of the list for potential logic errors during C* program debugging.

Fourth, C* provides very powerful and compact expressions for interprocessor communications using array syntax on parallel variables. We will only scratch the surface of this rich topic in the following discussion, which will concern relative addressing—that is, a processor naming a destination node relative to its own address in the processor array. Consider the following:

```
026>  shape [2000][2000]mat_shape;
027>  float:mat_shape  array_A, array_B;
028>  int:mat_shape  me0, me1;

029>  with( mat_shape )
030>  {
031>    me0 = pcoord(0);
032>    me1 = pcoord(1);
         .
         .
033>    [me1][me0]array_B = [me0][me1]array_A;
         .
034>  }
```

The reserved function **`pcoord`** tells each processor its coordinates in the **`current shape`**. Line 033>, for example, has the effect of taking the transpose of the matrix held in `array_A` and placing it in `array_B`. This will involve interprocessor communications, since data will flow from one place in the **`shape`** to another. Each of the following statements would have the same effect as line 033> :

```
035>  [me1][me0]array_B = array_A;

036>  array_B = [me1][me0]array_A;
```

The fact that statements 035> and 033> are equivalent shows that the ordering of **pcoord(i)** is from left to right through the **shape** dimensions.

Statement 035> is an example of a **get** statement: Go off to another processor, **get** the value it holds, and return it to me. Consider, for example, the statement

```
037>  array_A += [me0+1][me1+2]array_A;
```

Each processor obtains the value of the processor "one up and two to the right" and adds it to its own current value. The programmer can also control what is to happen at the edges of the **shape** grid—for example, wraparound, 0-borders, etc.

Up to this point, our examples illustrate the use of general communications—the *router*, in Thinking Machines parlance. There is another type of communications (the CM equivalent of the MasPar XNET) that is much more efficient than the router when it can be used. For example, line 037> could also have been accomplished by:

```
038>  array_A += [.+1][.+2]array_A;
```

Here, the "**.+1**" is shorthand for "**pcoord(0) + 1**," and ".+2" is shorthand for "**pcoord(1) + 2.**" Notice how "**.**" adopts the sense of the array dimension where it is used. This type of relative addressing within the **shape** is called *grid communications* in Thinking Machines parlance. Grid communications are very efficient because the data layout on the processor array is chosen so as to optimize these patterns. Even here, however, the situation is more complex than appears on the surface. Using virtual processors, some of the data elements in the parallel variable will share the same physical processor. Clearly, interprocessor communications that can be accomplished without leaving the physical processor can be completed with the least overhead. By using knowledge of the underlying physical architecture, a clever programmer can arrange data so as to stay on-chip as often as possible. The compiler, having no a priori knowledge of the actual communications patterns required in a particular instance, can only make its best guess at what will be efficient.

One important feature to observe in C* is that the programmer need not deal directly with the physical number of processors. In effect, the programmer is allowed to assume an unlimited number of processors—as large as the array suitable for the problem at hand. The terminology *virtual processors* is used to refer to this capability. It is the job of the compiler and the run-time system to map the logical data array onto the physical processor array. All of the functionality—broadcast and reduction operations, interprocessor communications, library routines, context, etc.—is made to work correctly on parallel variables (with **shape**) of any dimension and size, regardless of the physical number of processors available.

The solution to the sample problem illustrates many of the features of C* described above. It also illustrates the parallel file system. The large scores array is decoupled from the smaller data arrays and is placed in a separate file for rapid access. Other things to notice as we proceed through the detailed code are:

- the single thread of control characteristic of classic SIMD programming
- use of ordinary scalar variables and operations
- use of **shape** to declare parallel variables
- use of virtual processors, so that the actual physical size of the processor array is not known or used during the solution
- how virtual processors are completely integrated into all aspects of system operation: I/O, broadcast and reduction operations, interprocessor communications, etc.
- use of both parallel and scalar I/O functionality
- the elegant use of indirect **shape** array syntax to accomplish the histogram computation
- efficient parallelization of the summation prefix computation using the **scan** parallel prefix subroutine

Finally, we note that the sample solution as presented is specific to the CM-5. The CM-2 requires that the size of the dimensions for a **shape** must be a power of 2—2,048, 4,096, etc. The programmer is responsible for choosing an allowed dimension that is at least as large as the actual array size being used. Since the arrays can be allocated at run time, this is usually not burdensome, and the code can adjust for arrays whose size is not known until the code is executed.

6.3.2 Annotations

lines 3–5: The CM header files.

line 6: A single thread of control, in the classic SIMD style.

lines 7–12: These are scalar variables that carry over from the sample problem.

lines 13–14: The calculation of the histogram and percentile arrays will take place on the processor array, but the output of the data will be from the scalar unit. This is the space to hold the data when it moves *from* the processor array *to* the scalar unit prior to output; hence, the name change. Note that space for the scores, histogram, and percentile arrays will be allocated dynamically when needed (lines 37–39 below).

lines 15–16: In this solution, we will assume that the large scores array is held in a parallel file for very high-performance I/O to the processor array. Thus, there are two files involved: the file (termed the configuration file) that holds the number of scores and to which scalar I/O will be directed and the parallel file from which the scores array will be read and to which the scaled scores array will be written. These two variables hold the data (name and file descriptor) for the parallel file.

lines 17–23: The user is prompted for the file name of the file that holds the number of scores. All I/O to this file will be performed by the scalar unit. Terminal I/O is handled as usual by the scalar unit.

lines 24–30: The user is prompted for the name of the parallel file that holds the scores array. The CM parallel file service library is used to open the file. I/O to this file will be at full parallel I/O rates.

lines 31–32: The number of scores is read in from the scalar configuration file.

line 33: We guard this section of code with a test to ensure that there are data in the parallel file to process. This test ends at line 68.

lines 35–36: Recall that parallel variables residing on the processor array are declared using a **shape**. The **shape** indicates the number of dimensions and the size along each dimension. In our case, there are two **shape**s of interest: first, the scores array, which is treated as a one-dimensional array with length `num_scores`, and, second, the percentile and histogram arrays, which are also treated as one-dimensional arrays but with length 1601. These two lines of code specify and give names to the **shape**s for these arrays. The space for the arrays is allocated when the parallel variables themselves are declared, in lines 37–39 below. This nicely decouples the **shape** of the parallel variable from its data type and storage requirements.

Notice that the sizes of the **shape**s do not need to match the physical number of processors in the processor array. This is the "virtual processor" feature of C*. The programmer can write code, in effect, assuming as large a processor array as necessary to handle the data arrays being manipulated. As noted above, if this code were intended for execution on the CM-2, the array dimensions would have to be powers of 2—presumably chosen large enough to hold the desired array size.

lines 37–39: Three parallel variables are declared, and space is allocated. The variable `scores` is declared using the `scores_shape` **`shape`** specified at line 35. The `histogram` and `percentile` variables are declared using the `hist_shape` **`shape`** specified at line 36. These declarations replace the static declarations and `malloc` from the sample problem code. The variables will last as long as the block in which they reside—that is, until line 69. This can be important in SIMD machines where (at least conceptually) each processor in the large processor array has a (relatively) small amount of memory. Managing the memory efficiently can be a significant aspect of SIMD-style programming. The approach taken here allocates not permanently at the beginning but dynamically only when needed.

line 40: The reserved word **`with`** is used to set the *current shape*. For example, subroutines are typically written to operate on data structures whose **`shape`** is not known until run time. Variables can be declared in the subroutine using the **`current shape`**; the user can then call the subroutine with whatever parallel variables are appropriate to the application. The brackets at lines 41 and 53 enclose a code region in which the **`current shape`** is `scores_shape`, declared at line 37.

line 42: An optimized data read operation from the parallel file that holds the scores array. The **`shape`** of the `scores` parallel variable is used at run time to distribute the data. Even if there are not as many physical processors as there are data elements in the shape, the system will take care of distributing the data across the processor array in a reasonable manner; the user is not responsible for explicit data partitioning.

line 43: A global minimum operation on the scores array, storing the result in the scalar variable `min_scores`. The mixture of parallel and scalar variables indicates that a reduction operation is involved.

line 44: Similarly, a global maximum operation on the scores array.

lines 45–46: Two global sums of the scores array. Note the explicit typecasting to promote the integer variables to `doubles` for the summation. Again, the results are stored in scalar variables located at the scalar processor.

line 47: This single line of code accomplishes the histogram calculation. Each `scores` value is used as the address of a processor holding the histogram array. The effect of this line of code is to increment each processor by 1 exactly as many times as its associated value appears in the scores array. Internally, a **`send_with_add`** operation is occurring. Each (virtual) processor, in effect, examines its value of `scores` and sends a "1" to the processor with the corresponding address (which, in turn, accumulates the values as they arrive).

The use of C-like array addressing, but using the **shape** brackets that precede the parallel variable, is the ordinary way of referring to data in *another* processor's address space. Reserved words are available to refer to one's own address and, hence (with arithmetic), to processors at relative addresses. See Section 6.2.1 for a more complete discussion of this syntax.

lines 48–49: Standard C operations on scalar variables performed in the scalar unit.

line 50: Classic SIMD array syntax. The variable `scores` is a parallel variable. This line of code operates on all the elements of `scores` in parallel, concurrently. Note the explicit typecasting. The scalar variable `average` is truncated and then *broadcast* to all the processors in the array for use on their local `scores` values. In this case, the mixture of parallel and scalar variables resulted in a broadcast operation.

line 51: An optimized parallel write back to the parallel data file. It was not necessary to seek to the end, since the file pointer was already there as a result of the read operation at line 42. In the sample problem, this was the last operation to be performed. In this solution, we have two separate files, and it makes sense to go ahead and complete operations on the parallel file at this point.

line 52: Close the parallel file.

line 54: Establish the **current shape** as `hist_shape`. This will extend to line 61.

line 56: A new parallel variable is declared, and space is allocated. It will remain allocated until line 61.

line 57: The **scan** operator has long been the standard prefix operator on Connection Machine systems. A number of variations of **scan** are supported—hence, the various arguments to the call. In this case, a summation prefix is being performed on the histogram array and is stored in the just-declared `prefix_hist` parallel variable. Other prefix options include logicals, multiplication, segmenting the **scan** (that is, setting barriers in the array at which the prefix starts over), direction (top to bottom instead of bottom to top), etc. On the original CM-1 and CM-2, both of which had an SIMD hardware architecture, **scan** was among the most powerful and frequently used operators. On the CM-5, which has a DM-MIMD hardware architecture, other alternatives may be preferred from a performance standpoint. The C* language, however, makes no distinction regarding the hardware platform.

line 58: The `prefix_hist` array is scaled and stored to the percentile array—again, classic SIMD array syntax in which all the elements in the parallel variables are acted on concurrently.

lines 59–60: The parallel variables `percentile` and `histogram` are moved *from* the processor array *to* the scalar unit prior to output. After these lines of code, the scalar arrays `histogram_buff` and `percentile_buf`, in the scalar unit, hold the correct values of the histogram and percentile, respectively. At this point, all the parallel processing on the processor array is complete.

lines 62–67: Standard, sequential C code, executed on scalar variables in the scalar unit. The results are being written out to the scalar configuration file.

line 68: Closing the "if" test opened at line 33. Again, standard sequential scalar code.

lines 69–71: Standard scalar code. Close the file and exit.

6.3.3 Alternatives and Considerations

The C* language was originally developed for the CM-2, which has a classic SIMD hardware architecture. It has since been ported to the current CM-5, which has a DM-MIMD hardware architecture. This is the best example we have seen so far of how the software programming paradigm is truly independent of the underlying hardware. As we saw in Chapter 5, a message-passing paradigm is the closest "natural" fit to a DM-MIMD machine, but we also saw the associated difficulties in data decomposition and synchronization. The C* language (such as FORTRAN 90 and HPF) is an array language that can execute on a variety of hardware architectures.

The perceptive reader may wonder, for example, how the role of "scalar unit" is implemented in a DM-MIMD machine or how such highly synchronized activities as global broadcasts and reductions can be efficiently implemented. The CM-5 has included some additional hardware capabilities (including controllers and a low-latency network connecting each controller to its assigned processors) to improve the efficiency of these operations. Even so, many of the operations (**`scan`** is a good example) that are extremely efficient and optimized for the CM-2 may not be the most efficient choice on the CM-5. Similarly, the CM-5 does a number of things that are not easily (if at all) expressible in the array syntax of C*. The bottom line is that, even using the same language C* in each case, efficient code written for an SIMD architecture (such as the CM-2) might very well be different from the code written for a DM-MIMD machine (such as the CM-5). A standard language only solves *part* of the problem; efficient algorithms must adapt to the strengths and weaknesses of the underlying target hardware.

The CM-5 also supports a standard message-passing library. The solution to the sample problem using this library would look nothing like the C* version but would more closely resemble the solutions in Chapter 5. Would the message-passing solution be more efficient than the C* solution? Perhaps, but the amount of improvement will be highly problem-specific and must also be balanced against overall ease of programming. The power and elegance of statements such as `043> – 047>` in the sample solution may be worth a bit of performance overhead.

Summary of Chapter 6

The expressive power of the languages that provide *operators* on *large arrays* of data has been the major focus of this chapter. While the various dialects of FORTRAN remain the most commonly used approach (certainly in the scientific and technical communities), we have seen in this chapter two C-based languages that effectively use array syntax. We observed the close relationship between this approach (often called *data parallel* programming) and an underlying SIMD hardware architecture. This relationship is explicit in the case of the MPL language from MasPar (the MP-1 is an SIMD machine). However, C* on the CM-5 shows that array syntax also maps well onto distributed memory MIMD machines (at least to ones such as the CM-5 that have a very rapid synchronization mechanism).

7

Linda

The fourth paradigm to be considered is Linda. The Linda environment for parallel applications was developed and popularized by David Gelernter, a professor at Yale University. It is remarkably simple and flexible and has been successfully hosted on a variety of platforms, including both shared memory and distributed memory MIMD machines. Besides its intrinsic interest, it is included here because it is an example of a software package that enables the use of a network of workstations as a single parallel "computing device."

There is increasing commercial interest in such a capability. As microprocessors continue along their extraordinary performance growth curve through the 1990s, an LAN of workstations can comprise, in aggregate, hundreds of MFLOPs (or more) of computing power. In many shops, these processors sit idle during off-hours, and production jobs are routinely shipped off to the computing center for processing. The idea is that these unused cycles could be put to work, thereby off-loading some of the work from the mainframes and perhaps even improving job turnaround time and accessiblity of resulting data. In addition, many shops would prefer increased autonomy and decreased dependence on centralized facilities—a major subtheme of open systems architectures.

To make this work, however, software is required that allows the programmer to treat the distributed workstations as a single entity. In particular, processes must be created and executed on the various workstations, and these processes must communicate and coordinate. The LAN provides the physical mechanism for such coordination, but the programming language should provide an easily understood and flexible interface to those facilities, shielding the programmer as much as possible from the low-level implementation details. It is this use of Linda that will be of particular interest in this chapter.

We will begin with a brief overview and primer in Section 7.1. Next, in Section 7.2, the example problem as reworked in Linda will be presented and discussed. Finally, in Section 7.3, we present a discussion of some of the alternative approaches available and the practical considerations surrounding their use.

7.1 A LINDA PRIMER

Conceptually, the idea underlying Linda is a *shared bulletin board.* This is illustrated in Figure 7-1.

Linda comprises a small collection of routines that permit independently executing processes to communicate with each other using the bulletin board. By incorporating these routines—as we shall see, they are just function calls in C—a process can post messages to the bulletin board, retrieve messages and data from the bulletin board, and cause the execution of new processes. The implementation details are hidden from the programmer, who simply uses the routines as a facility for coordinating work among many concurrently running processes.

In Linda, messages are called *tuples,* and the bulletin board is often referred to as *tuple space.* A tuple is a list of values—constants or variables—whose first entry is a character string that serves as the *identifier* for the tuple. The pro-

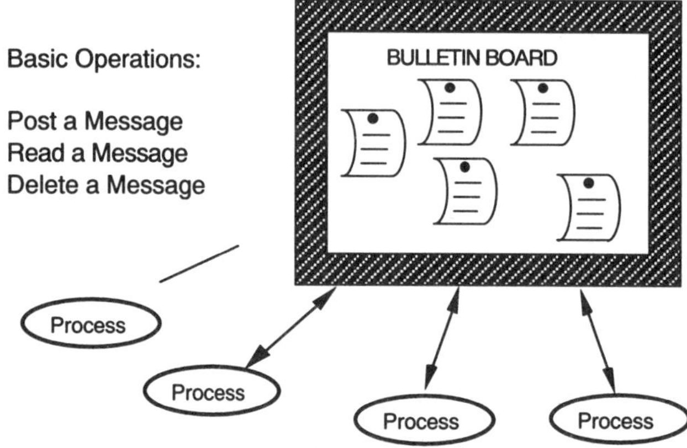

Figure 7.1. The basic operations in Linda

grammer creates the identifier and uses it to select which messages currently on the bulletin board are of interest. For example, suppose a subroutine calculates the volume of a box given its `width`, `length`, and `height`. It might go to the bulletin board looking for a tuple with the identifier `Dimensions` in order to obtain the values to do the calculation. Such a tuple might look like

```
("Dimensions",  2.4,  3.7,  1.9 )
```

The Linda routine that posts a tuple to the bulletin board is called **`out`**. For example, the line of code

```
out("Dimensions", 2.4,  3.7,  1.9 )
```

causes the tuple to the posted to the bulletin board. Once the tuple is on the bulletin board, it can be referenced by other routines—for example, a routine to calculate the volume of the box or a routine to calculate its area.

There are two routines available to read messages from the bulletin board: **`in`** and **`rd`**. The only difference between them is that **`in`** also has the side effect of deleting the message from the bulletin board, whereas **`rd`** merely copies the message, allowing it to remain on the bulletin board to be read by other processes. Both routines supply an identifier that is used by the Linda system to search for a matching tuple. The values in that tuple can then be assigned to local variables in the calling routine. Consider, for example, the line of code:

```
in("Dimensions",  ?width,  ?length,  ?height );
```

Here, `width`, `length`, and `height` are local variables in the calling subroutine. When this line of code is executed, the effect will be: (1) the new value of `width` will be `2.4`; (2) the new value of `length` will be `3.7`; (3) the new value of `height` will be `1.9`; and (4) the tuple will be deleted from the bulletin board. The action of the function **`rd`** is similar except that the final step (deletion of the message) is omitted. An example:

```
rd("Dimensions",  ?width,  ?length,  ?height );
```

The "**`?`**" attached to the variables indicates that the values in the matching tuple are to be assigned to these variables in the indicated order. Without the "**`?`**", a field is used as part of the matching criteria, such as the "`Dimensions`" identifier. For example, suppose there are several tuples on the bulletin board all with the same identifier "`Dimensions`," but only the tuple whose middle value is, say, `3.0` is desired. The call

```
in("Dimensions",  ?width,  3.0,  ?height );
```

will achieve this result.

Example: Consider the following code fragments from two processes, one called **main_program** and the other called **volume_calculator**.

```
code fragment from  main_program:

06>     out( "Dimensions",  2.7,  3.4,  3.6 );
07>     in(  "Volume",  ?volume  );
```

```
code fragment from  volume_calculator:

08>     in(  "Dimensions",  ?width,  ?length,  ?height );
09>     out( "Volume",  width * length * height );
```

Assuming that both processes are running independently and concurrently, the following describes what will occur. In line 06>, the process **main_program** posts the tuple

```
10>          ("Dimensions", 2.7, 3.4, 3.6 )
```

to the bulletin board. In line 08>, the process **volume_calculator** retrieves the tuple, deletes it, and assigns the values to its local variables `width`, `length`, and `height`. In line 09>, it then posts a new tuple to the bulletin board. This tuple looks like:

```
11>          ("Volume",  33.048 )  .
```

Finally, in step 07>, the process **main_program** retrieves this tuple from the bulletin board, assigns the value to its local variable `volume`, and deletes the message. The value of `volume` at the end of this process is 33.048. ■

The discerning reader will wonder how the correct order of these operations is assured. For example, what if the executing process **volume calculator** reaches line 08> in its processin *before* the **main_program** reaches line 06> in its. The answer is that both **in** and **rd** are *blocking* routines. The Linda system will search the bulletin board looking for a match with the identifier. If no match is found, *processing suspends* until a message appears on the bulletin board that *does* match the identifier. In the case above, if line 08> is reached before line 06>, no tuple will exist that has the `"Dimensions"` identifier, and **volume_calculator** will halt until such a tuple appears on the bulletin board (namely, until process **main_program** reaches line 06> and posts the message). This blocking feature of **in** and **rd** is used for synchronization—that is, ensuring that events occur in the proper order. This is entirely analogous to the blocking **nread** we encounterd in the message-passing example of Chapter 5. Note that the same phenomenon occurs between lines `07>` and `09>`: Line `07>` will not complete until the message produced by line `09>` has been posted.

The final operation that rounds out the Linda suite is **`eval`**. Its task is to cause the execution of a process and to post the results of that process to the bulletin board when it completes. An example might be:

```
12> eval("Area", cal_area( radius ) );
```

The effect of this line of code is as follows. First, `radius` is a local variable in the calling routine, and it is being passed to the function **`cal_area`**. This function is caused to execute, independently of the calling process and concurrently with it. This is very different from a normal subroutine call. In a subroutine call, control passes *from* the calling routine *to* the called routine; in effect, the calling routine suspends operation until the called routine completes and returns. In **`eval`**, on the other hand, we now have two distinct, parallel streams of execution where before there had been only one (the effect is similar to a `fork` call in UNIX). Indeed, the function in which this line of code exists will immediately continue on with its processing, and the results produced by **`cal_area`** will only be visible to the calling routine through the bulletin board.

When **`cal_area`** completes, a tuple is posted to the bulletin board. If the purpose of **`cal_area`** is to calculate the area of circle, and the value of `radius` is `2.0` when this line of code is executed, then the tuple would be:

```
13> ("Area",  12.56637 ).
```

Since this tuple only appears on the bulletin board *after* **`cal_area`** completes, its existence can be used to signal other processes that **`cal_area`** is done.

One natural programming style for Linda is for the progammer to conceive of independent, identical tasks that can concurrently process distinct portions of the underlying data and that use the bulletin board for communication and synchronization. Thus, instead of using shared data values (shared memory model) or process to process messages (message-passing model), Linda uses the bulletin board for communications. This is an SPMD (*S*ingle *P*rogram *M*ultiple *D*ata) approach, similar to those we have seen before. Multiple calls to **`eval`** with the same function name and different arguments have the effect of initiating the concurrent, independent execution of multiple copies of the function. We will see this technique in the sample problem.

7.2 THE SAMPLE PROBLEM IN LINDA

In this section, we will present a parallelized solution to the sample problem written in Linda. The author wishes to thank the technical staff at Scientific Computing Associates for help in preparing this solution. SCA has developed and markets a version of Linda that runs on networks of workstations, and the solution presented is based on this product.

In Section 7.2.1, we give a brief overview of the parallelization strategy and working assumptions about the operational environment. In Section 7.2.2, we present the detailed annotations to the solution code, which can be found in Appendix H.

7.2.1 An Overview of the Strategy

For this instance of the problem, we are assuming that Linda is running on a network of workstations—say, an EtherNet or FDDI LAN. We are assuming that the number of workstations available to participate in the solution is small—say, on the order of four to ten and definitely less than dozens. We are also assuming a shared network file system equally accessible to all the workstations.

The solution partitions the large file that contains the scores and gives to each workstation a part of this file to process. The large file is partitioned evenly (as evenly as possible) over the workstations, and each workstation pretends, for the moment, that it has the entire file, not just a part of it, to process. This allows reuse of a large amount of the original code and makes all the processes identical except for the data on which they are operating (a classic SPMD approach).

Once local values for max, min, sum, and histograms have been calculated on each workstation, the global values must be computed and distributed. The approach taken is a ring arrangement, and Figure 7-2 illustrates how a global minimum, for example, can be computed from the values held in five processors.

Each processor (except the first) does the same thing—read in from tuple space (using **`in`**) the best value so far obtained, compare this to its own local value, and then post the result to the bulletin board (using **`out`**). The correct *order* is ensured by attaching the processor ID to each posted message. By using the ID as part of the matching criteria, only one (and the *right* one) processor will extract data from the bulletin board at each stage. The others will be blocked, since the id field of the **`in`** operation they have initiated does not match the current tuple. This imposes a natural sequential order, as shown in Figure 7-2.

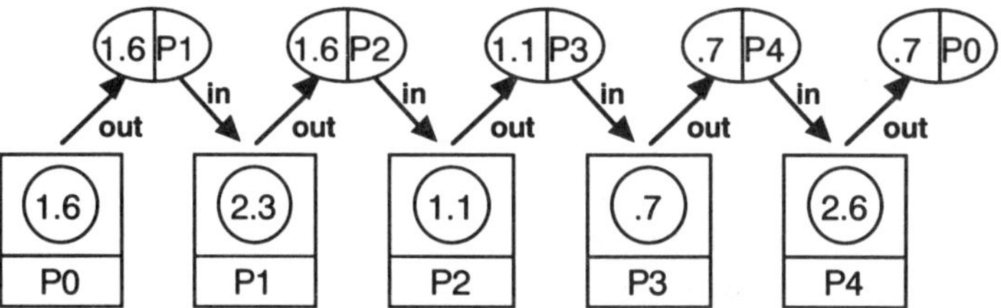

Figure 7.2 Example of computing a global minimum in a ring

While each of the reduction operations is logically independent, the solution code combines all of them—min, max, sum, sum of squares, and the histogram—into a single subroutine called **`merge`**.

For output, all the data are written from a single processor—processor 0, the master workstation that initiated the entire computation. The only difficulty is that the scaled scores array is still partitioned among the other workstations. These workstations post their locally held subarrays to the bulletin board (using **`out`**) and also attach their own ID's. Processor 0 can then match the ID's, one by one in order, pulling the subarrays off the bulletin board (using **`in`**) to ensure that the data are output to the file in the correct order.

Things to notice as we proceed through the detailed code are:

- how process ID's are used, in combination with the matching and blocking properties of **`rd`** and **`in`**, to ensure the proper execution sequence
- the SPMD nature of the solution—all the workstations are running *identical* versions of the **`compute/merge`** executables
- the code is *independent* of the actual number of workstations that may be available
- a large amount of the code from the sequential version can be reused

7.2.2 Annotations

lines 116–131: This is the main driver that gets everything started. It is executed on one of the workstations like an ordinary C program. Its top-level flow is:

- declare local variables (lines 116–119)
- obtain from Linda environment the number of processors (that is, workstations) available (lines 120–121)
- query the user for the file name containing the scores and post this to the bulletin board (lines 122–124)

- cause the main computational routine, **`compute,`** to execute on each of the other workstations (lines 125–118)
- cause **`compute`** to execute on itself and then exit (lines 129–131)

lines 120–121: The **standard UNIX `getenv()`**routine provides access to details about the hardware configuration—in this instance, the number of workstations available to take part in the computation. We will see the variable `nw` (= number of workers) used in the loop in lines 125–128. It is also sent to all the instances of **`compute`** that are created. Note that the actual number of processors is a *run-time variable.* The code is written in such a way that it will run successfully on any number of processors (although there are implementation decisions that make it most efficient when that number is small). Thus, this code will execute correctly, without recompilation, should the number of workstations on the LAN change. The only change required would be in the data structures referenced by **`getenv()`**.

line 124: This posts the file name to the bulletin board, under the tuple identifier "`file name.`" The **`compute`** routines running on each of the workstations will then copy (but not remove) this name (line 17). This is an example of how one routine can *broadcast* data to all the others, using the bulletin board.

lines 125–129: Comparing with line 4 in **`compute`**, we see that `(nw–1)` instances of compute are created and begin executing, one on each of the other workstations in the cluster. Each is told the value `nw` (= NW, the total number of workers in the cluster), and each is assigned a separate value of `i` (= ID, the unique instance ID for each copy of **`compute`**). It is therefore possible to refer to the separate, parallel instances of **`compute`** by their unique ID's. Note that the *user* has chosen this naming scheme. While this approach is typical of SPMD codes, there is nothing in Linda that requires it. The numbering is C-like, beginning with `0` and extending through `(nw–1)`. Also, note that a call to **`eval`** is *not* required to get **`compute`** running on the workstation executing **`main`**—a simple subroutine call suffices. This illustrates well the difference between the two: **`eval`** causes separate, parallel execution on a different processor; the subroutine call passes control downward on the calling processor.

lines 4–82: This is the workhorse, where the majority of the computation takes place. Separate, parallel instances of **`compute`** execute independently on each of the workstations, using the bulletin board to coordinate and communicate. The top-level flow is:

- declare local variables (lines 4–16)

- get the file name from tuple space, open the file, use ID and NW to compute which portion of the file to read in, and get the data (lines 17–30)
- calculate the local values of max, min, etc., using the portion of the data read in (lines 31–44)
- call **merge** to consolidate the local values into global values (line 45)
- calculate the average, the percentiles, and the portion of the scaled array locally held (lines 46–58)
- one processor does the output to the file, obtaining the portions of the scaled scores array from the other processors (lines 59–79)
- close file and return (lines 80–82)

line 4: The instances of **compute** are created in lines 125–128, each instance receiving a different value of ID ranging from `0` to `(nw-1)`. The variable `NW` holds the total number of workstations being used.

line 15: These are the new variables added to the program as the result of parallelization. Note that the meaning of `num_scores` has changed—in the original program, it was the total number of scores in the file; in this program, it is the number of scores processed *by this workstation*, and the variable `total_scores` holds the aggregate value. The other variables will be used in lines 24–28 to compute how many records to give to each workstation.

line 17: Find out the file name. This value was posted to tuple space by the main program in line 124. Since everybody needs this data, **rd** is used (so that the tuple is not deleted).

lines 18–22: Every process opens the file, not just one. In a shared memory/multitasking environment, a single "`open`" might suffice, but not here. Note that each process also closes the file (line 80). The **lexit(-1)** call is Linda-specific. Ordinarily, when a process executes as the result of an **eval** call, it returns a value that is posted in a tuple to the bulletin board. The use of **lexit** ensures that this occurs, even though the process terminated without completing. Replacing line 21 with the line

```
21>                return( -1 );
```

would have the same effect: It posts the tuple

```
("worker", -1 )
```

to the bulletin board. Should line 20 be executed, the stream would be routed back to the original processor and would appear on the user's screen, *not* on the screen of the workstation where the copy of **compute** is executed. This is convenient, since it ensures a single logical path to the initiating user's terminal irrespective of how many workstations are involved.

lines 24–28: The number of workstations, `NW`, may not divide evenly into the total number of records, `total_scores`. Thus, some workstations may receive one record more than the others. These lines make this calculation, determine the actual records (that is, starting record and number) to be read by each processor, and allocate the memory.

lines 29–30: These lines position the file pointer to the initial score value and read in the correct number of values. Note that because of the calculation in lines 24–28, each workstation will read in a different set of records beginning at different starting points in the file. This is the implementation of the basic parallelization strategy—give separate subsets of the data to each of the different processors.

lines 31–44: Identical to the sample problem code but operating only on the subset of data held by each workstation.

line 45: The function of **`merge`** will be discussed at greater length below. Note that **`merge`** is local to the **`compute`** executable, so that passing addesses makes sense (it *doesn't* make sense when moving data between workstations). Before **`merge`** is called, the variables and arrays (`min_scores`, `max_scores`, `sum_scores`, `sumsq_scores`, and `histogram`) have been separately computed in each workstation. When **`merge`** is complete, the values are no longer the local values but the true global values—for example, `min scores` is not the minimum of the scores in *one* workstation but the minimum of the scores across *all* the workstations. Further, every one of the workstations (that is, each instance of **`compare`**) will have the global values—it is as if *both* a combination *and* a broadcast have occurred. The variable for which this is needed is `sum_scores`. Each workstation must compute the `average` (using `sum_scores`, in line 46) and must then use `average` to scale its portion of the scores array (line 58).

lines 46–58: Identical to the sample problem code, except that `num_scores` (which now has the meaning of the number of scores held by each processor) is replaced by `total_scores` (which was read by each processor in line 23 and is the total number of scores in the entire array).

lines 59–79: This is where output occurs. The strategy is to have all the output done by one processor—processor 0, where the computation originated. The global values are held by all processors, including processor 0, and this part of the code is identical to the sample problem code. However, the scaled scores array (as modified in line 58) is still partitioned across the LAN; each workstation holds one subset of the scaled array corresponding to the portion it originally read in (lines 29 and 30). Thus, a kind of collation is required. Processor 0 will obtain, one after the other, the portions of the scaled array held by each processor and will write the data one by one to the file. This is accomplished in lines 70–79, which are discussed at greater length below.

lines 59–75: Only processor 0 will execute this part of the code.

lines 61–67: Identical to the sample problem code. The global values are appended to the file.

line 68: Processor 0 appends its own portion (the initial subset) of the scaled scores array to the file.

lines 70–74: For processor ID's from `1` through `(nw–1)`, processor 0 retrieves the corresponding subset of the scaled scores array from the bulletin board. These subarrays have been previously placed in tuple space by the workstations (line 78). By matching on ID (note that the variable `i` in the call to **`in`** is *not* preceded by a **`?`**), the correct order of removal is ensured: first `i` = `1`, next `i` = `2`, and so on. As each subset of records is consumed, it is written out to the file (line 73). Also notice that the variable `num_scores` is now doing double duty; it is altered with each call to **`in`** to reflect the number of items in the array being removed from tuple space. The mechanism (invisible to the programmer and part of the service provided by the Linda system) by which the data move *from* the other workstations *to* workstation 0 is message traffic over the LAN.

Also note that unlike ordinary C usage, arrays of data cannot be passed "by reference"—that is, by passing the *address* of the array's first element. This is because the address space of one processor has no meaning to another processor on the LAN. Passing of data in arrays, to and from the bulletin board, requires an actual copying of the data. This situation is an artifact of the assumed implementation. A shared memory implementation of Linda could use other, more efficient, means to pass large data arrays.

lines 76–79: This portion of code is executed by the processors other than processor 0. Each posts its portion of the scaled scores array to the bulletin board (using **`out`**). An ID tag is also included for use by processor 0 to ensure the correct order for consuming the data (line 72).

lines 80–82: Ordinarily, when a process exits as the result of a call to **`eval`**, a tuple is posted to the bulletin board. The **`eval`** call in line 117 is what initiated the various copies of **`compute`**, and we see that when **`compute`** exits, the tuple

```
("worker", 0)
```

will be placed into tuple space. Should it be needed, line 81 could be replaced by

```
81>    return( ID );
```

Then, the various tuples created by the multiple calls to **eval** would be distinguishable. For example, the processor with `ID = 2` would post the tuple

```
("worker", 2)
```

when it exits, and the calling process (if required) would have the information that the various executables it had created had completed.

lines 84–115: The **merge** routine combines the partial results held in each processor into global results. A ring structure is used (see Figure 7-2), although there are many other possible implementations.

line 84: The **merge** routine is a true subroutine to **compute** and is part of the same executable module and address space; hence, the passing of addresses in the calling sequence makes sense. These addresses are local to each processor and have no global significance across the cluster.

lines 85–87: When values are pulled off the bulletin board, local temporary storage must be provided to hold them. They can then be compared to the values computed on the subset of data processed by each copy of **compute**.

line 88: If there is only one processor, its local values are already the global ones.

lines 89–90: Compute one's successor in the ring. The last processor completes the ring by naming processor 0 as its successor.

lines 91–105: This portion of the code implements the reduction operations (see Figure 7-2). Each processor waits (since **in** is blocking) for its predecessor in the ring to update the variables and post the result to the bulletin board. It then removes the data, updates it, and posts the results back to the bulletin board to be consumed by its successor. Processor 0 gets things started by posting its own current values, which are then consumed by processor 1, etc. The blocking feature of **in** and the fact that the processors are matching on ID (note that the `next` field in line 108 is *not* preceded by a **?**) together ensure the proper sequence of **in**s and **out**s.

lines 91–94: Processor 0 starts the sequence. As noted at line 72 above, the histogram array must be physically copied when data move between processors across the LAN.

lines 95–105: Here is what the other processors do.

line 97: Get the current data from your predecessor, posted either in line 93 (if you are processor 1) or in line 104 (if you are any other processor). Read these data into temporary storage created for this purpose in lines 85–87.

lines 98–103: Compare locally held values against the current best (lines 98–99), or add the current sum into your local values (lines 100–103).

line 104: Post the updated values (computed in lines 98–103) back to the bulletin board, using the `next` field to signal your successor along the ring that it is ready for processing. Note that the last processor in the ring will have the complete results and posts them with `next = 0` (to be consumed by processor 0 in line 108 below).

lines 106–113: The data are now broadcast back to the full ring. Note that instead of the one by one approach used here, a technique such as that used in lines 124-127 (which gave a copy of the file name to each instance of **`compute`**) could also have been used. We could replace lines 108–113 by the single line:

```
108>  rd("hist", 0, ? *min, ? *max,
                    ? *s, ? *ss, ? histogram: );
```

omitting lines 109–112 entirely. The difficulty with this approach is that all the workstations would contend simultaneously for access to the same bulletin board entry held in a remote workstation on the LAN. While the Linda system will resolve this contention and complete the operation correctly, the sequence as provided ensures that each **`in`** operation does not contend with others for use of LAN bandwidth; that is, it imposes an orderly, sequential structure on access to the shared LAN resource.

lines 114–115: This returns control back to **`compute`** at the point where **`merge`** was called in line 45.

7.3 OBSERVATIONS AND CONSIDERATIONS

This section is a potpourri of comments of the "what if" variety. The attempt is to put the detailed problem solution into a larger context. What are some of the alternatives that are available but not illustrated by the example? What are the practical factors in an operational setting that might affect choice of algorithm? What would Linda look like on other types of architectures?

We begin by considering the I/O portion of the sample problem. The example problem is I/O bound. The operations of reading in the data from the file sequentially over the LAN and then writing the results back out over the LAN will dominate all other aspects of the run time. This is true both in the sequential version and in the Linda parallel version, because in both the access to the file is sequential—not more than one active process can access the file at one time. Instead of having, say, one long "read" of 2 million entries, we have (with, say, a five-processor cluster) five successive reads of 400,000 entries each—and no savings. Similarly, on output, the "write" operations are sequentialized.

The only way to improve I/O performance on this problem is to have multiple, distinct files open concurrently, with each file accessed by a separate processor. If the LAN is used for this purpose, however, little will be gained, since the LAN bandwidth is likely to have been the bottleneck in the first place. It is better for each workstation to have its own private disk and to decompose the data array into pieces—one subarray file per local disk. Each workstation could then access its own portion of the data independently of and concurrently with the others. Similarly, on output, each could write its portion of the scaled array back to the local file. On a real application, it is likely that this improvement alone would have the greatest overall impact on run time.

The sample solution chose not to parallelize the sum-prefix loop (lines 51–56) that computes the percentile array. This is entirely reasonable, both because the array size is so small (only 1601 entries) and because of the high overhead of communications on the LAN. In this operational setting, no performance advantage accrues to parallelizing this loop. Altered circumstances might make it appropriate.

Some features of the solution reflect the distributed memory nature of the architecture. For example, each workstation reads its own portion of the large array into its own private memory. In a shared memory implementation, a single "read" would place the array in shared memory, and the workers could simply be pointed to the portion of the array on which each is to work. Similarly, when the ring structure is utilized to perform the global reduction operations in **`merge`**, the passing of data from one instance of **`compute`** to another would proceed much more rapidly on an SMP, since the shared memory (rather than the LAN) could be used for communications. In general, the bulletin board operations will all proceed more rapidly on a shared memory architecture.

Conceptually, the bulletin board is a shared resource to which all processes have equal access. The concept more closely matches that of a shared memory hardware architecture than that of a distributed memory environment. A little thought will show that the "bulletin board" concept, on an LAN of workstations, is an abstraction that requires a fair amount of overhead to implement. When a process on one workstation posts a tuple using **out**, for example, how are the other workstations to know that this has occurred and that the tuple exists? Clearly, a protocol of data exchanges among the workstations is required. The user is shielded from the details of this protocol by the Linda abstraction, but it is easy to see that profligate use of the bulletin board in this environment will have performance impacts. The careful algorithm designer, therefore, will look for approaches that keep **in**s and **out**s to a minimum. This is the exact analogue, in a message-passing system, to keeping the message traffic to a minimum.

This, in turn, shows why parallel language standardization only gets you part of the way. The algorithmic approach will typically vary to reflect the performance realities of the underlying hardware architecture, and these algorithmic changes are not alleviated by language standards. A problem solved on a shared memory system and then again on a distributed memory system, can have quite different solutions on the two architectures despite the fact that standard Linda had been used in both cases.

Another related factor is that when an **in** or **rd** occurs for a tuple posted by a remote workstation, the data must be physically copied from the originator's address space to the consumer's address space, using the LAN as the data transfer mechanism. This means that there is a performance penalty for posting and consuming large data arrays. In the sample problem, the most significant impact of this occurs in lines 70–79, where the subarrays for output are first copied to processor 0's memory and then written out to the file. The data thus passes across the LAN twice—first, from processor K to processor 0 and then from processor 0 to the file. A more efficient approach is for each processor in turn (say, using the ring structure) to write its own subarray to the output file. A `seek` to end of file would position the file pointer correctly, and the data could be appended directly by each workstation rather than having to first go through processor 0.

All these matters become simpler (in the sense of having less performance impact) in a shared memory implementation, because the data transfer overheads are correspondingly reduced.

Summary of Chapter 7

The Linda environment provides a simple, flexible tool for parallelizing applications across an LAN of workstations. The shared bulletin board at the heart of the Linda abstraction shields the programmer from many low-level details and is a powerful mechanism for coordinating the various concurrent tasks. We have also seen some of the performance implications in I/O and in interprocessor communications over the LAN. Finally, a true shared memory architecture (SMP) to support the bulletin board abstraction has performance advantages in reduced communications overhead and flexible data sharing.

8

The Development Environment for Parallel Software

This chapter focuses on software tools that can assist in the development, debugging, testing, and optimization of parallel code for MPPs. Before looking at specifics, however, a general assessment is in order. All vendors of parallel systems provide a software development environment. In most cases, the tools were first written to assist in-house development efforts leading up to system release. This will give the reader the sense of the *type of programmer* (both in training and function) for which the tools were originally created. A typical profile for such a programmer would include: an excellent undergraduate (and often graduate) education in electrical engineering or one of the "hard" sciences, thorough familiarity with UNIX and C, comfort with assembly (and even microcoding) when necessary, and a good understanding of compilers and their inner workings.

> ***Example:*** Thinking Machines Corp. won the Gordon Bell award in 1990 by achieving a sustained rate of over 14 GFLOPs for a seismic code running on their CM-2. Guy Steele, who was as responsible as anyone at TMC for this accomplishment, characterized the approach they took: "We taught the compiler a few tricks." Here is an organization able and willing to rewrite a compiler as part of an optimization effort. The degree of surprise at such a feat (some readers will merely nod, others flinch) is your first pop-quiz regarding the suitability of your organization for the transition to MPP! ■

In short, the tool set provided by parallel vendors reflects its heritage: the needs and skills of a group attracted to parallel processing for the technical challenge and with the background and temperament to work "close to the hardware." Programmers coming from such a background will feel right at home. The tools have the "feel" of UNIX and are often straightforward extensions of well-known UNIX utilities (like **`db`** and **`prof`**). However, programmers coming to a parallel machine from the more user-friendly, bulletproof, pragmatic, and solution-oriented background characteristic of the commercial world may find things a bit austere. This cultural disconnect has not helped market acceptance of MPP technology.

The goal of this chapter is to provide an overview, focusing on what is *actually being provided* by vendors rather than on what is theoretically possible. An excellent source for additional information is hands-on demonstrations by the vendors. A manager will also want to give the intended programmers an initial cook's tour of the system, ensuring that the level of comfort (or discomfort) is tolerable and assessing the need for additional training. Most vendors provide training courses (a week is typical) that include hands-on experience with the software development support tools. It might even be useful to attend such a course as part of the hardware selection process *before* the decision to buy is made. Experience is the only way to know for sure how well the tools mesh with an organization's existing style. This chapter should provide at least a general sense of what to expect. The references give information about the extensive literature in this area of research [20–26].

8.1 COMPILERS

As we saw in Chapters 4 through 7, MPP vendors often provide access to the hardware capabilities of the machine via a library of routines optimized for common functions. On this view, the compiler is little more than a librarian, selecting and linking the building blocks indicated by the source code. To program the machine in this style requires familiarity with the library; the programmer picks and chooses from the library a sequence of highly optimized routines that together accomplish the desired task. The kinds of features we might ordinarily expect of a compiler/linker—register optimization, assembly listings, space versus speed optimization—are not an issue. The efficiency of the resulting code depends not on compiler features per se but on the appropriate choice and arrangement of hardware capabilities by the programmer using the library. The term *automatic parallelization* is not really applicable in this case; the programmer is involved but has a toolbox of optimized routines to perform commonly used functions.

A step closer to automation is the use of operations on large arrays typical of SIMD or vectorizing languages (such as C* or FORTRAN 90; see Chapter 6)—the so-called *data parallel* approach to parallel progamming. The ability of a language and its compiler to efficiently support such capabilities is widely viewed as essential to broad acceptance by programmers of MPP technology. We have already seen, in Chapter 6, the types of language syntax available to express these operations, which are most naturally mapped onto an SIMD hardware architecture. The problems facing a compiler that attempts to map such language features onto MIMD machines are considerable and differ sharply between the shared memory and the DM-MIMD cases. We'll look at each in turn.

On shared memory machines, the job is to break up the work into separate control streams, assigning to each a separate portion of the large array. Because the array is held in a *shared* memory space, the array need not be physically decomposed; however, the portion of the array assigned to each control must be computed—a function we might term *data decomposition.* In this case, automation means turning over to the compiler such decisions as the number of processes to create (spawn) and the details of how the array is to be partitioned among them. Working in conjuction with a run-time system, this decision may not be made until the actual time of execution (based, for example, on system loading) and, hence, may (and generally will) differ from run to run. The biggest potential difficulty is that the temporal order in which operations are executed can differ from one run to the next. For exact operations (logical and integer), this may not be a problem. For floating point it can be, since floating point arithmetic only approximates the ideal of associativity for addition and multiplication. As another example, if the operation is to terminate as soon as a "success" is found, changing the order of the events can change the point in the array at which processing stops. This indeterminacy in the execution arising from automatic decomposition can be a source of considerable difficulty in debugging, since the symptoms of embedded logic errors may only arise during particular configurations (e.g., number of processors) and, hence, can be difficult to recreate.

It is typical that symmetric multiprocessors make use of large caches local to each processor to improve performance (recall Figure 3-11 and the discussion of cache coherence in Section 3.5.2). One factor that can dramatically affect overall run time, and for which compiler assistance would be welcome, is in managing data decomposition so as to optimize cache hit rates. For example, if the stride (distance between successive data addresses in vector operations) is large, then the principle of data locality (on which cache performance relies) is violated, and poor performance results. In such a case, it is sometimes possible to rearrange the computation (for example, by decomposing the data structure in a different way) so as to circumvent this difficulty. Depending on the specifics of the problem, a compiler may or may not be able to detect the possibility of such a restructuring and provide it. As noted in Section 3.5.2, shared memory machines with large local caches are architecturally very similar to DM-MIMD machines. As a result, compiler techniques developed for one may be transferable to the other.

In some shared memory machines, special low-latency registers, called *switches*, are provided to reduce memory contention for semaphores on locks protecting shared variables. Access to these registers is typically made available to the programmer through a subroutine library, and the compiler may also make use of this library in implementing synchronized access (e.g., critical regions; see Chapter 4).

Much of the research in automatic parallelization over the past 15 years has focused on large arrays in a shared memory context. In part, this is due to the interest from the scientific and engineering communities, the largest consumers of supercomputing cycles. In part, it has to do with the closely allied need for vectorization. The FORTRAN DO loop over a large array is taken as the archetypical parallelizing entity. David Kuch and Ken Kennedy have been leaders in this field, and the technology and algorithms they developed have been incorporated in several compilers and code analysis tools. Another attempt in this direction was the Myrias machine. We saw in Chapter 4 the kind of compiler assistance provided by SMP vendors (in this case, Silicon Graphics). The tools are primarily intended for the relatively small number of processors characteristic of shared memory architectures.

Turning now to SIMD and DM-MIMD machines, the situation is quite different. It becomes the compiler's responsibility to physically decompose the single logical data structure and to distribute it across the processor array. This requires automatically selecting and inserting operators (for example) for global reduction, broadcast, and interprocessor communications. These capabilities are implemented using library functions, and automatic parallelization now refers to making the compiler responsible for deciding when and where to use the library and for inserting these calls as appropriate. The user may assist the compiler in this by providing hints or directives—perhaps even interactively; or, the compiler may make these decisions automatically. The algorithms used by the compiler to partition the data, assign it to processors in the array, and insert library functions can, therefore, substantially affect overall performance.

From a programmer's view, this compiler assistance can be a mixed blessing. Certainly, it can permit a programmer quickly to get a version of the code up and running. However, the algorithms used by the compiler to make these decisions are necessarily limited to a few general prototype cases. These may or may not be optimal for the intended use, and sooner or later questions will arise about how the logical to physical assignment was made and how to override that assignment in specific cases. Programmers may (rather, *will*) manipulate the compiler, twisting natural stuctures into bizarre forms to induce the compiler to select the data layout and library routines the programmer really wants. The result is that the advantage of the automatic compiler assist has been lost.

We see here the same tension—programming ease versus performance—discussed in Chapter 3. The compiler can usually do *something*. Except in the simplest cases, however, the programmer (using specific knowledge of the application) can usually do *more* but only at the expense of additional coding effort to partition the data sets and arrange optimal data transfer strategies.

Another compiler issue is unique to DM-MIMD machines. Recall that, typically, a DM-MIMD machine consists of a large number of stand-alone microprocessors, each running a program instance independently from other array nodes. Part of the compiler's job on such a machine is to generate object code that will execute on the node microprocessor—a task identical to that of an ordinary sequential compiler for such a microprocessor. The registers and instruction set of the microprocessor (typically a high-performance RISC architecture) are the target. The microprocessor compiler provided by the MPP vendor is often a third-party product with an instruction-generation back end customized to whatever microprocessor the MPP is using for its processors. Efficient code for the node microprocessor is critical to performance. We should also expect the same standard services (assembly listings, register optimizations, ability to link in macros and assembly routines, etc.) provided by any other microprocessor compiler.

When DM-MIMD vendors discuss their compilers, therefore, it is important to be clear about the difference between low-level microprocessor code generation, on the one hand, and top-level data and control decomposition and control, on the other. How has the vendor broken out these distinct functions, and how much responsibility (and control) is given to the programmer?

In a DM-MIMD machine that includes a heterogeneous mix of node processors, a separate compiler for each processor type will be required. Similarly, if the front end is explicitly used in the program, separate compilation for the host processor will be required. This is also an issue on systems (such as PVM [18, 19]) intended to run on a network (LAN) containing a heterogeneous mix of processors. A separate compilation for each target hardware platform is then required. Configuration management and naming conventions for this hodgepodge of load modules can be challenging (see Section 12.4).

8.2 DEBUGGING PARALLEL CODE

There are a number of coding errors unique to parallel machines, whose detection and resolution may require special debugging services. The next three sections describe these special features for each of the three major MPP programming paradigms.

First, however, it is worth noting that the debugging environment provided by MPP vendors is, generally speaking, quite good. It is possible to set breakpoints in running code, to single-step execution from the source code, and to interrogate values symbolically. All the features of a symbolic source-level debugger, such as **db**, can be expected. Separate windows can reference the source, the shell executing the debugger, and the contents of the several node processors. In an MIMD environment (SM or DM), the separate control streams can be single-stepped individually or in concert. In addition, the programmer can, if necessary, insert diagnostic terminal output that includes, for example, the process/processor id so that the progress of individul nodes can be interactively traced.

In a large processor array, of course, it is easy to become swamped with debugging output. One aspect of the art of debugging parallel code is to keep the output to a minimum and to locally monitor isolated node behavior symptomatic of the general problem. The tools, in other words, must be used with care. The data to do the debugging are available in a user-friendly interactive windows environment; it is up to the programmer to use the tool well. References [22] and [25] provide a good discussion of the issues involved in visually presenting the necessary information in a usable manner.

To say that the debugging tools are adequate, however, says nothing concerning the difficulty of the task. The question—*Is parallel code harder to debug than sequential code?*—must, in most instances, be answered affirmatively. While the difficulty can often be considerably reduced by using defensive coding practices, the number of types of errors, and their complexity, is increased in a parallel environment. Timing and synchronization errors are especially detrimental, since they may arise only sporadically and, hence, may be difficult to reproduce (that is, the order of operations in an MIMD parallel environment is often *nondeterministic*, so that errors that depend on a particular allowed but erroneous sequence will only occur some of the time—the occasions on which the erroneous ordering is actually achieved).

From programmers with experience on parallel machines, however, all these difficulties, daunting as they may be, are mild compared with the fact that the evidence of error in a parallel machine is so often highly *nonlocal*. By this, I mean that the effects of an error may only show up at a time and place, in program execution, quite distant from where the actual error occurred. A typical scenario might be:

- an error occurs in processor A
- data resulting from the error are sent, via interprocessor communications, to processor B
- Processor B correctly processes the erroneous data and sends it on (via interprocessor communications) to processor C
- Processor C then bombs—that is, the actual symptom of the error occurs in Processor C, at least two removes away from processor A where the actual mistake occurred

The displacement—temporal and spatial—of the symptom from its underlying cause is a potential source of great difficulty in debugging parallel code that is virtually unknown in the sequential world. From long experience, parallel programmers write extremely defensive code that permits such potentially lengthy causal sequences to be unraveled. There is, in fact, very little that a debugging tool can do to help in such a case; programmer experience and insight are required.

A more general problem arises due to the interaction between the debugger and compiler optimizations; that is, optimizing compilers are often free to restructure code (subject, for example, to the rules of logic governing mathematical operations) so as to make the resulting object module more efficient (faster runtime) without sacrificing accuracy (that is, the restructured code should, from a mathematical viewpoint, give the same answer as the original). The difficulty with such optimizations is that the connection between the source code (which is where the debugger runs) and the underlying object code may have been broken; that is, the source code suggests a certain sequence of operations that the compiler has foregone in order to achieve greater processing speed.

Such optimizations are already common in sequential codes (e.g., RISC microprocessors or vectorizing machines). The situation only becomes worse in the parallel case, particularly when the compiler has been allowed to make data partitioning and process creation decisions automatically. The whole notion of "single-stepping" through a section of code at the source level may make little sense in the restructured and optimized object code that has been created by the compiler.

8.2.1 SIMD Debuggers

The advantage of the SIMD environment is that, since there is only one control stream, the debugger need only keep track of a single symbol table. Scalar values, at the controller, fit easily into the ordinary sequential model. Values located out on the array can be interrogated by their array index; since the compiler has mapped the logical array onto the physical array, the information needed to reverse the mapping is available so that selected values can be retrieved from the array for interactive inspection.

There are two difficulties that are unique to the SIMD environment and for which special provision must be made in the debugger. The first is in interprocessor communications. On a *send* operation, for example, every node must name its associated destination node. The same code, executing on different nodes, must arrive at the correct answer in each case. Such relative addressing is easy in some cases (e.g., *my north neighbor* in a 2-D mesh—all nodes send one step *up*). It can be more complicated in other cases, where the destination node depends not only on the id of the source node but on the data it holds. Validating that all the nodes are calculating the correct address and sending the correct data can be difficult.

To help with this, it may be useful to have a test, performed locally at each node, to decide whether the addressing has been carried out correctly for that node. All nodes execute the test, and those that fail raise a flag. The debugger then interrogates the flagged nodes, presenting to the user local values for inspection. If, for example, a correct implementation should result in every node receiving exactly one message, a local message count could flag cases where 0 or 2+ messages were received.

A second source of error in SIMD implementations is context; that is, the set of processors that are awake at any moment. As we saw (Sections 3.2.1 and 6.1.1), value-dependent branches in the instruction stream result in some processors going to sleep while others remain awake. The complication is that context is inherited, so that subsequent nested tests may cause additional processors to be rendered temporarily inactive. In a subroutine call, for example, the subroutine inherits the context of the calling routine, may change it internally, and then resets it upon completion.

A common source of error is for the programmer to lose track of the current context. Incorrect assumptions are then made about active and inactive processors. To help in this, the debugger should be able to supply information about context at any point in the control flow. The depth of the stack that holds the current and inherited context and the status of the local copy of this stack held by each processor should be available for inspection. If a processor is not in its expected state (awake or asleep, respectively), the programmer has evidence that something is wrong. For experienced SIMD programmers, the *first* thing to check when a program goes south is the context.

A final source of error on SIMD machines, but one that the debugger can't help much with, concerns programmer misunderstanding of the uses of the library routines for standard operations. There may be several parameters, each controlling a different aspect of the operation. Care must be taken to set these parameters correctly, and reliance on documentation is not as good as running some sample test cases to verify expected behavior.

8.2.2 Message-Passing Debuggers

The simplicity of a single control stream in SIMD turns to potential anarchy in the MIMD environment. There are as many control streams as there are processors, and the debugger must provide the means to monitor and direct each of them.

For simplicity, let us assume that the SPMD programming model is in use, so that each processor in the array is running a copy of the single master source program. Then, a breakpoint set in the source code should apply to all the processors in the array and should amount to a global *sync* operation; all processors should come to that point and wait for further instructions. One useful capability is for the debugger to interrogate the full array, reporting any processors that have not reached the breakpoint. This can help in finding cases where a processor has taken an unexpected branch through the code and is now out of synchronization with the other processors in the array.

It is also helpful to single-step a single processor, observing its behavior in detail. This can reduce the amount of output debug data (watching one representative node is easier than watching 1,000 all at once). Frequently placed global sync points can ensure that the rest of the array does not run on ahead of the slowest one, so that in effect the single-stepping of one processor forces a similar slowing down across the entire array, as the other processors wait for the one being interrogated.

One of the most difficult bugs to find in an MIMD environment is the bug that depends on the order in which events occur. For many, many runs, no problem appears, because the time order of events matches the implicit but unstated programmer assumptions. Then, for whatever reason (say, data dependency), the messages arrive at their destination nodes in a different order, and an error appears.

Defensive coding (e.g., validating the address of the sender or the sequence number of the message) is the best way to avoid such bugs. The debugger can also help by keeping a log of message traffic at each node and by making available the status of the pending message buffer at any point in the processing flow; that is, the user is allowed to suspend processing flow and examine what messages are pending in the message buffer before continuing. This can help in tracking down logic errors based on an implicit assumption about the sequence of arrival of messages. Creative use of the type field in the message send and receive commands can also provide useful evidence (see Chapter 5). Finally, some errors arise because the amount of pending message traffic exceeds the allocated message buffer area. Correct sizing of the message buffer is part of the tuning of the program. By giving visibility into each of the node processors, the debugger can assist in this operation.

The typical development sequence on a DM-MIMD machine is to get the code running first on a single node and then gradually increase the number of nodes. The ability to simulate multiple nodes (such simulators are provided by some vendors) can also help, since expensive machine cycles are not wasted in the debugging stages of code development. Similarly, a small version of the machine (that is, a machine with only a small number of nodes) may be dedicated to program development, only transitioning development to the large array for final testing. It is the author's experience that some timing-dependent bugs only show up when the full array is executing on a realistic data set and on the full array.

8.2.3 Shared Memory Debuggers

Although the shared memory paradigm is in some ways the simplest, shared memory programs can be the most difficult to debug. The very fact of globally shared variables means that if the value of the variable ends up wrong, it is difficult to decide who is the culprit—*all* processes have access. It is similar to the problem of debugging a global data structure in sequential code (say, a FORTRAN COMMON block). Any routine referencing the common area *could be* responsible for errors that occur, and deciding which one *is* responsible can be a nightmare.

More troubling than global variables are synchronization problems. Even experienced programmers sometimes forget to enforce sequential access to a shared variable using a lock or semaphore. For 99 times in a row, the code works fine because the access pattern matches the programmer's implicit assumption. Then, on the hundredth time, the program goes south. Further, it is impossible to debug because on the next execution the program runs fine again! In nondeterministic situations such as this one, it is impossible (or, at least, very difficult) to systematically recreate the error. This is further complicated when automatic array parallelization (perhaps utilizing run-time system weighting factors) has been used. The actual number of processes and processors varies from run to run and can be affected by the data size and system loading. Reproducibility, the bedrock of any debugging effort, cannot be achieved.

One debugging capability that can help is a log of access patterns to a critical shared variable—say, a lock guarding a global summation variable. The programmer can examine the log, looking for anomalous or out of sequence behavior. (Of course, this won't help if the bug occurred because the lock was omitted in the first place.) Another debugging capability is the ability to interrogate and single-step each of the multiple logical processes independently. This is easier when the program has created them itself—the compiler is then in control, and the appropriate symbol tables can be deterministically referenced. When the creation of processes is dynamic and variable from run to run, the debugging task is much more difficult.

The difficulties mentioned here are, at least in part, a reason why many SMPs are used exclusively to run single processor user jobs. Spreading a job across multiple processors is still not an easy thing to do, even in a shared memory environment.

8.3 PROFILERS AND LOAD BALANCING

In Section 2.3.3, we described the difficulty facing the parallel programmer in ensuring that the total work load is evenly distributed across the processing array. Since the clock measuring the elapsed processing time continues to tick until the last processor is complete, an imbalanced load can result in many processors remaining idle until the last few stragglers finally cross the finish line. The same type of problem was also described in Section 3.3.2, where the notion of *synchronization points* was introduced (see Figure 3-7). Such points mark the transition, in a DM-MIMD machine, between local unsynchronized processing and a global coordinated activity. Again, the global activity cannot begin until all processors have reported in, and the fastest (that is, the earliest to complete) must wait idly until the slowest has completed.

One benefit of a profiler on an MPP is to graphically display processor behavior in such a way that imbalances of this sort can be readily detected. Ideally, the display should be interactive, allowing the programmer to watch the behavior of the array as it approaches synchronization points and to obtain measures of disparity between first, average, and latest arrivals. Two problems, however, make such a display difficult to produce. First, in a true MPP application with hundreds or thousands of processors, there is no easy way to fit so much data on a single screen. Second, in many cases, load imbalances occur at millisecond (or even microsecond) time scales. The fact that most of the processors are spending a high percentage of their time idling will be lost to a human observer as the machine sails through perhaps dozens of synchronization points in the blink of an eye.

The only realistic approach to this kind of performance monitoring is through a detailed log of processor activity—referencing the local clock on individual processors as key events (completion of local task, completion of synchronization, completion of global task, etc.) occur. The profiler can then, after the fact, analyze and display this log data at scales appropriate to the events being monitored.

A related and important measure concerns how much time the processor spends in communication—sending data to other processors and waiting for and receiving data from other processors. This time spent in interprocessor communications is generally part of the nonparallelizable part of a problem and, hence, contributes to reduced speed-up and loss of efficiency (see Section 2.2). One goal in parallel applications is to keep the number of data transfers as low as possible and to keep the amount of data transferred relatively high; in other words, a few long messages are preferred to many short ones. The reason is not hard to find: Each message has a fixed start-up overhead that must be paid no matter its length. A long message can amortize this overhead over a larger number of bytes. A performance monitor can track, at very fine time granularity, the number of message transfers and the actual, measured amount of time they consume.

A third area (besides load balancing and interprocessor communications) where a profiler is useful is in I/O operations. It can certainly happen that I/O dominates a complete end to end run on an MPP. Often, vendors report benchmark results in which timing begins *after* the data are in main memory and ends just *before* data are to be written out. Alternatively, they may create a benchmark where the data are generated internally, perhaps using a random number generator. By avoiding explicit attention to I/O, such benchmarks can make the machine appear much better than it really will be in a practical setting. Notice, for example, that MPPs have little or no advantage over other architectures when it comes to disk access. All architectures utilize essentially the same storage technologies, so that such critical parameters as access latency and data transfer rates are not likely to be cost or performance discriminators.

We will now consider the state of profiler software for each of the three major classes of parallel architecture. In the SIMD case, there is a single control stream, usually closely coupled to a UNIX front end. Thus, standard UNIX tools carry over naturally: Array operations appear to the profiler as one more type of timeable entity. Further, it is an easy matter for the programmer to instrument the code, pulling off and storing the global clock state at significant events.

More difficult for SIMD machines is a measure of how much of the machine is "asleep" as the application proceeds. Recall that data-dependent code branches can result in large numbers of processors waiting while the branch taken by only a few is executed. Collecting statistics on such inefficiencies can be problematic. Code must be inserted to count the number of active processors, and the execution of this code can interfere with timing analysis. Automated support for such analysis is generally not provided; the programmer is expected to augment the code as needed to obtain this information.

Turning next to DM-MIMD, there is good support for what is least important. Recall that a processing node in this architecture is indistinguishable, in most respects, from an ordinary microprocessor. Thus, all the standard software profiling tools to monitor performance at each individual node are readily available. It is easy to collect and display statistics on such matters as the amount of time spent in subroutines, the operating system, and major code segments. What can be much more useful, however, is measurement of the temporal disparity among processors reaching synchronization points, since this relates directly to load balancing. Similarly, a log of all message traffic—including count, size, type, and destination of messages in and out—can be useful in applications where data flow between processors is data dependent and unstructured (e.g., in event-driven simulations). In these and similar cases, the profiling software provided by the vendor may be of little use; the programmer must instrument his or her code and provide additional software to display and interpret the potentially voluminous results.

Even more difficult to monitor is *contention* in the interconnection network. For example, how much of experienced message delay is due to messages contending for the same switching link? An answer to this question requires a log of the switch behavior during critical periods, and typically such data are simply not available. The programmer must infer the existence of the problem based on experienced delays and knowledge of where communicating nodes reside in the network topology. If the logical to physical mapping has been performed by a compiler, or if the message patterns are unstructured and data dependent, the detection and circumvention of this source of inefficiency can be very difficult. A similar situation arises when it is desired to overlap communications with useful computation or in the overlap of multiple communications with each other (see, for example [3]). Careful exploitation of such potential sources of increased efficiency can dramatically improve overall performance, but it is difficult to measure and display such interactions directly.

Finally, the situation with SMPs is mixed. The *task* composed of multiple concurrent *threads* is the basic entity known to the operating system, and profilers are geared to this aspect of the process. Since, however, a truly parallel task can create many threads, and since their assignment to physical processors is load and priority dependent, the actual run-time behavior of an application can be both unpredictable and unrepeatable. In this context, it is hard to get useful information about the behavior of the *ensemble* of threads (as opposed to the easier problem of timing events *within a single thread*). On some SMPs, for example, the decomposition of a task into threads is performed at run time based on system loading and can vary from run to run. In such a case, the benefit of a profiler is greatly reduced.

The small number of processors typical of SMPs simplifies the collection and display of profile data. Most profilers for SMPs also provide some capability for detecting the occurrence of *hot spots*—global variables, often lock-protected, to which many processors demand frequent access. This can congest the bus (because of many repeated failures by several processors to open the lock), and the reduced bandwidth can slow down the processor that currently owns the lock—a nasty feedback loop. Hot spots were an unanticipated consequence of the SMP architecture, and over the years SMP vendors have provided various approaches to detecting and avoiding their effects.

8.4 OTHER TOOLS

In this section, we will consider a miscellany of additional tools intended to ease the effort of porting or developing parallel code. The most valuable, if successful, is *automatic parallelization*. We will consider the two ways in which this term is used and vanture an opinion on the likely utility of this technology. A second set of tools provides interactive quidance to the programmer on parallelizing strategies, particularly in an MIMD context. Finally, we'll consider the potential of object-oriented techniques in a parallel environment.

8.4.1 Automatic Parallelization

We have already observed (Section 1.2.1) that the lack of quality application software remains the greatest obstacle to widespread commercial acceptance of MPPs. It follows that there has been considerable interest, both in academe and in the MPP industry, in developing compiler and related approaches capable of transforming an existing sequential code into a version that can run efficiently on a parallel machine. It is felt, with some justice, that such a tool would be the MPP equivalent of the Midas touch—every application it touches turns to (parallel) gold, with little or no effort or risk on the part of the user. In the ultimate version of this daydream, the user need only submit his or her dusty deck, and the automatic parallelization software both detects opportunities for concurrency and generates the parallel version, either in modified source code or in straight binary.

Despite enormous economic incentives, automatic parallelization of existing sequential code remains a technological impossibility. We shall return to this topic at greater length in Chapter 11. Our purpose here is to briefly indicate why progress in this area has been so modest.

The case is clearest if the target hardware is an SIMD machine. Sequential codes go to great lengths to avoid exactly the kinds of operations on which an SIMD machine excels: searching and sorting long lists, especially if most of the entries are known (statistically) to be valueless. SIMD is best at finding a needle in a haystack—that is, at trying something simple on lots of cases and extracting the few that succeed. The sequential approach considers all those failures too high a price to pay for the few successes and goes to considerable lengths to take a clever, optimal path through the space. SIMD is extravagant —try everything and see what works. There is, thus, a fundamental difference in the underlying algorithmic approach, which is as much philosophic as it is systematic, and which precludes an automatic conversion. Indeed, it is hard enough to overcome years of training in sequential techniques for human programmers. Capturing and formalizing this process in code is, without exaggeration, simply not within the current capabilities of compiler technology.

The situation is somewhat brighter for DM-MIMD machines but not by much. The key tasks are: (1) partition the data across the processor array; (2) identify the independent tasks to be performed; and (3) identify the required data exchange, synchronization, and global operations and construct the appropriate message-passing constructs to implement them. However, the original author of the code had no reason to consider these categories or to structure the code in such a way as to make independence of operations apparent. What is often required is a reworking of the underlying data structures, making links that are deeply embedded in the code logic (and, hence, impossible for a compiler to extract) explicit in the arrangement and values of the fields themselves. Knowing that a DM-MIMD machine is the target, one can arrange the logic, structures, and operations in a suitable manner. Without such knowledge, such an arrangement would only arise by chance—which means it would not arise at all.

In an SMP setting, a considerable amount of progress has been made in the analysis of FORTRAN loops (see, for example [20]). As we noted in Section 8.1, it is possible to analyze dependencies in loops and to break out separate *tasks* and *threads* (here used in the technical sense of *schedulable processing entity*) to handle different portions of the array on which the loop operates. The underlying shared memory greatly aids this process. The dataare not *physically* partitioned; it is *logically* partitioned with different subsets allocated to different logical threads simply by calculating array indices. Thus, the data are not physically moved or redistributed across multiple independent memory banks (as is required for DM-MIMD machines). The basic control structure is preserved, and if the compiler cannot detect the opportunity for multiple tasking in a particular loop, the code will still execute as an ordinary sequential process.

The amount of performance improvement to be gotten from this level of analysis is modest—certainly not the factors of hundreds or thouands that are the goal of MPP. The number of separate tasks that may be created and scheduled for a given loop is typically on the order two to ten, the tasks are ephemeral, and the technique does not scale to MPP levels of parallelism. On the other hand, the user can treat these optimizations as "for free" and may not even be aware that parallelization is occurring. Best of all, no change at all to the existing code is required.

A more telling indictment of this type of automatic parallelization is that almost without exception considerable performance gains are possible by a programmer restructuring the code so as to explicitly take advantage of parallel opportunities missed by the compiler. We are not referring here to assembly language. Rather, the data structures and control flow can be rearranged in such a way that the compiler can now recognize parallel opportunities that had previously been hidden. The programmer must view things from the point of view of the compiler—that is, must know the types of structures the compiler can recognize and optimize—and must recast the code using this more limited set of coding conventions. This is exactly analogous to the process a programmer must go through when targeting an SIMD or DM-MIMD machine, and it was in this sense we claimed above that automatic parallelization is a "technological impossiblity."

The appeal of FORTRAN 90, for example, is that the array operations it provides match very closely to the types of vectorization and multitasking optimizations an SMP compiler can recognize and provide. "Speaking" FORTRAN 90 means speaking a dialect highly compatible with SMP compiler capabilities. Optimizing an SMP based on a well-constructed FORTRAN 90 code is, therefore, a simpler task than optimization based on poorly structured legacy code. It is this more difficult second task that really deserves the name "automatic parallelization," although vendors frequently use the term in the more limited and easily accomplished first sense.

8.4.2 Interactive Parallelization

Faced with legacy code not constructed with concurrency in mind, a compiler must often pass over parallel opportunities because of insufficient information regarding data-dependent logic. For example, the *programmer* may know (because he or she knows the data) that the successive loop iterations are independent, but the *compiler* has no access to this information and, hence, must assume the worst case and not parallelize. Or, the *programmer* may know that the matrix is to be used solely for matrix-vector multiplication and, hence, should be spread across the array row-wise. The *compiler* cannot know this and, therefore, must either make an assumption (and pay the communications overhead penalty if it is wrong) or simply not attempt to make the distribution at all.

If there were a way for the compiler to tell the programmer why it failed to parallelize and for the programmer to indicate that parallelism is, in fact, allowable, or that a certain data distribution is indicated, *then* the compiler could provide substantial additional "automatic" parallelization. This is the basic idea behind interactive parallelizing tools. The compiler (or code analyzer) provides information on where it failed to parallelize or where it was unable to make data placement decisions, and the programmer responds with hints, directives, or even source code restructuring to help the compiler out of its quandary. With the additional information, the compiler can then take on the drudgery of multitasking, inserting message-passing directives, etc.

These tools are typically initialized by a preprocessing step, which analyzes global code dependencies (e.g., subroutine calling tree, COMMON block inclusions). The programmer may then refer to this analysis in attempting to understand code behavior and the opportunities for parallelization. This can be especially useful when the code is unfamiliar (as will be appreciated by anyone who has attempted to understand the purpose and structure of a code consisting of more than a few hundred lines). The FORGE tool from Applied Parallel Research is typical of the interactive approach to assisted parallelization.

8.4.3 Object-Oriented Approaches

It has been observed for some time [27] that there is a natural affinity between *objects* in the object-oriented programming style and *schedulable processes* in MIMD machines; that is, the object is considered to be a combination of code and data that can be activated, as needed, by other objects—the program consists of specifying the interactions between the objects. For example, in a DM-MIMD machine, it seems natural to place each object on a processor in the array and to maintain a global look-up table of which processor holds which objects. As the objects interact, they send messages (using addresses found in the global look-up table), which cause execution of other objects. A programming style that replicates large numbers of objects of a given type is also attractive, since it limits the coding effort to specifying a few basic object types.

On an SMP, the translation is even easier. Objects become schedulable entities entered on the operating system task queue, making calls to other objects and accessing globally available tables and data structures.

The premier example of this approach is the Time Warp parallel event-driven simulation system, in which the software objects correspond directly to the elements of the system being modeled. Military units in a battlefield scenario are a well-known example. Reference [16] provides an excellent introduction to this technology.

There has been considerable research on extending these ideas to a complete parallel programming environment. However, this research has not been translated into supported commercially available products. In the author's opinion, this approach constitutes an attractive programming style, particularly in cases where the underlying data structures are irregular (as in many applications of commercial interest) and for which array manipulations are not appropriate.

Summary of Chapter 8

This chapter has provided a brief overview of the types and quality of software tools currently available to support porting and development of parallel codes. A major theme has been the ability (rather, the *in*ability) of current compiler technology to provide automatic parallelization of legacy sequential code. On the other hand, newly developed code using appropriate syntax (e.g., data parallel array syntax) can shift to the compiler much of the low-level decomposition and message-passing arithmetic with the concomitant danger of potential loss of efficiency. The difficulties of debugging parallel code (particularly indeterminacy, timing errors, and nonlocal effects) were stressed. Profiling, load balancing, and interactive code analysis were briefly discussed. Perhaps the most important message in this chapter is the need for an organization to compare the capabilities offered by these tools against the development environment in which they will be used. Serious disconnects are cause for concern and should be thought through *before* a transition to parallel hardware occurs.

9

Operating System Issues

This chapter will consider a number of operating system issues that are unique to MPPs and that can impact both the performance and usability of an MPP in an open systems environment. Sections address multiple users, virtual memory, scheduling, virtual processors, and I/O considerations, with a final section that ties together and summarizes the impacts for open systems.

The focus is on MPPs, which translates (in the basic architecture taxonomy of Figure 1-2) to SIMD and/or DM-MIMD. For completeness, we begin with a few comments on operating systems for symmetric multiprocessors. Shared memory SMPs have been in the mainstream of processing for some time, and their operating systems are natural outgrowths of the time-sharing operating systems of the early 1970s. Instead of a single processor to service the job queue (in a batch environment), there are several. Parallelism occurs by running multiple independent jobs, concurrently, on several processors.

Should a job wish to parallelize *internally* on an SMP (that is, multiple threads with some amount of shared memory space executing concurrently within a single task), the libraries to support this from source code piggyback on the standard multitasking capabilities already provided by the operating system. It is even possible to use a UNIX script as the parallelizing language, with UNIX *pipes* or *sockets* as the interprocess communications mechanism. The complete application can then be thought of as a number of concurrently executing UNIX processes, logically linked together by the top-level script that spawns and controls them. This programming style has been around for a long time and is a quite reasonable mechanism for parallelizing an application on an SMP, particularly for those already accustomed to UNIX systems programming.

Example: The author vividly recalls the moment when the parallel processing light dawned on an experienced UNIX systems programmer: "Oh, all you're doing is spawning processes. We've been doing that for years!" Indeed. ■

The parallel language constructs considered in Chapter 4 attempt to move many of these functions into the source code, shielding the programmer from the operating system details. The chief advantage of parallelizing from the source is the ability to use a logically shared address space and perhaps some reduction in swapping overhead through the use of lightweight threads. The point is that organizations that already have an SMP (and a systems programmer with a little initiative) can, perhaps, use their existing operating system capabilities to do effective coarse-grained parallel processing.

9.1 MULTIPLE USERS

In some environments, the MPP will be viewed as a single-purpose production engine, dedicated to one (or a few) compute-intensive jobs. The processor services one job at a time on its queue and has no interactive component—a true batch-oriented style. Further, the job stream is controlled by the ADP center. In the extreme version, a user fills out a form to request that a job be run and submits it to the ADP center, which then arranges for execution and delivery (in hard copy?) of the data output.

This is typical of some shops, but is antithetical to an open systems view. In an open system, the MPP is more likely to be viewed as a computing resource directly available to users over the LAN with no intervention (other than top-level account monitoring) by system control personnel. Users (perhaps in the form of department-level programming staff) develop, compile, and run their own codes on their own data, often in a highly interactive setting. In this operational environment, the ability of the MPP to dynamically service multiple users according to a fair resource allocation policy may well be critical to user acceptance and full utilization.

Figure 9-1 shows a typical configuration. The users gain access to the MPP via an LAN interface to a front end. The front end (typically a UNIX server) provides services for code development (compilers, debuggers, etc.) and also attempts to assign space on the MPP to users wishing to execute programs. Figure 9-2 shows an alternative configuration. Here, an I/O subsystem interfaces both to the LAN and directly to the mass storage device. The interactive connection software now resides directly on the user workstation, and the

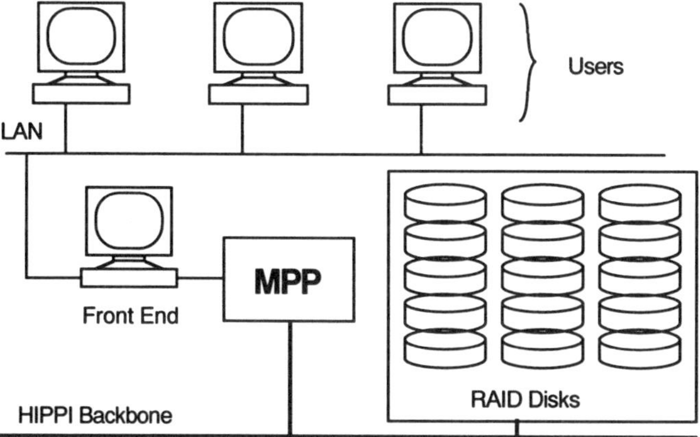

Figure 9-1. Typical MPP configuration in an open system

high speed of the I/O subsystem alleviates the potential congestion at the front end.

In an SIMD machine (see Figure 3-5), a *single* controller drives a large array of processors in slave-mode. The fact that there is a single controller limits the opportunities for sharing. Time-sharing (in the traditional sense of swap in/swap out) does not make any sense in this context, since not only the controller memory but also the memory in the array nodes would have to be separately managed and swapped. The inefficiencies in such a scheme have prevented SIMD vendors from supporting this type of sharing. On the other

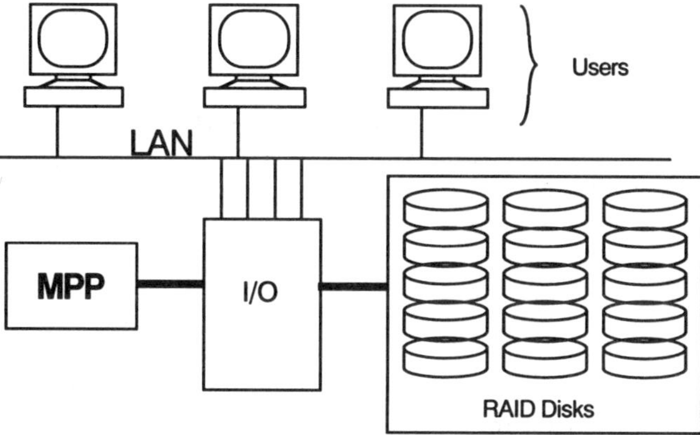

Figure 9-2. Use of an I/O subsystem

hand, some vendors support more than one controller and associate with each controller some fraction of the full array, ordinarily adjusting boundaries based on powers of two. For example, if four separate controllers are provided, then up to four separate user programs can be concurrently supported, each receiving one-fourth of the machine. Three users might be allocated, respectively, one-half, one-fourth, and one-fourth. A single large job could drive the complete array from a single controller. This form of *space-sharing* on an SIMD machine is illustrated in Figure 9-3.

In a UNIX environment, the SIMD MPP appears as a *device*, and the network allows the user (via remote log-in to the front end) to interact with the MPP. When multiple users are involved, the UNIX multitasking capabilities are then used to time-share the front end. Users may experience some degradation, since the front end is now a potential serial bottleneck. The high-speed HIPPI backbone, shown in Figure 9-1, supports high-bandwidth access to the mass storage devices. Running bulk I/O through the front end would *seriously degrade* performance. Similarly, a configuration such as the one shown in Figure 9-2 should be better able to support a large number of interactive users.

Turning now to DM-MIMD, it is possible, in theory, to partition the large array of processors into subarrays of sizes requested by the various users. Figure 9-4 shows a notional diagram of three users sharing a 24-node machine. One user has half the machine in a four-by-three configuration. Another user has been assigned three nodes in a one-by-three configuration. A third user has been assigned four nodes in a two-by-two configuration. There are five remaining unused nodes.

The reader will immediately sense some of the difficulties that can arise. We have shown the interconnection network as a two-diminsional mesh for simplicity. Suppose the next user wants four nodes (note that five are available) but needs them (based on his or her program logic) in a two-by-two or

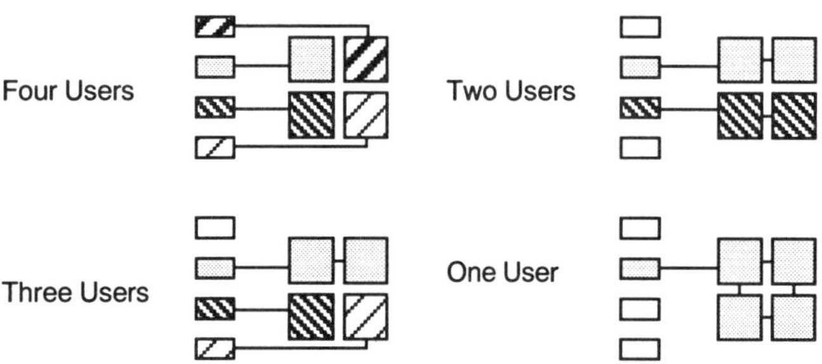

FIgure 9-3. Space-sharing in an SIMD machine

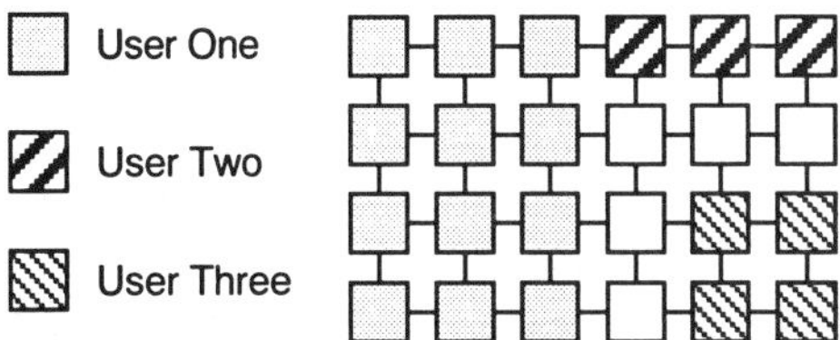

Figure 9-4. Space-sharing on a DM-MIMD

a four-by-one configuration. Even though enough nodes are available, the desired configuration is not, and the user must wait until one of the current users has finished. In more complex topologies, the same problems arise. For example, in a hypercube network topology, users will request subarrays in the configuration of hypercubes (of dimension less than the full dimension of the hardware). Only by deliberately keeping the underlying network topology invisible to the user can these potential problems be avoided. In such an approach, it would not matter where the nodes are in the network; they could be randomly scattered, as Figure 9-5 illustrates.

As we have seen, efficient code typically takes the network topology into account and, hence, requires that the underlying hardware be in a specific configuration. While it is possible to write programs so that the configuration is a run-time variable (that is, the same code works on a variety of, for example, hypercube dimensions or mesh sizes), the code will typically expect a specified configuration, not some randomly selected assortment of nodes with no spacial relationship in the underlying network topology.

Also note that in Figure 9-4, a given job uses only a well-contained subset of the network. One user need not access a portion of the network (that is, the links that connect the nodes together) that has been assigned to a different user. That is not true in Figure 9-5. Nodes assigned to, for example, User Two will need to use network links held by other users in order to communicate. This sharing can become visible to the other users in the form of

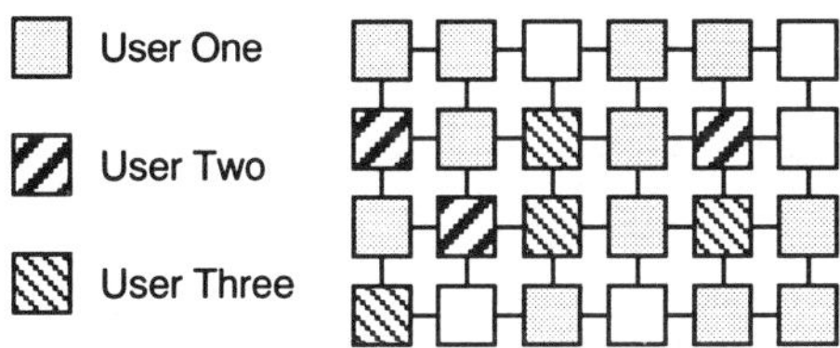

Figure 9-5. Space-sharing when the network topology does not matter

decreased performance; some of "their" bandwidth is being taken by another user. There are also security ramifications. Partitioning users from each other in the Figure 9-4 arrangement is potentially much simpler than in the Figure 9-5 arrangement. For example, we would not expect faulty code in one isolated subarray, which shares no resources with other assigned subarrays, to affect user jobs executing elsewhere in the machine.

It will be the operating system's responsibility to keep track of the current assignment of nodes, releasing nodes when a user's job is complete and making them available in the desired configurations as new user requests come in. It will also need to do accounting, if required, and may use a packing algorithm to optimally select from the available possibilities the node assignment that leaves the most options open for future requests. It may also take priority into account and will attempt to minimize fragmentation of the array.

9.2 VIRTUAL ADDRESS SPACES

Programmers and users of sequential processors and shared memory SMPs have come to expect the convenience of working with very large address spaces—spaces much larger than the physical memory in the machines. A combination of hardware and operating system software inserts a level of indirection between the logical address issued by the running code and the physical address where the referenced variable is held. This intermediate layer can detect when the referenced value is not currently in memory and can suspend processing until the variable has been accessed (from secondary storage). Statistically, codes have enough *locality of reference* so that the desired variable is already in memory most of the time. This permits the code to run (with some slight degradation) as if the physical memory were much larger than it really is. A caching scheme uses the same ideas. The cache is smaller, but faster, than main memory. Similarly, main memory is smaller, but faster, than secondary storage (see Figure 3-8).

The great advantage of virtual memory is that the user need not take the physical size of memory explicitly into account in designing the program. The virtual memory capability also meshes nicely with other goals of modern operating systems. For example, by monitoring all memory references (so as to detect those not currently in main memory), the virtual memory mechanism can enforce security and user separation capabilities. Multiple users on the machine are kept isolated by using the virtual memory mapping facilities to map each user's logical address space onto distinct and protected physical areas.

The use of virtual memory in MPPs is best characterized as theoretically possible but currently impractical. We will consider SIMD and DM-MIMD separately. For an SIMD machine, it is not clear exactly what virtual memory might mean. When the controller issues an address to the processor array, all processors are to fetch/store to a local instance of that address. If the address lies outside the physical address space of one node, it will lie outside the address space of all the nodes, and the controller could, and should, have known this. In other words, the controller should have performed an I/O operation before the address was issued to ensure the required data were already in physical memory. If one considers virtual memory as a way to relieve the user from having to perform I/O explicitly (that is, I/O operations are triggered, when necessary, as a side effect of ordinary memory addressing), then virtual memory in an SIMD machine just doesn't match with the basic capabilities and philosophy of the machine architecture.

As a result, keeping track of physical memory in SIMD machines remains an important aspect of programming them. This is particularly true when dynamic memory allocation is required (that is, when the size of physical memory required is not actually known until run time). It can also become an issue when auxiliary data structures, used by the compiler but invisible to the user, are employed. In the best of worlds, a quick order of magnitude estimate can be used to compare program storage with available memory—hopefully showing that the program fits with plenty of room to spare. However, in codes that begin to stress the available physical memory, more elaborate precautions (memory bookkeeping and warning messages) must be taken. We will return to this in Section 9.4.

Turning now to DM-MIMD machines, while virtual memory for the individual array processors is possible, there are many reasons why it should not be used. The most important is the likelihood of severe performance impact. For example, typical DM-MIMD processing begins by loading a copy of the object module (the machine-language version of the program) into each node. Since the SPMD programming model is used, the load module is identical for each processor, and a *broadcast* operation can be utilized to share the single I/O operation (retrieving the code from storage) across the entire array. In a virtual memory scheme, on the other hand, each processor would issue the first instruction of the program. The memory management unit (a separate one on each processor) would detect that the memory page holding the instruction is not yet in memory, and an I/O operation to retrieve the required page would be issued—a separate such operation for each processor in the array. The single I/O operation, shared via a broadcast, becomes a multitude of separate I/O requests. This "one becomes many" problem does not exist in a shared memory system, since replication of this sort (to multiple physical address spaces) is not required.

One suggested use for virtual memory capabilities in DM-MIMD machines is to use the addressing mechanism as the means for data transfer. The idea is that *all* memory locations are "mapped" onto the address space of each processor in the array. In effect, a processor can cause a message transaction to a remote processor just by issuing the address of the memory location held in that remote processor's memory. For a memory read, for example, the virtual memory hardware/OS facilities would (in this scheme): (1) detect that the memory reference is not local; (2) find (via a look-up table) the processor that holds the memory; (3) initiate message traffic to obtain the value; and (4) return it to the executing process. The effect is to turn the memory physically distributed across the array into a single large, shared address space. This concept, known (in an oxymoron of classic proportions) as *distributed shared memory* (DSM), is an attempt to avoid the programming difficulties of message passing by providing a single global shared address space. Its fatal weakness (as discussed in Section 3.5) is *nonuniformity* of memory references. References to memory locations held by remote processors can take orders of magnitude longer to complete than local references and, hence, can have grotesquely disabling levels of performance degradation. Reference [10] contains an excellent survey of the current state of research on DSMs. As might be imagined, the key issue is cache coherence strategies to ensure that local copies of the global address space are properly updated.

Since virtual memory is not available in a DM-MIMD context, the programmer must explicitly size and manage program memory in ways long obsolete in the sequential world. One significant impact is management of message buffers. Typically, messages are received into operating system spaces and then copied to the user area when the program reaches the appropriate receive operation. Similarly, when a message send command is issued by the user program, the data are typically copied from user space to operating system areas prior to physical transmission. The size and frequency of messages will dictate the appropriate size of buffer space needed to accommodate the traffic. Managing and sizing these buffer areas can be a significant aspect of debugging and optimization. This is a direct consequence of the absence of virtual memory capabilities.

To summarize, virtual memory (and its advantages) is not available for MPPs: This is due to fundamental architectural incompatibilty for SIMD machines and because inefficiencies arising from "one-becomes-many" and nonuniformity make implementations impractical for DM-MIMD machines. The only good thing that can be said in this regard is that MPPs are intended to have very large physical memories. More times than not, a programmer will have plenty of elbow room so that the limitations of physical memory will not be an issue.

9.3 SCHEDULING

Issues of scheduling and job priorities arise inevitably when a scarce resource is being shared among many users or for many tasks. In a time-sharing system, where jobs are allocated time slots on the CPU dynamically, one of the functions of the system manager is to set job priorities and the prioritization weighting scheme so as to maintain both fairness (as perceived by . . . ?) and overall throughput.

The most valuable resources on the machine are likely to be:

- CPU cycles
- main memory
- disk storage
- specialized I/O devices (frame buffers, plotters, etc.)

We'll deal with I/O in Section 9.5 and focus here on CPU cycles and associated main memory.

As we saw in Section 9.1, the most natural and widely available form of sharing in MPPs is space-sharing—allocating blocks (subarrays) of processors to different users. At any point, the machine may be servicing up to several users spread out across the machine, executing different jobs, and at various stages of completion. In addition, there may be other users on the queue waiting their turn on the machine. In an interactive environment, the latency on the queue may be a source of concern. Most of the time, users will not be pleased if they must frequently endure long waits before obtaining access to the machine. On the other hand, reduced waiting times almost certainly imply increased overhead, since rapid access means that resources are immediately available, which means (in turn) that they were not being used.

Another issue that arises in this environment is the single large job that requires the entire machine. Such a job may well be very high priority. Not infrequently, the goal of dramatically reducing run times on such a job (a very large sort, for example) initially motivates the acquisition of an MPP. In a prioritization scheme that waits until resources become available before a job is scheduled, one or two small jobs could conceivably prevent a more important larger job from gaining access. This problem is not faced by a virtual memory time-sharing system, since the physical size of the machine available at any instant is hidden behind the friendly abstraction of virtual memory.

A strategy for dealing with contention of this sort is *block* or *periods processing*. The idea is to turn space-sharing, at least for some portion of the day, into large block dedicated processing. For example, there may be, say, three large projects or jobs that can usefully consume the entire machine. Based on past experience, the required amount of run time for each job can be estimated, and blocks of dedicated time on the machine made available for each job. During a block of time, the entire machine, including its dedicated peripherals, is made available to a single user. At the end of this time, the current user is tidied up and moved off the hardware, and the next user can begin the next block of time. Mass storage devices with removable media may also help ensure both physical and logical isolation between successive users. While this type of scheduling has the disadvantage of "scheduled downtime"—that is, the intervals between successive users during which the switchover is made—the efficiencies of contention-free access to the complete machine can more than compensate.

In the author's experience, the management of such a scheme can be as simple as a weekly meeting between the system manager and the principal users to go over the major jobs to be run and to negotiate dedicated times for them. These times can be published, and the remaining time can then be made available for general access on a space-sharing basis. Such an approach can also simplify the accounting scheme (if machine time is billed), since billing the entire machine to a single user over a long block of time is considerably simpler than trying to subdivide the machine (some of which may not even be used) among a variety of users.

One of the side benefits of time-sharing is the ability to save the complete state of a process. This capability is required when the process is "swapped out" so that its state can later be restored when its turn comes to be rescheduled. The ability to save state in this way also supports two other useful capabilities:

- bumping low-priority jobs in favor of high-priority jobs
- automatic checkpoints

Neither of these capabilities is typically provided by the operating system of an MPP, in large part because it is so difficult to save state. For example, we noted how a single small job on an MPP, using only a small fraction of the total processor array, could delay a more important job that needed the entire machine. One might imagine an operating system capability to "save" the small job, bump it to disk, execute the large job, and then subsequently restore the small one using the saved state. At the moment, all one can do is imagine; such a capability is not provided by MPP vendors. For a similar reason, automatic checkpoint/restart is not offered. If user jobs require a checkpoint capability, they must supply it themselves, including the necessary code in their applications. This makes it more difficult, but not impossible, to schedule very long jobs—jobs that might run over several days, say, in the off-hours. There will be very little specialized OS support for managing the off-load/reload switchover stages for such an application.

To summarize, the problems of scheduling among multiple jobs and users, which are already complex in a time-sharing system, become even more complex on MPPs. This is a consequence of the underlying hardware architecture, which imposes limits on the ways in which the machine can be shared and makes it difficult or impossible to automatically save state for running processes. A manually (rather than automatically) enforced scheduling policy may be the simplest and most effective way to deal with large jobs that require contention-free use of the machine for long periods of time.

9.4 VIRTUAL PROCESSORS

To understand the power and utility of the notion of virtual processors, we must first go back to the material in Chapters 4 through 7 on programming approaches. Some approaches encouraged the programmer to deal exclusively with large arrays and not to "meddle" with the details of how these arrays are mapped onto the underlying hardware or how the various primitive array operations are implemented. The assumption underlying these approaches is that the programmer does not want to be concerned with the nitty-gritty details of the network topology, number of processors, interprocessor communications, etc. The concept of virtual processors is of no value. The programming abstraction is already at such a high level that hardware details (such as how many processors are physically being used) are invisible.

The other approach is much closer to the actual hardware. Here, the programmer takes responsiblity for explicity spreading the data across the processor array, implementing interprocessor communications explicity (rather than implicitly, using array operations), and typically going to some lengths to ensure that interprocessor communications are localized and free of contention. In this style, the number of processors and the geometric relationship among them in the underlying network interconnection scheme are of great importance. The programmer expects the machine (or subarray of the machine) to be in a configuration that matches the programming assumptions used to construct and optimize the code.

Example: Consider an array with, say, 2**22 = 4 million elements, and suppose the code in which the array is declared is to execute on a processor array with 2**10 = 1,000 processor nodes.

The first programming style allows the programmer to declare the array as:

```
#declare  FOUR_MILLION    4000000
#declare  NUM_PROC        1024
integer sample_array[ FOUR_MILLION ];
```

The compiler/operating system takes care of spreading the data across the underlying physical processor array. Indeed, the number of processors (NUM_PROC) does not explicitly appear at all in the array declaration or in the operations performed on it. The code should run, without alteration, on any size machine.

In the second scheme, the declaration might instead appear as

```
integer sample_array[ NUM_PROC ][ FOUR_MILLION/NUM_PROC ];
```

Here, the programmer is *expecting* to see a processor array with 1,024 processors and has explicitly constructed the code to reflect that fact. In this declaration, the data array will be spread by rows, one 4,000-long row per processor. Similarly, if the declaration had been

```
integer sample_array[ FOUR_MILLION/NUM_PROC ][ NUM_PROC ];
```

the large array would be spread by columns, one column per processor. In this case, each processor would receive not a contiguous sequential set of 4,000 elements but the 4,000-long "vector" of elements beginning at NUM_PROC and counting with a stride of NUM_PROC between successive elements.

Even more striking, the programmer might declare

```
integer sample_array[ FOUR_MILLION/NUM_PROC ];
```

Here, it is assumed that each processing node (of which the programmer expects to see NUM_PROC) need hold only the subset of the total data array appropriate to it. Space for the full array is allocated implicitly, since each processor will have its own local array of the declared size. The programmer will take care of whether the array is distributed by row or by column in the I/O portion of the code, where the data will be explicitly routed (by the programmer) to the desired node. ■

This example has shown how the characteristics of the processing array (in this case, the number of nodes) can be embedded in the code in certain programming styles. For such a style, the capability of virtual processors would permit the code, which has been designed for a specific size processor array, to, in fact, run on a different-size processor array. Presumably, this might be accomplished by inserting an extra loop, invisible to the user, allowing one physical processor to do the work of many. Data structures are then replicated in the physical node the requisite number of times, and message passing is altered to direct messages to the physical node on which the logical destination resides.

There are at least two reasons why such a capability might be of use. First, it allows the user to debug code intended for a large array using a small array. Less of the machine is needed to support the code development and debugging process, and, hence, more of the machine is available for other useful work. Also, depending on how machine time is billed, running code for a large array on a small one could save development cost. In the extreme case, a simulator for the large array might reside on a single workstation, separate from the physical MPP. Development and debug takes place on the inexpensive workstation.

The second use relates to scheduling. As we have seen, if code expects to see a certain number of processors in a specific configuration, it may be that the job must wait until enough other jobs are complete to free up a configuration of the desired type (see Figure 9-3). If, however, the operating system can emulate the larger configuration on a physically smaller one, it may be able to schedule the job earlier (though, of course, the total run time will suffer, since fewer physical nodes are being applied to the problem). In an ideal world, the job might even migrate to a larger subarray, in midprocess, when it becomes available (such an ideal world is not yet with us).

Vendors differ widely in their ability to support virtual processors, and even the terminology is not standard. For example, an MPP whose language completely shields the user from the run-time number of processors has many of the same advantages, though with the concomitant penalty of reduced potential for code optimization. It is better to have the hardware internals of the machine visible from the source code but with the ability, when necessary, to execute in a degraded mode on a smaller configuration. It is this second capability that deserves the name *virtual processors*.

9.5 I/O

A recurring theme of this book is the importance to MPP efficiency of a balanced and flexible I/O subsystem. A brief summary of issues would include:

- adequate bandwidth to and from peripheral storage devices
- adequate bandwidth to and from networks
- source-level libraries to parallelize I/O operations, spreading data across the array on input and merging it from array nodes on output
- sufficient on-line storage space
- sufficient back-up and archival storage space
- in real-time on-line systems, ability to meet latency requirements
- a familiar and flexible file system at the user and program interface
- sufficent variety in specialized peripherals (frame buffers, plotters, CAD/CAM workstations, etc.) to meet user requirements and adequate bandwidth to service them
- ability to interface to (read from and/or write to) existing legacy files and storage media (tapes, DASDs, CD-ROMs, etc.), including data format conversion if required
- system control to assign and monitor space usage on secondary storage
- security features to monitor, audit, and control access to system resources

Many of these issues are not unique to MPPs, but even those shared with other systems have unique characteristics in an MPP context. The reason for this is architectural. In an MPP with distinct private memories for each processor, performance hinges on getting the data to the right processor. A shared memory machine that provides uniform access to the shared address space does not have this problem. As long as the data are in the shared memory, any processor has access to any part of the data. The situation is different in an SIMD or DM-MIMD machine. If the data required by a processor are not already in its local memory, an expensive (that is, high-latency) data transfer is required. Depending on frequency and size, these data movement operations can potentially cripple MPP performance.

In the context of I/O, this means that as part of input, data must be routed to the correct processor. If the data are viewed (by the programmer) as a single long array (the typical file abstraction on UNIX machines), the MPP must have the ability to specify which subsets of the data are to be routed to which processors (*spreading* the data). Similarly, on output, the subsets contributed by each of the processors must be interleaved into a single stream for output (*merging* the data). The spreading and merging operations can be difficult to specify, since many different possibilities might be required depending on individual application characteristics. Limiting the range of options has the advantage of simplicity but the disadvantage of reduced flexibility and, hence, reduced performance on some applications.

Figures 9-6 and 9-7 illustrate these issues and how some MPPs attempt to resolve them. Figure 9-6 shows the typical arrangement in which a RAID (*R*edundant *A*rray of *I*nexpensive *D*isks) storage device is servicing an MPP. At the interface, a RAID meets ordinary standards: a high-bandwidth sequential data stream. Internally, that data stream is partitioned into numerous substreams by the RAID controller. The high bandwidth is achieved by merging (when data leave the RAID) or spreading (when data enter the RAID) the single high-bandwidth data path into multiple low-bandwidth paths routed to individual drives in the array. These drives are typically commodity Winchester drives typical of workstations or PCs. RAID storage devices achieve excellent reliability by encoding the data redundantly with error-correcting codes (ECCs). Loss of a disk unit does not mean loss of data, since the controller can use the ECC to correctly rebuild the data using the redundant information embedded in the code.

This concentration/spreading process is mirrored, in reverse, at the MPP. On input, the single data stream formed by the RAID must be spread across the MPP array. (The sprinkler tip on a garden watering can is a good analogy for this process.) On output, individual data streams from the MPP processors must be merged in a highly coordinated way into a single stream for shipment back to the RAID.

Figure 9-7 shows how some MPP vendors have shortcut this merge/spread process. Each processor in the MPP array (or, at least, some significant subset of processors) has direct access to its own data disk (typically an inexpensive Winchester, such as those used in a RAID). The "file" is physically spread across the set of disks and read or written by the processors completely in parallel. The sequential abstraction for the file is lost, but the data in the file are avail-

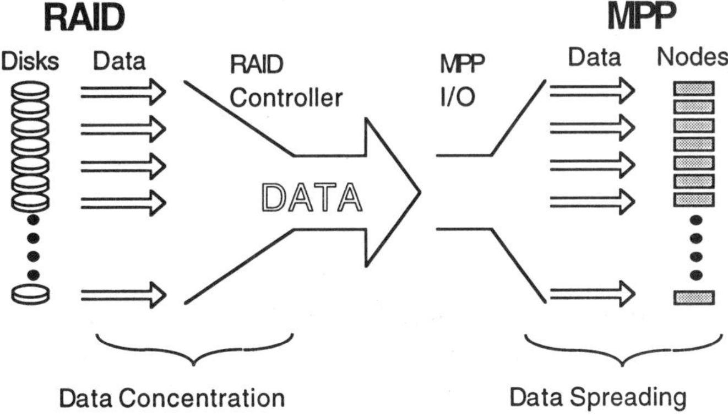

Figure 9-6. Data concentration and preading between a RAID and an MPP

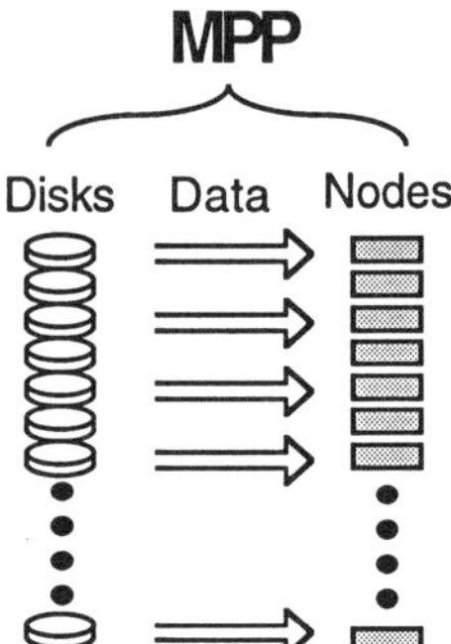

Figure 9-7. MPPs can emulate RAIDS using local disks

able at very high aggregate bandwidth (much like the wheelbarrows used by the soldiers in the wall-building example from Chapter 3). Rearrangement of the data among the processors is then accomplished using message passing over the interconnection network.

A potential difficulty for such a scheme is multiple users. As described above, a coordinated, synchronized activity by the entire array appears to be required. If multiple users each have separate, asynchronous jobs running, and each job has its own I/O requirements independent of the others, the approach appears to break down. The usual solution to this problem is to provide a separate subset of processors dedicated to I/O. These processors have direct disk access and maintain the file directories. When a group of processors in the array requires an I/O operation, communication with the I/O processors is established using the interconnection network. Particulars of the I/O operation (that is, how spreading and/or interleaving is to be accomplished) can be user-specified. The I/O processors are, thus, a resource shared by the array processors on an as-needed basis.

This same approach can be used to service peripherals and network interfaces. A group of processors (physically near the edge of the processor array) can be assigned (permanently or dynamically) as device drivers for HIPPI channels, frame buffers, plotters, tape drives, etc. This is illustrated in Figure 9-8. Data flow back and forth between these dedicated I/O processors and the array using the interconnection network, and protocols are provided by the operating system to handle the required merging and spreading.

A recurring theme has been the importance of good performance of data placement on the processor array. In simplest terms, we want the data as "close" to the processor that will operate on it as possible. The same issue applies when data are spread across multiple disks for I/O. Some disk/processor pairs

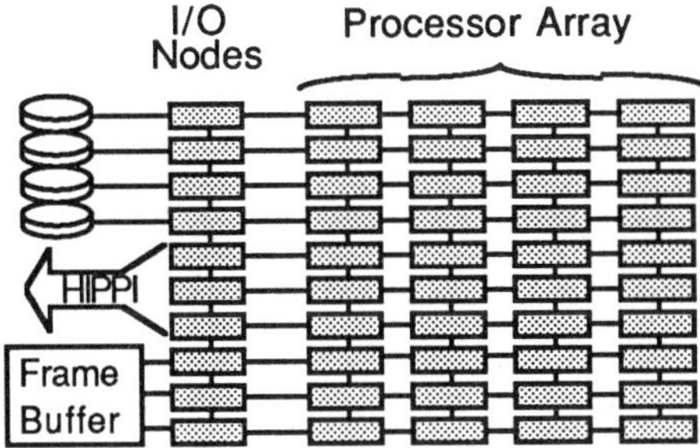

Figure 9-8. Use of dedicated nodes for I/O in an MPP

will be closer (i,e,. lower latency) than others. A complete program design will reflect this, consciously partitioning the data for efficient I/O. This is yet another factor that frustrates attempts at automatic parallelization of legacy codes.

A central message of Chapter 2 was that large MPP arrays need large problems in order to be used efficiently. In most instances, what *large* means is *large data sets.* This, in turn, often means large amounts of I/O. Unless the I/O portion of the problem is adequately addressed, the overall performance on the application can be poor. Typically, MPPs do not offer any performance advantage in the I/O part of the problem. While they can keep up with the fastest devices and networks, their performance boost is on the computational part of the problem, not the I/O part of the problem. If, for example, the data on which the MPP is to operate reside on low-speed devices (tapes, for example), the end to end application performance may be limited not so much by the MPP performance as by the limited bandwidth of the I/O devices. On the other hand, the very large main memory provided by MPPs can sometimes reduce the number of I/O stages required. In polyphase merging, typical of tape sorts, for example, the number of merging phases as well as the time spent in the initial sort can be reduced by using an MPP with a very large main memory. References [28] and [29] provide additional insight into I/O issues for MPP systems.

9.6 OPEN SYSTEMS

In this section, we will consider three alternative configurations for an MPP in an open systems architecture. All three have implications for the operating system.

First, the MPP may be a dedicated computing engine for some small number of highly computational-intensive applications. It is in this role that MPPs most often make their entrance into commercial processing. An organization has an application (say, a large sort routine or a linear programming problem), which is critical to the enterprise but which is straining the capabilities of the existing equipment. The MPP is viewed as a special-purpose processor dedicated to this application. The hope might be, for example, to bring the run time down from two weeks to less than a day for an application that must be run once a month. Processing time and resources currently devoted to this application are now available for other uses, and the additional time in the production schedule provides latitude for processes linked to this one, either as suppliers or consumers. In short, the MPP is viewed as *loosening* what had become a *tightly constrained* processing flow.

In this setting, I/O and the ability to interface to existing databases are the dominant considerations. We might envision the complete solution involving three steps each time the application is executed. In the first step, data are transferred from the current storage devices to the high-speed I/O devices directly attached to the MPP. A network interface will be required, and the transfer may also involve reformatting data so as to be compatible with the MPP. The second step is the processing phase, in which the MPP performs the required computation. Presumably, the program has been specially coded and optimized, and the intent is to spread this initial software development cost over tens or hundreds of runs during the effective life of the MPP. Finally, in the third step, the processed data must be returned to the operational environment, effectively reversing the transfer from the first step. Depending on the size of the databases and the bandwidth of the network, it is entirely possible that the first and third steps, in which the data are transferred to and from the MPP, could dominate the end to end processing time.

This operational scenario imposes the least pressure on the MPP and is also fully compatible with batch-oriented (that is, centralized and nonopen) architectures. Over time, the organization may envision additional compute-intensive applications migrating to the MPP. If the MPP's storage devices were, for example, to become standard for the facility, the overhead of Steps 1 and 3 could be dramatically reduced. Thus, the introduction of the MPP may, for some organizations, be the initial phase of an evolutionary process, which comprises the gradual withering away of traditional mainframes and the corresponding flourishing of the MPP and its associated peripherals. The speed and exact course of this process over time will, of course, be highly dependent on the specific requirements and operational characteristics of each organization.

A second role for the MPP in an open system is as an on-line server for the user population. It is in this role that the interactive capabilities—multiple users, virtual processors, multitask scheduling, etc.—become significant. If, for example, the MPP is viewed as a database engine (one of the roles in which MPPs have proven commercially successful), then report generation and SQL service to other applications in the open system are likely and natural capabilities. Of particular concern will be the scheduling function, which monitors MPP utilization and which can assign resources in a timely way to the highest-priority users.

This second role is in some ways the destiny of MPPs but is currently frustrated by the lack of good-quality application software (see Section 1.2). Since the users have no software to run, they see no use for an MPP. On the other hand, users are sensitive to cost and might welcome more rapid turnaround for the jobs and services they submit. An MPP, viewed not as a hardware architecture but as a performance booster, might well find an enthusiastic clientele. In such a case, the ability of the operating system to fairly arbitrate and support a variety of users will be critical to its overall utility and acceptance.

The third role is when the open system *becomes* the MPP! This is the intent of software such as Linda, Epress, or PVM. Workstations distributed across the LAN are viewed conceptuaxlly as processing nodes in an MPP, and the LAN is viewed as the interconnection network. Applications can then be written that are automatically distributed across the LAN and that steal available cycles from otherwise unused CPUs.

This is an attractive and low-cost way of introducing parallel processing into an open system. First, the caveat: This approach *cannot scale to supercomputing levels of performance.* The high latency and low bandwidth of LANs (relative to fully integrated MPPs) make the performance penalty for interprocessor communications extremely high. Further, the distributed I/O capabilities discussed in Section 9.5 are generally not available in these configurations, making I/O a potential bottleneck. Despite its limitations, however, for coarse-grained applications with modest I/O and interprocessor communications requirements, an LAN of workstations (particularly if they already exist) can be an effective parallel platform. For organizations considering such an approach, the UNIX operating system forms the software base on which the parallel development and execution environment is built.

Summary of Chapter 9

This chapter has provided a glimpse into the operating system issues that arise when an MPP is integrated into an ADP environment. A key theme has been the kinds of sharing that the MPP might be expected to support and the policies and capabilities that are then required. While the widespread use of UNIX among MPP vendors can ease one aspect of integration into an open system, there are other concerns—data format, distributed I/O, and scheduling, for example—that may need to be solved if the integration is to be seamless and effective. In an open system, it may even be possible to use the LAN of workstations *as* the MPP, provided proper OS and application development support is provided.

PART 3

Management Issues

When an organization is considering use of parallel processing (either moving an existing application to a parallel machine or developing a new application), there are typically a number of questions relating to performance and cost that must be answered before an informed decision can be made. The purpose of Part 3 is to present methodologies for gathering and evaluating this information. An appropriate subtitle for this material might be:*What every manager should think about before touching the MPP situation.*

The key issues under performance—that is, how fast the machine can be expected to execute—are considered in Chapter 10 on benchmarking. As will become apparent, there are a number of wrinkles in benchmarking parallel equipment that must be ironed out before reliable performance estimates can be obtained.

Very often with parallel machines, for which very little third-party application code exists, the driving factor for cost is software development. Chapter 11 considers this issue from two points of view: (1) when the job is to port an existing application, and (2) when the job is to develop a new application "from scratch." Each has unique characteristics—problems, tools, and methods of attack—that deserve attention *before* a project is undertaken. A highlight of the chapter is a carefully chosen set of examples, drawn from actual experience, which illustrates the lessons of this chapter in a concrete way.

The culmination of the book is Chapter 12, which presents a methodology for selecting the "right" parallel machine for an application. The methodology is comprehensive, and all aspects of the problem are incorporated in a structured manner. From one point of view, this entire book can be viewed as a tutorial presenting the information needed by a manager in order to carry out such an evaluation and selection process.

10

Benchmarking Parallel Applications

This chapter is the first of three grouped under the heading, Management Issues. The point of view for this material is that of an ADP manager considering the possibility of transitioning one or more applications to an MPP. This chapter will focus on performance. How fast will a given machine execute an application of interest? A suite of applications? How does this compare with other alternative machines? How will performance change as the problem size changes? As the machine size changes? What component of the execution time (I/O, interprocessor communications, computation, etc.) dominates and, hence, is the best target for hardware and/or software optimizations? How does delivered performance depend on the choice of algorithm? The choice of compiler? What is the relationship, if any, between *delivered* performance and *raw peak* performance?

All these questions are hard enough in the world of sequential processing, where instruction sets (RISC versus CISC), caching strategies, virtual memory, and optimizing compilers introduce complications that can mislead the unwary (see, for example [1] for a good overview of the pitfalls of benchmarks). For parallel processors, the problems of developing benchmarks that will accurately predict performance (or of extrapolating performance measures from published standard benchmarks) are even more difficult. Performance often depends critically on such factors as choice of algorithm, machine and data size, and I/O configuration. A good benchmarking strategy must take these into account and must be structured so that reasonable and supportable extrapolations can be made to full-up, end to end applications.

A further stress on the benchmarking process is that performance is often a greater concern for MPPs than it is for sequential machines. The motivation for an MPP, in many instances, is the need to dramatically reduce execution time on a particularly lengthy computation. Having a high degree of assurance that the intended improvement will be realized is critical to management's decision concerning a possible transition to MPP. The software risks of MPP are well known. Does the performance benefit outweigh these risks? Since performance for such applications is weighted more heavily in the trade-off evaluation, accuracy of performance estimates is correspondingly more important.

The dependence of parallel benchmarks both on machine size and on problem size is the topic of Section 10.1, followed by a discussion of the importance of choosing the "right" algorithm for the target hardware. The major parallel benchmarks (and their limitations) are then described in Section 10.3. The next two sections consider how the available information can be reliably extrapolated to full-up, end to end performance on a complete application. A final section then gives a "heads up" on how vendor sales literature should be understood and under what conditions it is (or is not) likely to be applicable to a given situation.

10.1 DEPENDENCE ON PROBLEM SIZE AND MACHINE SIZE

As we saw in Chapter 2, the efficiency of an MPP on a particular class of problem can vary greatly with changes both in the size of the problem and the size of the machine. This has significant implications both for designing parallel benchmarks and for interpreting benchmark results. Further, MPP performance can be dramatically affected both by I/O and by the amount of interprocessor communications. Well-designed parallel benchmarks should, if possible, break these components out for separate consideration. Finally, in many cases the delivered performance can be data dependent; the implications for parallel benchmarks are considered.

10.1.1 Amdahl's Law Revisited

We begin by recalling some material from Chapter 2 that will be useful in our discussion of parallel benchmarking. The key idea underlying Amdahl's Law is that the total execution time for a problem, when executed on a single processor, can be separated into two pieces. The first is the *parallel* part of the problem. This part of the problem can be speeded up by applying more processors: The more processors applied, the faster this part of the problem can be executed. The second is the *sequential* part of the problem. This part of the problem cannot be speeded up by adding more processors: No matter how many processors are put on the problem, the sequential part must still be executed, and this puts a hard lower bound on how much speed-up is achievable using parallelism alone. If, for example, the sequential part uses 20 percent of the total run time, then I can never reduce the run time below this 20 percent bound just by parallelizing. The best speed-up I can hope for is about 5×, *no matter how many processors I apply to the problem.* Briefly, Amdahl's Law says that the fraction of the problem that is sequential imposes a hard lower bound on achievable run time (and, hence, a hard upper bound on achievable speed-up), *independent* of the number of processors in the parallel array.

The next step in this argument is to estimate the actual fraction of a problem that is inherently sequential. The larger this fraction, the less efficiently a large parallel machine can be used. However, if this fraction is very small, it may be that large parallel processor arrays can be used very efficiently. A central message from Chapter 2 was that this fraction—the size of the sequential part of the problem relative to the total problem—*changes with the size of the problem.* Generally, the sequential part of a problem grows at a slower rate than the parallelizable part. Thus, as the problem size grows, the *fraction* of execution time spent in the sequential part can become arbitrarily small, allowing arbitrarily large parallel arrays to be applied efficiently. In short, *large parallel machines need large problems.*

This phenomenon takes place along two dimensions and can be briefly summarized by the following two rules:

Rule One: **Efficency decreases with machine size.** If the problem size is held constant and more processors are added, efficiency will decrease. In other words, achieved speed-up, as a fraction of theoretical best speed-up, will become worse and worse as the processor array size increases. This is just Amdahl's Law.

Rule Two: **Efficiency increases with problem size.** If the processor array size is held constant and the problem size is allowed to grow, efficiency will increase. In other words, the speed-up, as a fraction of theoretical best speed-up, will become better and better as the problem size increases. This is an observed property of many problems and is often related to differences in growth rates between the boundary (= sequential) and interior (= parallelizable) parts of a problem.

The implications of this observation for parallel benchmarking are clear. A complete assessment must balance the factors of efficiency, speed-up, hardware costs, and the size (or range of sizes) of the problem to be solved. It is important to have timing figures *both* over the range of problem sizes on which the application will be run *and* over the range of machine sizes (that is, number of processors) being considered (see Figure 10-1).

10.1.2 Measures of Effectiveness

The currency of performance measurement for high-end systems is *MFLOPs*—millions of floating point operations per second. Of late, *Gflops* (Giga-FLOPs, that is, billions of floating point operations per second) have appeared with increasing frequency, reflecting the peformance improvements achieved over the past decade. In this standard, the vendor counts *multiply* and/or *addition* operations against the total. Since these two operations may, in some machines, actually take different amounts of time, a bit of care may be required in interpreting the results. A further complication concerns the size of the data on which the operation is performed. A *single precision FLOP* is performed on a 32-bit (4-byte) data word, while a *double precision FLOP* is performed on a 64-bit (8-byte) data word. It is not unusual for a double precision FLOP to take up to twice as long as a single precision operation. On the other hand, this can be an advantage if the computation does not require double precision accuracy and, hence, can take advantage of the performance boost by working in single precision (this is a factor, since some machines only work in double precision and, hence, provide no performance advantage to single precision applications). When an MFLOP rate is reported, attention

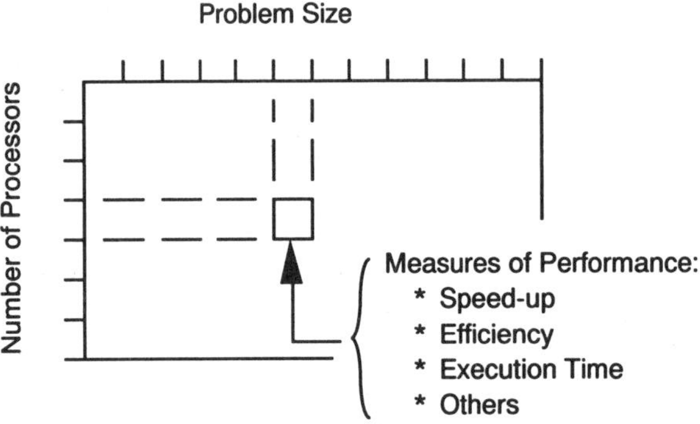

Figure 10-1. Parallel benchmarks must reflect both machine size and problem size

should be paid to whether single or double precision FLOPs were counted, taking into account the relation of this to the intended application(s).

There are two ways in which MFLOPs are typically reported: (1) as *peak* rates, and (2) as *measured* rates (measured by actually executing some piece of floating point-intensive code). It is not unusual for peak and measured performance to differ by factors of up to 10 or more, depending on how well the hardware characteristics of the machine match the logical requirements of the code being executed. Savvy organizations pay little attention to peak numbers, although vendors are fond of trotting them out as part of sales presentations. Rather, they focus on measured rates on codes that are as close as possible to the codes they intend to execute.

The biggest difficulty with MFLOPs as a measure is that one must actually count the number of floating point operations the code executes. While that may be possible for an extremely simple operation (like a matrix multiply), it is almost impossible (and largely unnecessary) for typical large-scale production codes. What can further complicate the issue is that the optimal algorithm used to perform the operation may differ from machine to machine. This is especially true for parallel machines, where some initial redundancy (say, in replicating shared data structures) can pay handsome dividends in reduced interprocessor communications. Thus, two differing machines may perform completely different numbers of floating point operations to achieve the same result, depending on what algorithm has been selected. In such a situation, the extra floating point operations should, it seems, not be counted as increased MFLOPs, since they were in some sense a superfluous artifact of the machine architecture and not an essential part of the function.

Thus, while MFLOPs continue to be widely used (because of the simplicity of the concept), this measure will be misleading without some additional understanding of exactly how it was obtained. Further, as we saw in the previous section, achieved MFLOPs on parallel processors can differ substantially based both on the size of the machine (that is, the number of processors) and on the size of the problem (say, the dimension of the matrix being inverted). In general, achieved MFLOPs *per processor* (a common measure of efficiency) will be best for larger problems and for smaller numbers of processors. Thus, a vendor might be tempted to measure MFLOPs on a single processor for a moderate- to large-size problem. The unwary might be lured into assuming that this rate will scale upwards to large arrays (it may or may not) or that it will hold for other problem sizes (again, it depends).

For all these reasons, MFLOP ratings have fallen into disfavor among the high-performance cognoscenti, to be replaced by *measured run time on customer-prepared benchmark code.* The point is simple. After all, what the customer really cares about is how fast the machine will actually execute the applications. It is better, then, to prepare a small but representative suite of kernel codes (executing against data sizes representative of the operational setting) executed on a variety of machine sizes representative of the configurations under consideration for procurement. In this way, all the pertinent factors (I/O, interprocessor communications, synchronization overhead, etc.) can be observed in the relative proportions characteristic of the true operational objective.

This, in turn, raises an important consideration that applies to high performance computing in general and to parallel processors in particular: Namely, when the benchmark is prepared, the vendor must be given the flexibility to select the algorithm that best takes advantage of the hardware architecture. Suppose, for example, that the kernel is an optimization routine. There are, in fact, a number of algorithms for performing optimization, all of which can give satisfactory (or even provably optimal) results but that differ dramatically in the internal details of their operation. So long as the algorithms agree on an input/output basis, a fair comparison should permit each vendor to select the algorithmic approach that best utilizes the machine features.

The objection may be raised, at this point, that such flexibility will require recoding. If the benchmark requires the vendor to run customer-supplied code *as is*, without modification, this reflects the situation where the customer is not willing to invest time or effort in recoding or optimization. Now, we have seen already that the parallel processing industry is at a substantial disadvantage when it comes to software and the porting of existing sequential code. Automatic parallelizing compilers are still R&D, and even the most sequential-like of machines (vectorizing machines) may require a good deal of tuning and code restructuring in order to take full advantage of the machine's performance potential. In short, if an organization is not willing even to consider some additional effort for code porting, algorithm restructuring, and optimization, it is not clear why it would be looking at a high-performance architecture in the first place.

A more reasonable approach is to allow the vendor to make algorithmic modifications and optimizations but to require an accompanying report listing what was done and the level of effort that was required. The vendor might even be willing to produce benchmark results for various versions of the code: (1) before any changes; (2) with minimal modification and (3) with full-up optimizations, for example. This would allow the customer to accurately weigh performance improvement against development cost, since the level of effort required to achieve the optimizations would be available.

Another commonly encountered but potentially misleading measure of performance is \$/MFLOP—intended to be a top-level summary of cost performance. All the problems we have already mentioned concerning the meaning of an MFLOP apply here, as well. (Is MFLOP peak or measured? Single or double precision? If measured, then on what size machine and on what size problem? How closely does the measured benchmark code reflect the intended application?) However, many of the same complications also apply to the measurement of cost—the "\$" in the numerator. What costs are to be included? Raw hardware purchase price is often just the tip of the iceberg. What about secondary storage? Software purchase, porting, or development? Maintenance? Future upgrades and expansions? A reliable measure of cost must consider the full life cycle and include likely impact on both the operational environment and, in many cases, on the organization and how it does its business. This last is a major theme of Tom Wheeler's book on open systems [30] and has the potential to be the most far-reaching of all impacts.

> ***Example***: Because of high-fidelity simulations made possible by supercomputers, it was determined that the logistics requirements for a military operation could be met, by improved scheduling, with seven fewer transport aircraft than a lower-fidelity worst-case simulation predicted. The cost savings resulting from fewer aircraft completely swamped the additional cost of the supercomputer. Further, the supercomputer is now integral to the scheduling process, resulting in far-reaching organizational changes (skill-mix and other staffing implications, for example). ■

Another misleading factor in the \$/MFLOP measure is that there are many problems that a small machine cannot do at all—say, because it does not have the storage or network interfaces required just to get at the data. How do you measure \$/MFLOP against a problem the small machine cannot execute? When MPP vendors (with some justification) peg microprocessors at the best cost/performance point, they may neglect this consideration. As problems become very large (and, hence, worthy of supercomputer levels of performance), the mix of I/O, networking, main memory, and clock rates changes. The mere ability to do certain types of large problems may (does!) require investment in capabilities that will necessarily drive the achieved cost/performance into a different regime. For MPP technology to realize its potential, it must not only achieve good \$/MFLOP measured solely on processor cost, but it must achieve good \$/MFLOP measured against total system cost, on actual applications, and including storage, networking, software development, porting, etc.

For large corporations, the investment in hardware is a minuscule part of the total operational budget. Such organizations are not as concerned about *cost/performance* as they are about *total delivered performance*—that is, they want to solve problems well beyond their current capabilities in order to create new markets. These are the situations best suited for MPP (see Section 1.3.1), since success will repay by orders of magnitude the initial hardware and software investment. As more high-quality software becomes available for MPPs, other organizations (for which hardware costs are a large share of the margin) can take advantage of cost/performance for MPPs in the more traditional sense.

As we noted in Chapter 1, facility impacts (such as power, maintenance, cooling, and reliability) are areas in which MPPs appear to have a substantial advantage over traditional mainframes and vectorizing supercomputers. A complete cost assessment should include these factors, which may help to offset software porting and development costs and, over the life of the machine, can dominate the cost. Even if the initial hardware procurement were free, there are many organizations that could not afford the maintenance, staffing, facility support, and upgrade costs for traditional supercomputers. For these organizations, an MPP may be the only feasible entry into high-performance computing based on facilties considerations alone.

Example: A supercomputer vendor had recently introduced a new model. A marketing representative remarked, "The first hurdle is to see if we can give one away." ■

The fact that MPPs are often available in scaled-down versions at entry-level prices well under $1 million is another consideration. This permits a strategy where initial software porting takes place on a small and inexpensive machine, with upgrades to supercomputer levels of performance to follow after proof of concept. This reduces the *risk* (a factor not captured in a raw $/MFLOP number) and may be more acceptable to management than a headlong plunge into MPP technology. For example, benchmarks reflecting the intended application areas can be developed and executed *in-house* and the necessary caveats on I/O and interprocessor communications explicitly understood and extrapolated. In the author's opinion, this is a nearly ideal approach, since it enables the organization to fully understand and become comfortable with the biggest risk area (the software) before committing large resources to hardware and facilities. We will have more to say on this subject in Chapter 12.

10.1.3 Specifying Machine Configurations

As we saw in the previous section, measured end to end performance on benchmarks constructed to approximate the target application code is the most reliable predictor of delivered performance. However, as we saw in Section 10.1.1. (itself a review of material in Chapter 2), the efficiency with which the machine is used (which is closely related to cost/performance) critically depends *both* on the size of the machine on which the benchmark is executed *and* on the size of the problem. In this section, we will consider how *machine size* should enter into the specification of reliable benchmarks.

There are four factors that should be specifically called out in specifying the machine configuration for the benchmark: the number of processors (array size); the amount of directly addressable memory (total, for shared memory machines, and per node for distributed memory machines); interprocessor communications (latency, bandwidth, topology, and routing); and I/O bandwidth. We will briefly discuss each in turn.

First, well-constructed parallel codes accept the number of processor nodes as a run-time variable; that is, the same compiled object code can execute on arrays containing varying numbers of processors. Typically, the user (or the operating system script) will specify the desired array size as part of the job start-up protocol. Depending on the vendor, there may be more or less flexibility in array dimensions that can be supported. Machines that use log-binary interconnection topologies (hypercubes, fat trees) are likely only to support a power of two (4, 8, 16, 32, etc.); meshes may be somewhat more flexible. The impact for the benchmark is that it should be executed on processor arrays of varying sizes. For a given problem size, two measurements suffice to estimate the sequential and parallel parts of the code (see Section 2.2.3); additional measurements can be handled by curve fitting. This, in turn, can be used to extrapolate performance to arrays of other sizes (for example, machine configurations that may not be physically available for benchmarking).

Example: A benchmark code is executed on processor arrays of sizes $N =$ 64 and 256, with measured run times:

$T_{64} = 12.3$ sec.
$T_{256} = 8.8$ sec.

Using the model $T_N = T_S + T_P/N$ (where T_S is the sequential part of the problem, and T_P is the parallel part), we can solve and find that

$T_S = 7.6$ sec.
$T_P = 300.8$ sec.

so that T_S is about 2.5 percent of the total. Notice that *quadrupling* the array size only decreases run time by about 28 percent—the effect of Amdahl's

Law for this problem size, which only has a modest amount of parallelism. Having calculated T_S and T_p, we can now estimate run times for array sizes not in the benchmark. For example, we would estimate

$$T_{32} = 7.6 + 300.8/32 = 17.0 \text{ sec.}$$

or

$$T_{1024} = 7.6 + 300.8/1024 = 7.9 \text{ sec.} \blacksquare$$

One difficulty that arises on shared memory SMPs is that the operating system, rather than the user, selects the number of processors to apply to a job, and this number can vary from run to run because of varying system loading. This can become a real headache in trying to reproduce and interpret benchmark results. This problem does not arise on MPPs; subarrays are dedicated to particular users, so that effects of sharing are far less pronounced.

Second, we consider memory specifications. It is well known that increased memory can have dramatic effects on run time, even when all other factors (processor speed, compiler optimizations, etc.) are held constant. In virtual memory machines, this is ordinarily the consequence of reduced *paging*. (Note: *Paging* occurs when the requested data are not already present in main memory, so that the operating system must first retrieve the data from secondary storage before the memory request can be satisfied. The additional time to perform this I/O operation can dramatically increase overall run time, if paging occurs frequently. The larger the main memory, the less likely paging will be needed and the faster the application executes.)

The effects of memory on run time in MPPs can also be substantial but for different reasons. For MPPs (as we saw in Section 3.4), the programmer is usually expected to be aware of physical memory limitations during code design and to tailor the algorithm and implementation accordingly. Having more memory means the ability to *replicate* shared data structures, such as look-up tables, rather than sharing them via message passing. Sizes for message buffers can also increase, meaning fewer and longer messages and reduced overhead. Increased memory also means the ability to hold a larger problem "in-core," so that the machine may be able to execute in problem size regimes more favorable to efficiency and, hence, cost performance.

Because MPPs use commodity DRAM for implementing main memory, they benefit from the recent market-induced exponential explosion in DRAM density and reduced price per bit. A complete benchmark will make some attempt to understand how performance can be expected to improve with coming generations of DRAMs. Unfortunately, no simple formula (such as that used above) is available to model these effects. The most reasonable approach is for software engineers familiar with both the machine and the algorithm implementation to construct a suitable model using engineering judgment and past experience. This is an area where specialized outside expertise might be of some value.

Third, the benchmark should take explicit account of interprocessor communications and synchronization overhead. The best situation is when the benchmark code, itself, is instrumented to record the number and lengths of messages, delays associated with sending and receiving messages, and delays associated with synchronization. These statistics can be obtained with operating system library calls and have negligible effect on overall execution. A difficulty arises if the high-level programming language hides these overheads (say, by allowing the programmer to use array operations directly, which the compiler then expands into the low-level message-passing primitives). Failing to understand, in some detail, what is happening at the machine level can result in unwelcome surprises.

An abstraction that is sometimes used by parallel software engineers is the ratio:

$$T_{comm}:T_{calc}.$$

The quantity T_{calc} refers to the elapsed time for a "typical" operation—a floating point addition, say, for scientific codes or a key compare for integer/character codes. The quantity T_{comm} refers to the time it takes to transfer a "typical" word of data from one processor to another. It usually combines latency, bandwidth, and the typical message size (number of bytes) into a single number. Models exist for program behavior (see, for example [2, Chapter 3]) that relate predicted performance both to the measured values of T_{calc} and T_{comm} and to their ratio. The intent of these measures is that they should depend only on the machine, not on the algorithm. If a given algorithm, then, knows the ratio of *required* calculations to *required* communications, an assessment of goodness of fit can be obtained.

In practice, T_{comm} in particular can vary remarkably depending on how the message passing is structured (optimizations for nearest-neighbor communications, message buffers, avoidance of synchronization, etc.). In the author's experience, the ratio $T_{comm}:T_{calc}$ has been most valuable as a top-level way of tracking overall progress in the MPP industry and of suggesting the potential for imbalance if the ratio becomes skewed (values of 3 to 7 for this ratio are representative of well-balanced machines).

Fourth, and finally, the benchmark should take explicit account of I/O and should require reporting of the secondary storage and/or network facilities employed. It will come as no surprise that many applications have substantial—even dominant—I/O processing requirements, and MPPs are no exception. A benchmark that runs entirely in-core (say, by first computing the values of a data set, rather than reading them in) can hide the flaws of an inadequate I/O subsystem.

This area has been a weakness for many MPP vendors for some time, and the charge of inadequate I/O capabilities—storage, bandwidth, network interfaces, and industrial-strength OS software—continues to dog the industry. If the *application* requires a certain level of I/O capability, then the *benchmark* had better stress and measure that part of the problem as well. As we saw in Section 9.5, for example, the I/O subsystems for MPPs have come a long way. By using ideas from RAID technology, files can be spread across large disk arrays with very good reliability and high, parallel sustained bandwidth. If this is a useful capability, then the benchmark should exercise and measure it. Transaction processing is another area where I/O rates can become a dominant factor. I/O can also affect applications where large amounts of data are to be transferred from existing legacy storage devices, over a network, to the MPP. Knowing how fast the MPP can process the data *once in memory* is only *part* of the total answer. Equally important is the software to spread the incoming sequential data stream across the array on input and to concentrate the separate data streams from the processors into a sequential output (see Figure 9.7). The benchmark can, thus, be used as a way of assessing the state, availability, and performance of needed OS capabilities.

The benchmark should also reflect the format characteristics of the data on which the application is to run (Big Endian versus Little Endian, ASCII versus EBCDIC, IEEE versus proprietary floating point formats, etc.). In some instances, these represent serious incompatibilities that can add both to development time and execution time (that is, the need to perform on-the-fly data format conversions).

A complete benchmark for an MPP should break out for separate inspection three times:

- processor run time
- interprocessor communications
- I/O

It should also report statistics on message traffic and should attempt to identify performance dependencies on the size of processor memory. As long as the accounting rules are agreed to in advance (what do you do, for example, when communications overlap processing?), these three measures will provide a solid basis for performance evaluation in support of MPP selection and sizing activities. Failure to pay attention to any of these is a prelude to potentially unwelcome surprises.

10.1.4 Specifying Problem Sizes

In Section 10.1.1, we stressed how the efficiency of an MPP depends critically on problem size. In a nutshell, the sequential and parallelizable parts of a problem typically grow at different rates: the parallelizable part (associated with the interior) growing faster than the sequential part (associated with the boundary). This means that their *ratio* changes, so that for large problems the sequential component can become an insignificant fraction of the total job. Finally, this implies that the bound on MPP speed-up and efficiency imposed by Amdahl's Law changes with problem size and often becomes a nonfactor for very large versions of the problem.

The major implication of this for benchmarking is that a well-designed benchmark for a parallel machine will not only be able to execute on various machine sizes (see Section 10.1.3) but will also be able to execute a variety of problem sizes. We refer back to Figure 10-1, which shows the desired case. Timing and other measures are obtained on a range of cases indexed *both* by number of processors *and* by the size of the problem.

Perhaps it is worthwhile to indicate what we mean by the general phrase, *problem size*. Many scientific codes (and coders) are inflexibly enamored of *data arrays* of whatever dimension. This infatuation, coupled with the fact that the National Laboratories and agencies are the major accounts for virtually all supercomputer vendors, has led to a preoccupation with benchmarks based on various types and sizes of *arrays*: matrices (sparse, symmetric, Hermitian, etc.); vectors; grids of space (2- or 3-D, sometimes with a time component) for finite element methods; sequences of samples (signal analysis); pixel arrays (image processing); etc. There is a school of thought that indicts FORTRAN for this unseemly fixation on arrays. After all, the array is about the only structure recognized by traditional FORTRAN, and FORTRAN is about the only language with which many researchers (for whom the very *idea* of computer science is professional anathema) are familiar. The adage says that if the only tool you have is a hammer, everything looks like a nail. By analogy, if the only data structure you know is an array . . . !

As a result, about the only meaning usually assigned to the phrase *problem size* in the scientific community is the *size of the array*, in each of its dimensions, on which the benchmark algorithm is to operate. While certainly adequate for such simple operations as inverting a double-precision matrix or implementing a Fast Fourier Transform (FFT) on 16-bit data, this is not adequate for the range of real-world applications faced by commercial enterprises.

Take *sorting* as a simple example. The scientific programming community will see this in simplistic terms: How many elements are in the array? In the real world, the number of items to be sorted can be overwhelmed, in terms of run time, by many other factors:

- What is the record length? Are the records variable length?
- What is the key size, and are there secondary or tertiary keys?
- Is the key in contiguous bytes or fields, or is it spread across the record?
- Can the file to be sorted fit in main memory? If not, how many "loads" are required to see all of it?
- Is it stored on a random access device or a serial device? What is the bandwidth of the device? What is its latency?
- Is the file already partially sorted?
- Is the file to be written back in sorted order, or is it simply to be fed into the next step of a larger job?
- Is the file under the control of a DBMS? an RDBMS? Is it the result of a join operation?

If problem size is to be a reflection of difficulty, then all these (and other) factors should be reflected when "sizing" a sort routine.

Of course, the easiest way to make a benchmark longer is to change the *number* of whatever it is the benchmark is operating on—records, values in an array, pixels, etc. From a mathematician's point of view (the author confesses to belonging to this dangerous breed), this is great, since wherever there is a *number* there must also be a *formula*. The reader will recall how, in the previous section, we used a simple model of parallel computation (based on separating a problem into its parallel and sequential components) to interpolate sampled execution times and extrapolate them to other array sizes. The number of processors, N, was the independent variable in this formula, and by simple, formal manipulations, we exposed and hoisted Amdahl's Law.

While we may thirst for a similar victory over problem sizes, no such simple program can succeed here. The key elements we seek are the growth rates of both the sequential and parallel components as problem size changes. It is the *ratio* of these that is critical to determining how much parallelism is in the problem, and what we need is a formula that expresses this ratio as a function of whatever we are using to count problem size.

Example: In the wall-building example from Chapter 2, the problem size was the length of the wall. Here, we had an extremely simple formula for run time based on L, the length of the wall in yards, and N, the number of soldiers. Assuming that a soldier can build one yard of wall per day and that each soldier needs six days to complete the ends (three days for each), then the number of days required to build a wall of length L with N soldiers is:

$$T_N = T_N(L) = 6 + L/N,$$

and the fraction of time in the sequential part (irrespective of N) is:

$$T_S / T_1 = 6/(6 + L).$$

Here, T_S is constant, independent of L. In more difficult cases, it might be a much more complicated function of L. Unless we adopt a model for the run time (and where is this to come from?), which would allow us to extract T_S mathematically, the problem of extrapolating to other size problems becomes less science and more guesswork. ■

Building such an execution time model, and solving for the missing variables based on measured performance on selected problem sizes, is the name of the game in parallel performance measurement. One approach is to use the techniques of complexity theory (that is, actually count the number of certain primitive operations performed by an algorithm, and use this as the independent variable for an execution time model).

Example: A certain parallel sorting algorithm is known, on the basis of a complexity analysis, to have a run-time model on L records and N processors given by:

$$T_N = T_N(L) = A + B * L * (lg(L/N) + lg(N))/N.$$

The two missing constants, A and B, are machine dependent and can be determined by picking two different choices for L and N, actually measuring T_N and solving the resulting equations for A and B. For example, suppose we run a set of $L = 100{,}000$ records on an $N = 64$-processor machine in $T_{64} = 18.40$ seconds, and a set of $L = 450{,}000$ records on an $N = 256$-processor machine in $T_{256} = 23.21$ seconds. We obtain

$$18.40 = A + B * 25{,}952$$
$$23.21 = A + B * 33{,}011$$

The reader can verify that from these equations,

$$A = .7 \text{ seconds}$$

and

$$B = .682 \text{ msec/record/processor}$$

With these in hand, performance estimates for other numbers of records and other sizes of processor arrays can be computed. For example, we would expect the machine to sort $L = 280{,}000$ records on an N = 32-node machine in

$$T_{32} = A + B * L * (lg(L/N) + lg(N))/N$$
$$= 108.7 \text{ seconds}$$

In practice, the growth formulas given by complexity arguments are too simple for the real world. Their theoretical elegance was purchased at the price of simplification. We will speak at greater length in Sections 10.3 and 10.4 about approaches for extrapolating results to different problem sizes. The two major points are: (1) variations of the benchmark should reflect the full range of factors that make the problem "hard", of which item count is only one, and (2) due to weaknesses in the models provided by complexity theory, the benchmark should be run against as many problem sizes as is reasonable.

Briefly, the more entries in the matrix from Figure 10-1 that can be filled in by actually executing the problem, the better.

10.1.5 Data-Dependent Benchmarks

One factor that complicates a benchmarking effort, and that can be misleading to the uninitiated, is the dependence of run time not on the algorithm or the machine but on the particular data values held in the structures on which the algorithm operates. A well-known example is *sorting*. Execution times for sorting arrays of the same length and record structure can vary dramatically depending on the particular *order* in which the values happen to lie in the file.

Continuing for a moment with the sorting example, some sorting algorithms are more susceptible than others to this phenomenon. *QuickSort*, for example, is far more variable in its response to data dependencies than is *MergeSort*. Thus, one can trade off an increase in the average (*expected*) run time against greater certainty (that is, reduced *variance*). This is illustrated in Figure 10-2. Algorithm I has a lower expected time to complete, but its larger standard deviation makes a worst-case scenario more likely. Algorithm II runs slower on average but has far less uncertainty.

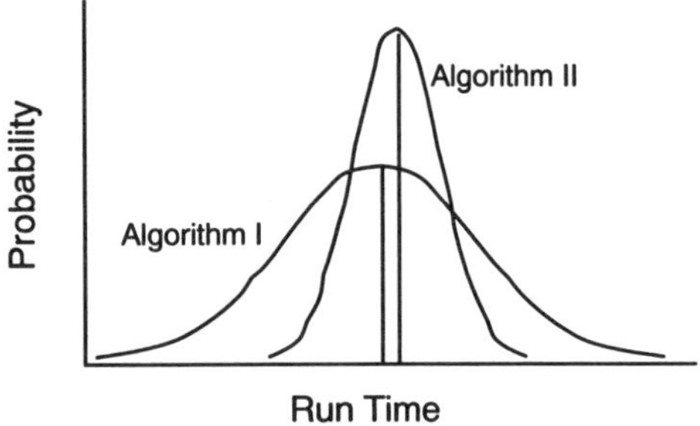

Figure 10-2. Trading off reduced increased run time for reduced variance

In numerical algorithms, an important source of data-dependent run-time variability has to do with *convergence*. A typical stopping condition for iterative algorithms is that the estimated error falls below some threshold. The iteration continues until this condition is achieved (or a loop count barrier is exceeded), and the number of iterations is the primary factor affecting run time. Depending on the actual data, the number of required iterations may be highly variable. Again, as with sorting, some algorithms may have the property that the number of iterations is deterministic and uniform, so that run-time variability is dramatically reduced.

While these general remarks apply to sequential as well as parallel algorithms, they can have a marked impact in the parallel case. We observed in Section 3.3.2, for example, how parallel algorithms on DM-MIMD architectures are often characterized by *synchronization points*. This is a point in the processing flow at which processors wait until it has been reached by all processors. Faster processors (that is, processors that, for reasons of data dependence, complete the processing stage more rapidly) must wait until the slower ones are done. Thus, the total time to complete this processing stage is the *maximum* time it takes any of the processors, not the *average*. The increased variability in Algorithm I in Figure 10-2 means that when replicated over many independent processors the *expected maximum* is greater than the corresponding maximum if Algorithm II is used.

The observation, then, is that parallel algorithms tend to exaggerate inherent data-dependent variabilities. Thus, algorithms that keep that variability low may be preferable, especially on very large processor arrays. Further, well-designed benchmarks for parallel machines should attempt to gauge this effect, so that it can be extrapolated to the intended operational setting. We will return to this subject again in Section 10.3.

> ***Example***: When John Gustafson and his coworkers at Sandia Laboratories were pursuing the first Gordon Bell award [3], they quickly realized the performance penalty associated with execution variability and synchronization overhead. One of the effects they noted was the number of cycles it took to perform a floating point multiply operation. This could vary, because the internal floating point representation was always normalized (initial zeroes behind the binary radix were shifted off and the exponent adjusted accordingly). The total time to execute a multiply was, thus, data dependent (depending on the number of shifts required) and over the course of computation could lead to variability in the execution times of otherwise deterministic algorithms. Of course, these researchers were intent on wringing the last .5 percent of performance from the

machine, but this example illustrates the kind of run-time uncertainty (and, in a parallel machine, consequent synchronization overhead) one can expect to encounter on large processor arrays. ■

Another situation where the "max versus average" phenomenon can strike is in memory utilization. It is not unusual for algorithms to dynamically construct auxiliary data structures during their execution, and the number and size of these structures can be data dependent. Distributed memory machines do not have a virtual memory capability, so it is important that enough physical memory be available in each node to handle the additional required space. In a shared memory machine, this variability is, to some extent, smoothed. The processors that need less in a statistical sense make room for those that need more. In a distributed memory machine, however, there is no way to know in advance which node will require the most memory, so that the individual node memories must be sized for the worst case, even though it may only be required infrequently. Again, a well-constructed benchmark will explicitly report memory utilization so that these effects, and their costs, can be understood.

Ideally, the benchmark will, therefore, be run not only over varying-size machines and varying-size data sets but also on a variety of data sets reflecting the statistical run time and memory usage variability of the intended operational environment. Yes, this is more work and more money, and it may not be required in simple cases. Nevertheless, simplistic "I can run 100 times faster with 100 nodes" extrapolation models can founder on exactly these considerations. At least, managers should be aware of the added source of risk if the benchmark does not reflect such variability and incorporate it as an evaluation factor of the selection and trade-off process.

10.2 PUBLICLY AVAILABLE PARALLEL BENCHMARKS

This section will briefly review the publicly available parallel benchmarks. A preliminary remark is in order. In the sequential world of commercial processing, the need for reliable industry-wide benchmarks has been recognized for some time. In the PC market, publications such as *PC Magazine* act as honest brokers for this function. For workstations, the major vendors set up and fund an independent organization that maintains and implements the Systems Performance Evaluation Cooperative (SPEC) algorithm suite. In the regime of on-line transaction processing (OLTP), audited comprehensive performance evaluations are conducted that take into account hardware, the

DBMS, archiving, roll-back, and realistic transaction rates. In all these cases, independence, objectivity, and technical comprehensiveness are the goal, and customers can have reasonable assurance of the accuracy and relevance of the published performance numbers.

The situation for benchmarks of parallel machines is not so benign. As we shall see, the available benchmarks are oriented to the scientific community and, hence, concentrate on matrix and array operations. Further, the difficulties we have already mentioned (selecting the right algorithm, data-dependent run-time variability, scaling factors reflecting both machine size and problem size, etc.) are beyond the scope of these efforts. To a certain degree, they act more as a scorecard in the leapfrog contest for holder of the title, *World's Fastest Supercomputer.* The relationship of these numbers to what can be operationally achieved is buried in all the details of system balance, I/O, interprocessor communications, and algorithm selection, none of which are shown by the top-level numbers. Nevertheless, these performance numbers continue to hold a certain perverse fascination thoughout the community, and so we pay them nodding recognition.

10.2.1 LINPACK Massively Parallel Computing

For a number of years, Jack Dongarra (currently at the Computer Science Department of the University of Tennessee) has acted as referee and honest broker for the supercomputer community, publishing a set of benchmark results relating to the LINPACK set of FORTRAN subroutines. Since many scientific codes use LINPACK kernels, and since this was about the only show in town for supercomputers to strut their stuff, and since (under the rather loose rules) the benchmark could be run not only by a vendor but also by an owner of the hardware, this has been a popular forum for following progress in the supercomputer marketplace.

When MPPs came on the scene, the Amdahl's Law effect associated with small problems immediately become apparent. The most widely used of the subroutines constituting the benchmark was the one that solved a set of linear equations (double precision = 64-bit arithmetic), and a dense matrix size of 100 × 100 was used. However, with the passage of time, this became unacceptably constricting even to vectorizing, modestly parallel shared memory machines. For example, an Amdahl's Law calculation for a 16-processor Cray C-90 shows a parallelizable part of only about 20.5 percent for the 100 × 100 case. The next step in the evolution of the benchmark was to boost the matrix size to 1,000 × 1,000. On this size problem, the Cray C-90 achieved an 11.1-fold speed-up on 16 processors, and the Amdahl's Law computation shows that the 1,000 × 1,000 case has a parallelizable part of about 97.1 percent—a classic instance of how the parallelizable part of a problem changes (and grows) with problem size.

However, 3 percent is still a lot of sequential processing for a massively parallel processor. It imposes a speed-up limit of about 30× to 35× and, hence, is biased against massive parallelism. As a result, yet another component was added to the LINPACK benchmark—the Massively Parallel Computing component. Here, the organization doing the benchmark is allowed to choose *whatever size problem it wants* and report results as achieved GFLOPs (double precision). More precisely, they report:

N	the number of processors used
R_{max}	the maximum achieved GFLOPs
N_{max}	the order of the matrix inverted
$N_{1/2}$	the matrix size at which half R_{max} is achieved
R_{peak}	the maximum possible GFLOPs of the machine

As of March 30, 1993, the list was topped by a 1,024-node CM-5 from Thinking Machines Corp., with values

N	1,024
R_{max}	59.7 GFLOPs
N_{max}	52,224
$N_{1/2}$	24,064
R_{peak}	131

These data inform the reader that should he or she wish to invert a double precision matrix of size 52,224 × 52,224, and should he or she be considering using a 1,024 processor CM-5 MPP, then a processing rate of 59.7 GFLOPs can be obtained. Since there are approximately 9.5×10^{13} floating point operations performed in this computation, this problem would be complete in approximately 26.5 minutes. Additionally, a processing rate half R_{max} (namely, 29.9 GFLOPs) can be had on a matrix dimensioned 24,064 × 24,064. The 9.3×10^{12} operations for this smaller problem would complete in approximately 5.4 minutes.

The virtues of this benchmark are that: (1) it allows the parallel processor to choose its own algorithm for the solution; (2) it allows the parallel processor to choose a problem large enough so that Amdahl's Law effects are neglible; and (3) it requires reporting of performance on a second size of the problem (namely, the problem size at which performance is cut in half) so that users can interpolate their own intended problem size based on those reported. The difficulties are: (1) it reports results as GFLOPs, a measure only applicable to scientific, floating point–intensive codes; (2) the selected algorithm (matrix inversion) is highly vectorizable; (3) no I/O is reported, and there is no indication of how much of the computation is taken up by interprocessor communications; and (4) there is no indication of how much optimization was incorporated or even which algorithm was used.

It may be objected (to my objections) that at least this allows us to compare machines, even if it does not allow us to actually predict delivered performance. This rests on a false premise—namely, that performance ratios between machines do not change as we move from problem to problem. In fact, different problems are more or less suitable to different machines, and a machine that performs poorly on, say, problem A may perform like a champ on problem B, while the reverse will hold for some other architecture. Simple scaling rules are the exception, not the rule, and (in the author's opinion) the LINPACK Massively Parallel Computing benchmark has more to do with pleasing the egos of the machine designers than with reporting anything very useful for prospective users.

The LINPACK benchmarks are publicly available from a number of sources, including *more@hpcwire.ans.net.*

10.2.2 SLALOM

The SLALOM (Scalable, Language-independent, Ames Laboratory, One-minute Measurement) benchmark was established and is supervised and maintained by John Gustafson and his staff at the Ames Laboratory-USDOE in Ames, Iowa. The basic idea is simple. An ordinary benchmark holds the problem size constant and asks various machines to attempt to run that problem faster and faster. The total number of floating point operations in the problem (the numerator in the MFLOPs/second unit of measure for processing rates) is held constant, and the run time (the denominator) is made as small as possible. In SLALOM, the denominator (that is, the run time) is held constant, and the size of the problem is allowed to increase; that is, machines are asked to work the *largest possible problem* in one minute.

This requires a problem that can easily scale to extremely large sizes—large enough to keep GFLOP machines busy for at least a minute—but that also can scale to small sizes—small enough, for example, that a PC could work a simple version in at most a minute. The problem chosen is a *radiosity* (that is, ray tracing) problem, and the "size" of the problem is scaled by the granularity to which the problem is solved. Any given solution will approximate the "true" solution by decomposing the surface (in this case, a simple six-surface box) into subregions called *patches*. The more patches, the closer the approximation is to the true value and the more calculations are required. A machine that can solve, say, a 100-patch version of the radiosity problem in one minute is significantly faster than one that only can solve a 20-patch version but significantly slower than a machine that can solve a 1,000-patch version. Thus, the number of patches becomes a measure of performance. Since there is also a simple formula to compute the number of floating point operations involved for a given number of patches, it is easy to convert patches to MFLOPs, remembering that the run time is always 60 seconds.

Like the MPP version of the LINPACK benchmark, the underlying motivation for a benchmark like SLALOM is that MPPs must be allowed to work a large enough problem so that Amdahl's Law effects become negligible. By holding execution time constant, and by allowing problem size to grow, SLALOM meets this requirement. However, like LINPACK, the radiosity application is representative of only a very narrow type of problem and in the end has more value as a scorekeeper in the race to a TFLOPs than as a realisitic predictor of delivered performance. A discussion of the design of SLALOM can be found in [31].

10.2.3 Others

Perhaps the most careful and comprehensive benchmarking of high-performance architectures was a year-long effort conducted at Cal Tech under the direction (initially) of Geoffrey Fox and (later) of Paul Messina. Funded by the National Science Foundation, the effort ported and executed a variety of scientific codes on a variety of machine architectures. Problem sizes and machine sizes (number of nodes) were varied (to account for Amdahl's Law effects), and the algorithms were adjusted from machine to machine to best suit architectural characteristics.

A complete description of this effort can be found in [32], which describes the applications included in the benchmarking effort (primarily scientific codes) and the machines (Crays, the CM-2, nCube, Sequent, Alliant, etc.). While the results are already out of date, the paper is an excellent introduction to what is required for a "fair" benchmark among a variety of parallel architectures and of how results should be reported and caveated. There has been no effort on the part of NSF or Cal Tech to update these benchmarks or keep them current.

Stanford University has maintained a continuing interest in distributed shared memory (DSM), most recently evidenced by the DASH (Directory

Architecture for SHared memory) prototype. Using a directory-based cache coherence scheme with substantial hardware assistance, a single coherent address space was implemented over 12 SGI multiprocessor boxes (48 processors total). In evaluating performance, the DASH team drew upon a group of parallel benchmark codes called SPLASH (Stanford ParalleL Applications for SHared memory). While these applications are not in a form suitable for direct implementation on DM-MIMD or SIMD machines, they do permit both problem size and the number of processors to vary, thereby directly addressing Amdahl's Law effects. A description of DASH and the performance measurement techniques employed (including a powerful profiling environment) can be found in [13].

Over the past 10 years, a substantial amount of literature dealing with measured performance on parallel architectures, has appeared. It seems that at least one good way to get a paper published nowadays is to port an existing piece of research software to a parallel box, and then report run time as a function of number of processors. Papers in this vein tend to be more interesting for the parallelizing software strategies employed than for the performance results reported. First, few universities can afford a full-up MPP and, hence, tend to have small parallel machines (say, 8 or 16 nodes). This, in turn, limits the size of problem that can reasonably be run, so that more often than not the results reflect performance on a problem size so small that not a great deal of parallelism is available. Further, since the universities are more interested in research than production, I/O, storage, and OS difficulties are often finessed, so that reliable extrapolation from reported results to predicted operational performance is not possible. In short, papers dealing with performance measurement on parallel architectures in academic publications and conferences tend to have only marginal, and highly caveated, relevance to an operational production setting.

A recent entry into the parallel benchmarking arena is a suite of benchmarks called ParkBench constructed by the Center for Research on Parallel Computation [33]. It is too early, at this writing, to be sure what impact this will ultimately have on the parallel processing community.

10.3 SCALING SEQUENTIAL PERFORMANCE TO PARALLEL PERFORMANCE

This section and the next take up the situation most often encountered—namely, when an organization does not have the resources (time, money, personnel, etc.) to undertake a full-up parallel benchmark but yet needs reliable performance estimates to support a rational selection of both parallel architecture and machine size. In this section, the situation is further simplified to applications that are *embarrassingly parallel.* By this, we mean that the total problem naturally decomposes into a large number of independent subproblems, each identical except for the data on which each subproblem is to execute. Little or no interprocessor communication is required—just load up each processor (in MIMD fashion) with its data, and let it run to completion. Examples include matrix multiplication, Monte Carlo simulations, statistical optimization techniques, image processing, and some types of database operations.

In these situations, it may be possible to reliably extrapolate performance from a single processor to quite large arrays. If, for example, measured performance is known for a single processor (say, the processor on which the application is currently executing), a simple execution model may be adequate. This is typical, for example, of applications where *throughput* is more important than *latency.*

Example: In automated fingerprint matching applications, the unknown fingerprint (called the *mark*) must be compared against a potentially large number of possible matches. A score (reflecting goodness of fit) is computed, and the top few candidates are then provided (in sorted order, best to least) to a human expert for final verification. The most difficult and time-consuming part of the task is the execution of the algorithm that computes the goodness of fit score; I/O and the other parts of the problem are insignificant by comparison. Now, the set of potential matches is given in advance, and the job can be viewed as the calculation of a score for each of them. Clearly, two machines could each take half the candidates, compute their scores concurrently, and be done in half the time. Or, following that thought, 100 machines could each take 1/100 of the candidates, process them concurrently (in parallel), and be done in 1/100 the time. ■

This is a classic example of an embarrassingly parallel problem. Amdahl's Law is a nonfactor, and we can expect nearly ideal speed-up for even large numbers of processors. For this type of problem, parallel performance can be reliably predicted just by knowing how fast a single processor can execute the matching algorithm (including I/O) on a single mark/candidate pair. Thus, the benchmarking effort need not go to the trouble of running on a large processor array. Running the matching code as a benchmark on a single processor will provide all the information necessary.

Things get even better in a simple case like this. It may well be that execution time is already known on a current uniprocessor platform—say, Processor A. Now, a good set of sequential uniprocessor benchmarks (e.g.,

SPECmarks and the like) exists in the public domain. These can be used to directly scale performance from Processor A to another uniprocessor—say, Processor B. With this estimate in hand, the simple scaling rules to a large parallel array consisting of Processor B nodes can be made. In short, reasonably reliable sizing can be done without elaborate benchmarking efforts, just using information already in hand.

Suppose that Processor A currently executes the matching algorithm at a rate of 18 candidate/match pairs per second. Further, suppose it is known that Processor B is about 3.6 times faster than Processor A, based on published SPECmarks. Thus, we would expect Processor B to process candidate/match pairs at a rate of approximately 3.6 * 18 ~ 65 candidate pairs per second. Now, suppose that the desired rate is 1,000 pairs per second. Then, we would expect a loosely coupled array of approximately 1,000/65 ~ 16 Processor B nodes to achieve this desired rate (provided that I/O bandwidth is also appropriately scaled). Throwing in 20 percent overhead (generous, in this simple example), a 20-node array would probably be more than adequate. Note that the only information necessary was: (1) the already known execution time for the current platform; (2) the sequential scaling factor using existing sequential benchmarks; and (3) the desired performance goal.

In embarrassingly parallel applications, the concerns and caveats expressed in Sections 10.1 and 10.2 are largely irrelevant. Since many useful applications are, in fact, embarrassingly parallel, the benchmarking and performance estimation problems may be considerably eased without sacrificing accuracy.

This simple analysis does *not* apply to a closely coupled shared memory architecture. Tasking and paging overheads in the operating system generally do *not* permit linear speed-up, and the simple model applied above does not hold. Even when the application appears to be perfectly parallelizable, the tasking and paging effects on an SMP will often introduce overheads that seriously degrade efficiency and, hence, cause serious undersizing of estimates if the simple speed-up model is used. On SMPs, it is critical that actual benchmarks be run on the target hardware with the intended operating system. It is not unusual to lose a factor of 2 in efficiency (that is, to run half as fast as a linear speed-up model would predict) when as few as eight processors are employed. DM-MIMD machines do not have this problem on embarrassingly parallel applications, since there is no possible interaction between the tasks (each task executes independently on its private node, with no interaction among processors). On SMPs, the tasks can and will interact, via the operating system, in complex ways not readily apparent at the application level.

To summarize, choose a level of benchmarking effort appropriate to the intended application. If the application is embarrassingly parallel (and many are), little or no additional effort may be required beyond simple scaling based on existing benchmarks on sequential machines and desired levels of performance. Such simple models are more appropriate for DM-MIMD architectures than for shared memory SMPs. Operating system overheads on SMPs can considerably complicate performance estimation, even in these simple cases.

10.4 ESTIMATING PERFORMANCE

In the previous section, we considered a situation (where the application was embarrassingly parallel, and the intended architecture was loosely coupled DM-MIMD) in which lengthy or elaborate benchmarks are simply not needed in order to obtain reasonably accurate performance estimates over a wide range of problem sizes. In this section, we consider another frequently encountered situation, namely, when it is not feasible to perform all the benchmarking one might otherwise desire. For example, the intended processor array size might not exist, or be available, to run the benchmark. Or, the benchmark code and associated data might be sensitive (or classified), so that benchmarking on vendor equipment would be unacceptable from a policy viewpoint. Or, the cost of porting the software might be too great, especially if the benchmark is part of a selection, and the target machine might not be purchased. For these and many other reasons, porting the benchmark code to the target hardware and executing it may not be an available option, so that something else has to be done.

Here, we are definitely leaving known territory and striking off into uncharted regions. Paper and pencil performance estimates are notoriously inaccurate, even on fairly straightforward sequential machines. When we add in the additional uncertainties of interprocessor communications and contention, synchronization overhead, and data-dependent run-time effects, the honest engineer will approach performance estimation on MPP with fear and trembling.

Having done my duty as an author with this comprehensive disclaimer, let me say that experience has shown it is not always necessary to just throw in the towel without a fight. Providing that data dependencies are not overwhelming, and that a *clear pattern* of synchronization and communications can be specified for an intended implementation, reasonably accurate execution models can be built that require only a limited amount of sequential benchmarking.

This is not a subject that can be profitably discussed in abstact terms. Everything depends on the details of the application *and* the target hardware. The best approach is to present a worked-out example that illustrates some of the major issues. The reader can then get a sense of the kinds of processes involved. The message (disclaimer aside) is that this is not always a completely intractable problem and that with some care management can obtain performance estimates with enough credibility to serve as a basis for sizing, selection, and procurement decisions.

Example: This extended example is drawn from orbitology. We want to compute time intervals during which pairs of orbiting satellites in a constellation have a direct line of sight, unobscured by the earth or its atmosphere. The intervals are to be computed during some larger time interval—say, over a two-week period, beginning at date D_B and ending at date $D_E = D_B + 14$ (measured in days). The basic capability at our disposal is an ephemeris generation routine—*EPH*(time)—which (when initialized with a description of a satellite's orbit) accepts a time as input and computes the exact position and velocity for that satellite as output. Thus, at any point in time we can compute exactly where each of the satellites is/will be and, hence (with some geometry and knowing a little about the shape and size of the earth), we can compute whether any pair of them can see each other.

Our approach will be to begin at time D_B and to step forward through time (until D_E is reached) using a delta time step that agrees with the accuracy requirements (that is, if I need to know the visibility intervals accurate to 30 seconds, my step size will be 15 seconds). At each iteration of the loop, I compute the positions of all the satellites at the new time and then examine them pair by pair to see if a line of sight exists. By keeping track of the times at which visibility starts and ends for each pair, I can obtain the desired visibility intervals.

To parallelize this application, we partition the problem *over time*; that is, we break the large time interval $[D_B, D_E]$ into equal subintervals and assign one time interval for each processor in the array. Each of the processors then computes the visibility intervals over the subinterval assigned to it. At the end, some "gluing" is needed to piece together visibility intervals spanning the artificial breakpoints introduced by our parallelization approach—an induced overhead at the boundary typical of parallelization based on data decomposition.

We propose an execution time model incorporating the following variables:

N	the number of processors
S	the number of satellites
K	the total number of time steps

Each of the *N* processors must compute the value of *EPH* for each of the *S* satellites at each of *K/N* time points. Thus, the total number of calls to *EPH* by each processor is:

$$(S * K)/N$$

Now, *K* itself depends on the length of the total time over which we are to compute and on the step size. For example, if we are considering a two-week (14-day) period and 15-second time steps, then

$$\begin{aligned} K &= \text{days} * \text{min/day} * \text{steps/min} \\ &= 14 * 1{,}440 * 4 \\ &= 80{,}640 \end{aligned}$$

If we are considering a constellation of 20 satellites, this is

$$K * S = 80{,}640 * 20 = 1{,}612{,}800$$

calls to *EPH*. We will be spreading these out evenly across the processor array. For example, if $N = 64$, each processor will receive/make

$$\begin{aligned} (S*K)/N &= 1{,}612{,}800/64 \\ &= 25{,}200 \end{aligned}$$

calls to *EPH*. Thus, a single measurement for one call to *EPH* can be used to estimate this part of the processing of the complete application. For example, if a call to *EPH* on one of the node processors takes 385 msec, then the total of 25,200 calls would take 161.7 minutes. Note that the only benchmark required for this estimate is a single instance of *EPH* on a single processor node.

At this point, a quick survey of the remaining required processing shows the need for: (1) input of the ephemeris data for the 20 satellites; (2) computation of the $S^2/2$ line of sight states for each of the *K/N* time steps; (3) performing the sequential "glue" operation over the array, whereby visibility intervals that have been split across processors are rejoined; and (4) output of the visibility intervals for each satellite pair. Now, compared to a call to the ephemeris generator *EPH*, the operation in (2) is apt to be extremely quick—say, on the order of .2 msec, so that all the 190 pairs can be examined in less than .04 msec for each time step, or about .8 minutes for the 64 processors. Similarly, estimating data sizes, latencies, and bandwidths, the reader will be easily convinced that both I/O stages (1) and (4) are well under 1 second. Finally, turning to (3), each processor (beginning with the last) sends to its predecessor information regarding potentially border-crossing visibility intervals. Estimating this data as a maximum of 30 bytes per pair for the 190 pairs, each processor must transmit about 6 KB to its neighbor. Even at an extremely conservative estimate of .1 msec latency and 1 MB/sec bandwidth, each of these transfers takes at most

.1 + .006 = .106 msec

for each of the 64 processors, or less than .1 second total.

In other words, run times for steps (1)–(4) are swamped by the run time of that portion of the algorithm devoted to calls to *EPH*. In effect, we can model the total run time as

.385 msec/call * (number of calls) + small overhead

Of course, we can reduce the number of calls each processor makes to *EPH* by increasing the number of processors. Increasing *N* will have the effect of increasing steps (1), (3), and (4), but, since they are already so small, this effect is of negligible practical significance. Thus, based on these figures, the analysis shows that the application should scale very well to large numbers of nodes and further gives a reliable basis for estimating the array size needed to obtain a given level of performance.

Now, if the numbers were different, the analysis might turn out quite another way. Suppose, for example, that a call to *EPH* took only .040 msec instead of .385 msec. This would have the effect of decreasing the portion of run time devoted to calls to *EPH* by a factor of 10, and the ratios between this component and the other components (1)–(4) now change. They potentially have a much greater impact (proportionately) on the overall run time, so that they would need to be specifically included in the run-time estimate. One could imagine, for example, an algorithm where interprocessor communications would be required, not once at the end but once per time step. In that case, it could become a significant contributer to the model. Even more complicated would be an algorithm in which interprocessor communications were not contention-free, nearest neighbor (as this problem is) but more general and, hence, subject to contention. If an analyis shows that overall run time can be substantially affected by the interprocessor communications, then an appropriate (and appropriately pessimistic) model must be constructed and included. ■

The basic approach should now be clear. The run-time model must incorporate (in a complexity analysis sense) the major operations in the algorithm as they will reside on the target hardware. This, in turn, means a *separate* model for each hardware platform being considered. The model should explicitly include I/O and interprocessor communications. Top-level order of magnitude estimates may show that some components of the model are inconsequential compared with others, permitting an initially complex model to be considerably simplified. The remaining portions of the model are then benchmarked or estimated to an accuracy appropriate for their overall impact on run time. It is also common practice to add on a "safety margin" of 20 to 50 percent to account for growth, elbow room, and errors in the estimation process. Management tolerance for this will be tempered by its impact on cost. For MPPs, however, hardware is typically a smaller fraction of total cost (including software, etc.) than it is for traditional architectures, so that this overhead may be less significant than it might at first appear.

In the author's experience, the goal of performance estimation on parallel machines has always been to find some manageable set of key software kernels (*EPH* in the above example) whose behavior dominates the total execution. When those can be found and benchmarked, and when the number of calls to them can be computed deterministically both as a function of problem size and machine size, then defensible estimates can be obtained. Anything that prevents such an approach—data dependence, uncertainty in message sizes or patterns, or inability to benchmark even single processor performance on the key kernels—detracts (perhaps fatally) from the accuracy and usefulness of the estimate.

The example presented above is based on a real problem. Performance estimates on several machines, with numbers of nodes varying from 4 to 256, were made. While only a few of these were ever validated against measured run times, in those cases the paper and pencil estimate was within 15 percent of the achieved performance and was actually a bit on the conservative side. If care is taken, and if the application has a sufficiently deterministic parallel structure, performance estimation is a reasonable (and often very cost-effective) alternative to benchmarking as part of the selection and sizing process.

10.5 QUESTIONS TO ASK VENDORS

Specifically, this section is a list of questions to ask vendors about their performance numbers.

1. If the benchmark involved floating point, was it single precision or double precision? It is best to have both measurements and to see what the penalty is for double precision (or, conversely, what the reward is for being able to use single precision).
2. Does the benchmark include any I/O operations? If not, why not? If so, does it break out I/O for separate consideration?

3. What is the largest machine (number of nodes) the benchmark has been run on? Are run time, speed-up, and efficiency figures available for that case?
4. What is the required memory for the benchmark? Does the problem fit entirely into main memory? If cache is used, does the problem fit entirely into cache?
5. Was there any extrapolation involved (i.e., running the problem on a small number of nodes and then scaling upwards)? Is so, what was it, and what assumptions were made to support the scaling model?
6. What language was the benchmark written in? Were any low-level (assembly, microcode) or tuned library routines involved? What compiler and optimization switches were used?
7. Was the benchmark run on a variety of problem sizes? If so, are performmance results available for all cases or only for the best?
8. How much interprocessor communications does this benchmark require? Are all the communications nearest neighbor in the underlying network topology? Does the benchmark produce estimates of the amount of time spent in interprocessor communications?
9. If the vendor attempts to estimate cost performance (say, as $/MFLOP), what costs were considered? In particular, did software development costs enter into the calculation?
10. What operating system was used? Were any operating system calls involved? How much job control software is required to run the benchmark?
11. Has the benchmark ever been run while other jobs/users were on the machine? If so, explain the performance impact.

Summary of Chapter 10

Benchmarking supports the twin goals of *comparing* alternate platforms and *sizing* a platform to meet requirements. This chapter has identified the unique issues that arise when benchmarking a parallel machine. Dependence of benchmark results both on machine size and problem size has been a major theme. Performance measures are needed that reflect efficiency (how much of the potential performance is lost due to Amdahl's Law). Cost/performance should honestly appraise the complete cost, including software development. The strengths and weaknesses of the major public MPP benchmarks were discussed. Vendors should be allowed both to select a size of the benchmark problem (generally, *large*) that shows the hardware to its best advantage and should be permitted to select an algorithmic approach that makes the best use of the architecture. While pencil and paper performance estimation has its limitations, Sections 10.3 and 10.4 suggest that for many parallel applications reliable performance estmates can be obtained with a minimum of additional benchmarking effort. Often, only knowledge of sequential node performance on a few key kernels is required. A recurring theme has also been to understand the component of total performance due to I/O and interprocessor communications. A checklist of "context" questions essential to a proper understanding of a published benchmark was provided in the final section. An introduction to the literature on benchmarking and performance estimation for MPPs may be found in several of the references, including [1, 31, 32, 33–4].

11

Porting and Developing Parallel Applications

As was stressed in Section 1.3, the Achilles' heel of parallel processing is the lack of third-party application software. While a great deal of algorithm development work has been going on in the National Labs and the academic research community, this is a far cry from the kind of turnkey, bulletproof software required for commercial production systems. Thus, the question that should never be far from the mind of a manager contemplating a shift of applications to a parallel machine is: *Where is the software coming from?*

Most organizations (rightly) have little interest in *writing* software. They would much prefer to buy it and run it. To an organization that has gone through the pain of procuring, customizing, and/or developing an application at some point in the past, the thought of reopening that can of worms is not a happy one. Only the clear and tangible benefits of greatly increased performance or greatly reduced cost could induce a practically minded organization to venture down this path. It is better to wait, thinks the manager, until the technology is mature and available off the shelf. For some organizations, however, the processing throughput requirement is *now*, and the option of waiting is simply not available. Like it or not, such organizations will face the software issue—either porting existing applications or developing new ones from scratch.

The two problems of *porting existing codes*, on the one hand, and *developing new codes*, on the other, are related but distinct, and our approach in this chapter will be to deal with them separately. The first section takes up issues of porting existing applications—what are the available strategies and their associated strengths and weaknesses. The second section concerns development of parallel codes—how hard is it, how different is it from sequential code development, what options are available, etc. The final section provides three case studies that illustrate major themes.

11.1 PORTING STRATEGIES

This section will discuss the various strategies that are available to port existing application code to a parallel architecture. The major options are indicated in Figure 11-1, and this will serve to organize our discussion. The first section (11.1.1) will consider automatic parallelization; the second (11.1.2), the use of parallel libraries. The third porting strategy, major recoding, is enough like from-scratch application development that we reserve its discussion for Section 11.2. However, a third subsection (11.1.3) is provided under this heading. It deals with some ways to make the porting task easier (or, at least, some things to avoid that would make it more difficult).

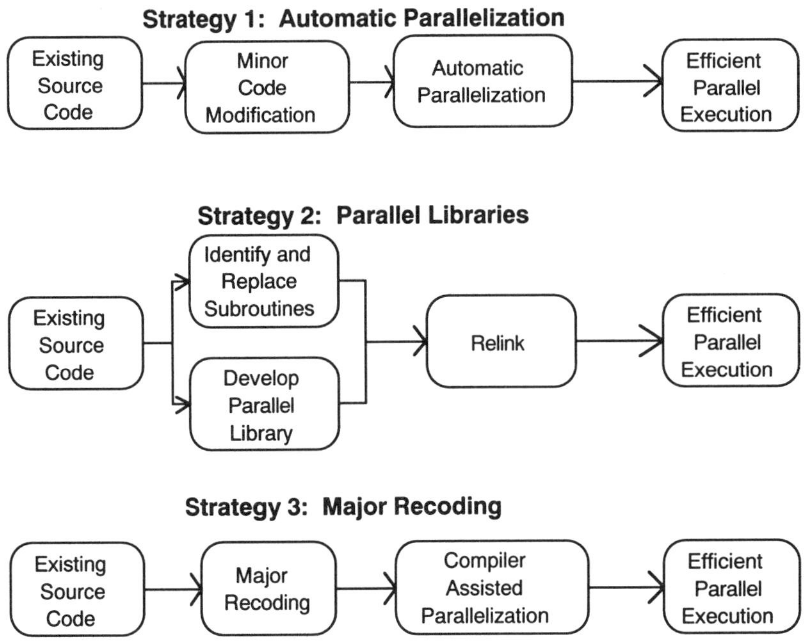

Figure 11-1. Porting strategies for efficient parallel execution

11.1.1 Automatic Parallelization

In Section 8.1, we reviewed the current state of parallelizing compilers. Briefly, the situation is as follows. Depending on the machine architecture, there are a number of tasks that must be accomplished in order to obtain an efficient parallel version of an application. For machines where the processor has local memory, data layout across the processor array is perhaps the most complex and least intuitive task to programmers with a sequential background. Even in shared memory machines, data layout and access patterns can be important but for a different reason. Here, it is necessary to make efficient use of the processor's local cache. Programs that manage to keep memory references tightly clustered in a small number of memory regions will use the cache (and the virtual memory paging scheme) much more efficiently than programs whose memory reference pattern is widely dispersed.

In addition to data layout, other parallelization tasks include: creation of multiple control streams, each responsible for part of the work (in MIMD machines); data exchange among cooperating processors; synchronization of access to shared memory locations (in shared memory models); and (most difficult of all) tailoring of the algorithm to take optimal advantage of the target hardware. These tasks are either not required by a sequential program or are greatly simplified.

The goal of automatic parallelization (or parallelizing compilers) is to relieve the programmer of as much responsibility as possible for these parallelizing tasks. In the rosiest scenario, the programmer need not worry about these matters at all. The compiler would (in such a world) accept "dusty deck" codes and produce efficient parallel object code without any (or, at least, very little) additional work by the programmer. This is the sense in which the phrase "automatic parallelization" is typically used. The more a compiler departs from this ideal, the less "automatic" it is.

How realistic is it to think a compiler for a parallel machine could perform such a task? As we discussed in Chapter 8, for various reasons this is a *very hard problem* and (in its general form) is well beyond the reach of current compiler technology. Vendors can, of course, construct carefully tailored small examples that their compilers can handle, but these must be considered toy problems and are hardly representative of the stresses that real, large codes would put on a parallelizing compiler. This is not to criticize. In the author's opinion, truly automatic parallelizing compilers are so far in the future as to be without effect for any practical current problem. Those who insist on waiting for this technology will find that parallel processing has long ago passed them by.

The practical consequence of this observation is that the first strategy in Figure 11-1 is just a pipe dream. Of course, if anyone could produce an efficient parallelizing compiler, his or her fortune would be made. There is a fabulous market for such a tool, and many gifted computer scientists and savvy parallel vendors have made valiant attempts on the problem—thus far, without noticeable success. We have included Strategy 1 in our catalog not because it is a realistic option but because some vendors talk as if it were, and some organizations appear to be ready to believe it. At least you are now warned!

The most promising option now being pursued is to try to formulate extensions to existing sequential languages (such as FORTRAN or C) that depart as little as possible from the sequential language standard on which they are based and yet supply enough additional information to allow the compiler to make reasonable choices about parallelization tasks. Both FORTRAN 90 and HPF (*H*igh *P*erformance *F*ORTRAN) are efforts in this direction. The idea is to make life easy for the parallel programmer by incorporating a few simple but powerful new primitives, easily learned and specified, that can permit the compiler to do most of the hard work (spreading the data across the processor array, inserting locks, inserting message-passing primitives, replicating shared data structures, etc.).

All the effort in this area, to date, has been in using FORTRAN-like arrays and array syntax for this purpose. This is because the major users of supercomputers are technical and scientific organizations (like the National Labs) who are accustomed to FORTRAN. The examples provided in Chapters 4 through 7 give a flavor for where things stand at the moment. The main point is that while these parallel languages do relieve the programmer of some of the low-level drudgery, they are still a far cry from the sequential languages they build on and, hence, from the "dusty deck" that is the wished-for ideal input to a fully automatic parallel compiler.

A useful convention would be to term compilers for these new languages "assisted parallelization" and reserve the word "automatic parallelization" for the real thing. Vendors are not always too scrupulous in their wording (no universally accepted terminology has emerged), and so the term "parallelizing compiler" is applied indiscriminately to a variety of more or less useful capabilities. One approach, for example, is a preprocessor whose objective is to accept "dusty deck" source code as input and to produce a corresponding source listing in the parallel language (which can then be fed to the "parallelizing" compiler). In fact, these tools are not successful without a substantial amount of programmer interaction. They are best thought of as interactive CASE tools to assist in code conversion rather than as "automatic compilers." This is not to undervalue their utility but only to properly assess their potential and capabilities.

The message of this section, then, is that Strategy 1 from Figure 11-1 is not a realistic option for porting of application code. We turn next to Strategy 2.

11.1.2 Parallel Libraries

Another possible approach to porting parallel code, and one that has a much better chance for success than the first, is the use of *parallel libraries.* The basic idea is fairly simple and has been used (in another guise) for optimizing sequential codes for some time. It rests on the observation, which is true for many codes, that a relatively large percentage of the run time may be spent in a relatively small percentage of the total code. In the purely sequential world, code optimization efforts focus on the computationally intensive parts of the code—the handful of scientific subroutines, say, where the majority of the work is done. An analogous approach may be taken for parallelization. Suppose that very fast parallelized versions are available for these subroutines. In the ideal case (of course, things are never this simple), one could substitute the parallel library versions for the sequential library versions. Even though the entire application has not been parallelized, the computationally demanding part has, and an effective compromise has been made between recoding effort and taking advantage of the performance boost offered by the parallel machine. So goes the argument.

This approach has been used for many years on vectorizing machines. Typically, the vectorized library already exists—a set of commonly used scientific subroutines already highly optimized for target hardware. A substantial performance boost is available by the simple expedient of linking in the new library of subroutines. Even if the desired subroutine does not already reside in the library, the programmer need only focus attention on a relatively small amount of code—the new version of the subroutine—rather than a complete rewrite.

This approach can also work reasonably well on shared memory machines. Multitasking/multithreading can take place internally to the subroutine and, hence, is completely invisible to the sequential code in which it resides. Indeed, the programmer need not even be aware that parallelism (respectively, vectorization) has occurred.

The reason why this approach can be successful for vector and shared memory machines is that the programming paradigm for these machines is so close to sequential. The choice to vectorize or to parallelize is made locally at the subroutine level and, hence, invisibly to the top-level control structure. Further, these machines are able to execute sequential portions of the code without modification (albeit, without speed-up), so that the portions of the code that do not parallelize do not prevent the software port from at least executing.

Were we to look closely at what it is about the underlying architecture for these machines that permits this approach to succeed, we would find that the key is the large, uniformly addressable memory. The program/programmer need not worry about *where* the data are. Any physical processor can access any memory location (or any part of an array in memory) without a penalty in additional latency. Thus, whatever data structures the programmer may have chosen for the sequential version can (usually) be accommodated by the parallel version. Things are not so easy when a distributed memory MPP—SIMD or DM-MIMD—is the target.

Suppose, for example, that the subroutine we wish to accelerate is a *sort* routine. In a shared memory machine, the array to be sorted has already been named and storage allocated. The parallel version of the sort routine will enlist several processors to assist in the sort operation, but no modification to the array itself, as a data structure, is required. If, however, a distributed memory MIMD machine is to be used to accomplish the sort, the first and most difficult problem to be overcome is that the data array must be physically distributed across the MPP processor array. How is this to happen?

Conceptually, we might think of the MPP as an *attached processor*. The original machine, instead of performing the operation itself, will ship the data off to the MPP for this part of the operation and then accept the processed code back when the operation is complete. This is illustrated in Figure 11-2. The execution of the new library subroutine consists of three pieces: (1) shipping the data (using what means?) to the MPP; (2) executing the function (in this case, a sort) on the MPP; and (3) shipping the data back from the MPP to the sequentially executing host.

There are a number of inefficiencies, which will be apparent to the reader, in this approach. First, how much extra time is spent in moving the data (maybe a lot, maybe not)? Do the data have to be moved every time the fast version of the subroutine is wanted (yes)? Are there data format conversion problems to be solved (maybe)? When I add in the overhead of the data transfer, how much time have I really saved (it depends)? And so forth. Attached processors have been around for a while (particularly array processors used in the late 1970s and early 1980s to accelerate scientific codes), and they have all suffered from these difficulties.

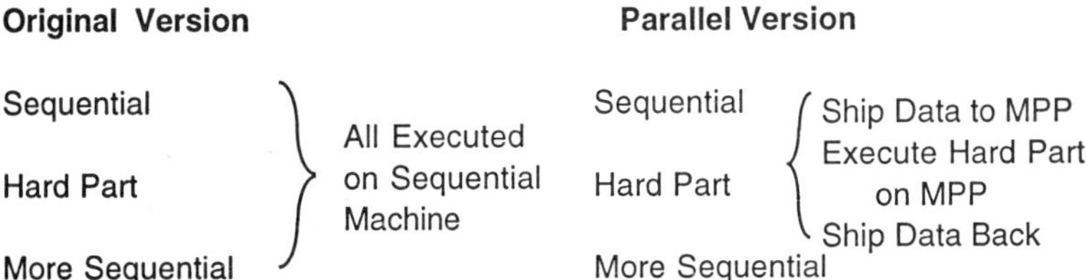

Figure 11-2. Using an MPP to speed up selected subroutines

Some vendors have adopted a marketing approach in which the MPP is viewed as an attached processor. For existing customers, the MPP is sold as an accelerator "for tough parts of the application," with (hopefully) most of the code remaining untouched. For new customers, the traditional product line benefits, since a "host" or "front end" will typically be required along with the MPP. Each organization can judge for itself whether such an approach. In making the assessment, remember that the Amdahl's Law phenomenon (see Chapter 2) is most pronounced when the sequential portion of the code (that is, the part that executes on the host) is greatest. The very *existence* of the host, therefore, is an indicator that (at least in its current form) the application has not been successfully parallelized and, hence, that an MPP may not be warranted. Based on this reasoning, a host+MPP solution is a tacit admission of failure, at least as far as parallelization is concerned. Of course, such failures are not necessarily seen as bad news to vendors of traditional equipment.

11.1.3 The Choice of Architecture

For a number of reasons, the choice of hardware architecture can have a substantial impact on the software porting effort. This section briefly summarizes the relevant issues.

The best situation is when the application is susceptible to coarse-grained, "natural" parallelism—say, running several instances of the same job concurrently and independently. Even if the application does not match this model perfectly, there may be an outer loop, with little or no dependence between iterations, that can be spread across multiple processors. In such a case, very little modification to the existing source code may be required—just some control logic to partition the work and collect results at the end. Entire sections of code and entire collections of related subroutines that perform low-level operations deep inside the outer loop may need no modification at all.

When this type of parallelism is possible, an MIMD machine—whether distributed memory or shared memory—is indicated. The reason is that the natural parallelism in the problem requires separate, independent control streams and, hence, separate controllers (that is, *M*ultiple *I*nstruction rather than *S*ingle *I*nstruction). Indeed, if the outer loop iterations are completely independent, an LAN of workstations with some shared control software may be the most cost-effective solution.

A second reason that the port to an MIMD machine may be easier is that MIMD machines can compile sequential code to run on separate processors. The parallelism in the problem can be imposed as an appliqué on top of the sequential language (FORTRAN or C) that serves as the base. The advantage of a parallel language is that the compiler can take over some of the low-level bookkeeping. The advantage of a sequential language with extensions is that large parts of the existing sequential code may be able to be reused.

> ***Example***: In Section 10.4, a scientific code, which generates ephemeris for satellites, was discussed—the code is initialized with parameters that characterize the satellite's orbit and, when called with *time* as the input, will return position and velocity as output. If many different satellites are involved, or if they are to be examined over separate and independent intervals of time, only the initializing data and input times need to vary—the underlying subroutine (which may constitute a large part of the application software, and which may consume a large part of the execution time) need not be altered *at all*. This is the basis for our claim, in Chapter 2, that the instructions to the individual wall builders may be reusable. ■

In an SIMD environment, code reuse is more complex. A translation into the parallel language for the machine will be required, and the data arrays in which the parallelism resides must be mapped onto the processor array. Typically, the controller of the SIMD machine will be able to compile and execute sequential code (generally, parallel languages for SIMD machines are supersets of the sequential languages on which they are based), but these sequential parts will be executed on the controller, not the processor array, so that no speed-up will be obtained. SIMD processors parallelize on the inner loop, using operations on entire arrays as the parallelizing mechanism. Since this is more distant from the sequential programming paradigm, correspondingly more work will be required during the port to expose and map these parallel opportunities. The bottom line is that in many cases the port to an SIMD machine can be more difficult than a port to an MIMD machine.

Within the MIMD world, the port to a shared memory machine (like a symmmetric multiprocessor) will probably be easier than the port to a distributed memory machine. The disadvantage of an SMP, as we have observed several times, is that SMPs do not scale to supercomputer levels of performance. Thus, porting using a shared memory paradigm limits scalability. Of course, for many applications the levels of performance and cost/performance provided by SMPs is perfectly adequate. Organizations that feel "the need for speed" may prefer to accept some additional effort during the initial software port in return for assured scalability to the highest levels of performance. Hardware costs should not be an issue: SMPs and DM-MIMD machines of comparable performance are comparably priced.

A general comment on *distributed heterogeneous processing*. This approach has received some attention lately—in the author's opinion, more than it deserves. The basic idea is that a complete application may have several phases or components. Suppose, hypothetically, that each phase is "best" suited to a particular type of hardware architecture. In a distributed heterogeneous environment, the idea is to ship the application around from machine to machine, letting each machine do the part of the computation for which it is best suited.

It seems hardly necessary to observe the difficulties that such an approach imposes. First, there is the operational and facilities overhead of all the different machines and their operating systems. Second, there is the processing overhead of moving the data around from machine to machine, including the potential difficulties of data format mismatches and conversions. Finally, there is the necessity of porting portions of the application to different architectures with different languages, data layouts, and control structures. The complexity grows exponentially, and the performance benefit is often marginal. For example, an effort was made at Carnegie-Mellon to have a Cray Y-MP cooperate with an SIMD Connection Machine. It is not a pretty story, though perhaps it qualifies as a triumph of the human spirit, akin to climbing Mt. Everest. In short, distributed heterogeneous processing is a situation most organizations will want to approach with caution.

In Chapter 12, a methodology will be presented to organize the hardware selection process. A major evaluation criterion for that methodology is the software cost—in our context, the cost of porting the application to the target hardware. As this section suggests, that cost, and the corresponding performance benefit, can vary from machine to machine and also from application to application. Thus, from a management point of view, the material in this section can be viewed as technical background contributing to the overall selection process, as described in Chapter 12. Software porting is *one factor among many others* to be considered in migrating an application to a parallel processor.

11.2 DEVELOPING PARALLEL APPLICATIONS

Developing new applications and porting old applications are quite different activities, and the difference is accentuated when the target machine is a parallel processor. On the one hand, development permits considerably more freedom in such matters as choice of language and design decisions. On the other hand, the lack of legacy code may make the task more difficult, since little of the code can be borrowed or modified. In the next few paragraphs, we will consider some of the unique aspects of the parallel application development effort:

- impact of the choice of hardware architecture
- impact of the choice of language
- retraining
- sizing and estimation
- impact of parallelism on software development methodology

The selection of the "right" parallel platform for the intended application can have a substantial impact both on the eventual performance obtained and on the difficulty or ease of the software development effort. In a nutshell, the hardware should "match" the intended type of parallelism in such a way that: (1) the application runs efficiently; (2) the level of effort to expose and express the parallelism is no harder than it need be; and (3) the architecture provides a credible growth path to projected future performance requirements. There is no "cookbook" answer for whether one or another hardware architecture best matches the application. A number of competing factors enter in—not least of which are factors regarding the stability of the vendor and level of technical risk an organization feels comfortable with. A systematic approach to assessing these types of questions is presented in Chapter 12. Suffice it here to note that the answer is seldom immediately obvious.

Example: The author has frequently been asked for a matrix that would list applications along one axis and hardware architecture types (SIMD, SMP, vector, DM-MIMD, etc.) along the other—the cells of the matrix being filled in with qualitative characterizations such as "good fit," "bad fit," etc. He has consistently (and for good reason) declined such a task. Everything depends on the particulars: problem size, machine size, the particular vendor and libraries provided, the operational setting (in particular, existing equipment and data characteristics), experience and biases of the programming staff, performance goals (absolute total performance or cost/performance), scalability requirements, etc. The only sensible approach seems to be to make a reasonably comprehensive set of evalutation criteria (including both performance and other issues); assign weights that express the organization's priorities (including tolerance for risk) and then systematically to make the comparisons. This is the essence of the methodology presented in Section 12.1.

One defensible comment is that far more applications are successfully parallelizable, and parallelizable on a wider range of parallel architectures, than would have been imagined, say, five years ago. As discussed in Chapter 2, the major issue is usually the *size* of the problem (parallel machines need large problems for best efficiency), not the algorithmic particulars of the application. The default position when considering a parallel machine should be that there is probably a solution available; the task then becomes determining how difficult it will be to code the solution and what level of performance can be expected.

The selection of a language can also have an impact on the coding effort. Chapters 4 through 7 and Section 8.1 serve to indicate the kinds of features and compiler capabilities that are now available. An advantage that development has over porting is that there is no incentive to select a parallel language merely because it closely matches a sequential language (in a software port, the desire is to match as closely as possible the language in which the application is currently written). Compilers for parallel machines are now able, in many cases, to take on some of the low-level drudgery such as data placement, synchronization, locks, and even multitasking. They are able to do this by using naturally parallel data constructs (arrays and primitive array operations) that are well-enough understood so that an automatic mapping to the hardware is possible. The programmer who finds the need to stray beyond this rather limited set of parallelizable array operations, however, will find the going rougher.

Portability of parallel code is not really an issue. As we noted in Section 1.3, language standards do not exist. Further, even if they did, an efficient version of an algorithm for one parallel machine might look very different from the implementation for a different machine. In many ways, porting from one parallel machine to another can be more difficult than porting from a sequential machine to a parallel one. Vendor claims that "parallel is parallel" can be dismissed.

If optimized library routines useful to the application are available, these can be an incentive both for hardware and for the implementation language selected.

We turn next to the issue of training/retraining—namely, getting the programming staff up to speed on the selected parallel platform. A frequent message of this book is that, if at all possible, a small initial prototype development effort is a particularly good way to introduce parallel processing to an organization. Figure 11-3 reflects the author's experience in the matter of retraining. The assumptions are that the programming staff are already experienced sequential programmers and that they have access to an analyst with experience on the target parallel machine. The point of the second assumption is that when a programmer encounters a new situation on the parallel machine, a walk down the hall and brief consultation will suffice to clear up the difficulty and get things moving again. Under these assumptions, experience has shown that about three months is enough time to get typical programmers/analysts acceptably productive on parallel hardware.

This is a fairly encouraging result and is much better than the dire predictions of the vendors of traditional architectures. In managing procurements, for example, contractors who bid parallel hardware need not be excessively penalized for requiring a very long learning curve. For organizations considering their own application development program, it means that a relatively small investment in retraining can result in an efficient parallel programming staff.

The preceding remarks bear on another issue that is frequently raised concerning parallel software: *Is parallel code harder to write than sequential code?* The answer (perhaps predictably) is—sometimes "yes" and sometimes "no." Where parallel languages gain is in the expressive power to directly manipulate large data arrays. Even sequential languages are now borrowing this capability to prevent the programmer from having to write long nested loops to sequentialize operations on the array that are "naturally" parallel. Where parallel languages lose is the necessity for synchronization and exchange of data

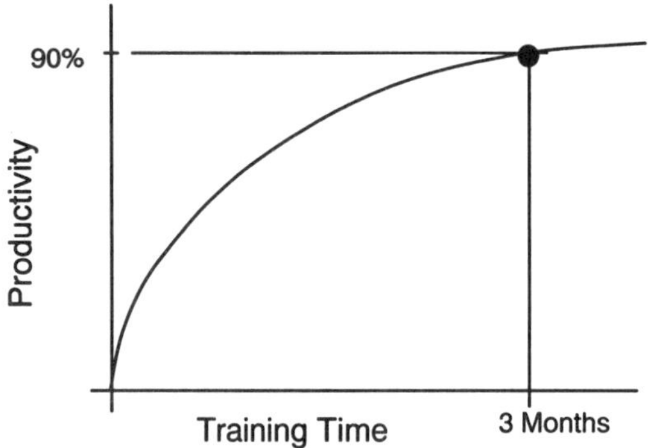

Figure 11-3. Productivity of new parallel programmers

among processes/processors. Even when these operations only amount to a small fraction of the run time, they can result in a substantial fraction of the total code. We have also mentioned (Section 8.2) the special difficulties associated with debugging parallel code, particularly in a shared memory environment where execution is not deterministic and where symptoms can appear and disappear in an apparently random fashion.

A summary assessment, while hard to defend with objective data, is that programmers will find the parallel environment more comfortable as they gain more experience. There are many examples in which once a programmer has learned the expressive features of a parallel language, he or she will be reluctant to return to the sequential paradigm (in much the same way that, once object-oriented programming is mastered, few programmers would wish to do without it). Most things one might wish to do on a parallel machine can be expressed fairly simply and, after a few months, the parallel programmer's toolkit is complete enough for most tasks. Of course, there will always be programmers anxious to conquer new territory or to squeeze the last 1 percent of performance from the machine. Trouble awaits these individuals even in the sequential world, although perhaps parallel processing has attracted more than its fair share of these programmers. Part of the attraction of parallelism to programmers is its newness and "high-tech" aura. One task of managing a software development effort on a parallel box is to get the staff over the "gee whiz" hump, so that the machine can be treated for what it is—a tool to get a job done, no more and no less.

We turn next to the potential difficulties of *sizing* a software development effort on a parallel machine. Experience both with the target system and with the type of application is the best guide, and this is another benefit of some initial prototyping on a small hardware configuration. It is well known for sequential codes that there are trade-offs between time spent in design and time spent in testing/debugging. This is exaggerated with parallel software, since the debugging effort can be considerably more difficult for parallel applications. Self-diagnosing, defensive code has correspondingly higher payoff in the parallel world, since the difficulty of diagnosing a core dump from an MPP is correspondingly higher. Depending on the constraints of the application, experience has shown a tendency to underestimate the difficulty of interfacing to other equipment, and the design and management of parallel I/O can be more complex than might appear, based on sequential precedents. These uncertainties are behind our recommendation regarding the appropriate software development methodology—the final topic of discussion.

A widely used software development methodology—the so-called *waterfall* methodology—takes a top-down approach: first design concept, then detailed

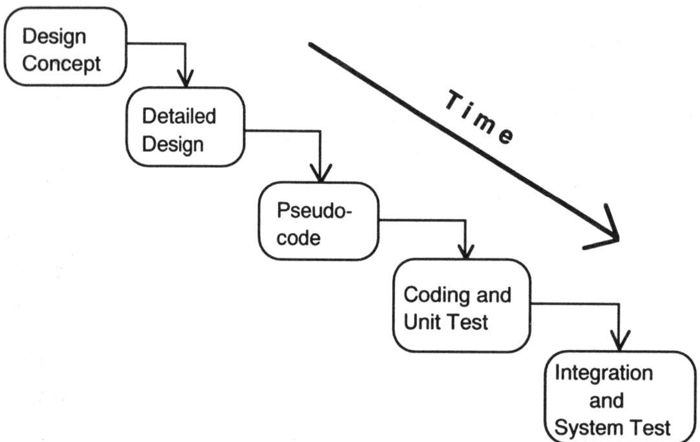

Figure 11-4. Standard waterfall software development methodology

design, then pseudocode, then implementation and unit testing, and finally integration and system testing. A set of design reviews and associated documentation is associated with completion of the various stages. This is shown in Figure 11-4.

A more appropriate management approach on a parallel machine is a *spiral methodology*. The basic idea is that key modules be prototyped—that is, coded, tested, and benchmarked—very early in the design cycle. Once the difficult "core" of the application is in hand, the more straightforward pieces that surround it can be incorporated incrementally. This approach is shown in Figure 11-5.

The point here is that working, hands-on experience with the parallel hardware and its development environment is likely to be critical to the success of the project and should be obtained as early as possible. Indeed, the core stage of the development effort could be a stand-alone prototype of the key computational kernels. The packaging, interfaces to other systems, and user interface (which is typically standard sequential code executed on the front

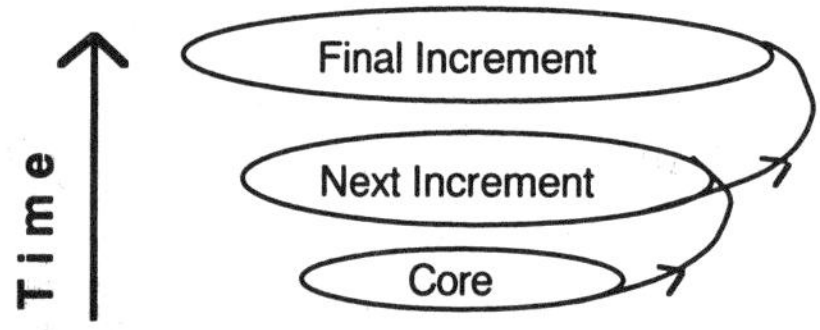

Figure 11-5. The spiral software development methodology

end or at the user's workstation) can then be added on incrementally once the overall design parameters have become clear.

One advantage of this approach is reduced risk. Design effort is not spent on matters such as interfaces until the proof of concept using the parallel processor is in hand. Also, building and testing the core kernels will support accuracy in both system hardware sizing and in level of effort sizing: Eexperience with the machine is the best foundation for sizing activities.

11.3 EXAMPLES

The goal of this section is to illustrate some of the ideas from this chapter using examples based on actual experience. The author has both participated in development/porting efforts and served as a consultant to such projects. The following three case studies should serve to put the general comments of the preceding sections into a more practical context.

The first two examples concern porting of codes to parallel machines—an SIMD array in the first case and a DM-MIMD message-passing machine in the second. The third example is based on a code development effort to produce a very large, very fast sorting routine.

11.3.1 Case 1: Porting an Image Processing Code to an SIMD Array

As we will see, this example has a surprise ending (*Ellery Queen* fans, alert!). First, a brief account of the circumstances surrounding the project. A suite of image processing (actually, image understanding) algorithms had been under development for some time in a research mode on a late 1970s/early 1980s minicomputer. The algorithms had reached a level of maturity that required validation against large collections of data to establish statistical significance. The difficulty was that on the older equipment the time to execute even a single image was on the order of dozens of hours. Clearly, a substantial performance boost was required.

A profile of the code by run time revealed that a great deal of time—well over 60 percent—was spent in relatively simple and widely used imagery operations: the Sobel edge finder, for example. These types of operations are known to be very effectively mapped onto SIMD 2-D meshes, such as the AMT DAP or the Martin Marietta GAPP. Such a strategy had other advantages. The software subroutine libraries for these machines already contain many of the primitive operators required, thereby saving on software development costs.

Thus, the SIMD approach seemed to be a good fit, and the system design began heading down this path.

Initial benchmarks were run on the SIMD array for the compute-intensive algorithms, and the results were very encouraging. Speed-ups of several thousand over the older equipment were achievable on several of the most lengthy subroutines. Operations that ran in hours on the older equipment could now be completed in a few seconds. The next step was to put together a complete end to end design for both hardware and software.

It is at this point that things started to get more complicated. The biggest problem was the remaining 40 percent of the run time that had not been addressed by the SIMD processor. On the 60 percent to which it was well suited, it was far superior to other alternatives. However, that only got us a little over halfway to the desired goal. The route of least resistance for the remaining 40 percent was high-end workstations. These microprocessor-based platforms were running about 20 times faster than the older equipment, were quite reasonably priced, and had good software development environments. A system design in which such a workstation (or two?) would take over the remaining part of the computation looked like a cost-effective approach. Again, some benchmarks were run on the workstations, and an end to end initial design using this concept was assembled.

Now, the desired performance goal for the project was a speed-up of about 100:1 over the older equipment. The SIMD processor could reduce 60 percent of the run time to effectively zero, but that still left 40 percent of the run time to account for. Assuming that the workstations were running at 20:1 over the minicomputers, analysis based on the benchmarks showed that it would take three workstations to bring the total run time down to the desired range. The initial sizing estimates thus suggested a configuration of three workstations and an SIMD processor.

The observant reader will have noticed that with a 20:1 speed-up per workstation only *five* workstations are needed to achieve the desired speed-up of 100:1 *without the SIMD processor at all.* The SIMD processor could be traded in for two more workstations while still meeting the overall performance goal!

Another observation confirmed this result. A timing analysis was done, using the 3WS+SIMD configuration, for a complete end to end run. We asked the question, How much of the time are each of the machines active? It turned out that the three workstations were active well over 85 percent of the time, while the SIMD processor was only active about 5 percent of the time. It could perform its part of the processing without even breathing hard and would spend most of its time waiting for things to do. The workstations, on the other hand, were fully loaded—not a balanced arrangement.

It seemed, based on this analysis, that the SIMD array would be able to handle up to 50 or so workstations before becoming saturated. However, as it turned out, this was not the case. The problem was movement of data between the workstations and the SIMD processor. The points at which the SIMD processor could be used were interspersed throughut the computation—stretches of sequential processing alternating with stretches of parallel processing. Thus, frequent data movement would be required between the workstations and the SIMD array. This added overhead that had not been considered in the initial analysis. When the data transfer was taken into account, the SIMD machine would have been active close to 80 percent of the time—most of it just doing data I/O. Further, the data transfers meant additional processing load on the workstations. Perhaps the initial estimate of three would no longer be enough, given the increased I/O involved.

At this point, the SIMD processor that had initially appeared so attractive began to feel more like an anchor than a balloon. An alternative approach was considered. Perhaps more of the processing could be shifted to the SIMD array. Instead of just using the software subroutine library already in existence, new parallel code could be developed for the remaining 40 percent of the code. The conclusion, after some analysis, was that while this might be successful in achieving the performance goals, it would require a very large additional effort for algorithm redesign. Perhaps as much as 95 percent of the code could be ported in this way but at the expense (and risk) of considerable additional software development. This was in sharp contrast to the workstations, which could run the existing code virtually without modification.

A side observation is appropriate here. Note that the performance goal for this project was not *reduced latency* but *increased throughput*. It was not necessary to have a single image processed as fast as possible but only to have many independent images processed more rapidly as a group. This is a classic instance of coarse-grained parallelism—parallelizing the *outer loop* instead of the *inner loop*. The SIMD processor was excellent at reducing the latency of its part of the computation, but that was not a direct requirement. By exploiting coarse-grained parallelism (processing several independent images concurrently on separate workstations instead of attempting to process a single image on the SIMD array), a simpler approach was possible.

The story has a happy ending. The coarse-grained approach to parallelism was adopted, and the initial plan to utilize the SIMD array to turbo-charge the application was abandoned. Five workstations turned out to be more than adequate: New microprocessor upgrades came along mid-project, and the 20:1 speed-up ratio originally estimated turned into 33:1 without any software redesign at all—just plugging in the new processor boards. Perhaps best of all, almost no software modifications were required—just what was needed to port from a proprietary operating system to UNIX.

In analyzing this project for lessons learned, four stand out. First, Amdahl's Law was a major factor. Only 60 percent of the code was parallelizable in the inner loop—a strong early signal that fine-grained parallelism might not be successful. Second, software development cost was a major factor. Sequential versions of the code already existed, and the cost of developing new parallel versions of the algorithms would have driven the total cost up when compared to other alternatives. Third, even given the high software costs, if *reduced latency* had been the driving requirement for this project, the SIMD solution would probably have won out. The coarse-grained workstation solution could only be successful because the requirement was stated in terms of the total time to process a *large group of independent images*, not the time to process a *single image*. Finally, by choosing the commercial off-the-shelf microprocessor-based solution, the project was able to benefit from the frequent performance improvements that characterize this extremely competitive segment of the market.

11.3.2 Case 2: Porting a Simulation to a Distributed Memory Hypercube

This project arose as part of a preproposal effort for a government contract. Like the previous case, the code had been developed on a late 1970s minicomputer, and the basic task was to obtain significant performance improvement as the program transitioned from a research to a production environment. The specific goal of the effort was to obtain benchmark data to support sizing and costing once the RFP was released.

Some background on the application may be useful. The intent of the code was to recreate, pixel by pixel, what would appear in the sensing array of an infrared sensor observing the surface of the earth from a high orbit. Each pixel (picture element) in the array would, during a scanning interval, receive photons that had journeyed up through the earth's atmosphere, encountering various kinds of phenomena along the way. The wavelength and intensity of the energy sensed by the pixel were, thus, a function of the scene being observed and the characteristics of the atmosphere through which the photons were to travel. The job of the simulation was to back-trace the ray terminating at each pixel along its path, summing and modifying energy contributions along the way, thereby determining the intensity of the energy at the pixel at that point in time. Models for the background radiation of the earth's surface (vegetation, snow, etc.), atmosphere (clouds, precipitation, etc.), and the infrared properties of the objects of interest in the simulation were provided by the code.

The target parallel processor for this project was a 32-node nCube 2. This is a classic distributed memory machine using a message-passing programming paradigm. We began by getting the code to execute on the workstation front end. Shifting to the UNIX environment from the proprietary baseline was not without its headaches, but within two man-weeks the code (about 15,000 lines of research FORTRAN) was running on the workstation front end. Our hope was that the calculations for each pixel in the sensor array would be independent and that this would provide the basis for parallelization. While this proved to be true, it was not the whole story.

It turned out that in order to calculate the value of any given pixel, entries into three other two-dimensional arrays had to be calculated—let's call these Array X, Array Y, and Array Z. The values in these arrays were static (that is, they did not change during the course of the calculation), and they could either be calculated up front before the main loop over pixels began, or they could be read in from a file (if the entries had been previously computed and stored). The index entry for each of the three arrays varied from pixel to pixel in an unpredictable manner, based on the actual trajectory of the ray. The top-level structure of the program then looked something like this:

```
Initialize Array X;
Initialize Array Y;
Initialize Array Z;

Loop over all pixels
{
Calculate index into Array X;
Calculate index into Array Y;
Calculate index into Array Z;
Using these values, compute pixel value;
}
```

Our parallelization strategy—hand different groups of pixels off to each processor in the processor array—hinged on being able to rapidly obtain the values held in each of the three arrays. If those data arrays were, themselves, spread accross multiple processors, then the only way to get the value would be via a message send/receive operation. The processor needing the array value (say, Array X [208,772]) would have to: (1) calculate the address of the processor holding the needed value; (2) send a message to that processor requesting the value; and (3) wait until the return message arrived in order to proceed. This would involve considerable message-passing overhead.

The solution to this potential difficulty was to *replicate* each of the three arrays—Array X, Array Y, and Array Z—in each processor's local memory. The machine on which we were working had 4 MB of DRAM memory for each processor. Each of the three arrays required about 450 KB—small enough to easily fit in the local processor memory and have plenty to spare for calculations. Thus, we gave each processor in the array its own, private copy of the three arrays: Array X, Array Y, and Array Z. In this regard, we were fortunate. Had the arrays been larger—say, on the order of several megabytes or more—this strategy of replication would not have worked, and we would have had to suffer the performance penalty of additional message-passing overhead.

In a way, our strategy with regard to the tables was not different from that of caches in an SMP. Each processor in an SMP has a large local cache, which holds the data being used by that processor. In the case of shared data structures (such as Arrays X, Y, and Z), each processor cache will have local copies of the tables, just as each processor on the nCube 2 array was given (in our approach) its own local copy of the three arrays. And, as in our case, if the cache is too small to hold the entire set of arrays, the code will experience frequent cache misses, slowing the computation.

The other issue worth noting was that the quality of the FORTRAN code made it very difficult to determine the control structure. The code we received was geared to the memory limitations of its original host, and, hence, the natural outer loop over pixels had been decomposed into two nested loops—one over columns of pixels and the other over the pixels in a given column. Further, there was no single data structure representing the entire pixel array. The columns were computed one by one, reusing the same data array and outputting the results to file as the processing for each column completed. The actual control structure contained in the code looked like:

```
Initialize Array X;
Initialize Array Y;
Initialize Array Z;

Loop over columns
{
Loop over the pixels in this column
{
```

```
{Compute the index into Array X;
Compute the index into Array Y;
Compute the index into Array Z;
Using these indices, compute the pixel value;
}   /*End loop over pixels*/

Output this column to file;

}   /*End loop over columns*/
```

Further, all these loops were implemented *not* by a FORTRAN DO loop but by complex GO TO structures. Once in the inner pixel loop, the processing of a single pixel was itself a fairly complex undertaking, involving multiple nested subroutine calls, conditional branching to handle special cases, and the like. I think it is safe to say that even though the parallelization structure turned out to be fairly intuitive once the code had been analyzed, there is no hope that a parallelizing compiler would have been able to automatically detect it. The point here is to emphasize that the porting strategy represented by "automatic parallelization" would not have succeeded in this case.

Once the code analysis was complete, the actual port to the nCube 2 was painless. Since each processor was to have its own copy of the three arrays, we let each processor calculate the values (this seems redundant, but since the calculation has to be done at least once anyway, no additional time is lost by having all the processors duplicate the effort, and we save the time it would take for a broadcast operation). Then, instead of having a given processor loop over the entire set of columns, a small amount of code was inserted to select the subset of pixel columns any given processor would compute (for example, when 32 processors were used, processor #7 would compute column 7, column 7 + 32 = 39, column 7 + 32 + 32 = 71, etc.). Some care was taken on output to ensure that the columns were being written to file in the correct order—that is, as processors completed a given column, they would wait their turn to output the results so that the order of the columns output to the file was correct.

The total effort, including the initial port to the UNIX front end, was about six man-weeks. Over 99 percent of the code was able to be reused *without modification.* Less than 150 additional lines of code had to be written, and less than 50 lines of code had to be modified. The majority of the effort was in understanding the control structure of the code, validating that we had not missed any dependency (when there are global COMMON blocks, as in FORTRAN, there is the possiblity of subtle dependencies), and testing. Of this, two man-weeks were attributable to senior staff experienced with the nCube, the rest to less experienced junior staff.

As a final footnote, the timing results agreed with theory to an amazing degree. The basic timing model for the code, where N was the number of processors, was:

$$\text{Total Time} = C_1 + C_2/N.$$

The constant C_1 represents the constant time to compute the three arrays, which has to be done once no matter how many processors are involved. The constant C_2 represents the time to do all the columns on a single processor. As the number of processors increases, the number of columns done by any given processor decreases, exactly as the formula predicts. Another way of representing this is:

$$\text{Total Time} = C_1 + C_3 * (\text{Number of Columns}).$$

Here, C_3 represents the time to process a single column of pixels on a single processor. The more processors, the fewer columns any given processor has to compute and the faster the run completes.

Using these results, the size of a machine to achieve any given level of performance can be accurately predicted and the processor reliably sized. Further, the porting effort gave us experience regarding the difficulty of the port (not very) and the potential for additional speed-up by modifying and improving the existing code in the transition to a production environment (lots).

11.3.3 A Large Development Effort

In software development, the word "large" has different connotations to different organizations. To be specific, the project described here has the following general characteristics (current at this writing):

- the project is well into its third year, with an ongoing staff of 10 analysts and programmers
- the target machine is a CM-2—a large SIMD supercomputer
- over 200,000 lines of code have been developed (including design, code, test, and integrate)
- a typical data set on which the code operates is tens of gigabytes, and many of the algorithms are out of core (that is, efficient I/O is a major driver in achieving good performance)

- the application is almost entirely integer/logical (that is, no floating point)
- no commercial DBMS software has been used

The purpose of the following discussion is to partially substantiate, based on actual experience from this project, some of the general guidance and recommendations found elsewhere in the book. While details of the application have been omitted in deference to our client, enough about the history and experience of the project can be related to serve as a good "reality check."

The genesis of the project was the experience of users of the then-current system. Some useful SQL queries either could not be processed at all or took inordinately long to complete (e.g., 12 to 140 hours). Our company suggested that a parallel supercomputer could, perhaps, offer two to three orders of magnitude performance improvement (that is, 100× to 1,000×). The users immediately sensed the potential for a "breakthrough" in their way of doing business. Not only would the current set of queries become feasible, but (almost at once) entirely new search approaches suggested themselves. The "impossible" had suddenly come within reach, provided that the advertised capability could be achieved.

A limited-scope pilot demonstration project was initiated, much like the core level of the spiral methodology shown in Figure 11-5. Key algorithms included a very large sort and a graph link analysis routine.

The inital demonstration concentrated on the algorithms rather than the user interface. The key question to answer was: *Can the desired levels of performance actually be achieved?* The interface was the minimum needed to drive the system. It rapidly became clear (as initial projections had suggested) that properly handling data I/O was key to project success. Much of the code design focused on optimizing the parallel aspects of the Data Vault—Thinking Machine's proprietary RAID disk system. During this phase, a core of five senior analysts was involved. A sample data set was provided by the client for development purposes.

Despite the very bare user interface, the initial demonstration was an unqualified success. The performance goals were achieved. More important, however, was the response from the user community. Users were brought in to go through the demo and see first hand the capabilities that were now available. In case after case, the response was: "This is really great, but can you also do . . . ?"—the wish list of an analyst community currently constrained by technology limitations. The users were engaged and were already generating the set of requirements for the next phase.

There were two major objectives for the second phase (see Figure 11-5). First, it was necessary to wrap the technology in a more friendly, familiar package and to add the support features (data updates, back-ups, remote access, etc.) necessary to support a production environment. Second, it was necessary to extend the existing set of algorithms to support additional capabilities suggested by the user community during the demonstration.

The key ideas for the implementation are shown in Figure 11-6. Users at the customer facility generate SQL queries via their standard workstation interface. Logic then determines whether to route the query to the existing mainframe or to the supercomputer. A T1 line (in this case, encrypted) links the user facility to the remote supercomputer facility where the CM-2 resides. The CM-2 uses its own local version of the database, stored on the Data Vault, to complete the query and return the response. The user, in effect, does not "see" the parallel processor at all—except that some queries that formerly took a long time to complete now are completed very rapidly.

It will be observed that in this design the data physically reside in two different places: in the disk system for the existing mainframe and in the Data Vault. A requirement for the design is to maintain coherency between these two copies, including updates. One feature that eased this task is that for this application, updates are relatively infrequent—say, once a month—and can be handled as one-time batch jobs (as opposed, for example, to an OLTP system where updates are continually occurring). Also, not shown in Figure 11-6 are the ongoing software development activities at the supercomputer facility. The CM-2 must support not only production but also debugging and testing of new algorithms.

The second major focus of the next phase was to increase the functionality of the software prepared for the initial demonstration. This aspect of the pro-

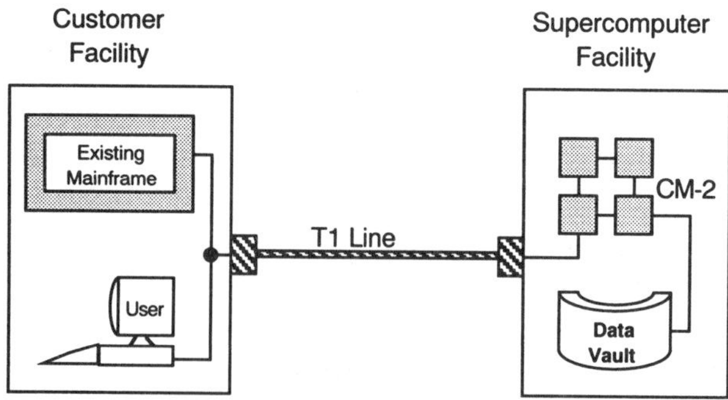

Figure 11-6. Design for production system

gram—developing algorithms and software to support new user requirements as they arise—is ongoing and increasingly important. At any given point in time, two or three new algorithms are under development, and it is this aspect of the work that requires a continuing high level of programmer support. As a result, and without overstating the case, the staff supporting this project have developed a number of state-of-the-art algorithms in parallel graph and link analysis—the major driver for this application. These algorithms are new—that is, they cannot be found in any textbook—and are highly optimized to the data characteristics and requirements of the client as well as to the hardware idiosyncrasies of the CM-2.

In this context, I asked the project manager to assess his experience in software development against the general comments made elsewhere in the book. The two areas where his experience most diverged were debugging and the learning curve. In the first instance, he felt that the picture of debugging presented in Chapter 7 is a bit too rosy. For a complex algorithm, standard practice in his organization is to code the algorithm *twice*: once for the CM-2 and a second time using a sequential version. This forces the programmer to think through the problem independently a second time, and it also provides code to *test* the results of the parallel version. In his opinion, the subtleties of parallel code are substantially greater than those for sequential code and require correspondingly more elaborate development, test, and debug disciplines.

One reason for this is lack of *intuition* about parallel behavior. An experienced C programmer, for example, ordinarily has the ability to "read" someone else's code fairly quickly. There are standard techniques that are recognizable from past experience, so that the translation from code to heuristics is familiar—the reader of the code feels on firm ground, based on past experience. The situation in parallel code can be quite different. It is often impossible to discern the intent and effect of a line of code without a detailed, handworked tracing of the internal logic—and, in particular, the effects of *context* and *interprocessor communications*. This complicates and lengthens code review and makes it more likely that mistakes will slip past unnoticed. Even the most experienced algorithm designers (and, in our organization, this includes doctorate-level mathematicians) make logic errors in tight parallel code that they would never make with sequential code. Note, however, that this project has a "research" aspect, and the goal is to push the performance envelope in a way that, perhaps, would not be so significant for less aggressive programs.

The second area of disagreement was with regard to the length of time it takes to get a new programmer up to speed on the parallel machine. Over the past two years, this project has amassed a large library of specialized subroutines. These are the working toolkit of the existing staff and contain many "solved problems" or templates for solutions that can be reused as new algorithms are undertaken A large hurdle facing a newcomer to the project is to become familiar with this legacy code. My estimate (90 percent efficient in three months—see Figure 11-3) only reflects the time to become familiar with the *language*. Becoming familiar with the existing library and being able to utilize it effectively lengthens the learning process to as much as six months.

An area where previous remarks are borne out concerns porting of the parallel code. A technical challenge facing this project over the next 18 months is the migration of code to the next-generation parallel processor. Much of the existing code is highly optimized to the hardware architecture of the CM-2. The performance of the CM-2 is being surpassed by the next generation of parallel processors, including, for example, the recently introduced CM-5 from Thinking Machines. Unfortunately, the hardware internals of the CM-5 are very different from the CM-2. The immediate impact to the program is that a software port from the CM-2 to, say, a CM-5 will be far from trivial. Even though the C* language (the implementation language for this project; see Section 6.3) is available on both machines, the algorithm internals may require coding changes if the CM-5 hardware is to be optimally utilized. A major theme of Chapter 3—that programmer consciousness of hardware can affect parallel algorithm design, independent of the choice of language—thus has the potential to seriously complicate the port.

Summary of Chapter 11

We have separately considered two issues: (1) porting an existing sequential application to a parallel machine, and (2) developing a new application "from scratch." Automatic parallelization—the most sought-after approach to the first issue—has been seen to be unrealistic, and the difficulties of libraries and using the MPP as an attached processor have also been discussed. New developments, however, present a less formidable problem and one in which MPPs need not be greatly penalized when compared with sequential alternatives. These observations were then illustrated using three case studies.

12

Matching Applications to Architectures

This chapter has some claim to being the culmination of the book. All the topics we have discussed thus far come into play, and support for this chapter has guided the author both in selecting material and in the depth of discussion. The premise is that the reader is (or will be) faced with a decision about incorporating parallel technology and has a number of questions to answer regarding this decision. In the author's experience, these questions often coalesce into two:

- What is the best architecture (SIMD, DM-MIMD, SMP, etc.) for the application (or collection of applications)?
- What size machine will meet the performance requirements (latency, throughput)?

The purpose of this chapter is to present a *methodology* to answer these questions. The goals include *completeness* (so that management has reasonable assurance that no major evaluation area has been left out), *flexibility* (so that an organization can tailor the specifics of the methodology to its particular setting), *visibility* (so that the answer that emerges is easily traced to the components that generated it), and *practical utility* (so that management has confidence the numbers generated by the methodology are grounded in reality, not theory).

This methodology has been employed by the author on behalf of a number of organizations representing a variety of goals and requirements—commercial, military, and government. While the approach overlaps the selection and sizing activities for conventional machines, it contains unique structural features particularly adapted to evaluation of parallel and high-performance architectures. This is not a rote procedure that can be followed in a cookbook manner by junior staff. Good results will require engineering judgment and the ability to clearly envision the eventual implementation in its operational context.

Successful use of the methodology depends, in part, on involvement by management. Part of management's role is to ensure that the available engineering effort is focused on the issues of greatest potential impact—that is, those on which the eventual decision is likely to hinge. Management must also clearly communicate its goals and priorities. The methodology is flexible in its ability to weight some evaluation criteria more heavily than others. The choice of weighting assignments is the specific formal mechanism by which management priorities (cost, performance, reliability, etc.) enter the methodology. Technical staff implementing the methodology will require guidance on how these assignments are to be made. Finally, there will be some areas where judgment, particularly concerning potential risks, is required. For example, how does one evaluate the *business risk* associated with a small high-tech start-up against the advantages of the technology being offered? Only management can assess its tolerance for this sort of risk and make the associated trade-offs.

The first section (Section 12.1) presents the framework for the methodology and describes the various engineering activities and products associated with it. This is followed by a discussion of transition and integration issues, including three illustrative case studies. Many of the potential "gotcha's" lying in wait for the parallel pioneer are illustrated with anecdotes and examples. Pay heed!

12.1 A METHODOLOGY

At the point where this methodology comes into play, an organization will already be fairly well along the road toward a parallel processing solution. In particular, one or a few target applications will be in mind that could benefit from a substantial performance boost, and, for whatever reason—cost, space, inability to meet target performance goals, etc.—a conventional solution has flaws that prevent it from completely addressing the need. Further, the organization is at least provisionally aware of the potential performance and cost/performance advantages of a parallel architecture. The problem now becomes:

(1) which machine is the *best* match (where *best* has to be broadly enough defined to include all major requirements) for the applications, and (2) how *large* a machine is/will be needed (where *large* is broadly enough defined to include clock rate, number of processors, interprocessor communications, I/O bandwidth, and secondary storage).

The key observation underlying the methodology is that often an evaluation of parallel machines focuses too narrowly on *performance.* A balanced evaluation must include other criteria, as well, and must accurately convey the complete picture—software costs, integration and transition problems, staffing and retraining, maintenance, etc. In order to make this balance explicit, the methodology breaks the evaluation criteria into two groups: performance evalution criteria (how well does a given machine perform on a given application) in one group and nonperformance evaluation criteria in the other. Figure 12-1 shows the skeleton of the methodology.

The boxes marked A in Figure 12-1 concern performance issues. The column associated with a type A cell is labeled with an application or algorithm of interest; the row is labeled with an architecture (that is, machine) included in the evaluation. The cell entry contains measures regarding how well the machine is able the execute the algorithm. Section 12.1.1 discusses issues concerning how to fill in the type A cells.

The boxes marked B in Figure 12-1 concern issues not directly related to execution timings. This is where all the other factors enter into the evalutation, and Section 12.1.2 discusses them. Finally, techniques for combining these "apples and oranges" measures into a single summary evaluation will be discussed in Section 12.1.3.

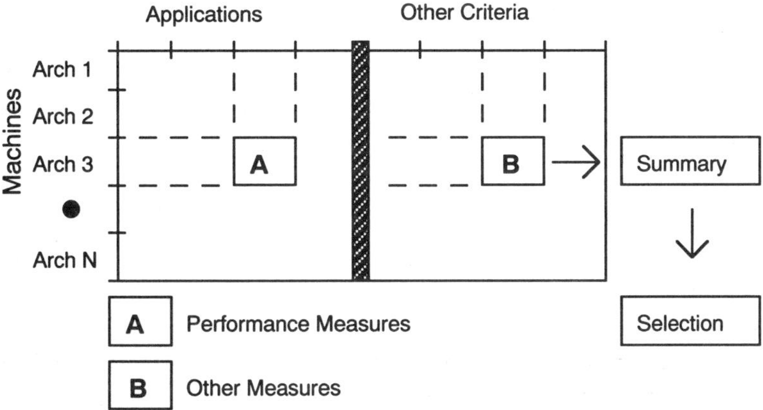

Figure 12-1. Methodology for algorithm-architecture evaluation

From a management point of view, four major tasks can be identified:

- obtaining performance measures associated with the type A cells (see Section 12.1.1)
- obtaining data associated with the type B cells (see Section 12.1.2)
- formulating summary evaluations for each of the architectures included in the study (see Section 12.1.3)
- reaching a consensus on the final recommendation (see Section 12.1.3)

The task dependencies are shown in Figure 12-2. While the level of effort, skills mix, schedule details, and decision mechanisms vary from case to case, this general structure has been flexible enough to accommodate a variety of implementations of the methodology. Typically, deliverables (briefings, reports, demos, etc.) are specified at the completion milestones for each of the tasks.

12.1.1 Performance Measures

The methodology requires a systematic assessment of expected performance against a candidate set of applications and/or algorithms. This is just benchmarking by another name, and the material in Chapter 10 provides a more detailed discussion of the issues that arise in benchmarking advanced architectures. Our purpose here is to remind the reader of the major observations made there and to put the material into the context of the evaluation methodology.

The most meaningful measures of performance are closely tied to specific applications, e.g., how long does it take machine X to execute application Y, where Y is familiar to the user population. The *operational impact* of the capability is brought home in a way users can relate to. While peak MFLOP ratings, for example, make good advertising copy, no one ever ran a business by

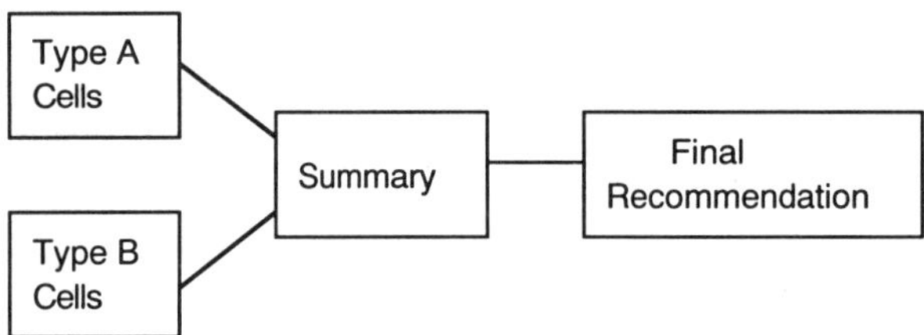

Figure 12-2. Methodology task dependencies

delivering MFLOPs. The performance measures that are reported and used in the selection should directly reflect the experience and goals of the users.

In some cases, it may even be possible to put a dollar value on the increased performance. For example, in an engineering design shop, ability to more rapidly evaluate soft copy models of components may translate directly into decreased time to market—a measurable benefit. Or, in a financial setting, there may be products (e.g., reports, analysis) depending on very large databases where timeliness is critical to the product's value. The ability to generate the report in, say, hours rather than days may make all the difference in its utility to the customer and, hence, in its market value. Again, supercomputing levels of performance can translate directly into measurable profit.

In other cases, the connection to profitability may be more tenuous. R&D efforts have this quality—the eventual outcome of the project is uncertain. The value of the supercomputer may be, for example, to enable more options to be evaluated or to permit a more complete analysis than would otherwise be possible. The supercomputer thus becomes a productivity-enhancing tool, enabling researchers to improve both the breadth and depth of their investigations. The uncertainty inherent in judging the eventual pay-off makes the supercomputer a harder sale in this type of environment.

One approach to performance measures that can make a dramatic impression on management is the ability to do the *same* job for substantially *less cost.* Mainframes are expensive, and there is increasing pressure on ADP shops to take advantage of the price/performance advantages of microprocessor-based technologies. This may take the form of workstations or symmetric multiprocessors (SMPs) in a client/server setting, or it may take the form of a large parallel processor executing the compute-intensive portions of the work load. In either case, the issues of distributed/concurrent/parallel processing are key, and the benefit that is expected is a substantial improvement in equipment purchase and maintenance costs. In on-line transaction processing, for example, a ratio of 50:1 in $/TPS can pay for a lot of one-time software development, which can then be recouped many times over the life of the system. This type of comparison holds the required level of performance constant and asks for the least expensive configuration that can achieve that level of perfomance. The ability of many parallel machines to scale smoothly from modest to extremely high performance levels (by adding additional processors in a "buy by the pound" manner) can give MPPs a competetive advantage over more conventional approaches.

In Chapter 10, we mentioned the importance of several issues in benchmarking parallel machines. We summarize the major ones here:

- Choose the algorithmic approach best suited to each architecture. If this requires some recoding, the level of effort (both time and expertise) to do the modification should be reported and factored into overall cost. However, allowing the vendors to make adjustments to the algorithms so as to take advantage of the machine's performance will present a truer picture of the performance potential.
- If possible, obtain separate timings for interproccessor communications, I/O, and computation portions of the application. This will indicate what aspects of the machine are being stressed and will support scaling estimates.
- If pencil and paper estimation is involved (and, in the author's opinion, this is a reasonable approach in situations where cost/schedule to complete the evaluation are critical), use performance models that include all the major stages of the algorithm and that reflect the manner in which the applications will actually be mapped onto the parallel hardware. Benchmarking small software kernels, and then using scaling models that accurately reflect relative performance, can be a rapid, inexpensive, and reliable technique.
- When using cost/performance as the measure, be sure to include *all* the potential costs, including software development. Section 12.2 indicates some costs that might be overlooked by the inexperienced.
- Be sure that the size of the machine and the size of the benchmark are well matched. As the discussion on Amdahl's Law shows, parallel machines that are inefficient on small versions of a problem can be used very efficiently on large versions. The best situation is to actually vary both the problem size and the machine size (number of processors) to obtain hard data on the scaling factors along both dimensions. The additional work may be offset with increased accuracy and reliability in performance estimates. Also, one result of the evaluation will be a recommendation on the size of machine (number of processors), and executing a variety of problems on a variety of configurations is the best way to get this information.
- In the best situation, an organization will have the opportunity to acquire a small initial version of a parallel machine and begin to become familiar with it. Small prototypes, which give programmers a chance to learn the programming style and operating system, are excellent learning mechanisms. The prototype then serves as a basis for performance estimation and can also provide useful experience in sizing the effort required by a software port. This experience is also the most reliable way

of learning about the kinds of optimizations that are appropriate for the intended application. Finally, a working prototype that can be shown to users is the most effective way to sell them on the usefulness of the technology. We will have more to say on these topics in Section 12.2.

12.1.2 Other Measures

The type B cells in the methodology capture the characteristics of the machine not directly related to performance on applications. A partial list of topics is shown in Figure 12-3. The importance of these factors (and others, not shown) will vary from organization to organization. In this section, we will comment briefly on these issues from the point of view of parallel processing.

First, recall from Chapter 1 that the VLSI technology used to implement MPPs is dissimilar from that used in traditional mainframes and vector supercomputers. Small footprint, modest heat dissipation, and very high availability are characteristic of the CMOS/DRAM chip types used in parallel processors. It is unlikely that power/cooling/footprint constraints will disqualify an MPP from further consideration, and, in fact, newcomers to this technology may be pleasantly surprised by how forgiving MPPs can be in this regard.

Second, it is likely that the most significant obstacle facing an MPP procurement is application software—where is it coming from? This is a consistent and recurring theme of this book, and any organization serious about parallel processing as an option must face this question honestly. Application software can be both the source of greatest cost (easily outstripping hardware, depending on the porting effort required) and can also be the source of great

Physical and Facility	Application Software
Reliability	Cost
Networking	Procurement Options
I/O and Secondary Storage	Accounting Services
Security and Auditing	Customer Service
Retraining	Compatibility with Existing Equipment
Risk	

Figure 12-3. Nonperformance evaluation criteria

est risk. The transition plan must make adequate provision, both in schedule and budget, for development or porting. Chapter 11 discusses these issues in greater detail.

Third, the customer service provided by MPP vendors is not what many organizations have become accustomed to from vendors of traditional equipment. This is an unavoidable consequence of the small size and technical focus of these companies. In general, larger vendors have been in the business longer, understand customer needs and requirements better, and have considerably more marketing savvy than do MPP vendors. Of course, these services show up, one way or another, in increased cost, but for many organizations these costs are well spent. A related issue concerns flexibility in procurement options—lease, lease with option to buy, discount policy, upgrades, etc. Because they are smaller and live closer to the margin, MPP vendors tend to have less flexibility in tailoring procurement options to customer needs. The flip side, of course, is that they also have less overhead and are using very inexpensive VLSI technologies, and this is reflected in considerably lower cost per MFLOP. A systematic look at these factors should be included as part of the evaluation process.

Fourth, the operating system for MPP systems is universally some flavor of UNIX. This is a good match for an open, distributed system, and MPPs fit naturally as servers into such an environment. However, some services characteristic of mainframe environments (extensive security and auditing capabilities, checkpoint/restart, extensive support for tapes, etc.) may not be provided or may be provided at lowered levels of functionality. If operating system services such as these are a key requirement, this should be reflected in the evaluation criteria.

Fifth, *risk* should be explicitly included in the evaluation process. Perhaps the greatest source of risk is selecting the wrong vendor, where "wrong" means one that will not be commercially successful. The author's crystal ball in this regard is no better than anyone else's, but a large percentage of commercial sales (as opposed to government R&D contracts) should be considered a healthy sign. Eventually, MPPs will have to prove their worth in the commercial market. The government labs and agencies are small when compared to the commercial world, and the vision and business plan of high-performance computer vendors should be broad enough to reflect both. A close look at the financial health of an MPP vendor and an assessment of the business savvy of its top management should be a part of any major procurement.

The sources of information for these evaluation criteria include: vendor literature and sales presentations, trade shows, the trade press, and Internet bulletin boards. The task of gathering and evaluating this information can be formidable for an organization just becoming acquainted with parallel technology. Consulting services are available to rapidly bring an organization up to speed by providing an initial technology survey covering the major MPP vendors, their product offerings, and relevant strengths and weaknesses. Services are also available to conduct benchmarking, develop prototypes, and port application software. Thus, an organization may choose to bring in outside expertise in parallel processing, rather than develop an independent capability, both to support the acquisition and evaluation phase and to jump-start the application software development process.

A final word of caution. In the author's experience, the most difficult task in the evaluation is to maintain a proper balance—a proper *tension*—between the undoubted performance (and cost/performance) advantages of MPPs, on the one hand, and the undoubted software headaches, on the other. To focus only on one or the other aspect is to risk losing perspective and, hence, misjudging the potential role MPP can play. The intent of the methodology is to maintain that tension in its proper proportions. Neither the young professionals greedy for GFLOPs nor the old guard clinging to their mainframes has the complete picture. This is one reason why a gradual, "start small" approach to transition is so attractive: It permits the new technology to demonstrate its potential in a nonthreatening context, while permitting both the technical staff and management to more accurately size up the software effort and potential performance gains. In other words, it is a way of building consensus both about the costs and benefits of the technology. Of course, some organizations have such large and well-defined performance requirements that an MPP solution is clearly the only alternative—like it or not. Others, however, will have options available in how and when a transition might occur. Care during the evaluation process can prevent both precipitous commitment and missed competitive advantage—the Scylla and Charybdis of all new technologies, including MPPs.

12.1.3 Combining Measures for a Unified Result

The previous two sections described the type A and type B cells from the methodology (see Figures 12-1 and 12-2), concerned with the two significant types of evaluation criteria. This section discusses the final process of combining the results for the various systems into a single unified result. The biggest difficulty is that the various measures (run time, efficiency, mean time to failure, amortized dollars, etc.) are in incompatible units. This makes simple summation across a row meaningless without additional work. Further, the priorities of the organization must also be reflected. Is operating system compatibility, for example, a show-stopper or a "nice to have"? Is software development cost critical or merely annoying? Is absolute performance on a single dedicated application the driver, or is balanced performance in a time-shared environment over a varied user population the goal? The methodology must be (and is) flexible to reflect these varying priorities.

We suggest two complementary techniques for dealing with these difficulties. First, minimum requirements should be identified. Overall cost might be one such area: the amortized cost of the system, including maintenance, software, customer support, etc., must not exceed $X per year over the next five years. This bounds the problem in a useful way so that solutions well outside the acceptable bounds can be rapidly eliminated from further consideration. Of course, costs less than this limit are even better, but the evaluator and vendors have a sense of scope of the acceptable solutions. Or, for example, must the application must run to completion within Y hours? Again, faster solutions are better, but a useful bound has been set to help direct the search to the most useful areas. Certain kinds of functionality may be required: The machine must support an HIPPI interface or must be able to utilize TCP/IP over the organization's existing LAN. Systems unable to meet these requirements can be eliminated at once without spending superfluous effort in additional evaluation.

A second technique that has been successful on these types of evaluations is a *total pool* of available points, spread across the evaluation criteria so as to reflect the organization's priorities. Where delivered performance is the overriding objective, the type A boxes would receive the lion's share of the weighting—for example, 250 points each for the three major application targets for the MPP, with another 250 for the type B boxes. Where ease of use, software porting, additional functionality, etc., are most important, the type B boxes would be correspondingly emphasized. Indeed, at a top level, the relative importance of the two areas—performance and nonperformance criteria—is the most useful way for management to indicate to the evaluation team its overriding priorities.

In each area, the rules for assigning the available points must be agreed to *in advance*. When cost is a major factor, it is important that machines of like abilities be compared. For example, the amount of memory in the machine is often a major cost driver. Thus, machine configurations with similar amounts of memory should be compared. Again, with, say, 250 points available for performance on an application, the rules for awarding the points based on achieved performance must be specified—say, a sliding scale from 0 to 250 points based on achieved run time from 10 hours (= 0 points) down to 20 minutes (= 250 points). Figure 12-4 illustrates the idea.

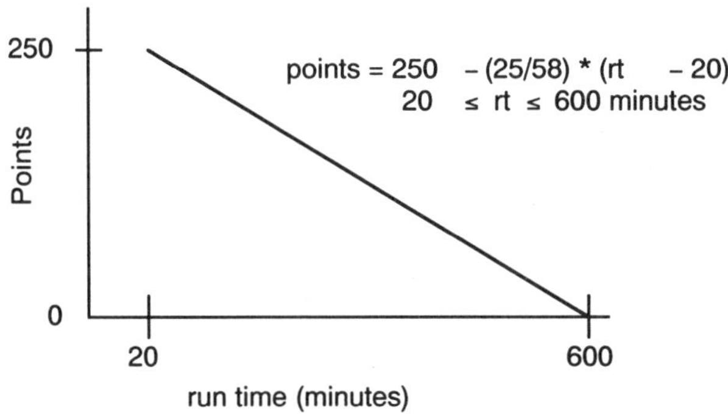

Figure 12-4. Sample scale for converting run time to evaluation points

Similar scales can be developed for other evaluation areas—cost, reliability, functional features (10 points each for checkpoint/restart, IEEE floating point, a graphics library, etc.), security, and so forth. Since the point weights and the measure-to-points conversion rules are at the heart of the evaluation, they will be the subject of debate and negotiation, and there may be pressure to change the rules as advocates of one or another system perceive they are doing more or less well than competitors. Hopefully, enough objectivity can be maintained so that the methodology does not become a political tool to be manipulated. This is contrary to its intent, which is to faithfully reflect the organization's priorities. Like any approach where judgment and qualitative assessments are involved, the methodology is subject to distortion.

When presenting the results to management, it is important that back-up charts are available to explain exactly how the various numbers were obtained. It is also wise to give some indication of sensitivity (e.g., if the weights were changed in such and such a way, system Y would come out ahead of system X). The methodology is not intended to force a decision but to clarify where major differences between the systems exist and to give management assurance that no major areas have been omitted. Also, when subjective evaluations have been made (e.g., vendor Y appears to be a more risky business venture than vendor Z), the reasons for the judgment should be explicitly presented, especially when the overall recommendation is hinges on the result. In the author's experience, it is not uncommon that the issue of software comes to dominate the discussion. To prepare for this, it would be wise to keep a record of the experience of the software engineers in porting or developing the benchmark code. This may be valuable in giving management an accurate sense of the size of the software development/porting effort that lies ahead.

12.2 INTEGRATING A PARALLEL MACHINE INTO EXISTING OPERATIONS

In this section, we will illustrate the issues that arise during transition and integration by means of three representative examples. In the first, the MPP is intended as a special-purpose device assigned to production runs of a single compute-intensive application. In the second, a modest-size MPP is included as a server in an open systems environment. In the third, an LAN of workstations becomes the parallel processor. Each example illustrates different aspects of the general integration problem.

12.2.1 Case 1: Turbo-Charging a Mainframe Application

The first example arises when some aspect of an application—sorting is a typical example—has reached the point that traditional solutions are no longer working. The MPP is viewed as a fix for a specific problem, and the goal is to off-load the computational crunch onto the MPP. This has three benefits: (1) the complete run gets done sooner, since the most time-consuming part of it has been "turbo-charged" by the MPP; (2) by off-loading this part of the problem, the mainframe is able to take on additional work; and (3) since only a piece of the application has been transferred to the MPP, most of the existing application software can still be run on the mainframe with attendant savings in software development. A notional hardware configuration is shown in Figure 12-5.

The most significant issues to be overcome are:

- data transfer from existing storage media (disk, tape) to the MPP
- software development to perform the operation on the MPP
- data transfer back to the mainframe environment in a format usable by the application

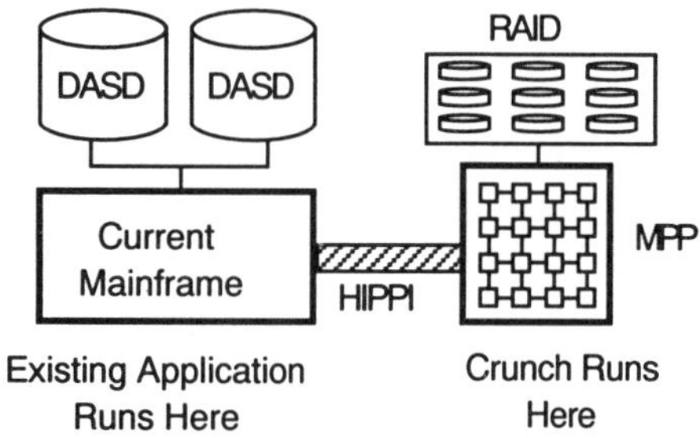

Figure 12-5. Using an MPP to turbo-charge an application

If this looks a bit like "input, processing, and output," the similarity is not by accident.

Regarding the input phase, the data residing in the mainframe environment are structured optimally for the existing application, not for the benefit of the MPP. The restructuring that may be required (particularly the issue of distributing the various records optimally across the processors) can be done on either side of the interface, but it is probably best to do it on the MPP, using the high-performance interconnection network of the MPP to perform the rearragement preparatory to execution of the algorithm. Thus, the job on the mainframe side is to get the data into the form of a single flat file and transfer it across the link (HIPPI is commonly used for this purpose) to the MPP.

If the application is too large to run in core, the MPP will utilize its own specialized high-performance secondary storage devices (e.g., RAID disks) for buffering and to hold intermediate results. The arrangement and use of this space is part of the software development activity on the MPP side of the interface. However, depending on the available networking and database sharing capabilities, it is possible (via a shared file system) to use the secondary storage device as the data transfer mechanism. Such a capability is not yet "off the shelf" from MPP vendors. The path of least resistance, at the moment, is to treat the incoming data as essentially an unstructured byte stream and to impose additional structure via the application software running on the MPP. In this situation, minimal effort should be required on the mainframe side of the interface—enough to assemble the data in whatever form is convenient and ship it across the network interface.

Turning now to actual processing on the MPP, the incoming data must be spread in a suitable fashion both across the processor array and in fast secondary storage. For out of core algorithms, this second factor can be critical to overall performance, since we would prefer that each array processor or group of processors have independent, concurrent, and contention-free access to the portion of intermediate results it needs. In particular, we do not want to serialize/deserialize the I/O operations once the application data are on the MPP side of the interface.

Another potential difficulty is a mismatch between data formats. The three that are most often encountered are:

- Big-endian/Little-endian
- ASCII/EBCDIC
- Floating point

While data format conversion routines are not difficult to write, they are annoying and must be done in both directions. Existing libraries written for one collating sequence, for example, may no longer work for data encoded using a different scheme. Similarly, nonportable usages based on programmer knowledge (i.e., assumptions) about the byte order of data types can cause difficulties.

In our sorting example, specific code must be written for the MPP to handle long, variable-length records and to extract the keys from the proper fields. Database utilities for this purpose do not exist—the code must be developed from scratch, and this will require detailed knowledge of the data storage and encoding techniques employed by the database manager on the mainframe side of the interface. This, of course, is in addition to the algorithm itself, which must be written to take maximal advantage of the MPP hardware.

The road back to the mainframe is similarly fraught with difficulty. Once one has gone to all the trouble of moving data to the MPP in a format and with a structure suitable for its operations, there will be a natural inclination to leave it there as long as possible—that is, to perform as much of the application as is reasonable before returning the massaged data back to the mainframe. An amoeba-like swallowing up of neighboring (in the production flow) phases will appear more attractive, and the boundary between the mainframe and MPP portions of the work can become cloudy. Further, once the advantages of the MPP on the selected application become known among users, demand for its services is likely to increase, complicating life on both sides of the interface. If the MPP has its own complement of peripherals for report generation and networking, the role of the mainframe in the end to end application can appear increasingly superfluous. The bottom line, here, is that there may well arise a strong argument that the path *back* to the mainframe should be, shall we say, gracefully excised. If it is not already clear, the author has a certain affinity for this point of view.

12.2.2 Case 2: The MPP as Server in an Open System

The second example arises when an MPP (or SMP) is added to an existing LAN of workstations as a computational server. The idea is that certain applications may be compute-bound when executed on the workstation and, hence, can be effectively migrated to a compute server. Conceptually, the user causes the application to execute on the MPP and receives the results (via the LAN) for display and local analysis. The intent is to share the MPP's computational resources over a wide user base, resulting in efficiencies of scale and improving productivity for the individual users on the network.

A notional hardware configuration is shown in Figure 12-6. While the figure shows FDDI as the LAN implementation, other choices are available (e.g.,

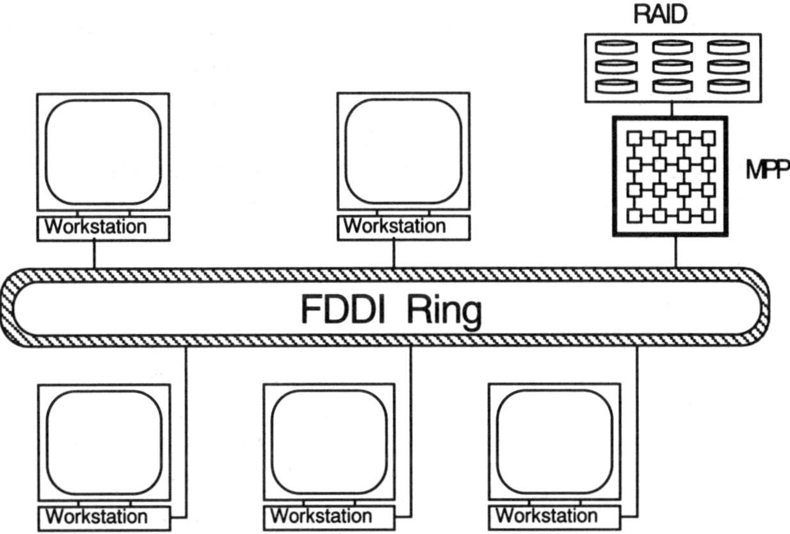

Figure 12-6. An MPP as a compute server

EtherNet or vendor proprietary). The advent of affordable SONET/ATM networks is likely to revolutionize this type of architecture over the next five to ten years, as inexpensive high-performance (that is, multi-GByte) switches become widely available to the commercial market.

The most significant issues to address are:

- sharing the MPP's resources
- development of application software
- interface difficulties (format, standards)

A typical setting for this configuration might be an engineering shop where users perform, say, structural analysis on components using CAD/CAM software at high-performance workstations. It is typical that certain portions of the computation (say, matrix inversion for FEM solvers) consume the majority of computational time once the model itself has been initialized. It makes sense to move this part of the problem to a central server where it can be completed rapidly and shared by multiple users.

In such a setting, sharing the MPP's resources can become a major requirement. An SIMD machine, for example, architecturally can only support a single instruction stream (that is, user job) at a time, so that sharing must take the form of a job queue serviced sequentially. MIMD machines are more flexible. Since they can support multiple independent instruction streams (one per controller), it is possible to space-share the machine. Subarrays can be independently allocated to different users (see Figure 9-4), each executing a different job. A significant part of the integration task will be to establish both the mechanisms and the policy to control this type of sharing. Applications that can make use of high-speed peripheral storage may find themselves competing for this resource—a situation already familiar to many ADP centers.

Security (in the form of isolation) may also become an issue. A rogue program in one user's partition should not affect the running (say, by requiring system reboot) of a program in another user's partition. Not all MIMD vendors are equally adept at providing such isolation. When such separation is critical, it is not uncommon to find MIMD vendors recommending one at a time sequential job servicing similar to an SIMD environment.

It is likely that application software will be a major concern. With one important exception (SMPs, to be discussed shortly), the organization will be faced with a code porting or code development task. Even if users are accustomed to code development, some amount of retraining for the parallel architecture will be required. Other organizations will have centralized programmer support, which can assist the client users in the software port. The integration/transition plan must provide resources—time and personnel—for this purpose. This is one reason why an incremental, start slow and grow approach to MPPs makes sense. A small machine suffices to get the software porting/development effort started on one (or a few) high-profile applications. A working prototype, with scaling data indicating achievable performance on larger configurations, serves as the springboard to demonstrate utility to the user community and to enlist their support. This strategy has been successfully used in a variety of environments and, when it can be adopted, is probably the most likely either to succeed or to avoid a large and costly failure.

This configuration has been specifically targeted by almost every workstation vendor. These vendors have all introduced parallel servers in the form of symmetric multiprocessors (SMPs). The hardware architecture for these machines is a cache coherent shared memory, and the operating system is a modified multiprocessor version of UNIX. They have a number of advantages over distributed memory MIMD or SIMD MPPs.

First, the microprocessor used in a vendor's SMP matches the processor in the associated workstation. This means that the sequential version of the workstation software will run, without modificiation, on the SMP (of course, not parallelized but used in a space-sharing multitasking mode). Thus, the SMP comes with a built-in set of application software—the same set that already runs on the workstations.

Second, the vendor will ensure a reasonable level of connectivity between its workstations and the SMP it provides. Network protocols, shared files and/ or databases, remote procedure call, and other useful capabilities will be bundled in the package. It may even be possible to use the SMP as a driver for several "dumb" X-terminals—the application software runs on the SMP server, and the X-terminal provides the user interface [30].

Third, as we have discussed in the sections on programming models, the shared memory paradigm is the closest to traditional sequential programming. Should parallel software porting or development be required, the task is apt to be easiest on a shared memory machine.

Fourth, some organizations have found software license fee advantages by using an SMP. While a single copy for an SMP may be more expensive than a single copy for a workstation, the SMP copy can service many different users, and some cost savings may accrue.

It should be stressed that at the moment the application software for SMPs is essentially sequential. The multiple processors are assigned to separate independent jobs on which they execute sequentially and independently. Truly parallel applications, which use several processors concurrently to speed up the execution, are not generally available, even on SMPs. Another disadvantage to SMPs is scalability. For reasons discussed at some length is Section 3.5, the *shared memory programming* model is only useful if it is matched by a *uniform memory access hardware* model—one in which all memory accesses have essentially equal latency. The current generation of SMPs, using very large caches (up to 4 MB of SRAM), reaches as high as 30 to 40 processors before running out of memory bandwidth, and there is no reasonable prospect of extending much beyond this limit. Applications that can make use of up to hundreds of processors (or more) must pursue a different approach.

Turning now to interface issues (data formats, operating system compatibility, etc.), the advantage of SMPs has been noted. Each workstation vendor offers its own SMP and software that interfaces seamlessly with its own workstations. An organization with an existing investment in the hardware of a given vendor may choose to avoid potential interface issues by not switching horses. An organization that has conscientiously adopted a multivendor, open approach will be better able to pick and choose the most cost-effective solution. Even the most standards-conscious shop, however, can experience annoyances—data format conversion being a typical and frequent example.

A final comment on the situation in which users are to develop their own parallel applications. For many MPP vendors, it is perhaps not a good idea to mix development and production on the same machine. Even on systems where multiple users are space-sharing a machine using multiple subarrays, parallel applications on one subarray can, for a variety of reasons, affect (or even cause to abort) applications on a different subarray. The most reasonable approach, given the current state of OS software for MPPs, is to institute operational policy that segregates the two types of activities. This is another advantage of having a small version of the MPP hardware—it permits parallel software development work without a large hardware expense. In the meantime, a larger configuration of the machine can be dedicated to user production codes. Another alternative is simulator software running on, say, a workstation. Again, debugging and OS aborts are circumscribed in an environment that is less costly and that does not affect production runs.

12.2.3 Case 3: The LAN *Is* the MPP

An increasingly popular variation on the parallel processing theme is to turn an existing LAN of workstations—hopefully, all the same vendor and OS—into a single computing resource. The idea is that a single application can be parallelized by assigning different parts of the application to different processors on the LAN. Since these processors are running a time-sharing system (UNIX), available cycles, which would otherwise be wasted, on these processors can be "invisibly" put to use. The basic configuation is the same as Figure 12-5, except that the MPP has been omitted. The term *cluster* is increasingly used for such a configuration.

As an example, suppose the LAN has, say, 20 workstations. A user on one of the workstations develops a parallel application that can use, say, the services of 10 other processors. Using the LAN as the communications mechanism, a protocol is exercised (invisibly to the local users) in which the current usage level across the network is interrogated. Those processors with the largest number of available cycles then agree (via the protocol) to participate in the distributed computation. Executables and data are either downloaded from host or accessed via a shared file system. They are executed as background processes that need never come to the attention of the users on whose workstations they execute. They simply share the machine in the background, via the UNIX time-sharing capabilities, until the distributed application is complete, at which point they output results and exit. Further, the LAN serves as the mechanism when processors need to communicate (like the soldiers in the wall-building example who share a common boundary).

The advantages of such an approach are clear. First, little or no additional hardware need be procured—only the software that provides the user programmer interface to the LAN and OS facilities. Several such packages are now available—Express from ParaSoft, Linda from SCA, and PVM from Oak Ridge Labs are perhaps the best known. While the LAN is not the sort of high-performance interconnect that would permit massive parallelism, for applications that are very coarse-grained and require only minimal coordination among processors, the LAN may be perfectly adequate. Finally, since the cycles being used in the the application are (at least theoretically) currently going for no-ops, the hope is to experience a performance boost for the parallelized application without impacting the performance of other currently running applications.

Our intention for the remainder of this section is to indicate in a general manner some of the considerations that should be taken into account when considering such an approach. They fall into three areas:

- application software
- impact on users
- scalability

First, no application software is available for such an environment; it must be developed in-house. The packages that implement the parallelism are essentially libraries of subroutines that implement the network and OS interfaces. Thus, the standard compilers (usually C or FORTRAN) available on the workstation can be used.

A typical case is a user running a Monte Carlo simulation. The more trials, the better, and the trials are independent. Thus, the LAN parallelization tools can be used to run multiple copies of the existing Monte Carlo code on as many other workstations as are available. The parallelization tools provide the ability to distribute and coordinate the concurrent execution and to assemble final results. Little interprocessor communications are required other than the initial downloading of the executable and the final assembling of results.

In considering whether an application might be appropriate for this kind of parallelism, the dominant issues will be interprocessor communications and I/O. The LAN is the interprocessor communication mechanism. The more message traffic generated by the application, the more stress is put on the LAN. Further, by parallel processor standards, even the most powerful LANs are very high latency/low bandwidth devices. Relatively long delays will be associated with data exchanges, and, hence, the most efficient applications will be those that require almost no interprocessor communications. A similar concern applies to I/O. How is the data to get to the various workstations executing the application? If the initiating host first does the I/O and then distributes the data, a sequential bottleneck arises. On the other hand, if the processors do their own I/O, the application may require modification to allow this to occur and physical rearrangement of the data around the LAN may be required. In either case, the LAN may (will) be additionally loaded by the I/O operations. Some care should be taken, during initial benchmarking, to size these portions of the problem so as to ensure that LAN bandwidth saturation is not likely to occur and to estimate the likely performance degradation associated with interprocessor communications.

The second major consideration in such an environment is the likely impact (perhaps unintended) on the users. Here are some examples of potential unintended consequences:

- The background process, even if set at a low priority, will, to some extent, compete with the local user's applications for CPU cycles. Even if the workstation is lightly loaded when execution of the parallel application begins, it may not remain that way.
- A more likely performance impact is due to memory utilization. While it is true that UNIX implements a virtual memory, applications run faster when there is less paging. The background process may compete with the local user's application for physical memory, causing an increased number of page faults and reducing responsiveness. This can be particularly noticeable in applications with a large interactive graphics content.
- If the parallel application requires secondary storage (for intermediate files or even for paging), it can slow performance at the workstation.
- The parallel application can even impact workstations on which it does not reside by flooding or saturating the LAN.
- Local workstation users with private files may feel (with whatever justification) uneasy about sharing resources with "imported" applications. Paranoia (some would say reasonable caution) regarding viruses, for example, can make users mistrustful about such a configuration.

The point here is that the execution of the parallel application may not be as "invisible" as the ideal model would suggest. One approach that has been used in some organizations is to restrict execution of parallel applications to off-hours, when the LAN is not otherwise in use. Another unexpected "gotcha" can come during application development and debugging. If care is not paid to default file allocations, error messages and other annoying side effects of debugging may show up at the local workstation OS rather than the initiator. Care is therefore required to ensure that local users are shielded from the impact of parallel application debugging.

Finally, the issue of scalability of parallel applications in LAN environments is likely, sooner or later, to become an issue. Implementations that work well across, say, four or five workstation processors can rapidly degrade as the number of processors increases to, say, 10, or 20, or 50. The application developer, on the other hand, will almost surely feel the "need for speed" and be anxious to expand a small and manageable success into something greater. Generally speaking, the mind-set and implementation constraints associated with the high latency, low bandwidth of an LAN lead to implementation approaches that will not scale to large configurations. This does not mean that the application is not parallelizable (even to large machines) but that the LAN as MPP is not really a scalable architecture.

The advent of SONET/ATM will substantially impact this type of architecture over the next few years. An LAN implemented using this technology will be able to support the rapid exchange of truly phenomenal amounts of data (on the order of a few gigabytes per second of bandwidth). However, message start-up latencies are not likely to improve much over current implementations (on the order of a few milliseconds). Relatively coarse-grained applications, which only require a few large data transfers, will flourish in such an environment, since the cost of the ATM solution will be much better than the low-latency interconnects characteristic of top-end MPPs. Applications (such as sorting), which require frequent small messages with very low latencies, are less amenable to this approach.

We have frequently mentioned in this chapter the value of beginning with small prototypes of parallel applications to demonstrate proof of principle. An LAN of workstations can be used in this way. The eventual target platform may be a fully integrated DM-MIMD, but the inital data decomposition, message-passing requirements, and debugging can often be worked out in the LAN environment. So long as some care is taken to ensure transferability to the MPP, this can be a very reasonable, inexpensive approach to getting some initial experience with a parallel software environment.

Summary of Chapter 12

A systematic methodology has been presented that permits a balanced, comprehensive assessment of the relative strengths of various parallel architectures when considered as solutions to a specific application. While performance (that is, speed of execution) is important, it is only one factor among many if the eventual implementation is to be successful in its intended operational environment. Ways of measuring both performance and nonperformance evaluation criteria, and of combining these "apples and oranges" results into a complete assessment, have been considered. A second major section illustrated some of these ideas by discussing three typical MPP implementation strategies and the factors that should be included in the evaluation process. A recurring theme has been the value of "starting small," gaining experience with the software issues, and convincing users of the utility of the MPP by building working, scalable prototypes.

Appendix A

The Sample Problem

In order to focus our attention on some of the issues that arise in developing code for an MPP, we have constructed a "toy" problem. It includes instances of the following operations:

- terminal I/O
- file I/O
- scalar and vector operations
- dynamic memory allocation
- broadcast and reduction
- index-dependent loops

The problem is to calculate some statistics, a histogram, and a percentile array for a large number of SAT scores. The scores are assumed to lie in a range from 0 to 1600 and are to be found in a file whose name will be supplied at run time by the user. The first entry in the file is an integer (32 bit) containing the total number of scores held in the file. Our assumption is that this could be a very large number (up to several millions). Memory to hold the array is allocated, and the file is read in. A single pass is made down the array, calculating: (1) the maximum and minimum of the scores; (2) the sum of the scores (for later use in calculating the average); (3) the sum of the squares of the scores (for later use in calculating the standard deviation); and (4) a histogram array (that is, for each possible value from 0 to 1600, a count of how many scores took on that value). Following this pass through the array, the average and standard deviations are computed. Next, a percentile array is computed; that is, for each score from 0 to 1600, the percentage of scores *less* than the given score is found. The iterative relationship

$$\text{percentile}[N] = \text{percentile}[N-1] + \text{histogram}[N-1]/\text{Total} * 100\%\ ,$$
$$1 \le N \le 1600,\ \text{percentile}[0] = 0$$

is used, where:

percentile: the array holding the score percentiles

histogram: computed in the initial pass through the large array

The dependence of element N on element $(N-1)$ poses a problem for certain vector operations. This is an example of a *prefix* operation, which can be successfully parallelized. Next, the values of the array are replaced by their difference from the average (rounded to an integer); that is, each score in the array is replaced by (score – average). The max, min, average, standard deviation, histogram array, percentile array, and recalculated array are then appended to the file, which is then closed, and the program exits.

LISTING FOR SAMPLE PROBLEM

```
#include <stdio.h.>
#include <math.h>

void main()  {

char file_name[128];
FILE * file1;
int * scores;
int num_scores, max_scores, min_scores;
int average_int;
float temp1, temp2;
double sum_scores, sumsq_scores;
double average, standard_dev;
int histogram[1601];
float percentile[1601];

register int i, curr_score;

/*  Prompt user for file name. */

printf
```

```
("Enter the name of the file containing the scores\n");
scanf("%s", file_name);

/* Open file for update */

if(  ( file1 = fopen( file_name, "a+b" ) ) == NULL )
{
printf("Cannot open file.\n");
exit(-1);
}

/*  Initialize the file pointer. */

fseek( file1, 0L, 0 );

/*  Read in total number of scores in the file  */

fread( &num_scores, sizeof( int ), 1, file1 );

/*  Allocate memory to hold the array  */

scores = ( int * )malloc( num_scores * sizeof( int ) );

/*  Read in the array  */

fread( scores, sizeof( int ), num_scores, file1 );

/* Initialize variables  */

max_scores = -1;
min_scores = 1601;
sum_scores = 0.;
sumsq_scores = 0.;

for( i=0; i<=1600; i++ )  histogram[ i ] = 0;

/*  Loop over all the scores, updating max, min,
    sum, sum of squares, and histogram. */

for( i=0; i<num_scores; i++ )
{
curr_score = scores[i];
if( curr_score < min_scores ) min_scores =
```

```
    curr_score;
if( curr_score > max_scores ) max_scores =
    curr_score;
sum_scores += (double)curr_score;
sumsq_scores += (double)curr_score
                * (double)curr_score;
histogram[ curr_score ] += 1;
}

/*  Calculate the average and standard deviation. */

average = sum_scores/num_scores;
standard_dev =
  sqrt( sumsq_scores/num_scores - average*average );

/* Initialize variables prior to percentile
    calculation. */

percentile[0] = 0.;
temp1 = percentile[0];
temp2 = 100./(float)num_scores;

/*  Loop over histogram array, calculating its percent,
      and summing into the next entry of the
      percentile array. Convert percentile values to
      an integer. */

for( i=1;  i<=1600;  i++ )
{
percentile[i] = temp1 + temp2 * histogram[i-1];
temp1 = percentile[i];
percentile[i] = floor( percentile[i] );
}

/*  Round average to an integer.  */

average_int = ( int )(  average + .5 );

/*  Loop over the scores array, subtracting the
      average from each entry. */

for(i=0;  i<num_scores; i++ )  scores[i] -= average_int;
```

```
    /*  Position file pointer to end_of_file,
        preparatory to appending data. */

 fseek( file1, 0L, SEEK_END );

    /*  Append to file each of the required
        values and arrays. */

 fwrite(  &min_scores, sizeof( int ), 1, file1 );
 fwrite(  &max_scores, sizeof( int ), 1, file1 );
 fwrite(  &average_int, sizeof( int ), 1, file1 );
 fwrite(  &standard_dev, sizeof( float ), 1, file1 );
 fwrite(  histogram, sizeof( int ), 1601, file1 );
 fwrite(  percentile, sizeof( float ), 1601, file1 );
 fwrite(  scores, sizeof( int ), num_scores, file1 );

    /*  Close file and exit. */

 fclose( file1 );

 exit( 0 );

 }
```

Appendix B

SGI Challenge

```
#include <stdio.h.>
#include <math.h>

void main()  {

char file_name[128];
FILE * file1;
int * scores;
int num_scores, max_scores, min_scores;
int average_int;
float temp1, temp2;
double sum_scores, sumsq_scores;
double average, standard_dev;
int histogram[1601];
float percentile[1601];

/*  Both i and curr_score will become local
    variables in threads created later in
    program.  */

register int i, curr_score;

/*  Here are the declarations of the other
    local variables we'll need.  */

int l_max, l_min, l_avrg_int;
```

```
016>  double l_sumsc, l_sumsq;
017>  double l_avrg;
018>  int l_hist[1601];

      /*  From here to line 33, the code is identical
          to the sample problem and executes sequentially
          on a single processor. In particular, the file
          I/O and memory allocation are all sequential.

          Prompt user for file_name.
      */

019>  printf
      ("Enter the name of the file containing the scores\n");
020>  scanf("%s", file_name);

      /*  Open file for update */

021>  if(  ( file1 = fopen( file name, "a+b" ) ) == NULL )
022>  {
023>    printf("Cannot open file.\n");
024>    exit(-1);
025>  }

      /*  Read in total number of scores in the file  */

026>  fread( &num_scores, sizeof( int ), 1, file1 );

      /*  Allocate memory to hold the array  */

027>  scores = ( int * )malloc( num_scores * sizeof
        ( int ) );

      /*  Read in the array  */

028>  fread( scores, sizeof( int ), num_scores, file1 );

      /*  Initialize the shared, global variables.  */

029>  max_scores = -1;
030>  min_scores = 1601;
031>  sum_scores = 0.;
```

```
sumsq_scores = 0.;
/*  We could move this initialization loop inside
    the parallel region and parallelize it using a
    pfor pragma. This way it is closer to the
    original code.
*/

for( i=0; i<=1600; i++ )  histogram[ i ] = 0;

/*  Begin parallel portion here. */

#pragma parallel

/*  Here are the variables that are shared across
    all the threads created by the parallel pragma.
    The variables default to shared, but we will
    explicitly declare them anyway. We use the "\"
    character to override the end-of-line, since
    ANSI syntax specifies that the prgama statement
    only extends to the first end-of-line.
    Alternatively, we could have replicated the
    pragma statement, once for each shared variable.
*/

#pragma shared ( scores,            \
                 min_scores,        \
                 max_scores,        \
                 sum_scores,        \
                 sumsq_scores,      \
                 histogram,         \
                 average,           \
                 num_scores         )

/*  Here are the variables that will be local to
    each thread.  Separate copies of these
    variables will be automatically created in the
    private address space of each thread.  We will
    see below why average should have its local
    surrogate.
*/
```

```
036>  #pragma local   ( i,              \
                        curr_score,     \
                        l_min,          \
                        l_max,          \
                        l_sumsc,        \
                        l_sumsq,        \
                        l_hist,         \
                        l_avrg   )

      /*  Open the parallel region.  The scope extends to
          line  72.
      */

037>  {

      /*  First, each thread initializes its local
          variables prior to entering the "for" loop over
          the scores array.
      */

038>  l_min = 1601;
039>  l_max = -1;
040>  l_sumsc = 0.;
041>  l_sumsq = 0.;

      /*  Don't parallelize this loop, since each thread
          has to initialize its own copy of the local
          l_hist array.
      */

042>  for(i=0; i<1601; i++) l_hist[i] = 0;

      /*  Now, parallelize the main "for" loop over the
          scores array, using the  pfor  pragma.
      */

043>  #pragma pfor iterate (i=0; num_scores; 1)

      /*  This bracket will control the scope of
          influence of the pfor pragma.  It terminates at
          line  54  below.  Strictly, the "{" and "}" are
          not needed, since there is only a single "for"
          statement in the block (compare with lines
          67–69 below).
```

```
     */
{

     /*  The meaning of the "for" loop has now changed.
         Each thread will only execute some of the
         iterations, not all of them. The values held
         by local variables (such as l_max) in each
         thread will only reflect the subset of the
         scores seen by the thread. The compiler
         automatically makes the decision concerning
         which subset is assigned to each thread. Notice
         the similarity between this loop and the main
         loop from the sample problem.
     */

for( i=0; i<num_scores; i++ )
{
   curr_score = scores[i];
   if( curr_score < l_min ) l_min = curr_score;
   if( curr_score > l_max ) l_max = curr_score;
   l_sumsc += (double)curr_score;
   l_sumsq += (double)curr_score
            * (double)curr_score;
   l_hist[ curr_score ] += 1;
}

     /*  Now, close the pfor pragma.  */

}

     /*  At this point, each thread has local variables
         with values reflecting the subset of the scores
         array processed by the thread. We now must
         combine the results together. The critical
         pragma ensures one by one sequential access of
         the threads to the section of code it guards.
     */

#pragma critical

     /*  Open the region designated critical. Each
         thread will execute this complete section one
         by one in order, the next thread not starting
         until the previous one has finished.
```

```
     */
056> {

057> if ( l_min < min_scores ) min_scores = l_min;
058> if ( l_max > max_scores ) max_scores = l_max;
059> sum_scores += l_sumsc;
060> sumsq_scores += l_sumsq;
061> for( i=0; i<num_scores; i++ )
062>           histogram[ i ] += l_hist[ i ];

063> }

     /* At this point, the correct global values of
        max, min, sum, sum of squares, and histogram
        are held in the shared variables. Each thread
        will now compute (redundantly) a local instance
        of average – l_avrg. The standard deviation
        calculation has been moved outside the scope of
        the parallel pragma. If a single global value
        of average were wanted here, we would have to
        restrict execution to a single processor. This
        way is easier.

        First, we have to synchronize, because we don't
        want any thread to use the value of sum_scores
        until we know that each thread has contributed
        its part.
     */

064> #pragma synchronize

     /* Now, it's safe for each thread to calculate its
        own local copy of l_avrg.
     */

065> l_avrg = sum_scores/num_scores;

     /* We choose not to parallelize the percentile
        calculation, though there are approaches to do
        so. However, we do want to parallelize the
        scaling of the scores array, so we move it
        here, prior to closing the scope of the
        parallel pragma opened at line 37.

        Round l_avrg to an integer.
```

```
   */
l_avrg_int = ( int )( l_avrg + .5 );

/*  Another pfor pragma, but this time easier.
    This parallelizes the scaling of the scores
    array.  */

#pragma pfor iterate (i=0; num_scores; 1)
for(i=0;  i<num_scores;  i++ )
             scores[i] -= l_avrg_int;

/*  Now, use the one processor pragma to copy the
    local value of l_avrg to the global value,
    prior to leaving the parallel region. Whichever
    thread reaches this point in the execution
    first will execute it, and the others will skip
    it.
*/

#pragma  one processor
                average = l_avrg;

/*  We are now done with the parallel region. The
    remainder of the code will excute sequentially
    on a single processor.
*/

}

/*  First, do the stuff we moved outside the
    parallel region:  the standard deviation
    calculation ....
*/

standard_dev =
 sqrt( sumsq_scores/num_scores - average*average);

/*  .... and the percentile calculation.  */

percentile[0] = 0.;
temp1 = percentile[0];
temp2 = 100./(float)num_scores;

for( i=1;  i<=1600;  i++ )
```

```
{
  percentile[i] = temp1 + temp2 * histogram[i-1];
  temp1 = percentile[i];
  percentile[i] = floor( percentile[i] );
}

/*  Everything else is the same.

    Position file pointer to end_of_file,
    preparatory to appending data.
*/

fseek( file1, 0L, SEEK_END );

/*  Append to file each of the required values and
    arrays.  */

fwrite(  &min_scores, sizeof( int ), 1, file1 );
fwrite(  &max_scores, sizeof( int ), 1, file1 );
fwrite(  &average, sizeof( double ), 1, file1 );
fwrite(  &standard_dev, sizeof( double ), 1, file1 );
fwrite(  histogram, sizeof( int ), 1601, file1 );
fwrite(  percentile, sizeof( float ), 1601, file1 );
fwrite(  scores, sizeof( int ), num_scores, file1 );

/*  Close file and exit.  */

fclose( file1 );

exit( 0 );

}
```

Appendix C

nCube

```
#include <stdio.h>
#include <math.h>

/*  Header for nube library.  */

#include <nCube.h>

void main()  {

char file_name[128];
FILE * file1;
int num_scores;
int * scores;
int max_scores, min_scores;
int average_int;
float temp1, temp2;
double sum_scores, sumsq_scores;
double average, standard_dev;
int histogram[1601];
register int i, curr_score;

/*  Here are the additional variables needed for
    the parallelized version.
*/

int me, pid, hid, dim;int array_size, my_offset;
int num_start, num_here;
int target = -1;
```

```
int msgtyp = -1;
int mask = -1;

/*  Each processor in the array finds out its node
    number <me> and the dimension of the array
    <dim> and calculates the array size based
    on the dimension.
*/

whoami( &me, &pid, &hid, &dim );

array_size =  1 << dim;

/*  All nodes get the same file name, so set the
    I/O mode to nglobal.
*/

nglobal();

printf
("Enter the name of the file with the scores.\n");

scanf("%s", file_name);

/*  Each node will open the file separately and
    get different values from it. So, shift the
    I/O mode to nlocal.
*/

nlocal();

if( (file1 = fopen( file name, "r+b") ) == NULL )
{
  printf("Node %d cannot open file.\n", me);
  exit(-1);
}

fread( &num_scores, sizeof( int ), 1, file1 );

/*  At this point, each node has the total number
    of scores in the file. The next library routine
    does the arithmetic to split the large scores
    array into equal subarrays.
*/
```

```
partld( me, array_size, 0, &num_start, &num_here, 0 );

/*  Each node now allocates only the amount of
    memory it needs to hold its portion of the
    scores array.
*/

scores = (int *)malloc( num_here * sizeof( int ) );

/*  Now, each node reads in only that part of the
    scores array calculated by the call to partld.
    Each node repositions its file pointer to the
    begining of the file (SEEK_SET).  Remember,
    there is one integer value, num_scores,  at the
    beginning of the array.
*/

fseek(file1, (1+num_start) * sizeof( int ),
  SEEK_SET );

fread( scores, sizeof( int ), num_here, file1 );

/*  The input is now complete.  Each node knows the
    total number of scores in the array and has
    read in its own portion of the array for
    processing.

    Now, each node initializes the variables
    and computes statistics on the locally held
    subarray.
*/

max_scores = -1;
min_scores = 1601;
sum_scores = 0.;
sumsq_scores = 0.;

for(i=0; i<=1600; i++ ) histogram[i] = 0;

for( i=0; i<num_here; i++)
{
  curr_score = scores[i];
  if(curr_score < min_scores) min_scores = curr_score;
  if(curr_score > max_scores) max_scores = curr_score;
```

```
    sum_scores += (double) curr_score;
    sumsq_scores += (double) curr_score + (double)
      curr_score;
    histogram[ curr_score ] += 1;
}

/*  Each node now has local values for max_scores,
    min_scores, sum_scores, sumsq_scores, and
    the histogram array. These must now be combined
    into global values. Each will be done
    separately, using the appropriate nCube library
    routine. But see below for an alternative
    approach.
*/

min_scores = imin(min_scores, target, msgtyp, mask);
max_scores = imax(max_scores, target, msgtyp, mask);
sum_scores = dsum(sum_scores, target, msgtyp, mask);
sumsq_scores = dsum(sumsq_scores,
        target, msgtyp, mask);
nisumn(histogram, 1601, target, msgtyp, mask);

/*  Alternatively, a subroutine call could be made
    that would coalesce all the five global
    operations into a single call. This would look
    like:

find_global_values( &max_scores,
                    &min_scores,
                    &sum_scores,
                    &sumsq_scores,
                    histogram   );

    This subroutine is presented and commented
    immediately after the main program.

    Note that all the nodes have the global values.
    It is as if both a reduction operation (to find
    the global value) and a broadcast operation (to
    make the value available to each node) has
    taken place. The logic in the subroutine will
    explain how this occurs without added overhead.
```

```
        Now, compute the average and standard
        deviation, just as in the sample problem.
    */

057>  average = sum_scores/num_socres;
058>  standard_dev =
       sqrt( sumsq_scores/num_scores - average*average );

      /*  Because the percentile array is so short, no
          attempt is made to parallelize it directly.
          For a longer array, however, summation prefix
          can be parallelized.
      */

059>  percentile[0] = 0.;
060>  temp1 = percentile[0];

061>  temp2 = 100./(float) num_scores;
062>  for(i=1; i<=1601; i++)
063>  {
064>    percentile[ i ] = temp1 + temp2 * histogram[ i-1 ];
065>    temp1 = percentile[ i ];
066>    percentile[ i ] = floor( percentile[ i ] );
067>  }

      /*  Now, each node will scale that portion of the
          scores array allocated to it. Later, in line
          82, each node will also separately output the
          subarray at the correct position in the file.
      */

068>  average_int = (int)( average + .5 );
069>  for( i=0; i<num_here; i++ ) scores[ i ] -=
        average_int;

      /*  Ready for output. The first few values are the
          same for all nodes, so we reset the I/O mode to
          nglobal and reposition the file before writing.
      */

070>  global();
071>  fseek( file1, 0L, SEEK_END );
```

```
fwrite( &min_scores, sizeof( int ), 1, file1 );
fwrite( &max_scores, sizeof( int ), 1, file1 );
fwrite( &average, sizeof( double ), 1, file1 );
 fwrite( &standard_dev, sizeof( double ), 1, file1 );
fwrite( histogram, sizeof( int ), 1601, file1 );
fwrite( percentile, sizeof( float ), 1601, file1 );

/*  Clear the I/O buffer prior to one by one
    output.
*/

fflush( file1 );

/*  Reset I/O mode to nlocal, for one at a time
    writing to the file.
*/

nlocal();

/*  Each node computes its correct offset into
    the file, including the initial number of
    scores, the original scores array, the
    values just written, and the values that
    precede it.
*/

my_offset =
  ( 1 + num_scores + 1 + 1 + 1601 ) * sizeof( int )
                  +
  ( 1 + 1 ) * sizeof( double )
                  +
  ( 1601 ) * sizeof( float )
                  +
  ( num_start ) * sizeof( int );

/*  Position the file pointer correctly,...*/

fseek( file1, my_offset, SEEK_SET );

/*  ...and write the data.  */

fwrite( scores, sizeof( int ), num_here, file1 );

/*  Each node closes the file and exits. */
```

```
083>  fclose( file1 );
084>  exit( 0 );
085>  }

      /*  We supply here an alternative subroutine for
          computing the global values of max, min, sum,
          sumsq, and histogram. This makes explicit use
          of the nread and nwrite routines and
          illustrates how the hypercube topology enables
          logarithmic and contention-free combining/
          reduction operations. This could be used by
          deleting lines 51-55 and inserting line 56
          instead.
      */

086>  void find_global_values( int * max,
                               int * min,
                               double * sum,
                               double * sumsq,
                               int * hist   )   {

      /*  This structure packs the five values into
          a single data entity to facilitate the
          construction of a message.
      */

087>  struct sample_message( int  m_max;
                             int  m_min;
                             double m_sum;
                             double m_sumsq;
                             int  m_hist[1601];
                           );

      /*  We'll need two copies: one to hold the
          current best and the other to receive
          the data from neighboring nodes as the
          algorithm progresses.
      */

088>  struct sample_message temp_message input_message;
089>  int me, pid, hid, dim;
090>  int array_size, my_neighbor, msg_typ;
```

```
091>  register int i, j;

      /*  First, get context.  These could have been
          passed in as parameters, but this way
          is just as easy.
      */

      whoami( &me, &pid, &hid, &dim );

092>  /*  Now, pack the values into the message
          structure.
      */

093>  temp_message.m_max = *max;
094>  temp_message.m_min = *min;
095>  temp_message.m_sum = *sum;
096>  temp_message.m_sumsq = *sumsq;
097>  for(i=0; i<=1600; i++)
              temp_message.m_hist[ i ] = hist[ i ];

      /*  The msg_typ field will need a dummy
          value, common to all the nodes.
      */

098>  msg_typ = 2;

      /*  Now, loop over the dimensions of the cube,
          exchanging current values with your neighbor,
          and updating them.
      */

099>  for(i=0; i<dim; i++)
0100>  {

       /* Name your neighbor along dimension i
           by toggling your ith bit!
       */

101>   my_neighbor = me ^ (1 << i);

       /*  Send the current values to your neighbor
           along the ith dimension.
       */
```

```
102>    nwrite(  my_neighbor,
                 &temp_message,
                 sizeof( sample_message );
                 msg_typ );

        /*  Now, receive the message sent by your neighbor.
            Be sure to match on who sent it to you, so you
            don't receive the messages out of order.
        */

103>    nread(   &input_message,
                 sizeof( sample_message ),
                 &my_neighbor,
                 &msg_type );

        /*  Now, update the values in temp_message
            against the values in input_message
            you just got from your neighbor.
        */

104>    if( input_message.m_max > temp_message.m_max )
                temp_message.m_max = input_message.m_max;

105>    if( input_message.m_min < temp_message. m_min )
                temp_message.m_min = input_message.m_min;

106>    temp_message.m_sum += input_message.m_sum;

107>    temp_message.m_sumsq += input_message.m_sumsq;

108>    for( j=0; j<=1600; j++ )
          temp_message.m_hist[j] +=
                input_message.m_hist[j];

        /*  Ready for the next neighbor.  */

109>     }

         /* At this point, temp_message contains the
            global values. Unpack, assign to the input
            variables, and return.
         */
```

```
*max = temp_message.m_max;
*min = temp_message.m_min;
*sum = temp_message.m_sum;
*sumsq = temp_message.m_sumsq;
for(i=0; i<=1600; i++)
          hist[i] = temp_message.m_hist[i];

return;

}
```

Appendix D

Express

```
#include <stdio.h>
#include <math.h>

/*  Header for the Express library.  */

#include <express.h>

/*  Define a global structure that will hold
    the context. The fields for this structure
    are defined in <express.h> and include
    the node number and array size.
*/

struct nodenv cparm;

void main()  {

/*  These declarations are the same as the
    sample problem.
*/

char file_name[128];
FILE * file1;
int num_scores;
int * scores;
int max_scores, min_scores;
```

```
011>  int average_int;

      /*  temp1 is no longer needed.  */

012>  float temp2;
013>  double sum_scores, sumsq_scores;
014>  double average, standard_dev;
015>  int histogram[1601];
016>  float percentile[1601];
017>  register i, curr_score;

      /*  Here are the additional variables introduced
          for the parallel version.
      */

018>  double pref_sum;
019>  int nvals, lo_index, myslot, score_vals;
020>  int score_first, percent_vals, percent_first;

      /*  Get the context, using the global structure
          declared in line 4.
      */

021>  exparam( &cparm );

      /*  The default I/O mode is "fsingl".
      */

022>  printf(
      "Enter the name of the file containing the scores.\n");

023>  scanf("%s", file_name);

024>  if(  (file1 = fopen( file_name, "a+b" ) ) == NULL )
025>  {
026>    printf("Cannot open file.\n");
027>    exit( -1 );
028>  }

      /*  Initialize the file pointer.  */

029>  fseek( file1, 0L, 0 );
```

```
fread( &num_scores, sizeof( int ), 1 file1 );

     /*  All nodes now know the total number of scores
         in the scores array, their own node number, and
         the size of the processor array. The next two
         lines instruct Express to treat the machine as
         a one-dimensional array and compute the optimal
         logical to physical mapping for the hardware.
     */

exgridinit( 1, &cparm.nprocs );
exgridcoord( cparm.procnum, &myslot );

     /*  Each processor now knows its logical position
         <myslot> in the processor array. The next two
         calls logically partition the scores array
         across the processor array. The result is that
         each node will know the first element in the
         scores array to process, <score_first>, and
         the total number of scores to process,
         <score_vals>.
     */

excalweight( 1000, EXP_FLTOPS );
exgridsize( cparm.procnum, &num_scores,
                     &score_vals, &score_first );

     /*  Each node allocates only the amount of memory
         it needs to hold the portion of the scores
         array it will receive.
     */

scores = (int *)malloc( score_vals * sizeof(int) );

     /*  Now, each node will read its own portion of the
         scores file. The programmer does not need to
         seek to the correct position – the Express
         library takes care of the details.

         First, shift from "fsingl" (the default) to
         "fmulti" so that each node can perform its
         own independent I/O operation.
     */
```

```
036>  fmulti( file1 );

      /*  Use the logical value myslot computed at
          line 32 to specify how EXPRESS should
          distribute the data across the processor array —
          in this case, in the same order as the logical
          order of the array.
      */

037>  forder( file1, myslot );

      /*  The  fread operation will now partition the
          scores array correctly.
      */

038>  fread( scores, sizeof( int ), score_vals, file1 );

      /*  Initialize statistic variables and compute
          statistics but only on the portion of the
          scores array held locally.
      */

039>  max_scores = -1;
040>  min_scores = 1601;
041>  sum_scores = 0.;
042>  sumsq_scores = 0.
043>  for( i=0; i<=1600; i++ ) histogram[i] = 0.;
044>  for( i=0; i<score_vals; i++ )
045>  {
046>    curr_score = scores[i];
047>    if(curr_score < min_scores) min_scores =
                 curr_score;
048>    if(curr_score > max_scores) max_scores =
               curr_score;
049>    sum_scores += (double)curr_score;
050>    sumsq_scores +=
               (double)curr_score * (double)curr_score;
051>    histogram[ curr_score ] += 1;
052>  }

      /*  Each node has the statistics corresponding to
          its subset of the complete scores array. Use
          the Express library to compute global values.
      */
```

```
053>  excombop( &min_scores, 1, EXP_INT_TYPE, EXP_MIN_OP );
054>  excombop( &max_scores, 1, EXP_INT_TYPE, EXP_MAX_OP );
055>  excombop( &sum_scores, 1, EXP_DOUBLE_TYPE,
      EXP_SUM_OP );
056>  excompop( &sumsq_scores, 1, EXP_DOUBLE_TYPE,
      EXP_SUM_OP );
057>  excombop( histogram, 1601, EXP_INT_TYPE, EXP_SUM_OP );

      /*  Every node now has the correct global values.
          Compute the average and standard deviation.
      */

058>  average = sum_scores/num_scores;
059>  standard_dev =
         sqrt( sumsq_scores/num_scores - average*average );

      /*  Lines 60-72 parallelize the percentile
          calculation using a summation prefix operation.

          First, logically partition the histogram array
          across the processor array.
      */

060>  nvals = 1601;
061>  exgridsize( cparm.procnum, &nvals,
                      &percent_vals, &percent_first );

      /*  Initialize percentile array and constants.
          The temp1 variable is no longer needed,
          since we will truncate the percentile
          array in a different loop (lines 71-72).
          The initialization for the local percentile
          calculation is different for the first
          logical processor than for the others.
      */

062>  temp2 = 100./ (float)sum_scores;
063>  if( myslot = 0 ) percentile[0] = 0.;
064>  else
065>    percentile[0] = temp2 * histogram[percent_first - 1];

      /*  A full 1601 memory spaces were allocated for
          percentile at line 16. Each node will only
          use the first few of these, from <0> up to
```

```
    <percent_vals>. The histogram indices are
    offset to the correct point in the array,
    <percent_first>, while the percentile indices
    start at the index <0> in each node.
*/

for( i=1; i<percent_vals; i++ )
  percentile[i] =
    percentile[i-1] +
       temp2 * histogram[percent_first+i-1];

/*  Now, use the final values in each partial array
    to perform a global summation prefix across the
    processor array. The Express library performs
    this prefix operation.
*/

pref_sum = (double)percentile[ percent_vals - 1 ];
exprefop( &pref_sum, EXP_DOUBLE_TYPE,
                EXP_SUM_OP, myslot );

/*  The local arrays can now be updated.  First,
    adjust pref_sum, ....
*/

pref_sum -= (double)percentile[ percent_vals - 1 ];

/*  ... and then truncate the updated percentile
    values for the assigned portion of the
    percentile array.
*/

for(i=0; i<percent_vals; i++)
  percentile[i] = floor( percentile[i] + pref_sum );

/*  Each node now scales the subset of the scores
    array it holds.
*/
average_int = (int)( average + .5 );
for(i=0; i<score_vals; i++) scores[ i] -=
 average_int;

/*  Ready for output. The first few data items are
    to be written only once, so shift to "fsingl"
    I/O mode.
*/
```

```
075>  fsingl( file1 );

      /*  The same as the sample problem.  */

076>  fseek( file1, 0L, SEEK_END );
077>  fwrite( &min_scores, sizeof(int), 1, file1 );
078>  fwrite( &max_scores, sizeof(int), 1, file1 );
079>  fwrite( &average, sizeof( double ), 1, file1 );
080>  fwrite( &standard_dev, sizeof( double ), 1, file1 );
081>  fwrite( histogram, sizeof( int ), 1601, file1 );

      /*  Both the percentile and scaled scores arrays
          are partitioned across the processor array. We
          first shift back to "fmulti" I/O mode.
      */

082>  fmulti( file1 );

      /*  Next, output the percentile array. Note that
          each node holds its portion of the percentile
          array at the beginning of the array and that
          the I/O subsystem takes care of ensuring that
          the fwrites are properly interleaved into the
          sequential file. This was determined by the
          forder  call at line 37.
      */

083>  fwrite(percentile, sizeof(int), percent_vals,
      file1);

      /*  Clear the buffer, .... */

084>  fflush( file1 );

      /*  ...and repeat the process for the scores array. */

085>  fwrite( scores, sizeof( int ), score_vals, file1 );

      /*  Close the file and exit.  */

086>  fclose( file1 );

087>  exit(0);
088>  }
```

Appendix E

Intel Paragon

```
#include <stdio.h>
#include <math.h>

/*  Paragon message-passing library. */

#include <nx.h>

/*  Paragon file I/O library.  */

#include <fcntl.h>

/*  Classic SPMD:  a single program, copies
    of which run on each of the nodes.
*/

void main()  {

/*  Variable declarations.  */

char file_name[128];

/*  Standard C file I/O not used, so FILE *
    declaration is omitted.  Instead, ...
*/

int file1;
int * scores;
int num_scores, max_scores, min_scores;
int average_int;
```

```
011>  float temp1, temp2;
012>  double sum_scores, sumsq_scores;
013>  float average, standard_dev;
014>  int histogram[1601];
015>  float percentile[1601];

016>  register int i, curr_score;

      /*  Here are the additional declarations needed for
          the parallel version.
      */

017>  int MSG_TYPE1 = 1;
018>  int MSG_TYPE2 = 2;
019>  PID = 0;
020>  int mynum, nprocs;
021>  int my_scores, r_scores;
022>  int itmp;
023>  double dtmp;
024>  int work[1601];

      /*  First, get context:  the number of nodes
          and the local node id.
      */

025>  mynum = mynode();
026>  nprocs = numnodes();

      /*  Node 0 prompts the user for the file name and

          then broadcasts it to all the other nodes in
          the array using csend.
      */

027>  if( mynum == 0 )
028>  {
029>    printf( "Enter name of the scores file.\n");
030>    scanf("%s", file_name);
031>    csend( MSG_TYPE1, file_name, sizeof( file_name ),
                    -1,  PID );
032>  }

      /*  The rest of the nodes receive the file name
          broadcast by Node 0 at line 31
      */
033>  else
034>  {
```

```
035>     crecv( MSG_TYPE1, file_name, sizeof( file_name ) );
036>   }

       /*  All nodes open the file using the Paragon
           file open utility.
       */

037>   if( (file1 = open(file_name, O_RDWR) ) == NULL )
038>   {
039>     printf("Node %d cannot open file.\n", mynum);
040>     exit(-1);
041>   }

       /*  Two I/O modes will be used. Both behave like
           the fmulti() mode from Express, in that all
           reads and writes result in distinct (not
           shared) I/O operations. In the M_LOG mode, the
           order in which the various nodes read or write
           the file is not specified. In M_SYNC mode (see
           line 56 below), the order is forced to
           correspond to the node numbering scheme: node 1
           first, then node 2, etc.
       */

042>   setiomode( file1, M_LOG );

       /*  Since we only want to read in one value, only
           one node executes the read operation. Without
           the guarding "if" test, all nodes would issue
           the read, and the file pointer would move deep
           into the scores array.
       */

043>   if( nynum == 0 )
044>   {
045>     cread(file1, &num_scores, sizeof(int) );

         /*  Now, broadcast the value of num_scores to the
             rest of the array.
         */

046>     csend(MSG_TYPE2, &num_scores, sizeof(int), -1, PID);
047>   }
       /*  Meanwhile, the other nodes receive broadcast
           messages generated at line 46.
       */
```

```
else
{
  crecv( MSG_TYPE2, &num_scores, sizeof(int), -1, PID);
}

/*  At this point, all the nodes have the value of
    num_scores.  Each computes the size of the
    subset of the scores array it will process.
*/

my_scores = num_scores / nprocs;
r_scores  = num_scores % nprocs;
my_scores += (mynum < r_scores) ? 1 : 0;

/*  Allocate just the amount of memory needed to
    hold the subset of the scores array needed
    by this node.
*/

scores = (int *)malloc( sizeof(int) * my_scores );

/*  We now shift to the M_SYNC mode to guarantee
    the order in which the scores are partitioned
    among the array processors.
*/

setiomode( file1, M_SYNC );

/*  This statement will be executed by all the
    nodes, and the I/O subsytem will ensure that
    the data are partitioned in order: the first
    set of data to Node 1, the second set to Node
    2, and so on.
*/

cread( file1, scores, sizeof(int) * my_scores );

/*  Each node computes the statistics using its own
    subset of the scores array.
*/

min_scores = 1601;
max_scores = -1;
sum_scores = sumsq_scores = 0.;
for( i=0; i<1601; i++ ) histogram[i] = 0;
```

```
for( i=0; i<my_scores; i++ )
{
  curr_score = scores[ i ];
  if(curr_score < min_scores) min_scores =
     curr_score;
  if(curr_score > max_scores) max_scores =
     curr_score;
  sum_scores += (double)curr_score;
  sumsq_scores +=
         (double)curr_score * (double)curr_score;
  histogram[ curr_score ] += 1;
}

/*  The local values of the statistics must now be
    combined into global values. The Paragon
    library routines are used. Notice how the
    calling program provides temporary work space:
    itmp, dtmp, and work.
*/

gilow( &min_scores, 1, &itmp );
gihigh( &max_scores, 1, &itmp );
gdsum( &sum_scores, 1, &dtmp );
gdsum( &sumsq_scores, 1, &dtmp );
gisum( histogram, 1601, work );

/*  All nodes now have the correct global values of
    the statistics variables. Each now computes the
    average and standard deviation.
*/

average = sum_scores/num_scores;
standard_dev =
  sqrt( sumsq_scores/num_scores - average*average );

/*  We choose not to parallelize the summation
    prefix operation.
*/

percentile[0] = 0.;
temp1 = 0.;
temp2 = 100./(float)num_scores;

for(i=1; i<=1601; i++)
{
```

```
083>     percentile[i] = templ + temp2 * histogram[i-1];
084>     templ = percentile[i];
085>     percentile[i] = floor( percentile[i] );
086>   }

       /*  Each node now scales its own portion of the
           scores array.
       */

087>   average_int = (int)( average + .5 );

088>   for(i=0; i<my_scores; i++) scores[i] -= average_int;

       /*  Now, for output.  Node 0 outputs the items
           that are not distributed.
       */

089>   if( nynum == 0 )
090>   {
091>     lseek( filel, 0L, SEEK_END );
092>     cwrite( filel, &min_scores, sizeof(int) );
093>     cwrite( filel, &max_scores, sizeof(int) );
094>     cwrite( filel, &average_int, sizeof(int) );
095>     cwrite( filel, &standard_dev, sizeof(double) );
096>     cwrite( filel, histogram, sizeof(int)*1601 );
097>     cwrite( filel, percentile, sizeof(int)*1601 );
098>   }

       /*  Now, all the nodes must participate in writing
           out the scaled scores array. Since the I/O mode
           has been set to M_SYNC at line 56, the Paragon
           I/O subsystem will ensure that the order of
           writing back to file corresponds to the order
           in which the subsets were read from the file.
       */

099>   lseek( filel, 0L, SEEK_END );
100>   cwrite( filel, scores, sizeof(int) * my_scores );

       /*  Close file and exit.  */

101>   close( filel );
102>   exit(0);

103>   }
```

Appendix F

MasPar MP-1

```
#include <stdio.h>
#include <math.h>

/*  Header for MasPar libraries.  */

#include <mpl.h>

/*  There is a single program with a single
    control stream. Some instructions refer
    to the SIMD processor array and some to
    the scalar unit.
*/

main() {

/*  Here are the scalar variables, just as
    in the sample problem. They reside on
    the scalar front end. Some of them
    are no longer needed, and some are now
    parallel variables on the processor
    array.
*/

char file_name[128];
FILE * file1;
int num_scores, max_scores, min_scores;
int average_int;
double sum_scores, sumsq_scores;
```

```
double average, standard_dev;

register int i;

/*  The scalar curr_score is no longer needed but
    two others are.
*/

int tmp_int;
double tmp_sum;

/*  An integer variable to hold the number of
    scores in each processor.
*/

int local_scores, last_few;

/*  Here are the parallel variables. Note that
    the scores array, histogram array, and
    percentile array are all on the processor
    array. The plural key word is used for this
    purpose.

    First, an integer pointer is allocated in each
    processor for the subset of the scores array.
*/

plural int *scores;

/*  Since the size of the histogram and percentile
    arrays is smaller than the number of processors,
    there is no need to partition these arrays. The
    remaining variables are local to each
    processor.
*/

plural int histogram;
plural float percentile;
plural float temp2;
plural int curr_score, scanval, my_num;

/*  The next few lines are standard scalar code,
    executing on the scalar unit.
*/
printf("Enter the file name with the scores.\n");
```

```
021>  scanf("%s", file_name);
022>  if( ( file1 = fopen( file_name, "r+b" ) ) == NULL )
023>  {
024>    printf("Cannot open file\n");
025>    exit( -1 );
026>  }

027>  fread( &num_scores, sizeof( int ), 1, file1 );

      /*  The predefined variable nproc holds the
          total number of processors, and the predefined
          variable iproc holds the index of each
          processor, from 0 to (nproc - 1). The following
          code computes how many elements each processor
          will hold.
      */

028>  local_scores = num_scores/nproc +
        (num_scores % nproc == 0 ) ? 0 : 1 ;

      /*  Now, each processor allocates enough memory
          to hold its own part of the scores array.
      */

029>  scores = (plural int *)p_malloc(
               local_scores * sizeof(plural int) );

      /*  Initialize scores to -1.  We'll use this
          at line below to exclude values in
          processors that did not receive scores
          elements.
      */

030>  for( i=0; i<local_scores; i++) scores[i] = -1;

      /*  Now, do a parallel read directly from the file
          to the processors in the array. Each gets a
          separate, contiguous subset of scores. Some
          processors at the end of the array may not get
          any scores, and one will receive the last few,
          if the partitioning is not even. The actual
          number is returned by p_read into the plural
          variable my_num.
      */
```

```
031>  my_num = p_read(scores, sizeof(plural int),
                              local_scores, file1);

      /*  Initialize the global statistics.  This is
          scalar code.
      */

032>  min_scores = 1601;
033>  max_scores = -1;
034>  sum_scores = 0.;
035>  sumsq_scores = 0.;

      /*  Initialize the histogram array. This is
          parallel code. The compiler is able to do the
          scalar to plural typecasting automatically,
          treating 0 as if it were a plural variable.
      */

036>  histogram = 0;

      /*  Now, for each of the scores elements in the
          processor array, update the global variables.
      */

037>  for( i=0; i<local_scores; i++ )
038>  {
        /*  This line is parallel, across the entire array.
        */

039>  curr_score = scores[i];

      /*  If scores[i] did not receive a value from the
          file during the p_read at line 31, its value
          will be -1, and it should not participate in
          the reduction operations. Put these processors
          to sleep until line 51.
      */

040>  if( curr_score > (plural int)-1 )
041>  {

      /*  This block of code will only be executed by
          processors with score values greater than -1.
```

```
       First, update the global max. Note the mixture
       of parallel and scalar variables: tmp_int is a
       scalar; curr_score is plural, so a reduction is
       occurring.
    */

    tmp_int = reduceMax32( curr_score );
    if( tmp_int > max_scores ) max_scores = tmp_int;

    /*  Next, update the global min.  */

    tmp_int = reduceMin32( curr_score );
    if( tmp_int < min_scores ) min_scores = tmp_int;

    /*  Next, the global sum.  */

    tmp_sum = reduceAddd( (plural double)curr_score );
    sum_scores += tmp_sum;

    /*  Next, the sum of squares.  */

    tmp_sum = reduceAddd(
         (plural double)curr_score *
                    (plural double)curr_score  );
    sumsq_scores += tmp_sum;

    /*  Finally, use the router to send_with_add 1 to
        each element of the histogram array that
        corresponds to the scores value.
    */

    router[ curr_score ].histogram += 1;

    /*  Now, wake up everyone for the next iteration of
        the loop, ...
    */

    }

    /*  ...and repeat.  */
```

```
}

/*  At this point, the correct global statistics
    and the histogram have been calculated and are
    held in the scalar unit. Compute the average
    and standard deviation.
*/

average = sum_scores/num_scores;
standard_dev =
 ( sumsq_scores/num_scores - average*average );

/*  The histogram has already been calculated. An
    optimized library routine is available to
    perform the summation prefix operation as part
    of the percentile calculation. This is a
    parallel operation on the processor array and
    involves interprocessor communications.
*/

scanval = scanAdd( histogram );

/*  Now, adjust the scanval prefix array.  */

temp2 = (plural float)( 100./(float)num_scores );
percentile =
  floor( (plural float)scanval * temp2 );

/*  Finally, each processor scales its portion of
    the scores array.
*/

average_int = (int)( average + .5 );
for(i=0; i<local_scores; i++ )
                  scores[i] -= average_int;

/*  We're now ready for output.  */

fseek( file1, 0L, SEEK_END );

fwrite( &min_scores, sizeof( int ), 1, file1 );
fwrite( &max_scores, sizeof( int ). 1, file1 );
fwrite( &average, sizeof( double ), 1, file1 );
fwrite( &standard_dev, sizeof( double ), 1, file1 );
```

```
     /*  The array can be written out in parallel.
         Only processors from 0 through 1600 should
         participate.
     */

065> if( iproc < 1601 )
066> {
067>   p_write( &histogram, sizeof(plural int), 1, file1 );
068>   p_write( &percentile, sizeof(plural float), 1, file1);

     }

     /*  Now, only those processors with a full set of
         scores values should write to the file.
     */

069> if( my_num == (plural int)local_scores )
070> {
071>  p_write( scores, sizeof(plural int) * local_scores,
                                      1, file1 );
072> }

     /*  There may be one processor with the last few
         scores.  If so, it will be handled separately.
     */

073> last_few = num_scores % local_scores;

     /*  This "if" test is done on scalar variables
         in the scalar unit. If it fails, the block
         until line 80 will be skipped entirely. We're
         testing whether there are any scores left to
         print out.
     */

074> if( last_few > 0 )
075> {

     /*  This next "if" test is done in parallel on the
         array. Only one processor will pass the test;
         the rest will become inactive. This processor
         will write out the last few items of the scores
         array.
     */
```

```
if( my_num == (plural int)last_few )
{
  p_write( scores, sizeof(plural int) * my_num,
                              1, file1 );
}
}

/*  Close file, and exit.  */

fclose( file1 );
exit( 0 );

}
```

Appendix G

C* on the Connection Machine

```
#include <stdio.h>
#include <math.h>

/*  The CM header files.  */

#include <cscomm.h>
#include <cm/cmfs.h>
#include <cm/cm_file.h>

/*  A single control stream.  */

void main() {

/*  The scalar variables from the sample problem.
*/

char file_name[128];
FILE * file1;
int num_scores;
int max_scores, min_scores;
double sum_scores, sumsq_scores;
double average, standard_dev;

/*  These scalar arrays will be a staging area
    between the processor array and scalar I/O;
    hence, the name change.
*/
```

```
int histogram_buff[1601];
float percentile_buff[1601];

/*  Two other scalar variables to hold the name of
    the parallel file and its descriptor.
*/

char parallel_file_name[128];
int pfd;

/*  The parallel variables will be declared as they
    are needed.

    Get the file name that holds the total number
    of scores and open the file.
*/

printf("Enter the name of the configuration
  file.\n");
scanf("%s", file_name);
if( (file1 = fopen(file_name, "a+b") ) == NULL )
{
  printf("Cannot open configuration file.\n");
  exit(-1);
}

/*  Now, get the file name for the large parallel
    file that holds the scores data. Open it for
    parallel read/write using the CM file system.
*/

printf("Enter the file name of the parallel
file.\n");
scanf("%s", parallel_file_name);

if( ( pfd = CMFS_open( parallel_file_name,
                       CMFS_O_RDWR,
                       0666 )  )  <  0  )
{
  printf("Cannot open the parallel file.\n");
  exit(-1);
}

/*  Read in the total number of scores from the
    configuration file.
*/
```

```
031>  fseek( file1, 0L, SEEK_SET );
032>  fread( &num_scores, sizeof( int ), 1, file1 );

      /*  Now, start the parallel portion of the code. */

033>  if( num_scores > 0 )
034>  {

      /*  Only declare parallel variables when you need
          them. Two shapes are needed: one for the scores
          array and one for histogram and percentiles.
          The shape of the array does not depend on the
          data type of its elements. Both histogram and
          percentile will have hist_shape but with
          differing data types.
      */

035>  shape [num_scores]scores_shape;
036>  shape [ 1601 ]hist_shape;

      /*  Allocate memory for the three arrays: scores,
          histogram, and percentile. This memory remains
          until the block in which it resides closes at
          line 68.  A malloc is not needed. Note that
          histogram is initialized to 0 at line 38. Since
          these arrays have a shape, they will reside on
          the processor array, not the scalar unit.
      */

037>  int:scores_shape scores;
038>  int:hist_shape histogram = 0;
039>  float:hist_shape percentile;

      /*  We will use scores_shape as the default shape
          for the first calculation.
      */

040>  with( scores_shape )
041>  {

      /*  Read in the parallel file. Note that no
          explicit "folding" of the data onto the
          processor array is required – one of the
          benefits of virtual processors.
      */
```

```
042>   CMFS_read_file( pfd, &scores, sizeof( scores ) );

       /*  Perform the reduction operations on the scores
           array. First, the global minimum: ...
       */

043>   min_scores = <? scores;

       /*  ... next, the global max: ...   */

044>   max_scores = >? scores;

       /*  ... and finally, the global sums.   */

045>   sum_scores = += (double:scores_shape)scores;
046>   sumsq_scores = +=
       ( (double:scores_shape)scores * scores );

       /*  Now, for the histogram calculation — an elegant
           and powerful expression!
       */

047>   [scores]histogram += (int:scores_shape) 1;

       /*  Two ordinary scalar expressions.   */

048>   average = sum_scores/num_scores;
049>   standard_dev =
         sqrt( sumsq_scores/num_scores - average*average);

       /*  Scale the scores array. Note the promotion of
           data types: Average starts out as a scalar
           double but ends up as a parallel int with
           scores_shape.
       */

050>   scores = scores - (int:scores_shape)(average + .5);

       /*  Now, append the scaled scores array back to the
           parallel file and close it.
       */
```

```
051>  CMFS_write_file( pfd, &scores, sizeof(scores) );
052>  CMFS_close( pfd );

      /*  We are now done with scores_shape. Close the
          "with" block from line 40.
      */

053>  }

      /*  Change the current shape to hist_shape.  */

054>  with( hist_shape )
055>  {
        /*  We'll need a variable to hold the prefix sums
              of the histogram array.
        */

056>  int:hist_shape prefix_hist;

      /*  This performs the summation prefix on the
          histogram array. The scan operation on the CM
          has a number of fields that control details of
          its behavior.
      */

057>  prefix_hist = scan( histogram,
                          0,
                          CMC_combiner_add,
                          CMC_upward,
                          CMC_none,
                          NULL,
                          CMC_exclusive  );


      /*  Scale and truncate to obtain percentile. */

058>  percentile = floor(
         prefix_hist * 100. / (float)num_scores )  );

      /*  Move percentile and histogram up to the scalar
          unit for output to the configuration file.
      */
```

```
059>    read_from_pvar( histogram_buff, histogram );
060>    read_from_pvar( percentile_buff, percentile );

        /*  Done with the parallel computation.  Close the
            "with" block at line 54.
        */

061>    }

        /*  The rest is scalar output to the configuration
            file.
        */

062>    fwrite( &min_scores, sizeof( int ), 1, file1 );
063>    fwrite( &max_scores, sizeof( int ), 1, file1 );
064>    fwrite( &average, sizeof( double ), 1, file1 );
065>    fwrite( &standard_dev, sizeof( double ), 1, file1 );
066>    fwrite( histogram_buff, sizeof( int ), 1601, file1 );
067>    fwrite( percentile_buff, sizeof( float ), 1601,
          file1 );

        /*  Closing the "if" test at line 33.  */

068>    }

        /*  Close file and exit. */

069>    fclose( file1 );
070>    exit( 0 );

071>    }
```

Appendix H

Linda

```
#include <stdio.h.>
#include <math.h>

/*  Here are the Linda declarations.  */

#include <linda.h>

/*  The major work is done in this routine and
    in the merge routine, which follows. This
    routine is replicated, once per workstation,
    each workstation operating on a different part
    of the input data. The merge routine then
    combines the local results together.
*/

int compute( int ID,  int NW )  {

char file name[128];
FILE * file1;
int * scores;
int num_scores, max_scores, min_scores;
int average_int;
float temp1, temp2;
double sum_scores, sumsq_scores;
double average, standard_dev;
int histogram[1601];
float percentile[1601];
int even_split, left_overs, offset, total_scores;
```

```
register int i, curr_score;

/*  Get the name of the input file from tuple
    space.  */
rd( “file name”, ? file name: );

/* Open file for update */

if(  ( file1 = fopen( file_name, “a+b” ) ) == NULL )
{
  printf(“Cannot open file.\n”);
  lexit(-1);
}

/*  Split up the scores among the workers.
    Note the difference between total_scores and
    num_scores.
*/

fread( &total_scores, sizeof( int ), 1, file1 );
even_split = total_scores/NW;
left_overs = total_scores - even_split*NW;
num_scores = even_split + ( ID < left_overs );
offset = even_split * ID  +
    ( ( ID < left_overs ) ? ID : left_overs );
scores = (int *)malloc( num_scores * sizeof(int) );

/*  Read in this worker's slice of the score file.
    First, position file pointer to correct
    starting place, ....
*/

fseek( file1, (long)(offset*sizeof(int)), 1 );

 /*  ..and then read in the scores.  */

fread( scores, sizeof( int ), num_scores, file1 );

/* Initialize variables  */

max_scores = -1;
min_scores = 1601;
sum_scores = 0.;
sumsq_scores = 0.;0
```

```
035>  for( i=0; i<=1600; i++ )  histogram[ i ] = 0;

      /*  Loop over all the scores, updating max, min,
          sum, sum of squares, and histogram.  */
036>  for( i=0; i<num_scores; i++ )
037>  {
038>    curr_score = scores[i];
039>    if( curr_score < min_scores ) min_scores =
          curr_score;
040>    if( curr_score > max_scores ) max_scores =
          curr_score;
041>  sum_scores += (double)curr_score;
042>  sumsq_scores += (double)curr_score
                     * (double)curr_score;
043>  histogram[ curr_score ] += 1;
044>  }

      /*  Now, merge the values for all the workers.  */

045>  merge( &min_scores, &max_scores, &sum_scores,
           &sumsq_scores, histogram,  ID,  NW  );

      /*  At this point, all workers have the global
          values for min, max, sum, sum of squares, and
          the histogram. This will enable each worker to
          scale its own portion of the scores array, in
          lines 57-58 below, using the global average.

          Now, calculate the global average and standard
          deviation.
      */

046>  average = sum_scores/total_scores;
047>  standard_dev =
       sqrt( sumsq_scores/total_scores - average*average );

      /*  Now, the percentile calculation.  Note that
          this is done redundantly (but without
          added run time) by all the workers.
          First, initialize the variables,...
      */

048>  percentile[0] = 0.;
```

```
temp1 = percentile[0];
temp2 = 100./(float)num_scores;

/*  ..and then loop over histogram array,
    calculating its percent, and summing into the
    next entry of the percentile array. Convert
    percentile values to an integer.
*/
for( i=1;  i<=1600;  i++ )
{
  percentile[i] = temp1 + temp2 * histogram[i-1];
  temp1 = percentile[i];
  percentile[i] = floor( percentile[i] );
}

/*  Round average to an integer  */

average_int = ( int )(  average + .5 );

/*  Loop over the portion of the scores array held
    by this worker, subtracting the average from
    each entry. Because each worker received the
    global value of sum_scores in the merge
    operation, each can scale its own piece of the
    scores array.
 */

for(i=0; i<num_scores; i++ ) scores[i] -=
 average_int;

/*  Now, outut the result. Worker 0 will first
    write the global items and will then consume
    the portion of the recalculated scores array
    held by the other workers.
*/

if( ID == 0 )
{

/*  Here's the part that worker 0 does.
    First, position file pointer to end_of_file,
    preparatory to appending data.
*/
```

```
061>  fseek( file1, 0L, SEEK_END );

      /*  Now, append to file each of the global
          results, ...
      */

062>  fwrite(  &min_scores, sizeof( int ), 1, file1 );
063>  fwrite(  &max_scores, sizeof( int ), 1, file1 );
064>  fwrite(  &average, sizeof( double ), 1, file1 );
065>  fwrite(  &standard_dev, sizeof( double ), 1, file1 );
066>  fwrite(  histogram, sizeof( int ), 1601, file1 );
067>  fwrite(  percentile, sizeof( float ), 1601, file1 );

      /*  ..and its own portion of the modified scores
            array.
      */

068>  fwrite( scores, sizeof( int ), num_scores, file1 );

      /*  Now, consume the portions of the modified
          scores array held by the other workers and
          write them to the file.  */

070>  for( i = 1; i < NW;  ++i )
071>  {
072>     in("scores", i, ? scores:num_scores );
073>     fwrite(scores, sizeof( int ), num_scores, file1);
074>  }

075>  }
076>  else
077>  {

      /*  Here's the part done by the other workers. Each
          posts its part of the scores array to tuple
          space, where it is consumed by worker 0 in line
          72 .  */

078>    out("scores", ID, scores:num_scores );

079>  }

      /*  Finally, each worker closes the file it
          opened in line 18 and returns.
*/
```

```
fclose( file1 );

return( 0 );

}

/* Here is the merge routine which combines
   the partial results held by each worker into
   global results.  */

#define  LAST          (NW - 1)

void merge(  int * min,
             int * max,
             double * s,
             double * ss,
             int * histogram,
             int ID,
             int NW      )    {

int temp_hist[1601];
double  tsum, tsumsq;
int  i, next, tmax, tmin;

/* If there's only one worker, the local values
   are already the global ones.
*/

if( NW == 1 ) return;

/*  A ring will be used, each worker consuming
    the results produced by the one behind it.
    Worker 0 gets things started, and the last
    worker will end up with the complete answer.
*/

next = ID + 1;
if( next == NW )  next = 0;

/*  The last processor will pass things back to
    processor 0.
*/
```

```
if( ID == 0 )
{

/*  Worker 0 gets things started  */

 out("hist", next, *min, *max, *s,
                   *ss, histogram:1601);

}
else
{
/*  Each other worker waits (remember, in is
    blocking) its turn to receive the results from
    its predecessor in the ring, update them, and
    pass them to its successor. The results from
    the predecessor are read into temporary
    variables and used to update the locally
    computed values.
*/

  in("hist", ID, ? tmin, ? tmax, ? tsum,
                 ? tsumsq, ? temp_hist: );
  if( *min > tmin ) *min = tmin;
  if( *max < tmax ) *max = tmax;
  *s += tsum;
  *ss +=  tsumsq;

/*  The locally held histogram entries must be
    summed into the global one.
*/

  for(i = 0; i <= 1600; i++ )
            histogram[ i ] += temp_hist[ i ];

/*  Now, each worker posts the updated results on
    to the next worker.  */

 out("hist", next, *min, *max,
         *s, *ss, histogram:1601);
}

/*  At this point, the last worker in the ring has
    the complete set of values and has posted them
```

```
        for consumption by worker 0. However, the other
        workers need to know at least the value for the
        sum, because each must compute the global
        average. Therefore, we will pass the complete
        set of results along to all the workers.
    */

    if( ID !=  LAST )
    {
      in("hist", ID, ? *min, ? *max,
                              ? *s, ? *ss, ? histogram: );

    /*  The temporary variables are no longer needed,
        since these are the true answers. Now, pass
        the data along to your successor, except don't
        bother about the LAST worker, who already
        has the results.  */

    if( next != LAST )
    {
      out("hist", next, *min, *max,
                            *s, *ss, histogram:1601 );
    }
    }

    return;

    }

    /*  Here is the main program, executed on one of
        the workstations, that gets everything started.
    */

    void main()  {

    char *buf, file_name[128], *getenv();
    int  compute( int, int );
    int i, nw;

    /*  This call returns the actual number of
        processors that are available to participate in
        the computation.
    */
```

```
buf = getenv("NUM_WORKERS");
nw = (buf) ? atoi(buf) : 1;

/*  The file name will be solicited from the user,
    and then posted in tuple space for all the
    workers.
*/

printf
  ("Enter the name of the file holding the
 scores.\n");
scanf("%s", file_name);
out("file name", file_name:strlen(file_name)+1 );

/*  Here is where the other workers are created.
*/

for( i = 1; i < nw; i++ );
{
   eval("worker", compute( i, nw ) );
}

/*  This processor now becomes worker 0.  */

compute( 0, nw );

/*  No checking is needed for the tuple posted
    when  compute  completes.
*/

exit(0);

}
```

Appendix I

Two Recent Machines

Since the time the bulk of this book was written (the spring and summer of 1993), two parallel machines have been introduced that merit additional discussion. IBM introduced the *SP1* and *SP2* (the *SP* in the designation stands for *Scalable POWERParallel*); and Convex introduced the *Exemplar* series. Both these machines qualify as MPPs (although, at 128 maximum nodes, they fall toward the low end of the MPP spectrum), and both come from vendors that, up to this time, had been considered to be firmly entrenched in the sequential/vector camp of high-performance computing. The entry of these vendors into the parallel processing arena (as well as, for example, the T-3D from Cray Research) is additional evidence that the architectural tide for high-performance computing has turned toward massive parallelism based on microprocessors. The following two sections will briefly describe each of these machines, with a final section summarizing and contrasting the two architectures.

I.1 THE SP-SERIES FROM IBM

Using the top-level architecture taxonomy from Chapter 3, the SP-series are classic distributed memory MIMD machines. The two major components of such a machine are the architecture of the processing nodes and the interprocessor communications network. We'll discuss each in turn and then conclude with some comments on software and I/O.

Node Architecture

The processors in the SP-series are IBM RS-6000 microprocessors. Customers have several options: the 62 MHz or the 66 MHz clock; one or two processors per "drawer" (IBM uses the terminology "thin" or "wide" for this distinction); the amount of cache and core memory (up to 2 GB per node in the wide configuration); and the amount of disk storage per node (up to 8 GB per node in the wide configuration). Note that, because the RS-6000 has a super-scalar RISC architecture, peak MFLOP rates are a factor of four better than clock rate—266 MFLOP peak on the 66 MHz version.

Each processing node *must have* an associated disk. The advantage of this is that it permits AIX (IBM's version of UNIX) to implement local virtual memory at each node. That is, the local disk provides AIX with private, nonshared disk buffer space to implement a virtual memory capability at each processor node. This virtual memory address space is completely local to the processor node; it *does not* extend across multiple nodes. Because each node has a large local virtual address space, applications written for a single ordinary RS-6000 workstation can execute, unaltered, on SP processor nodes. As a point of reference, one can think of a single SP processor node as an RS-6000 workstation without the display. This analogy is also supported by the fact that each processor node is provided with its own I/O capability: up to eight microchannel slots per node in the "wide" version, with a variety of controllers and adapters available for connectivity and storage. The image is one in which the processor nodes are thought of as "stand-alone" computers loosely connected by a communications facility (which we will discuss in more detail later).

The price paid for the local disks is lack of packaging density. Since each SP processor node must have a disk, the board real estate that would otherwise have been available for additional processors and network hardware must, instead, be devoted to the disks. This becomes evident, for example, in the cabinetry. A single 36" × 44" × 79" cabinet can only house a maximum of 16 "thin" node processors at two per drawer (or eight "wide" nodes, at one per drawer). This, in turn, means that (according to sales literature) current versions of the SP series top out at 128 nodes, configured across nine cabinets (the ninth cabinet houses additional switch circuitry). The "MFLOP/pound" ratio for these machine is conservative when compared, for example, to machines such as nCube or MasPar that have taken a more dense packaging strategy. For example, a 512-node system (IBM plans to deliver such a system to Cornell) would occupy 32 cabinets, plus additional cabinets for added levels of the switch. Fortunate the organization with such space and infrastructure.

Interprocessor Communications

As noted in Chapter 3, a key hardware feature in MPP architectures is the interprocessor communications network. The SP series permits the customer some flexibility in selecting the desired level of interprocessor communication capability. At the inexpensive end of this spectrum, the machine can be configured to use standard LAN technology (EtherNet or FDDI) for connectivity. This has the advantage that if the application does not require a high-performance network, the cost of the network is avoided. Such a configuration may reasonably be thought of as an LAN of workstations *without monitors.* The overhead of cabinetry and interactive video displays for each processor is avoided. The term "cluster" fits such a configuration very well. Rather than being spatially spread across the desks and offices of many users, the processors are tightly bunched (that is, *clustered*) in a single box and, hence, can be a central processing resource easily shared by many users.

As explained in greater detail in Chapter 3, an architecture that uses shared, one at a time communications services (such as an LAN) cannot scale to supercomputer levels of performance. On the other hand, many potential customers for parallel systems do not require supercomputers. Further, such a machine can support initial prototyping and software development without requiring a large initial investment in hardware—a technology transfer strategy recommended in Chapters 11 and 12.

For customers interested in larger configurations and greater performance, the SP series provides the *High Performance Switch* (*HPS*). Processor nodes access the switch through HPS Adapter Cards, and the switch itself (a multistage Omega network) is physically implemented on separate switch cards. IBM makes a point that their HPS network architecture bandwidth scales linearly with the number of processors—a growth rate not matched by, for example, two- or three-dimensional meshes. This increased bandwidth comes at the expense of superlinear growth in switch hardware. Additional switch "levels" are required as the number of processors increases, and these levels require their own separate cabinetry, power, and cabling. This shows up, for example, in the fact that a ninth cabinet is required for the 128-node version just to house the additional HPS switch hardware. The HPS physically separates the processing nodes from the network hardware an approach similar to that taken by the Intel Paragon, the CM-5, and the Cray T-3D. As discussed in Chapter 3, this permits the processor node architecture to evolve independently of the network architecture, but it also imposes penalties in decreased levels of hardware integration.

The performance of the HPS is only moderate by MPP standards. Significant improvements were made between the SP1 and SP2 generations. Many functions previously performed in software were moved into hardware, and the "application to application" latency was reduced to 40 microseconds.

(Note: The exact significance of the phrase "application to application" is not clear. It appears to mean the elapsed time, starting when one processor issues the operating system *send* to initiate a data transfer and ending when a corresponding *receive* issued by the destination processor can be satisfied. This would take into account the operating system overhead associated with copying the data to system space, formatting the message package, initiating the transmission, buffering the data in system space at the receiving node, and, finally, initiating the copy of the data into application space for use by the program.)

The use of an Omega-style interconnection network nicely illustrates some of the "speed vesus difficulty" issues discussed in Chapter 3. In this network, all processors may be considered *equally distant* from each other; that is, the experienced difference in latency between different pairs of communicating nodes is negligible. This means that for application programmers there is no performance advantage in worrying about "where the data is." Carefully arranging the computation so that communicating processors are nearby in the underlying network topology is without benefit; using latency as the measure of distance, all processors are "equally distant" from each other. Unfortunately, in the SP series, that distance (latency) is considerable. The price for "equal" is "equally long." In the world of supercomputing, 40 microseconds is a lifetime—upwards of 2,000 instructions per processor at current rates, or 256 KB operations over a 128-node array. Of course, if the application does not require fine-grained communications capability (that is, very many messages, each very small), then this latency will be less apparent. IBM stresses the development advantages to the programmer of not having to worry about positioning data across the network; they speak less about the performance penalties associated with high latency.

In terms of bandwidth (that is, the rate at which data can be transferred once a connection between nodes has been established), the HPS can support 40 MB per second concurrently for all non interfering pairs of communicating nodes. Again, this is modest by current MPP standards. This is an aggregate bisection bandwidth of just over 2.5 GB per second across the entire network (in the maximum 128-node configuration). Other features of the network include alternate paths (which reduces the likelihood of contention), wormhole routing (which eliminates store-and-forward latency penalties), and small packets (which more evenly spreads network resources across multiple, contending users).

I/O and Software

A full range of I/O capabilities is provided, including EtherNet, fast and wide

SCSI, FDDI, HIPPI, ESCON, ATM, and connectivity to other IBM product lines (e.g., S/370 and S/390). A distributed file system, which permits high aggregate data rates and is accessed over the HPs, is supported. Storage devices include standard disk drives, RAID, optical disks, and tapes.

System software is built around AIX, a full copy of which executes at each processing node. As mentioned above, virtual memory at each processor is provided, since each node has its own private, nonshared disk space. In addition, software is available for load balancing, a parallel message-passing library, debugging, profiling, and visualization. A number of third-party development tools are available, including Express from ParaSoft, Linda from SCA, PVM, and FORGE 90 from APR.

As noted in Chapter 2, database operations are inherently parallelizable. Three of the major suppliers of relational databases will provide fully parallelized products for the SP2. Oracle Corp. will provide Oracle7 Parallel Server; Sybase will provide the parallel Navigation Server; and ASK Group will provide OpenINGRES. IBM is also considering a parallelized version of DB2.

A number of fully parallelized engineering and scientific codes either have already been ported to the SP series or have announced the intention to port. This includes codes for molecular modeling, computational fluid dynamics, finite element analysis, electronic and circuit codes, and geological/seismic analysis.

The SP1 has been generally available since the fall of 1993. As of this writing, customer shipment of the full-up version of the SP2 has been announced for September 30, 1994.

I.2 EXEMPLAR SERIES FROM CONVEX CORP.

The Exemplar Series is the most recent example of the attempt to merge the programming advantages of shared memory with the scalability advantages of distributed memory. The KS-1 from Kendall Square and the DASH research machine from Stanford are other examples. The shared memory paradigm has many advantages—particularly, a market advantage in that it can execute existing sequential codes almost without modification. Distributed memory hardware, however, is the only realistic means to achieve the hundreds or thousands of processors necessary for the next generation of TFLOP computing. As explained in Section 3.5, the difficulty in marrying SM to DM is that, implicit in the SM paradigm, there is the notion of *uniform latency for memory references*. The SM paradigm encourages the programmer (and compiler) to treat all of the large, shared memory as if all memory locations are equally distant (measured in latency) from the processor. In a system where memory is physically distributed, however, that abstraction does not correspond to the physical reality. In reality, some memory references will be significantly closer to the processor than others—in particular, access to memory located in the *same* cabinet will have reduced latency when compared to memory located in a *remote* cabinet. Thus, unless explicit attention is paid to data layout so as to preserve locality of reference, codes written for these types of machines can be very inefficient.

System Architecture

An Exemplar system can be thought of as a three-level hierarchy:

Level One: Processor Node

Level Two: Hypernode = Multiple Processor Nodes (up to 8)

Level Three: System = Multiple Hypernodes (up to 16)

We'll discuss each level in turn. At the lowest level, the *processor node* is built around Hewlett-Packard's PA-RISC 7100 microprocessor. This is a state-of-the-art, 100-MHz processor with a peak rate of nearly 200 MFLOPs. It has a large existing base of system and application software. Large (1 MB) local data and instruction caches match the high processing rate to the slower retrieval rate of the large shared memory, implemented in DRAM. Care has been taken that existing UNIX-based applications can execute as sequential applications on a single processor node. Thus, the Exemplar can be used to increase throughput by concurrently executing independent sequential user applications.

The second level is the *hypernode,* which is best thought of as a stand-alone, cache-coherent symmetric multiprocessor (see Figure 3-11). Memory—up to 2 GB per hypernode—is interleaved across multiple physical banks and connected to the processors by a high-performance crossbar. Instead of "bus sniffing" (the most common approach to cache coherency in SMPs), Convex utilizes "agent cards" to ensure coherent memory both within a hypernode and between hypernodes. Up to eight processors per hypernode are supported.

Hypernodes also share I/O capabilities—up to 250 MB/second nonblocking I/O bandwidth to memory. DMA capabilities in the ports offload processors, and the full range of storage and connectivity options is available. Note that these facilities are shared within and between hypernodes.

At the topmost level, multiple hypernodes are interconnected by a low-latency network to create larger *systems.* This network may be thought of as four independent rings running through the array of hypernodes. The physical memory located in one hypernode can be directly referenced by a processor located in a physically distinct hypernode. Coherency of the memory is enforced by hardware and software using a protocol based on the IEEE-standard, Scalable Coherent Interface Technology. Note, however, that since the current version of SPP-UX is 32-bit, only 2 GB of this memory can be directly mapped into a processor's user address space, with an additional 2 GB available for the system (e.g., maintaining large local system caches of shared memory spaces). As noted in the brief introduction, memory references that must travel between physically distinct hypernodes will experience greatly increased latency when compared with those that remain within a hypernode. This is the penalty of nonuniform memory reference associated with marrying SM memory coherency to DM scalability.

In terms of packaging, a single 20" × 50" × 72" tower can house two hypernodes, for a total of 16 processor nodes per tower. Eight of these air-cooled towers are used to achieve the maximum 128-node version. This "MFLOP/pound" ratio is conservative by MPP standards.

System Software

Convex rightly considers the array of application and system software available for itssystem to be one of its greatest strengths. Note that much of this software is, in effect, sequential code that executes on a single node. Like the rest of the MPP industry, fully parallelized applications remain scarce. The programming model for the Exemplar is the standard "tasks/threads" model described in Chapter 4. Convex has a number of tools to assist in load balancing, parallelizing, debugging, and profiling. All of the caveats for such tools, as discussed in Chapters 8 and 9, apply. The operating system, SPP-UX, is a fully symmetric, parallelized version of UNIX (based on a Mach kernel), which is also compatible with HP-UX from Hewlett-Packard. A major design goal for the Exemplar was compatibility with the large existing base of application software available on the PA-RISC microprocessor. In addition, Convex has ported, parallelized, and optimized its extensive mathematical and engineering software library for the Exemplar.

I.3 SUMMARY AND COMPARISON

The two machines discussed in this appendix—the SP-series from IBM and the Exemplar from Convex—illustrate well many of the issues discussed elsewhere in this book. At the heart of both machines are processing nodes based on state-of-the art microprocessors: the 66 MHz RS-6000 Power2 from IBM used in the SP2 and the 100 MHz PA-RISC from Hewlett-Packard used in the Exemplar. Both vendors have taken a very conservative packaging approach, with top-end systems coming in at 128 processors packaged in eight large air-cooled cabinets. The SP2 can provide up to 512 MB for each of 128 thin nodes, for a maximum of 64 GB. The Exemplar can provide up to 2GB for each of 16 hypernodes, for a maximum of 32 GB. Both machines can support small configurations and can be used as throughput engines, acting as servers for stand-alone independent sequential programs. Both offer versions of UNIX as the system baseline, with extensions for parallelism as appropriate.

The major difference between the two is that the Exemplar provides hardware support for a fully coherent shared memory both within and across multiple cabinets, while the SP2 is a fully distributed, nonshared memory. The Exemplar, for example, shares I/O facilities within a hypernode, while I/O in the SP2 is based on microchannel slots on a per node basis. A single eight-processor Exemplar hypernode competes directly against symmetric multiprocessors (a market in which Convex has been successful for some time). By extending memory coherence across multiple cabinets (that is, marrying a shared memory system view to a distributed memory physical architecture), the Exemplar allows SMP applications to execute on much larger physical configurations. The SP-series from IBM does not provide a coherent shared memory, placing it firmly among distributed memory architectures with explicit message passing (rather than shared memory addresses) as the interprocessor communications mechanism. Substantial progress from the SP1 to the SP2 (primarily in the HPS Adapter Cards) resulted in significant improvements in application to application latency for the HPS. In the absence of detailed benchmarks, the interprocessor communication capabilities of the SP2 and the Exemplar appear to be roughly comparable, with the SP2 holding the edge in total bandwidth and the Exemplar having the edge in latency. Both machines have only moderate interprocessor communication capability by current MPP standards. The fact that interprocessor latencies are uniform in the Omega-type HPS is a programming advantage for the SP2. This is offset, however, by the shared memory paradigm in the Exemplar, which can also be programmed using message passing (e.g., PVM). Both systems offer software support for load balancing, debugging, profiling, and (subject to the provisos from Chapter 8) automatic assistance in parallelization. Application software for both systems comes primarily from sequential codes already developed for workstations using the respective microprocessors. Fully parallelized applications for both systems remain sparse.

References

1. White, S. W. et al. "How Does Processor MHz Relate to End-User Performance?" *IEEE Micro*, Part I, August 1993, pp. 8–16; Part II, October 1993, pp. 79–88.27.
2. Fox, Geoffrey et al. *Solving Problems on Concurrent Processors*. vol. 1. Englewood Cliffs, NJ: Prentice Hall, 1988.
3. Gustafson, J. L., G. R. Montry and R. E. Benner "Development of Parallel Methods for a 1024-Processor Hypercube." *SIAM Journal on Scientific and Statistical Computing* July 1988, pp. 609–638.
4. DeWitt, D., and J. Gray. "Parallel Database Systems: The Future of High-Performance Database Systems." *Communications of the ACM*, June 1992, pp. 85–98.
5. Valduriez, P. "Parallel Database Systems: Open Problems and New Issues." *Journal of Distributed and Parallel Databases*, April 1993, pp. 137–166.
6. Yang, M. K., and C. R. Das. "Evaluation of a Parallel Branch-and-Bound Algorithm on a Class of Multiprocessors." *IEEE Transaction on Parallel and Distributed Systems*, January 1994, pp. 74–86.
7. Valiant, L. G. "A Bridging Model for Parallel Computation." *Communications of the ACM*, August 1990, pp. 103–111.
8. Ni, L. M., and P. K. McKinley. "A Survey of Wormhole Routing Techniques in Direct Networks." *Computer*, February 1993, pp. 62–76.
9. Seitz, Charles. "Concurrent Architectures." Chap. 1 in *VLSI and Parallel Computation*, edited by R. Suaya and G. Birtwhistle. San Mateo, CA: Morgan Kaufmann, 1990.
10. Nitzberg, B., and V. Lo. "Distributed Shared Memory: A Survey of Issues and Algorithms." *Computer*, August 1991, pp. 52–60.
11. Chaiken, D. et al. "Directory-Based Cache Coherence in Large-Scale Multiprocessors." *Computer*, June 1990, pp. 49–58.

12. Hagersten, E. A. Landin, and S. Haridi. "DDM—A Cache-Only Memory Architecture." *Computer*, September 1992, pp. 44–54.

13. Hennessy, J. et al. "The DASH Prototype: Logic Overhead and Performance." *IEEE Transactions on Parallel and Distributed Systems*, January 1993, pp. 41–61.

14. Squillante, M. S., and E. D. Lazowska. "Using Processor-Cache Affinity Information in Shared-Memory Multiprocessor Scheduling." *IEEE Transactions on Parallel and Distributed Systems*, February 1993, pp. 131–143.

15. Stenstrom, P. "A Survey of Cache Coherence Schemes for Multiprocessors." *Computer*, June 1990, pp. 12–24.

16. Fujimoto, R. M. "Parallel Discrete Event Simulation." *Communications of the ACM*, October 1990, pp. 28–53.

17. Gustafson, J. L. et al. "A Radar Simulation Program for a 1024-Processor Hypercube." *Sandia Labs Technical Report*, June 1989.

18. Geist, G. A., and V. S. Sunderam. "Network-Based Concurrent Computing on the PVM System." *Concurrency: Practice and Experience*, June 1992, pp. 293–311.

19. Sunderam, V. S. "PVM: A Framework for Parallel Distributed Computing." *Concurrency: Practice and Experience*, December 1990, pp. 315–339.

20. Albert, E,, J. Lukas, and G. L. Steele. "Data Parallel Computers and the FORALL Statement." *Journal of Parallel and Distributed Computing*, October 1991, pp. 185–192.

21. Gabber, E., A. Averbuch, and A. Yehudai. "Portable, Parallelizing Pascal Compiler" *IEEE Software*, March 1993, pp. 71–81.

22. Kraemer, E., and J. T. Stasko. "The Visualization of Parallel Systems: An Overview." *Journal of Parallel and Distributed Systems*, June 1993, pp. 105–117

23. Kennedy, K., K. S. McKinley, and C.-W. Tseng. "Analysis and Transformation in an Interactive Parallel Programming Tool." *Concurrency: Practice and Experience*, October 1993, pp. 575–602.

24. Li, J., and M. Chen. "Compiling Communication-Efficient Programs for Massively Parallel Machines. "*IEEE Transactions on Parallel and Distributed Computing*" July 1991, pp. 361–376.

25. Miller, B. P. "What to Draw? When to Draw? An Essay on Parallel Program Visualization." *Journal of Parallel and Distributed Computing*, June 1993, pp. 265–269.

26. Pancake, C. M. "Software Support for Parallel Computing." *Communications of the ACM*, November 1991, pp. 52–64.

27. Agha, G. "Concurrent Object-Oriented Programming." *Communications of the ACM*, September 1990, pp. 97–101.

28. DeBenedictis, E., and J. del Rosario. "nCube Parallel I/O Software." *Proceedings of the Eleventh IEEE Conference on Computers and Communications*, April 1992.

29. del Rosario, J. M., and A. N. Choudhary. "High-Performance I/O for Massively Parallel Computers: Problems and Prospects." *Computer*, March 1994, pp. 59–68.

30. Wheeler, Tom. *Open Systems Handbook*, New York: Bantam Books, 1992.

31. Gustafson, J. L. et al. "The Design of a Scalable, Fixed-Time Computer Benchmark." *Journal of Parallel and Distributed Computing*, August 1991, pp. 388–401.

32. Messina, P. et al. "Benchmarking Advanced Architecture Computers." *Concurrency: Practice and Experience*, September 1990, pp. 195–255.

33. Center for Research on Parallel Computation. "Parkbench Committee Releases Parallel Benchmarks." *Parallel Computing Research*, October 1993, pp. 1–3.

34. Gupta, A., and V. Kumar. "The Scalability of FFT on Parallel Computers." *IEEE Transactions on Parallel and Distributed Systems*, August 1993, pp. 922–932.

35. Gupta, A., and V. Kumar. "Performance Properties of Large-Scale Parallel Systems." *Journal of Parallel and Distributed Systems*, November 1993, pp. 234–244.

36. Gustafson, J. L. "Reevaluating Amdahl's Law." *Communications of the ACM*, May 1988, pp. 532–533.

37. Johnnson, S. L. "Performance Modeling of Distributed Memory Architectures." *Journal of Parallel and Distributed Computing*, August 1991, pp. 300–312.

38. Karp, A. H., and H. P. Flatt. "Measuring Parallel Processor Performance." *Communications of the ACM*, May 1990, pp. 539–543.

39. Karp, A. H., D. Heller, and H. Simon. "1993 Gordon Bell Prize Winners." *Computer*, January 1994, pp. 69–75.

40. Marinescu, D. C., and J. R. Rice. "On High-Level Characterization of Parallelism." *Journal of Parallel and Distributed Computing*, January 1994, pp. 107–113.

    Messina, P. "Parallel Computing in the 1980s—One Person's View." *Concurrency: Practice and Experience*, December 1991, pp. 501–524.

41. Mueller-Thuns, R. B. et al. "Benchmarking Parallel Processing Platforms." *IEEE Transactions on Parallel and Distributed Systems*, August 1993, pp. 947–954.

Additional Reading

Akyildiz, I. F. et al. "The Effect of Memory Capacity on Time Warp Performance." *Journal of Parallel and Distributed Computing*, August 1993, pp. 411–422.

Bauer, Barr E. *Practical Parallel Programming*. New York: Academic Press, 1992.

Beavis, A., and C. Phillips. "Porting a Dusty Deck FORTRAN Program to a Shared-Memory Multiprocessor." *Concurrency: Practice and Experience*, December 1992, pp. 575–587.

Carriero, N., and D. Gelernter. "Linda in Context." *Communications of the ACM*, April 1989, pp. 444–458.

Carriero, N., and D. Gelernter. "Coordination Languages and Their Significance." *Communications of the ACM*, February 1992, pp. 97–107.

Chandy, K. M., and C. Kesselman. "Parallel Programming 2001." *IEEE Software*, November 1991, pp. 11–20.

Chatterjee, A., A. Khanna, and Y Hung. "ES-Kit: An Object-Oriented Distributed System." *Concurrency: Practice and Experience*, December 1991, pp. 525–540.

Dally, William. "Network and Processor Architecture for Message-Driven Computers." Chap. 2 in *VLSI and Parallel Computation*, (edited by R. Suaya and G. Birtwhistle. San Mateo, CA: Morgan Kaufmann, 1990.

DeBenedictis, E., and S. C. Johnson. "Extending UNIX for Scalable Computing." *Computer*, November 1993, pp. 43–53.

Duncan, R. "A Survey of Parallel Computer Architectures." *Computer*, February 1990, pp. 5–16.

Fox, Geoffrey. "Achievements and Prospects for Parallel Computing." *Concurrency: Practice and Experience*, December 1991, pp. 725–739.

Gaksli, D. D., and J.K. Peir. "Essential Issues in Multiprocessor Systems." *Computer*, June 1985, pp. 9–27.

Habiger, C. M., and R. M. Lea. "Hybrid WSI: A Massively Parallel Computing Technology?" *Computer*, April 1993, pp. 50–61.

Hillis, D., and G. Steele. "Data Parallel Algorithms." *Communications of the ACM*, December 1986, pp. 1170–1201.

Hwang, Kai. *Advanced Computer Architecture with Parallel Programming*. New York: McGraw-Hill, 1993.

Ja'Ja', Joseph. *An Introduction to Parallel Algorithms*. Reading, MA: Addison-Wesley, 1992.

Kermouch, Gerry. "Large Computers: Parallelism to the Fore." *IEEE Spectrum*, January 1994, pp. 46–49.

Kuo, S., and D. Moldovan. "The State of the Art in Parallel Production Systems." *Journal of Parallel and Distributed Computing*, May 1992, pp. 1–26.

Maly, W. "Prospects for WSIP: A Manufacturing Perspective." *Computer*, April 1992, pp. 58–65.

Russell, G. H., and P. J. Waterman. "Variations on UNIX for Parallel Processing Computers." *Communications of the ACM*, December 1987, pp. 1048–1055.

Schmidt, B. K., and V. S. Sunderam. "Empirical analysis of Overheads in Cluster Environments." *Concurrency: Practice and Experience*, February 1994, pp. 1–32.

Seitz, Charles. "The Cosmic Cube." *Communications of the ACM*, January 1985, pp. 22–33.

Siegel, H. J. et al. "Report of the Purude Workshop on Grand Challenges in Computer Architecture for the Support of High-Performance Computing." *Journal of Parallel and Distributed Computing*, November 1992, pp. 199–211.

Willebeek-LeMair, M. H., and A. P. Reeves. "Strategies for Dynamic Load Balancing on Highly Parallel Computers." IEEE *Transactions on Parallel and Distributed Systems*, September 1993, pp. 979–993.

Wyatt, B. B., K. Kavi, and S. Hufnagel. "Parallelism in Object-Oriented Languages: A Survey." *IEEE Software*, November 1992, pp. 56–66.

Index

A

Addresses, virtual address spaces, 220-223
Alliant, 18
Alpha (DEC), 70
Amdahl's law, 25, 238-240, 255
  definitions of, 32-37
  efficiency and, 41-43
  examples of, 37-41
    See also Efficiency
Ametek, 18
Architectures. See Hardware
Array instructions
  and benchmarking, 245-246
  in SIMD programming, 152-156
Array languages, 156-160
ATM/SONET, 17
Automatic parallelization, 208-211
  definition of, 196

B

BBN TC2000, 18
Benchmarking, 238-268
  Amdahl's law, 238-240
  applications to architecture, 295-315
  customer-supplied code and, 241-243
  data-dependent benchmarks, 252-254
LINPACK benchmark, 20, 255-258
  machine size and, 244-248
  measures of effectiveness, 240-244
  paging and, 246
  problem size, 249-252
  public benchmarks, 254-259
  SLALOM, 257-258
  sorting routines, 249-252
BiiN, 18
Bisection constant, definition of, 58
Boundary regions. See Synchronization points
Broadcast
  in SIMD programming, 153-155
  in SIMD systems, 64-65
Butterfly, 81

C

C* programming, 167-177
  program annotations, 172-176
  sample program, 363-368
C, 17
Cache memory
  coherency problem, 81
  in shared memory MIMD machines, 79-82
Challenge SMP, 98-106
Clock rate, 5-7
  and networking, 58-59

CMOS/DRAM approach, 8-9, 11, 27
  cost advantages of, 301
CM series computers
  advantages and disadvantages of, 66
  hardware development, 63
Coherency problem, in cache memory, 81
Communication, locality of, 28-30
Compilers, 196-200
  automatic parallelization, 209-211
  and DM-MIMD systems, 72
  interactive parallelization, 211-213
Computing speed
  of GFLOP computers, 4-5
  single vs. double precision, 240-242
    See also Benchmarking
Contention, definition of, 58
Context, in message passing, 113-115
Convergence, and data-dependent benchmarks, 253
Cosmic Cube, 127
COTS package, 69
  in message passing, 115
Cray C-90, 6
  benchmarks, 255-256
Cray Computer Corporation, 7, 20
Cray Research, 7, 10, 17-8, 22, 56, 79, 111
Cray, Seymour, 3, 7
Cray Y-MP, 6, 10, 52
Critical region, in shared memory, 98
Customer service, 302

D

Dally, Bill, 138
DASH (Directory of Architecture for SHared memory), 258-259
Database queries, parallelization of, 43-45
Data-dependent benchmarks, 252-254
Debugging, 200-205
  message-passing debuggers, 203-204
  SIMD systems, 202-203
DEC MasPar. See MasPar
Desktop supercomputers, 21
DM-MIMD systems, 111, 127-128, 215, 218-220
  advantages and disadvantages of, 71-73
  automatic parallelization, 209-211
  and C* programming language, 176-177
  compiler technology, 198-201
  components of, 67-71
  integration of, 309-311
  I/O subsystems, 228-231
  load balancing, 207
  object-oriented approaches, 212
  shared memory MIMDs compared to, 73-83
  SIMD systems compared to, 64-66
  synchronization points, 69-71
  taxonomy of, 53-54
  virtual address spaces, 221-223
    See also Hardware
$/MFLOP, 243, 299
Dongarra, Jack, 19-20, 255
Double precision, vs. single precision, 240-242
DSM (distributed shared memory), 258

E

Efficiency
  definition of, 35-37
  $/MFLOP, 243
  examples of, 37-40
  formula for, 33
  load balancing and, 47-49
  in parallel processing, 238-240
  porting strategies, 290-294
  speed-up and, 32-35
    See also Benchmarking

Emulation, of DM-MIMD systems, 72
EtherNet, 17, 55
Evaluation
of hardware, 296-315
methodology of, 296-303
See also Benchmarking
Exemplar Series (Convex), 383-386
Express programs, 17
description of, 127-132
program annotations, 132-137

F

Fast Fourier Transform (FFT), 249
FDDI, 17, 55
FDDI ring, 308-312
FORTRAN, 17-18, 92, 106-108, 131, 198, 249, 287
Fox, Geoffrey, 258
FPS, 18
Front end, in networking, 63

G

GaAs (gallium arsenide), 7
Gelernter, David, 179
GFLOP computers
memory bandwidth, 9-12
speed of, 4-5
See also Parallel processing
GFLOPs, definition of, 240
Global variables, in parallel processing software, 92-95
Gore, Albert, 22
Government, influences on development, 18, 22
Gray Code, 130
Gustafson, John, 60, 253, 257

H

Hardware
architecture diversity, 17-18
benchmarking factors, 244-248
clock rate barriers, 5-7
CMOS/DRAM approach, 8-9, 11
and compiler development, 72, 196-200
decision-making about, 295-316
DM-MIMD systems, 67-73
evaluation of, 296-315
Exemplar Series (Convex), 383-386
governmental influences on, 22-23
high-end systems, 19-21
impacts of architecture, 52-54
integration with mainframes, 306-308
I/O subsystems, 30-31, 70-71, 153-154, 216-217, 227-231, 248
low-end systems, 21
matching applications of, 295-316
memory bandwidth, 9-12
RAID (Redundant Array of Inexpensive Disks), 12, 228-231
replication of, 27-28
shared memory MIMD machines, 73-83
SIMD systems, 60-66, 152-157, 202-203, 207-208, 215, 217-220
SP-series (IBM), 379-383
trends in, 4-7
VLSI technology, 7-9
See also Amdahl's law; I/O subsystems; SIMD systems; SMPs (symmetric multiprocessors)
HIPPI backbone, 17, 55, 218, 304
Histogram values, calculation of, 145-147
HPCCI (High Performance Computing and Communications Initiative), 22

HPF (High Performance FORTRAN), 131-132
Hypercube topology, 57-59

I

Indirect addressing, with MP-1, 165-167
Intel, 20, 22, 111
  iWarp project, 18
Intel Paragon. See Paragon (Intel)
Interactive parallelization, 211-213
Interconnection network. See Networking
Interprocessor communications, SP-series (IBM), 380-382
I/O subsystems, 216-217, 227-231
  benchmarking and, 248
  in DM-MIMD architecture, 70-71
  Exemplar Series (Convex), 384-385
  in Express programming, 137-138
  in Linda programming, 192
  load balancing, 206-207
  in MPP development, 30-31
  in Paragon programming, 139-140
  in SIMD programming, 153-154
  SP-series (IBM), 382-383
iWarp project, 18, 56

K

KAP (Kuck & Associates), 106
KS-1 (Kendall Square Research), 82

L

LANs
  MPP as, 312-315
  operating system considerations, 216-220
    See also Networking
Latency
  latency hiding, 78-82
  switching latency, 57
  vs. throughput, 45-47
Lightweight processes, in parallel processing software, 90-92
Linda, 17, 179-194
  basic concepts, 180-183
  program annotations, 185-191
  sample program, 369-377
Link bandwidth, definition of, 57
Links, in networking, 58-60
LINPACK benchmark, 20, 255-258
Load balancing, 47-49, 205-208
Locality of communications. See Synchronization points
Locality of reference, 220
Local variables, 93-95
Locks, in DBMS, 95-98
Logical mapping, vs. physical mapping, 129-131
Logical processes, and shared memory, 89-92

M

Mainframe, parallel processing integration, 306-308
Mapping, logical vs. physical, 129-131
MasPar (DEC), 18, 157-158
  sample problem, 355-362
Massively parallel processing (MPP). See Parallel processing
Master-slave model, in message passing, 115
"Max versus average" phenomenon, 254
Memory
  cache memory, 79-80
  CMOS/DRAM approach, 8-9
  coherency problem, 81
  DASH (Directory of Architecture for SHared memory), 258-259
  in DM-MIMD systems, 71
  DSM (distributed shared memory), 258
  latency hiding, 78-82

max versus average phenomenon, 254
in shared memory MIMD machines, 73-77
See also Shared memory
Memory bandwidth, 9-12
of DM-MIMD architecture, 71
MergeSort, 252
Message passing, 111-145
basic processes, 111-116
context, 113
debuggers, 203-204
in Express programs, 127-132
and Intel Paragon, 138-145
in Linda, 180-183
logical vs. physical mapping, 129-131
master-slave model, 115
in nCube2 programs, 116-126
and Paragon (Intel) processors, 138-145
PVM (Parallel Virtual Machine) library, 147-148
receive routine, 114
send routine, 113
test routine, 115
Messina, Paul, 258
MFLOPs, definition of, 240
Microprocessors
in DM-MIMD systems, 71
VLSI technology, 7-9
See also Hardware
MIMD systems. See DM-MIMD systems
Monte Carlo simulation, 313-314
MPL programming, 157-172
basic concepts, 158-160
program annotations, 160-165
MPP (massively parallel processing). See Parallel processing
Multiflow, 18
Multiprocessors, single processor compared to, 88-89

N

National Labs, 22
nCube, 18, 20, 56, 70, 111
nCube2 processor
design of, 9, 287-289
parallelization strategy, 116-120
program annotations, 120-126
nCube programming, 329-340
Network bisection constant, 58
Networking
basic concepts, 55-60
LANs, 312-315
open system, 308-312
standards, 17
topology, 57
NFS, 17
Node architecture, SP-series (IBM), 379-380

O

Oak Ridge Labs, 17-18
Object-oriented approaches, 212
OLTP (on-line transaction processing), 254
Open systems, 231-233
parallel processing in, 308-312
Operating systems, 215-234
compiler technology, 72
I/O subsystems, 216-217, 227-231
multiple users, 216-220
open systems, 231-233
scheduling issues, 223-225
UNIX, 215, 218
virtual address spaces, 220-223
virtual processors, 225-227
Operational impact, definition of, 298
Oracle, 18

P

Packaging, of DM-MIMD systems, 71
Paging, 246

Paragon (Intel), 18, 56, 70, 138-145
  advantages of, 143-145
  program annotations, 140-143
Parallel applications, development of, 278-283
Parallel processing
  automatic parallelization, 208-211
  benchmarking, 238-268
  clock rate barriers, 5-7
  debugging code, 200-205
  efficiency, 32-37, 238-240, 243
  general vs. special purpose, 13
  interactive parallelization, 211-213
  I/O subsystems, 227-231
  lightweight processes, 90-92
  mainframe integration, 306-308
  market resistance, 12-19
  message passing, 111-145
  multiple users, 216-220
  in open system, 308-312
  open systems, 231-233
  operating systems, 215-234
  PRAM model, 107-108
  processing rates, 4-5
  RAID (Redundant Array of Inexpensive Disks), 12, 228-231
  reliability of, 7-9
  scaling sequential performance, 259-262
  scheduling issues, 223-225
  shared and global variables, 92-95
  simulation strategies, 286-290
  software availability, 14-19
  taxonomy of, 53-64
  technology trends, 4-12
  TeraFLOP computers, 19-21
  virtual address spaces, 220-223
    See also Benchmarking; Express; Message passing; Operating systems; Paragon (Intel); Software
Parallel variables, in C*, 167-172
ParaSoft Corp, 17, 127
    See also Express
Performance criteria
  clock rate and, 5-7
  $/MFLOP, 243
  estimates of, 262-266
  HPCCI (High Performance Computing and Communications Initiative), 22
  load balancing, 205-208
  measures of, 297-301
  methodology of evaluation, 296-303
  profiling, 206
  questions to ask vendors, 266-267
  scaling sequential performance, 259-262
  SPEC (Systems Performance Evaluation Cooperative), 254
Physical mapping, vs. logical mapping, 129-131
Point-to-point networks, 55-56
Porting strategies, 270-277
Power dissipation, 6
PRAM (parallel random access memory) model, 107-108
Problem size, 25
  benchmarking effects, 249-252, 256-258
  efficiency and, 41-43
    See also Amdahl's law; Efficiency
Processor independence, definition of, 58
Processor synchronization. See Synchronization points
Profilers, 205-208
Programming
  and array languages, 156-160
  in C*, 167-177, 363-368
  Express, 341-347
  in Linda, 369-377
  MasPar MP-1, 355-362
  in MPL, 157-172
  nCube, 329-340
  Paragon (Intel), 349-354

Public benchmarks, 254-259
PVM (Parallel Virtual Machine), 17-18, 147-148

Q

Queues, in message passing, 112-115
QuickSort, 252

R

Race condition, 97-98
RAID (Redundant Array of Inexpensive Disks), 12, 228-231
  and benchmarking, 248
Receive routine
  in message passing, 112-115
  in SIMD programming, 153-154
Reduction, in SIMD programming, 153-154
Reliability, of DM-MIMD systems, 71
Replication, in parallel processing, 26-28
Ring topology, 57-59

S

Sample problem, 317-321
  MasPar MP-1, 355-362
  nCube programming, 329-340
  Paragon (Intel), 349-354
  SGI Challenge, 323-330
Sample program, in Linda, 369-377
Sandia Laboratories, 253
SCA, 17
Scalar instructions
  in C*, 167-177
  in SIMD programming, 152-156
Schedulable processes, object-oriented, 212
Scheduling, operating systems and, 223-225
Seitz, Charles, 127, 138
Send routine
  in message passing, 112-115
  in SIMD programming, 153-154
Sequential performance, scaling to parallel, 259-262
Servers, FDDI ring, 308-312
SGI Challenge, 323-330
Shape, in C* programming, 167-172
Shared bulletin board, in Linda, 180-183
Shared memory, 87-109, 194, 215
  basic concepts, 88-98
  critical region, 98
  debuggers, 204-205
  lock outs, 95-98
  MIMD machines, 73-83
  PRAM model, 107-108
  race condition, 97-98
  SPLASH (Stanford ParalleL Applications for Shared memory), 259
  variables in, 92-95
    See also Array instructions
Shared memory debuggers, 204-205
Shared variables, in parallel processing software, 92-95
Sharing, capacity of DM-MIMD systems, 72
Silicon Graphics, 98-106
SIMD systems, 215, 217-220
  advantages of, 64-66
  array languages, 156-157
  broadcast operators, 64-65
  debugging, 202-203
  hardware configurations, 60-64
  integration of, 309-311
  I/O subsystems, 228-231
  load balancing, 207-208
  MPL programming, 157-172
  porting applications of, 283-286
  programming model, 152-156
  strengths and weaknesses of, 64-66
  synchronization of processors, 64-65

taxonomy of, 53-54
virtual address spaces, 221
See also Hardware
Simulation software, 286-290
Single precision, vs. double precision, 240-242
Single processor system, multiprocessor compared to, 88-89
SLALOM (Scalable, Language independent, Ames Laboratory, One-minute Measurement), 257-258
SMPs (symmetric multiprocessors), 12, 76-78, 87-109, 197-198, 215
automatic parallelization, 209-211
Challenge SMP, 98-106
cost advantages, 299
integration of, 310-312
KAP (Kuck & Associates), 106
lightweight processes, 90-92
load balancing, 208
lock outs, 95-98
logical processes and, 89-92
object-oriented approaches, 212
PRAM model, 107-108
shared and global variables, 92-95
Silicon Graphics, 98-106
single processor compared to, 88-89
SNA networks, 55
Software
compiler development, 72, 196-200
costs, 15
debugging parallel code, 200-205
development environment for, 195-213
Exemplar Series (Convex), 385
installed base, 14-15
large development project, 290-294
matching hardware to, 295-316
message-passing debuggers, 203-204
object-oriented approaches, 212
parallel application development, 278-283
porting strategies, 270-277
shared memory debuggers, 204-205
standards, 15-18
validation, 15
vendor instability, 16, 18-19
See also Message passing; Shared memory; specific software by name
SONET/ATM, 17, 315
Sorting, benchmarking speeds, 34-35, 249-252
SPARC (CM-5), 70
SPEC (Systems Performance Evaluation Cooperative), 254
Speed-up
calculations of, 35-37
definition of, 32-35
examples of, 37-40
SPLASH (Stanford ParalleL Applications for SHared memory), 259
SPMD (Single Program Multiple Data), 115, 143
and Linda, 183
SP-series (IBM), 379-383
interprocessor communications, 380-382
I/O subsystems, 382-383
Stanford University, 258-259
STRAND, 17
Switches, in networks, 55-59
Switching latency, definition of, 57
Symmetric multiprocessors. See SMPs (symmetric multiprocessors)
Synchronization points
and data-dependent benchmarks, 253
in DM-MIMD systems, 69-71
load balancing, 205-208

locality of communications, 28-30
in SIMD systems, 64-65

T

T-3D (Cray), 70
Tasks
load balancing, 208
in parallel processing software, 90-92
TC2000 computer, 81
TCP/IP, 17, 304
Test routine, in message passing, 115
TFLOP (TeraFLOP) computers, 7, 19-21, 70-71
Thinking Machines, 18, 20, 22, 111, 195, 256
Threads
load balancing, 208
in parallel processing software, 90-98
Three-dimensional mesh, 57-59
Topology, of networking, 57, 69
Tuples, in Linda, 180-183
Two-dimensional mesh, 57-59

U

UNIX, 16, 70, 87-88, 215, 218, 287, 302

V

Valient, Leslie, 51
Variables
in C*, 167-172
in parallel processing software, 92-95
in SIMD programming, 154-156
Variance, and data-dependent benchmarks, 252-253
Vectorizable loops, 52
Vectorization, in shared memory MIMD machines, 79
Vendors
customer service factors, 302
instability of, 16, 18-19
questions to ask, 266-267
Virtual address spaces, 220-223
Virtual memory, 220-223
definition of, 51
Virtual processors, 225-227
VLSI technology, 7-9, 301

W

WaveTracer, 18

X

XNET communications, on MasPar MP-1, 158-160